Beth Stroble

The Subjects in the Curriculum

SELECTED READINGS

FRANK L. STEEVES

The University of Vermont

The Odyssey Press, Inc.

New York

Printed in the United States

Library of Congress Catalog Card Number: 67–20379

A 0 9 8 7 6 5 4 3 2 1

Preface

At first glance, *The Subjects in the Curriculum* may appear to be a redundant title. Why not simply *The Subjects* or *The Curriculum*? To most people outside the field of professional education, the "subjects" and the "curriculum" are one and the same, and to talk about one within the other is to deal in educational confusion. This, in fact was the reaction of one of the writer's academic colleagues when reviewing an outline of this manuscript.

"I think I understand what you are trying to do," he said, "but I'm confused about your title. When I think of the curriculum I think about what is taught, that is, the subject matter. Therefore, to me your title says 'The Subjects in the Subjects' and appears illogical." The reviewer, a professor of English, was sincere in his comment but ignorant of the nature of curriculum study. To reply to his objection the writer turned to a well-known comprehensive textbook on curriculum development.

Passing it across the table he said, "Look up *English* in the index of this seven-hundred-page book and tell me what you find."

Within a few moments the English professor looked up in astonishment. "Why, *English* isn't in the index! What kind of curriculum study do you education people do when you even leave English out of your textbooks?" He tossed the volume to the table with a gesture of distaste. "Maybe this isn't typical though," he quickly added. "Do you have any others like this?"

With mounting irritation he examined a half-dozen additional texts concerned with curriculum development, curriculum planning, curriculum design, curriculum improvement, and other titles, all pointing in the direction of what might be termed curriculum theory. Where he found English at all it was to note, with additional words of criticism, that only one or two pages of the four hundred or more pages in each book was given to the subject which he considered paramount among all subjects. He noted, also, with a sort of negative satisfaction that such words as "mathematics," "history," "art," "biology," "physics," "chemistry," "music," "geography," and "economics" were either omitted from these indexes or given extremely brief mention.

"I must say I don't think much of the way you people approach curriculum study," he said when his examination was completed.

"How can you possibly study the curriculum without studying the subjects?"

The writer, who readily agreed with the implications of this question — or else he would not have compiled a collection of readings on the subjects — then produced several curriculum textbooks, mainly in secondary education, which do give as much as a full chapter to each of the major areas of subject matter. "You see," he explained, "some curriculum books do give separate chapters to such topics as English, mathematics, and so on. But all comprehensive textbooks on the curriculum have to deal with such topics as the social forces affecting the curriculum, historical development, the nature of culture, educational objectives, human development and the nature of learning, and similar topics. The educational problem is not merely to study English but to investigate the questions of what English, for what pupils, at what age, by what means, and for what reasons. Unless satisfactory answers for these questions can be found, it is futile to go on studying more and more English. Otherwise, we may find ourselves trying to teach the right English to the wrong pupils at the wrong time for invalid reasons. Or, the wrong English to the right pupils at the wrong time. Or some other teaching sequence in which error is built in. Surely, you will agree that curriculum study, as such, should be done by school people?"

The English professor quickly agreed with this question but continued to hold to his opinion that at least a minimal acquaintance with the nature and structure of each major subject area and with trends and problems in each area should be part of the mental equipment of all curriculum workers.

With consensus on this point the discussion ended, two major areas of agreement having been reached: (1) The curriculum is indeed something larger than a collection of subjects. Curriculum study does demand a knowledge of social and psychological forces affecting school work. The nature of learning is as crucial to a student of curriculum as is the nature of knowledge. (2) To the degree that the subjects and/or subject matter constitute the intellectual core of school work, the curriculum worker who lacks an understanding of the subjects is at a profound disadvantage.

It almost seems unnecessary to point out the lack of logic in one published curriculum book which gives seven pages to biology, two pages to chemistry, and none to physics, none to any specific foreign language, none to English, none to music, none to business education, none to geography, the grand total of two pages to history, and one page to mathematics. When we think of the vast changes in such areas as science, mathematics, and the foreign languages, we have to question the value of such texts to students and teachers. When we contemplate the problems facing the nation and the nation's schools in such areas as geography, industrial and vocational education, and democratic citizenship, it seems that specific information in these areas is essential in any book which purports to concern itself with the curriculum.

Sooner or later every curriculum director, supervisor, teacher, and administrator has to face the reality of dealing with subject matter. Priorities among subjects have to be stated in each local community. Space, time, and budget decisions have to be made in terms of the subjects to be offered in each school. The contents and emphases of each course have to be stated. Trends, issues, and problems in each field have to be known. Local decisions must be based upon knowledge of specific subject-matter developments.

For these reasons the present collection of readings is centered upon the subjects themselves. This book, then, is not presented as a comprehensive textbook for curriculum study, although it could be central to any course in which the instructor accepts the idea that the subjects are central in the curriculum. Also, of course, the book could be used as an adjunct volume where the basic comprehensive text omits specific subject-matter treatment. In any event, all peripheral topics have been eliminated from this anthology. The reader will find no selections on such topics as human development and learning, school organization, methods of teaching, history of education, and educational innovations, except where such innovations are directly pertinent to some particular subject area.

Further, no readings are included from such fields as testing, guidance, the school lunch program, and related topics which are not studied directly by pupils. Obviously, no one questions the value of an area such as guidance in today's educational world, and most broad definitions of the word "curriculum" include guidance services as well as a host of other school functions and activities. However, this book is concerned with the subjects in the curriculum, and guidance is not a subject to be studied directly by pupils. By and large, guidance is something done to and for pupils. It is studied by teachers and counselors. Its techniques are those of the guide, not of the one being guided. What the pupil learns about guidance as a subject is learned incidentally and not as a result of planned organization for the purposes of teaching and learning. The pupil does not learn guidance as a result of his experiences with his counselor any more than he learns dentistry as a result of his visits to the dentist. Hence, important as they are conceded to be, guidance and similar services are not accepted as subjects in the curriculum for treatment in this book.

Certain extracurricular or cocurricular topics are included, particularly where these out-of-class activities are closely allied with the class or laboratory program, as might be considered true of music and physical education. Also, a single reading on the school library is included because the school library *is* studied directly and used by all pupils. Further, the library seems to this writer to be central to all facets of the subject curriculum.

Each of the selected readings either presents the case for a specific subject or field commonly offered in the schools or discusses the major issues, problems, or trends in some particular field. The sequence in which the subjects are arranged is neither random nor entirely logical. A random sequence seemed ridiculous, and no logical arrangement would ever satisfy the initial premises accepted by all students of education.

English, the social studies, science, and mathematics are given first because these fields represent the core of any sound intellectual education at all grade levels and, collectively, provide the bases for further learning in all other areas. This statement does not diminish the importance of any other subject. *Importance* is not the question. This is merely to suggest that in order for an English-speaking child to learn a foreign language with any facility he first has to learn something about English. Before a pupil can go very far in industrial arts or vocational education he first needs some basis in mathematics and science. Driver education is accepted as a subject of increasing importance and of major concern in modern society. But, even here, good citizenship is conceded to be a major aspect of proper training, and literacy is expected by most states as a prerequisite for the driver's license. English, social studies, science, and mathematics are found in one form or another at all grade levels from kindergarten through college. Courses in these areas are taken by nearly all pupils at all grade levels. They are basic to further learning. Therefore, they are given first in the sequence of subjects in this book.

Beyond this point, the subjects are presented roughly in order of diminishing pupil enrollment and/or increasing technical specialization. Obviously, this is a somewhat artificial arrangement, and no conclusions concerning the value of a given subject can be drawn because of its location here. This comment includes those perhaps very important special subjects listed in the concluding section of the book under the heading "Specialized Subjects and Activities." Those included here are so listed either because they are offered in relatively few schools or because they are given well apart from the traditional academic program. Driver education, for example, is fast becoming an after-school, a summer school, or a part-time program requiring somewhat less formal study and leading to somewhat more restricted objectives than might be expected in the typical course in chemistry, history, or any other academic subject. Again, this says nothing about the importance or value of one subject versus another.

Because each of these carefully chosen readings speaks for itself there is no need for introductory comments by this writer, either for individual selections or for groups of selections centered around a given field. However, during the process of finding and evaluating writings for this book, many articles of similar or equal merit to those finally chosen were examined. Space limitation, of course, prevented use of all those distinctive selections that might well have been included. Consequently, brief lists of sources for further reading are included following each part of the book.

Finally, students and instructors using this or any other anthology are cautioned to remember that the collection of readings should not place a limitation on further study but should stimulate extensive reading for purposes of comparison and contrast. The anthology should not substitute for personal research; rather, it should encourage a closer look at the area under consideration. It is hoped that the readings in this book will lead both to further reading and to considerable thought about the nature of the subjects in the curriculum by professional practitioners and students in education.

F. L. S.

Acknowledgments

The editor gratefully acknowledges the cooperation of the authors and publishers who consented to have their writings reprinted in this book. It is especially appropriate that this cooperation be noted in a book of current readings, because without the willing consent of copyright holders, authors, and publishers, it would be impossible to build an anthology of contemporary interest. This acknowledgment extends to academic, professional, and public journals, to individuals, to professional associations, and to the business world. For example, the article which appears on page 398 of this publication was used by permission of the Visual Products Division of the Minnesota Mining and Manufacturing Company.

A particular expression of appreciation is due to Professor John L. Rowe of the University of North Dakota, who devoted many months of effort to the preparation of his original and authoritative manuscript presenting the case for business education. It was contributed to the present collection and appears in print for the first time as Reading number 38.

The editor would also like to express sincere appreciation to the ten teachers and school administrators who enrolled in his course on the secondary-school curriculum during the 1966 University of Vermont Summer Session at the Castleton State College. To a considerable degree, the members of this class allowed their own goals of summer study to be bent to the purposes of the present book. Both during and outside of class hours they gave much time to searching professional journals for appropriate selections at the Castleton State College Library and at the University of Vermont Library in Burlington. Hundreds of readings were examined, discussed, and evaluated by the members of this highly motivated seminar. Approximately half of the selections included in this book were first located through their effort.

Finally, during the always-exacting work of searching the journals and documents for selections appropriate to a specific collection, the assistance of dedicated librarians and library staff cannot be forgotten. While working in the libraries named above, and also while studying collections at the Boston University School of Education and in the Muger Memorial Library of Boston University, the editor was given assistance far beyond the call of normal professional duty.

The shortcomings of this anthology, of course, remain those of the editor. However, the existence of this collection is due to the cooperative effort of those whose writings appear in it as well as to the many others who helped to find and select these readings.

Contents

PART FOUR: Science

PART FIVE: Mathematics

PART SIX: Health, Physical Education, Recreation

PART SEVEN: Foreign Languages

PART EIGHT: Business Education

PART NINE: Industrial Arts and Vocational Education

PART TEN: Homemaking

PART ELEVEN: Art and Music

PART TWELVE: Specialized Subjects and Activities

PART ONE

The Subjects in the Curriculum: Two Viewpoints

---

1. The Use of the Disciplines as Curriculum Content

Philip H. Phenix

In 1956 I published a paper entitled "Key Concepts and the Crisis in Learning," in which I developed the thesis that economy and efficiency in learning, in a time of vast proliferation of knowledge, can best be achieved by attending to the "key concepts" in the several fields of

From Philip H. Phenix, "The Use of the Disciplines as Curriculum Content," *The Educational Forum*, March, 1962, 26: 273–280. Philip H. Phenix is Professor of Philosophy and Education at Teachers College, Columbia University. His special professional interests are in the theory of knowledge and in moral and religious philosophy. He is the author of many articles in professional journals and of the following books: *Intelligible Religion, Philosophy of Education, Religious Concerns in Contemporary Education, Education and the Common Good, Realms of Meaning, Man and His Becoming,* and *Education and the Worship of God.* He edited *Philosophies of Education.* Professor Phenix is eminently qualified to present the case for the use of the disciplines as curriculum content. This article is reprinted from *The Educational Forum* by the permission of the author and of Kappa Delta Pi, an Honor Society in Education, owners of the copyright.

learning. Since that time many important developments in curriculum studies have taken place along somewhat similar lines.

In recent years various study commissions have been at work reorganizing the subject matter of some of the major fields of learning, the T.E.P.S. commissions have worked for rapprochment between academic scholars and specialists in education, and leading investigators like Jerome Bruner have dealt with the importance of structure for the mastery of knowledge. The present paper seeks to develop some of these same themes, with special reference to the idea of the disciplines.

I

My thesis, briefly, is that *all* curriculum content should be drawn from the disciplines, or, to put it another way, that *only* knowledge contained in the disciplines is appropriate to the curriculum.

Exposition of this position requires first that we consider what is meant by a "discipline." The word "discipline" is derived from the Latin word *discipulus,* which means a disciple, that is, originally, one who receives instruction from another. *Discipulus* in turn stems from the verb *discere*, to learn. Etymologically, then, a discipline may be construed as knowledge the special property of which is its appropriateness for teaching and its availability for learning. A discipline is knowledge organized for instruction.

Basic to my theme is this affirmation: the distinguishing mark of any discipline is that the knowledge which comprises it is instructive — that it is peculiarly suited for teaching and learning. Implicit in this assertion is the recognition that there are kinds of knowledge which are not found within a discipline. Such non-disciplined knowledge is unsuitable for teaching and learning. It is not instructive. Given this understanding of what a discipline is, it follows at once that all teaching should be disciplined, that it is undesirable to have any instruction in matters which fall beyond the disciplines. This means that psychological needs, social problems, and any of a variety of patterns of material based on other than discipline content are not appropriate to the determination of what is taught — though obviously such non-disciplinary considerations *are* essential to decision about the *distribution* of discipline knowledge within the curriculum as a whole.

I hardly need to remind you that the position here taken is quite at odds with the one taken by many people both in the field of education and in the several disciplines. The common assumption of these people is that the disciplines are in the realm of pure knowledge — of specialized professional scholarship and research — and that ordinary education is quite a different sort of enterprise. The disciplines have a life of their own, it is held, and knowledge in them is not directly available for the purposes of instruction, but to be suitable for education must be translated and transformed so as to become useful and meaningful to ordinary learners. Thus, the argument goes, for the curriculum we should draw upon life situations, problems, projects, and the like, for the primary *content* of instruction, using the knowledge supplied by the disciplines as auxiliary material to be employed as required by the basic instructional process. The person is supposed to learn primarily from experience as it comes naturally and not as it is artificially conceptualized and organized in the academic fields.

Correspondingly, under this customary view, there are two disparate realms of method: there are methods of professional scholarship and research, and there are quite different methods of instruction. There is a specialized logic of the disciplines and there is a largely unrelated psycho-logic of teaching and learning. From this division arises the well-known bifurcation between the academic scholars and the professional educators. The former pride themselves on their erudition and despise or neglect pedagogy, while the latter busily pursue the problems of teaching and learning, often with little understanding or concern for the standards of rigorous scholarship.

This common dualism is destructive both to scholarship and to education. It presupposes a concept of the academic disciplines which has no relation to the instructiveness of the knowledge contained therein and a concept of teaching and learning disconnected from the essential structure of the products of disciplined inquiry. We need to recover the essential meaning of a discipline as a body of instructive knowledge. So understood, the disciplines will be seen as the clue to good teaching and learning, and instructiveness will be seen as the mark of a good discipline. Furthermore, scholars will learn once more to measure their success by their ability to teach, and teachers will again be judged by the depth of their understanding, and the academics and the educationists will dwell together in peace, if indeed any such distinction will any longer be required!

It is wrong to suppose that the more profound scholarly inquiry is the further removed it is from suitability for teaching purposes. On the contrary, profundity is in proportion to illuminative quality. The esoteric knowledge that is often described as profound is more aptly termed obscure. The characteristic feature of disciplined intelligence is that difficulties and confusions are overcome and understanding of the subject is thereby facilitated. In short, the test for quality in knowledge is its communicability. Knowledge which is hard to teach is for that reason inferior. Knowledge which readily enlightens the learner's understanding is superior.

Now what is it that makes knowledge instructive? How does undisciplined differ from disciplined understanding? There are three fundamental features, all of which contribute to the availability of knowledge for instruction and thus provide measures for degree and quality of discipline. These three are (1) analytic simplification, (2) synthetic coordination and (3) dynamism. Let us consider each criterion in turn.

II

First, analytic simplification. The primal essential for effective teaching is simplification. All intelligibility rests upon a radical reduction in the multiplicity of impressions which impinge upon the senses and the imagination. The infant begins life with the booming, buzzing confusion of which James spoke, and his learning consists in the growing ability to sort and select, that is, to simplify. The lower animals have built-in simplifiers in the instinctive mechanisms. Human beings have a much more interesting and powerful apparatus of simplification, through intelligence. The index of intelligence is of course, the power of symbolization. Symbols — preeminently but not exclusively those of language — are means of marking out useful and memorable features of experience for special notice. All significant words are such markers. Thus, the word "hand" designates a *kind* of object, to which an indefinite member of particular objects (hands) correspond. The point for emphasis is that a symbol — for example, a word — allows human beings drastically to reduce the complexity of their experience by subsuming an indefinite wealth of particulars under a single concept.

The secret of human learning is in generalization, that is, in transcending the multifariousness of raw experience. All thinking requires conceptualization. Concepts are classes of particulars. They are selections from the inchoate mass of impressions of certain features of things which enable them to be treated as a class rather than one by one. Thought proceeds by a process of rigorous selection, emphasis, and suppression of data. A person is intelligent to the degree that he actively discriminates in his entertainment of stimuli. In our pursuit of the full, rich life we may forget that the key to felicity and wisdom lies as much or more in our power of excluding as in receiving impressions. Our humanness rests upon a wise asceticism, not upon indiscriminate hospitality to every message impinging upon us from the world about us.

This simplification of experience through the use of symbols may be called analytic. The sorting out of classes of things is the process of analysis. It proceeds by the discrimination of similarities and differences, whereby entities may be divided and arranged in orderly fashion.

Analysis is possible only because the human mind is able to *abstract*, that is, to discern properties, qualities, or forms of things. Every concept is an abstraction — a drawing out of certain features of a class of things for purposes of generalization and grouping. The function of abstraction is to simplify — to reduce the complexity of unanalyzed experience by selecting certain shared properties of kinds of things and neglecting their other features.

It is commonly assumed that abstract thinking is difficult and complicated. This assumption betrays a misunderstanding of what abstraction is. Analytic abstraction is a way of thinking which aims at ease of comprehension and reduction of complexity. For this reason all learning — all growth in understanding — takes place through the use of simplifying concepts. It is the key to effectiveness of instruction.

All of this bears directly on the question of the place of the disciplines in teaching and learning. A discipline is essentially nothing more than an extension of ordinary conceptualization. It is a conceptual system whose office is to gather a large group of cognitive elements into a common framework of ideas. That is, its goal is the simplification of understanding. This is the function of the techniques, models, and theories which are characteristic of any discipline. They economize thought by showing how diverse and apparently disparate elements of experience can be subsumed under common interpretive and explanatory schemes.

Thus, contrary to the popular assumption, knowledge does not become more and more complicated as one goes deeper into a discipline. If it is a real discipline and not merely a field for the display of erudition, the further one goes in it the more pervasive are the simplicities which analysis reveals. For example, how grand and liberating is the simplicity afforded by the atomic theory of matter as one seeks to comprehend the endless complexity of the world of material substances! Again, how much simpler Copernicus made the understanding of the apparent motions of the stars and planets, and how much easier Darwin made the comprehension of the varieties of living things!

The test of a good discipline is whether or not it simplifies understanding. When a field of study only adds new burdens and multiplies complexities, it is not properly called a discipline. Likewise, when a real discipline in certain directions begins to spawn concepts and theories which on balance are a burden and hindrance to insight, in those areas it degenerates into undisciplined thinking.

One of the greatest barriers to progress in learning is the failure to catch the vision of simplicity which the disciplines promise. When students (and their teachers) consider the movement from elementary to advanced stages in a subject as requiring the taking on of more and more burdens of knowledge, of ever-increasing complexity, just as physically one becomes with exercise capable of carrying increasingly heavy loads, it is little wonder that they so often resist instruction and postpone learning as long as possible. If, on the other hand, it can be made clear that, like Christian in Bunyan's allegory, the academic pilgrimage aims at release from the burdens of merely accumulated experience and leads to intellectual salvation through the insightful and revelatory concepts and theories contained in the traditions of the disciplines, how eager students become to learn and how ready to exchange their hampering ignorance for liberating understanding!

III

Let us now turn, more briefly, to the second feature of a discipline which makes knowledge in it instructive, namely, synthetic coordination. A discipline is a conceptual structure whose function is not only to simplify understanding but also to reveal significant patterns and relationships. Analysis is not an end in itself; it is the basis of synthesis. By synthesis is meant the construction of new wholes, the coordination of elements into significant coherent structures. Disciplined thinking is *organized* thinking. Differences and distinctions are recognized within an ordered framework which permits synoptic vision.

Such synthetic coordination is not opposed in tendency to analytic simplifications; both are aspects of a common process of intelligible ordering. The perception of meaningful differences is possible only against some common measure. Thus, the notion of parts within an ordered whole involves both the differentiation which is presupposed by the idea of parts and the unity which is implied by the idea of a whole. A discipline is a synthetic structure of concepts made possible by the discrimination of similarities through analysis. It is a hierarchy of ideas ordered as a unity-in-difference.

It is only in this sense that disciplined knowledge can be called complex. The simplifications of abstraction make possible the construction of cognitive complexes — i.e., the weaving together of ideas into coherent wholes. Concepts are no longer entertained in isolation, but are seen in their interconnections and relationships.

What occurs in disciplined thinking is a reconstruction of experience. The brute multiplicity of primordial experience is simplified by conceptual abstraction, and these abstractions are then synthesized into more and more comprehensive patterns of coordination. In this way naive experience is transformed from a meaningless hodge-podge of impressions into a relatively meaningful pattern of understanding.

Herein lies the great pedagogical virtue of a discipline. Whatever is taught within a discipline framework draws strength and interest from its membership within a family of ideas. Each new idea is illuminated by ideas previously acquired. A discipline is a community of concepts. Just as human beings cannot thrive in isolation, but require the support of other persons in mutual association, so do isolated ideas wither and die, while ideas comprehended within the unity of a discipline tend to remain vivid and powerful within the understanding.

IV

The third quality of knowledge in a discipline I have called its dynamism. By this is meant the power of leading on to further understanding. A discipline is a *living* body of knowledge, containing within itself a principle of growth. Its concepts do not merely simplify and coordinate; they also invite further analysis and synthesis. A discipline contains a *lure to discovery*. Its ideas excite the imagination to further exploration. Its concepts suggest new constructs which provide larger generalizations and re-constituted modes of coordination.

James B. Conant has pointed to this dynamism as a distinguishing feature of scientific knowledge. Science is an enterprise in which fruitfulness is the mark of a good conceptual scheme. Theories which merely coordinate and organize a given body of data but do not stimulate further experimentation and inquiry are scientifically unimportant. This principle may also be taken as definitive for any discipline. Instructiveness is proportionate to fruitfulness. Knowledge which only organizes the data of experience but does not excite further questions and inquiries is relatively undisciplined knowledge. Disciplined ideas not only constitute families of concepts, but these families beget progeny. They have generative power. This is why they are instructive. They lead on and out: they educate.

There is, of course, no sharp dividing line between disciplined and non-disciplined knowledge. There are on the one extreme isolated bits of information which are not within any organized discipline, and on the other extreme there are precisely articulated theoretical structures which are readily recognized as disciplined according to the meaning developed above. In between are bodies of knowledge which have all degrees of discipline. Perhaps it would be well also to speak of weak disciplines and strong disciplines, the difference being in the degree to which their contents satisfy the three criteria for instructiveness earlier stated. Thus, mathematics, with powerful analytic tools and the dynamic for endless fruitful elaborations, by the present criteria would appear to be a stronger discipline than most present-day political science, which (from my limited knowledge of it) seems to have relatively few unifying concepts and theoretical schemes permitting wide synthesis and creative expansion. Again, I would rate comparative linguistics which seems to possess a powerful and productive set of concepts as a stronger discipline than esthetics, which still operates largely in terms of individual subjective judgements about particular objects, one by one.

A distinction may also be useful between a discipline and an area of study. Not all areas of study are disciplines, since not all of them display analytic, synthetic, and dynamic qualities. Thus, it seems to me that "education" is an area of study rather than a discipline. Within this area disciplined learning is possible. For example, I think a good case can be made for a discipline of curriculum, or of educational psychology, or of educational philosophy — though I would not wish to rate these disciplines as to strength. Similarly, "business" and "social studies" appear to be areas of study rather than disciplines. Not everyone that cries "discipline, discipline" shall enter the kingdom of learning, but only those who can show analytic simplification, synthetic coordination, and dynamism in their knowledge schemes.

My theme has been that the curriculum should consist entirely of knowledge which comes from the disciplines, for the reason that the disciplines reveal knowledge in its teachable forms. We should not try to teach anything which has not been found actually instructive through the labors of hosts of dedicated inquirers. Education should be conceived as a *guided recapitulation of the processes of inquiry which gave rise to the fruitful bodies of organized knowledge comprising the established disciplines.*

In this brief analysis there has been no time to consider the problem of levels. I do not intend to suggest that that the whole conceptual apparatus of a discipline should be brought to bear on teaching at every level of education. There are elementary and advanced stages of disciplined inquiry. The great simplicities, the comprehensive syntheses, and the powerful dynamisms usually belong to the more advanced stages. Nevertheless, from the very earliest years on up, it is only discipline knowledge which should be taught in the curriculum. Every discipline has in it beginning concepts and more developed concepts, all of which belong to the discipline authentically and properly. There is no place in the curriculum for ideas which are regarded as suitable for teaching because of the supposed nature, needs, and interests of the learner, but which do not belong within the regular structure of the disciplines, for the disciplines are in their essential nature bodies of knowledge organized for the most effective instruction.

This view asserts the identity of the psycho-logic of teaching and learning with the logic of the disciplines, contrary to many of the current theories of the teaching-learning process. Or, it might be more generally acceptable among educators to say that the view measures the logic (and the authenticity) of a discipline by its instructiveness.

V

In closing, one further point can only be indicated here, without development or detailed defense. The priority and primacy of the disciplines in education are greatly buttressed by a realistic view of knowledge, as opposed to a nominalistic one. In realism it is asserted that concepts and theories disclose the real nature of things, while in nominalism it is affirmed that the structure of thought is a matter of human convention. Academic and educational nominalists believe that experience can be categorized and concepts organized in endless ways, according to the inclination and decision and for the convenience of individuals and societies. Furthermore, it is held, scholars can choose their own special ways of organizing knowledge and educators can choose other ways, the differences corresponding to the disparity in purposes in the two groups. Thus arise the supposed contrasts between the logic of the disciplines and the psycho-logic of the educative process.

Such nominalism is rejected in the realistic view here proposed. From a realistic standpoint nominalism is epistemologically impious and pedagogically disastrous, a source of internecine strife and intellectual estrangement. There is a logos of being which it is the office of reason to discover. The structure of things is revealed, not invented, and it is the business of inquiry to open that structure to general understanding through the formation of appropriate concepts and theories. Truth is rich and varied, but it is not arbitrary. The nature of things is *given*, not chosen, and if man is to gain insight he must employ the right concepts and methods. Only by obedience to the truth thus discovered can he learn or teach.

In short, authentic disciplines are at one and the same time approximations to the given orders of reality and disclosures of the paths by which persons may come to realize truth in their own being; which is simply to say that the disciplines are the sole proper source of the curriculum.

I think it is the special province of people in the schools of education to see clearly the relationship between discipline knowledge on the one hand and the tasks of teaching and learning on the other, and the interrelations between the fields of knowledge within the curriculum as a whole. In the light of these visions, educators can help the disciplines to be more true to their own essential nature and instruction to find once again its proper resource.

2. What to Teach?

Dorothy McClure Fraser and Thomas G. Pullen, Jr.

Today a variety of factors converge to create a demand for reassessing the school curriculum. The continuing revolution in science and technology, changing patterns of economic life, the expanded role of government in an increasingly interdependent yet fragmented society, and conflicts concerning values have brought dramatic changes and tensions in American life and culture.

In view of this situation, it is not surprising that many of the current concerns about the public schools are focused on the content that is taught or is not taught. These concerns range over a broad diversity of questions, criticisms, and proposed solutions. Most of these criticisms and proposals are intended to illuminate the central problem of achieving excellence in individual and national life.

Further, most of these concerns revolve around the Spencerian question, "What knowledge is of most worth?" But we must put this question in a context of time and place: What knowledge is of most worth for American youth in the latter part of the twentieth century?

It is not possible to give a specific prescription that would be valid for all the youth of America, for there is no uniform outline of "what to teach" that would be appropriate for all the children and youth in our

From Dorothy McClure Fraser and Thomas G. Pullen, Jr., "What to Teach?" *NEA Journal,* October, 1962, 34–36, Vol. 51. Dorothy McClure Fraser is Professor of Education and Coordinator of Social Sciences, Teacher Education Program, Hunter College of the City University of New York. She is a past-president of the National Council for the Social Studies and has published many articles on curriculum in educational journals and yearbooks. She is the author of textbooks in elementary school social studies and of a college textbook in social studies curriculum and methods. Thomas G. Pullen, Jr., was State Superintendent of Schools in Maryland at the time this article was published. Now President of the University of Baltimore, he has received many distinguished awards and honors for forty years of leadership and service in American education. He, also, is widely known as an author. Professor Fraser and President Pullen present the case for what to teach in terms of the children and youth who are to be taught. This article is reprinted by permission of the *Journal* of the National Education Association and of the authors.

public schools. It is possible, however, to identify and comment on some outstanding curriculum issues of the 1960's.

First: *Who should make curriculum decisions?* A considerable segment of educational opinion holds that the local school staff should make operational decisions about curriculum, but should stay within the framework set by the state educational authorities and draw on all available sources.

While mathematics, physics, or shorthand are not "local," the way such subjects can be taught most effectively will vary with the pupils' backgrounds. The major body of such subjects as history, geography, music, and literature is also not local, but a local and regional aspect of each of these fields may be worthy of study by children and youth of the locality. The local school staff can plan and implement the curriculum most effectively for the students in the local school.

Rarely, however, should the local staff attack a curriculum problem as if it were making the first effort to solve it. Instead, the staff should study work that has been done on the problem in other schools, judiciously screen recommendations by national study groups and professional organizations, and consider other information that is available.

Sometimes, teachers may need to choose among alternative programs developed by nationally oriented projects and then adapt the selected program to local conditions. The local staff also should draw on the resources of nearby institutions of higher learning — resources that too often are overlooked.

This kind of local curriculum planning is feasible only if teacher time and adequate resources are provided for in the budget. If curriculum planning is carried on as an afterhours activity, with no provision for materials and working facilities, haphazard and superficial results can be expected. Some local curriculum planning programs have been ineffective or even harmful because too much was attempted with too few resources.

Local curriculum development *must* be supported with adequate funds. Balanced curriculum planning has been weakened, in the opinion of many educators, by special federal aid measures such as the National Defense Education Act that limit support to projects in a few curriculum fields. Educators recognize that such projects have strengthened certain fields in the school program, but they are aware that the parts of the curriculum not receiving such support are standing still or slipping backward in many schools. A promising development is the more recent support by foundations of comprehensive models of curriculum planning proceeding on a broader base than has been characteristic of those supported in the past.

Curriculum = all those learning experiences for which the school accepts responsibilit

The NEA and the Council of Chief State School Officers have pointed out the dangers inherent in a proliferation of special federal aid laws and have been urging the Congress to substitute general federal aid for the present patchwork of special aid measures.

Second: *How can schools effectively use the recommendations from nationally oriented curriculum projects in specific subject fields?* Educators will be foolish if they either swallow the recommendations in one gulp or if they reject them offhand because they suspect that these proposals represent the views of special interest groups. Most of the nationally oriented curriculum projects have had rich resources available to them. In many of the projects, some experimental trial of recommendations has been made in selected schools, but the extent and soundness of the experiments have varied from project to project.

To use the results of such projects wisely, educators need to study them critically and then select and adapt projects suitable for the students — or selected groups of students — in their particular school. Questions should be asked: For what group of students was the project developed? — just for the college-capable? or for those with a broad range of ability? What effect would the project's recommendations have on the balance of the pupil's total school program, and how would they affect the continuity of his learning in the subject as he moves through the K-12 program?

And, before introducing materials from one of the nationally oriented studies, the staff should plan how it will evaluate the effects of these materials on student learning in order to decide whether or not to continue using them.

Third: *How can the curriculum be developed to meet the needs of all members of the school population?* Much of the recent and current concern about curriculum content has been focused on the college-capable student and on the upper sector of that group, the gifted. Our nation can no longer afford the waste of superior talent that has occurred too often in the past. Grave injustice has been done to many talented youngsters by providing inadequate opportunities for them.

The schools need to do even more than they are now doing for the youngster with superior ability. But as a matter of national policy and of human values, the schools must also do more for the children and youth who, for one reason or another, are not college-bound or who do not demonstrate superior academic ability on the measures we have available.

Recent studies of creativity suggest that we, as educators, have been overlooking an important kind of gifted student because we have relied too heavily on conventional measures of ability. Some of the recent work with underprivileged youngsters also suggests that we have been overlooking important human resources because of inadequate measures for

program design depends on students - their backgrounds, their differences; their aims identification. The search for talent, however, must not blind us to the urgency of providing for the typical and slow learners who also are future voters and who deserve full opportunity to develop their abilities.

One other thought on this issue: Individual differences indicate that the needs of all youth cannot be met by a single, uniform curriculum — educational equality does not necessarily mean identical opportunity. Setting up special programs for identified groups of children may be helpful, but this will not in itself solve the problem. Indeed, special programs may blind the teacher to the range of abilities and needs that exists in every class group, no matter on what basis the grouping has been done. There is need for continued search for ways of developing the school curriculum for individuals within the context of universal education.

The fourth and fifth issues are closely related. They are: *What should be included and excluded in planning the school curriculum?* and *What priorities and balance should be established in the instructional program?*

Some people, both educators and laymen, hold that the school has taken upon itself tasks which are properly the responsibility of other social institutions, such as the family and the church, and that in doing so the school neglects its primary responsibility, the intellectual development of children and youth. Others reply that many of youth's needs are not in fact taken care of by other institutions in society, no matter how desirable it is that they should be, and that the school can make little progress in encouraging the student's intellectual development without helping him to solve his problems of emotional and social adjustment. (Maslow's hierarchy of needs)

Opinions also vary on the priorities among the range of subjects that could be taught by the school. Shall increased emphasis and time in the school program be given to the sciences and to advanced mathematics? Shall English no longer be a required subject each year in the secondary school, or shall the time devoted to English be expanded?

Shall foreign language study begin in the elementary school for all children of average and superior ability? If so, what languages shall be stressed? How much time should be given to social studies subjects, and which of the social sciences should be emphasized? What is the place of the "practical" subjects, the applied sciences and arts, in the education of youth? And so on.

It seems a reasonable conclusion that schools in different communities with different student bodies must answer both the question of inclusion-exclusion and that of priorities and balance according to the needs of the immediate situation. To a considerable degree, a school's curriculum must be planned with regard to the background children bring with

Community will influ what's taught but curric must be balanced!

them to school, what children need in order to make progress in learning, and what kinds of long-range goals they already hold or can be encouraged to set for themselves.

The suburban high school which sends eighty percent or more of its graduates to college will inevitably require curriculums and balance different from those in the school which serves an underprivileged area where a high percentage of youngsters drop out at the legal school-leaving age.

The sixth issue may be receiving more discussion than any of the others: *To what extent should the content, structure, and organization of the academic disciplines determine the content and nature of the academic subjects in the instructional program in the schools?*

Curriculum decisions must take three factors into account: the learner's abilities and needs, society's demands on the schools, and the organized bodies of content — the disciplines. Traditionally, the disciplines provided the pattern for the school curriculum. In the twentieth century, however, study of human development, educational psychology, and educational sociology resulted in a new approach to curriculum planning. The needs of society and of the learner were emphasized.

The disciplines came to be viewed as reservoirs from which pertinent materials were selected and organized into curriculums that were considered appropriate for a changing society and for new conceptions of the learner's characteristics. The new curriculums contained a greater range of content than those they replaced. They provided organized or structured learning, but the basis of the organization was not that of the traditional disciplines.

In the past decade, pressures have developed for returning to the disciplines as the major basis for structuring the school curriculum. It is urged that young children can and should be taught the "structures of knowledge" — the overarching concepts and generalizations of the disciplines. Thus, it is argued, the child will achieve at an early age a conceptual framework which will enable him to see relationships among specific facts and which will make the facts more meaningful and thereby easier to retain.

Educators have long understood that pupils learn more effectively when the specifics they study are placed within a meaningful structure. There is no disagreement between them and academic specialists over the importance of organized, or structured, learning. Disagreements do arise, however, about what kind of structure or organization of knowledge has meaning and usefulness for the elementary or secondary school pupil.

Many of the current proposals which suggest that school subjects be organized around the structures of the disciplines seem to imply a deceptively simple procedure: The first step would be to have scholars in the various disciplines list the basic structures of their fields. Then units of instruction would be developed to present these generalizations and principles to pupils at as early an age as possible.

There are several problems with such a procedure. In the first place, in many of the disciplines there is no agreement among the scholars as to what are the basic structures of their field. The specific guidance that is assumed to be available is not, in fact, at hand.

A second problem is that there is a hierarchy of concepts and generalizations within each discipline, ranging from the more specific and concrete to the more general and abstract. Concepts and generalizations that children or even high school students can grasp may have little resemblance to those that are everyday intellectual tools for scholars or for the mature adult. To introduce the scholar's concepts and generalizations may only confuse the immature student, for if he learns them only at a verbal level he will deal with them almost as though they were nonsense syllables.

Finally, even if the structures of a particular discipline can be agreed upon and it is proven that pupils can grasp them, there still remains the question of whether such study is the best use of pupils' time at their particular stage of development. Is there other learning that they need more at their age? Would they grasp the concepts and generalizations of the academic scholars more quickly and with more understanding at a later time?

As these and related issues concerning what to teach are considered, there are several groups that should participate in the process. They include classroom teachers, school administrators, academic scholars, scholars in professional education, and informed lay persons. Each has a special contribution to make and each must respect and utilize the contributions of the others. Only through such cooperative efforts can our schools provide instructional programs that will meet the demands of the 1960's — and of the decades to come.

For Further Reading

Association for Supervision and Curriculum Development, *Balance in the Curriculum,* 1961 Yearbook, ASCD, National Education Association, Washington, D.C., 1961.

Beauchamp, George A., *Planning the Elementary School Curriculum,* Allyn and Bacon, Inc., Boston, 1956.

Breslow, Alice, et al., "Forces Influencing Curriculum," *Review of Educational Research,* June, 1960, 30: 199–225.

Clark, Leonard H., Raymond L. Klein, and John B. Burks, *The American Secondary School Curriculum,* The Macmillan Company, New York, 1965. (Chapters 8–16 are devoted to specific subject fields.)

Douglass, Harl R., (ed.), *The High School Curriculum,* Third edition, The Ronald Press Company, New York, 1964. (Chapters 15–25 concern specific subject fields.)

Educational Policies Commission, *Central Purpose in American Education,* National Education Association, Washington, D.C., 1961.

Fraser, Dorothy M., *Deciding What to Teach,* Project on the Instructional Program of the Public Schools, National Education Association, Washington, D.C., 1963.

Goodlad, John I., (ed.), *The Changing American School,* the Sixty-fifth Yearbook of the National Society for the Study of Education, Part II, The University of Chicago Press, Chicago, 1966.

Goodlad, John I., and M. Frances Klein, "What's Happening in Curriculum Development," *Nation's Schools,* April, 1966, 70–73, Vol. 77.

Goodlad, John I., Renata Von Stoephasius, and M. Frances Klein, *The Changing School Curriculum,* The Fund for the Advancement of Education, 477 Madison Avenue, New York, 1966.

Greer, Edith S., and Richard M. Harbeck, *What High School Pupils Study,* U.S. Department of Health, Education and Welfare, Office of Education, Government Printing Office, Washington, D.C., 1962.

Heath, Robert W., (ed.), *New Curricula,* Harper & Row, New York, 1964.

Huebner, Dwayne, (ed.), *A Reassessment of the Curriculum,* Bureau of Publications, Teachers College, Columbia University, New York, 1964.

Journal of Education, April, 1966, Vol. 148, No. 4. (Theme of the issue "Prospectus for Revolution in Secondary Education." Articles on English, foreign languages, social studies, mathematics, science, economics, and pre-teaching field experiences.)

National Association of Secondary School Principals, *Bulletin,* November, 1963, Vol. 47, No. 286. (This issue is organized into twelve sections dealing with curriculum planning and development. Each section includes three articles, one presenting issues in the field, the second discussing developments, and the third giving a principal's view of his role in meeting current problems in the area.)

Scheffler, Israel, *Conditions of Knowledge,* Scott, Foresman and Company, Fair Lawn, New Jersey, 1965.

The Teachers College Journal, October, 1964, 36: 1–59. (Theme of the issue: "What's Good About American Public Education." Forty articles, twelve of which concern specific curriculum issues and subjects.)

PART TWO

English and the Language Arts

3. What Is English?

Thomas G. Devine

When the Board of Directors of the National Council of Teachers of English met in Cleveland in the Fall of 1965, the Chairman of the Resolutions Committee, Yale's Edward Gordon, proposed that the officers and members of the Council give serious thought to resolving the question "What is English?" To observers outside of English—and numerous publishers' representatives and journalists were present—the question appeared both impertinent and trivial. Many wondered how an area of study entrenched in secondary education since before the turn of the century could lack definition; others doubted the possibility that a fifty-five year old professional organization, embracing more than one hundred and

From Thomas G. Devine, "What Is 'English'?" *Journal of Education,* April, 1966, 7–11, Vol. 146. Thomas G. Devine is Associate Professor of English Education, Boston University, School of Education. He is co-author of a junior high school reading-literature series; author of many teachers' guides, workbooks, recordings, and other teaching materials in secondary school English; and a Director of the National Council of Teachers of English. This article is reprinted by permission of the *Journal of Education,* a publication of the Boston University School of Education.

ten thousand teachers of English, could seriously entertain the question. To thoughtful teachers of English, however, the question was neither impertinent nor idle. English has lacked a definition acceptable both by the profession and the public: the term has meant too many things to too many people.

The concept of English — as a "subject-matter field," as an "area of study," as a "discipline" — has indeed been nebulous. At various points in its history in the secondary schools, English has been defined as a relative handful of specific literary selections and an odd-lot of grammatical "rules"; at other times lines of demarcation have been extended to include "world" literature, the study of motion pictures, acceptable telephone manners, semantics, and propaganda analysis; for many years it was conceived quite simply as the skills involved in reading, writing, speaking, and listening; at the present time, for some teachers at least, English embraces mastery of the International Phonetic Alphabet and an introduction to the grammar of Swahili. And — it should be noted — throughout its history in the schools English has been equated, by many teachers and parents, directly and unequivocally, with grammar ("English *is* grammar, and that's all there is to that!")

What, then, is English? As the 1964 NCTE resolution indicates, none of the concepts and definitions of the past half century seems generally satisfying. Teachers of English to culturally deprived ninth-grade boys reading at fourth- and fifth-grade levels are not apt to accept the notion that English necessarily involves the teaching of the IPA, literary genres, and one of the more esoteric modern grammars; teachers of college-preparatory students in upper-middle class communities are rarely satisfied with the reading-writing-speaking-listening concept when this involves — as it often does — units in telephone etiquette and propaganda analysis.

There are at least two reasons why an answer to the question seems to be needed. First, a teacher's concept of English influences the daily practices in his classroom, and these, in turn, seem to affect the present and future behavior of students. Second, the concept of English shared by the profession today will influence, if not determine, curriculum planning, the kind of research done in the area, the preparation of textbooks and other instructional materials, and teacher-preparation programs. Both of these reasons for sharpening our concept of English were valid in past decades, but they have an imperative ring to them today when our culture is rapidly changing, when the secondary school curriculum generally is in a state of flux, and when vast sums of money, from both government and private sources, are available to initiate and influence change.

II

Insights into the question "What is English?" and into its possible answers may be derived from a number of approaches, ranging from surveys of expert and lay opinion to explorations of the philosophic underpinnings of American education and use of techniques of logical and semantic analysis. The approach selected here seems to have the virtues of both simplicity and — it is hoped — fruitfulness. The writer has chosen, arbitrarily, four influential reports on the teaching of secondary school English and examined them in order (1) to draw possible inferences about the ways English has been viewed in the United States during the past half century, and (2) to suggest ways in which teachers and educational theorists may look at English in the next decade.

The Hosic Report (1917). To understand how English was conceived before the turn of the century, one may, with considerable profit, turn to Eaton's *College Requirements in English Entrance Examinations* (1), a description of entrance requirements of major colleges in the United States during the last decade of the nineteenth century. Secondary school English seems then to have been characterized by much analysis, both grammatical and rhetorical, of selected literary classics, with much attention directed to exegesis, to parsing, and to diagramming sentences. Considerable time seems to have been spent on detailed classifications of figures of speech, on formal rhetorical devices, on literary history and biography, and on critical commentaries on literary classics. English was conceived, in short, in essentialist terms (2). Emphasis was upon time-tested content, upon orderly sequence, upon inherited principles, upon guided discipline. English was a discipline to be mastered by learners rather than a general name for a host of useful communication skills to enrich the lives of students.

In the early years of the century, the adequacy of such a program in English was questioned by both a committee of the National Education Association concerned with college entrance requirements and by a similar committee operating under the auspices of the newly established NCTE. In 1911 both committees merged, and in 1917 a report, compiled by James Fleming Hosic, was issued which challenged the concept of English shaped — if not, indeed, decreed — by the prevailing college entrance examinations (3). The Hosic Report, noting the growth in numbers and in quality of secondary school students, recommended that the English program be diversified to provide for a variety of students. It recommended, further, that there be no limited set of curriculum essentials in English, that English be conceived as less a body of facts to be learned than a complex of competencies to be acquired. English is *best* conceived, the report noted, not as a subject of instruction, subdivided into language, literature, and composition, but rather as the study and practice of basic communication skills in reading, writing, speaking, and listening.

An Experience Curriculum in English (1935). Throughout the 1920's, the recommendations of the Hosic Report had a marked influence upon the preparation of textbooks and curriculum guides, upon teacher-preparation programs, and upon classroom practices. The concept of English developed in the 1917 report was further refined and elaborated with the publication, in 1935, of *An Experience Curriculum in English* (4). The Curriculum Commission of NCTE, under the direction of NCTE Executive Secretary W. Wilbur Hatfield, noted the "folly" of attempting to create a single English curriculum for all secondary school students in the United States. As the preface of the report indicates, instead of a single curriculum centered on language, composition, and literature, the English curriculum needs to be diversified. The Curriculum Commission recommended that teachers seek out "experience strands," that is, series of similar types of experiences gradually increasing in scope and difficulty through the grade levels. Such strands might serve, it is pointed out, as the structure for the English program. An examination of the strands of experience in Oral Composition reveals much about the concept of English underlying the thinking of the authors of the report. They are: Conversing, Telephoning, Discussing and Planning, Telling Stories, Dramatizing, Reporting, Speaking to Large Groups.

The English Language Arts (1952). The war, a changed and changing social order, and new understandings of learning and human development encouraged the NCTE to establish, in the late 1940's, an expanded Commission on the English Curriculum. The work of this commission led, in 1952, to the first volume of the NCTE Curriculum Series, *The English Language Arts* (5). This report was designed (1) to present an overview of current practices, (2) to bring the best thinking of the field to bear on major issues, and (3) to describe a method of approach to curriculum building. It does all these, and, in the process, extends the concept of English, found in the Hosic Report and developed in the 1935 NCTE report, to include study in listening, in semantics, and in the mass modes of communication. As defined by implication in *The English Language Arts,* English is reading, writing, speaking, and listening. The best current information about methodology, and about curriculum building, is utilized in the report to make the underlying concept of English dramatically alive and useful. The concept, while too catholic for some, was able to satisfy large numbers of teachers of English. But not for long.

The English Language Arts of 1952 failed to have the impact on practice and theory of either the Hosic Report or *An Experience Curriculum in English.* Although one of its implied objectives was to pull together current thinking on English and present a concept of English which would embrace a multitude of approaches, the 1952 report was the victim of its age. At the time when its effect should have been reverberating through the profession, sputnik went up, articulate, often well-financed, anti-progressive voices in education and in society took the opportunity to react to two decades of changes in America and in American schools, and *The English Language Arts,* instead of unifying thinking and enriching and enlarging the concept of English, became itself the symbol of only one kind of thinking about English.

Freedom and Discipline in English (1965). In September, 1959, the College Entrance Examination Board appointed its own Commission on English and charged it with the awesome task of improving the teaching of English in American schools and colleges. The Board was concerned, its spokesman noted, that English, in trying to meet needs not met elsewhere in the secondary schools, was becoming too diffuse, was in danger of losing its identity. The Commission set out to answer the question "What is English?" and came to the conclusion that the English language constituted the core of the subject. Its report, *Freedom and Discipline in English* (6), while confining its attention to college preparatory students, spells out an answer to the question in detail: it recommends that the English program be defined as the study of language, literature, and composition, with language as the core of the program, and that matters not clearly related to such study be excluded from the curriculum.

III

A re-examination of the Hosic Report, of *An Experience Curriculum in English,* of *The English Language Arts,* of *Freedom and Discipline in English* — especially if the four reports, representing, as they do, some four decades of thinking about English teaching, are re-examined together — encourages one to draw inferences about the concept of English in our time. Two such inferences are drawn here.

It would seem, first, that there are two, almost diametrically opposed, concepts of English current in the twentieth century. On the one hand is the view that English is a discipline, that is, that it is a clearly developed branch of knowledge, characterized to include the study of language, literature, and composition. On the other hand is the view that English is, rather, a *broad field* embracing a range of competencies in reading, writing, speaking, and listening. Those who believe that English is a discipline — usually college teachers of English and secondary school teachers of college-preparatory students — are essentialists: to them, English constitutes a body of knowledge, existing independent of men and women (and boys and girls) which, if mastered, will enable them somehow better to understand and cope with reality. Those who see English as a general area of studies seem to believe that the term "English" serves (and this is, of course, a simplification) to unify and to bring coherence to a body of skills in communication in self-perception, and in self-understanding. The term *English Language Arts,* still used in elementary education, may best characterize this point of view.

A second inference to be drawn from a re-examination of the four reports is that the pendulum — to revive an effective metaphor — has swung back. At the turn of the century, English was conceived as a discipline. During the first five decades of the century, it was believed (at least by those who wrote the reports) to be a complex of skills to enhance and enrich the lives of students. The last report considered conceives of English as a discipline. The pendulum seems to have returned to its 1900 starting place.

What, then, once again, is English? Is it a clearly defined discipline? Is it a term embracing a galaxy of communication skills? As teachers of English move into the last third of the century, a period promising revolutionary changes in secondary education, must they define their area of studies by whatever concept seems in vogue at the moment? Must they be influenced by the position of the pendulum?

The nature of the questions which evolve from the initial query, "What is English?," seems to indicate that no pat, generally acceptable answers will present themselves in the next decades. However, the re-examination of the four reports and of the questions raised by that re-examination suggest — at least to this writer — that teachers of English (and theorists about the teaching of English) might be guided by two simple recommendations. First, writers of English textbooks, planners of English curricula, and teachers of English should be reminded that they, more than others in secondary education, are apt to be trapped by the *faulty dilemma.* At the present time, there are two concepts of English prevalent; they seem to be diametrically opposed. It would be convenient to take an either-or point of view and choose one or the other concept to guide one's thinking. The danger here, as always when the trap of the faulty dilemma presents itself, is that one overlooks options. There may be *other* concepts of English. The doors of the mind need to be kept open so that other concepts may be examined when they are presented.

(Aside from the matter of possible options, it may be said that teachers who make the choice one way or the other will certainly do a disservice for their students. Those who teach English as if it were a clearly delineated body of knowledge will slight students who *need* teen-age novels, instruction in televiewing, lessons in using the telephone and in writing job applications. Those who view English as communication skills only will do an injustice to a "discipline" that has survived since Aristotle's *Rhetoric,* the grammar of John Wallis, and the writings of Northrop Frye.)

Those involved in the teaching of English need to be reminded, too, that, like all their fellows in the twentieth century, they must develop their *tolerance for ambiguity.* The concept of English as a clear-cut discipline is widely shared in the profession. Many of the most effective teachers and writers in the field believe that English does have well-defined lines of demarcation separating it from other fields or disciplines. On the other hand, many other successful teachers feel that these lines are too sharply drawn and that, for *their* students, English must include a multitude of communication skills. While it is imperative that secondary school students develop important understandings about the nature and art of language, it is also imperative that secondary school students learn to read newspapers, listen to television commercials, speak at rallies and PTA meetings, and write letters to the editor, — and to the small-loan department of their bank. Teachers of English need to recognize that English is all these things — and maybe more. Their best protection, from a mental-health point of view, may be to develop their own ambiguity tolerance.

The best protection for English as the profession plans for the last third of the century may be teachers who recognize the pitfalls of the faulty dilemma, who develop a tolerance for ambiguity, who recognize that English may be — whatever it is — bigger than them, than their century, and than those who write about it.

REFERENCES

1. Eaton, Arthur W. *College Requirements in English Entrance Examination.* Boston: Ginn, 1894.
2. Brameld, Theodore. *Philosophies of Education in Cultural Perspective,* New York: Holt, 1955, p. 204.
3. Hosic, James F. (compiler). *Reorganization of English in Secondary Schools.* Washington: U.S. Bureau of Education, 1917.

4. Curriculum Commission of the National Council of Teachers of English, *An Experience Curriculum in English,* New York: Appleton-Century-Crofts, 1935.
5. Commission on the English Curriculum of the National Council of Teachers of English, *The English Language Arts,* New York: Appleton-Century-Crofts, 1952.
6. Commission on English, *Freedom and Discipline in English,* New York: College Entrance Examination Board, 1965.

4. Some Basic Issues in the Teaching of English

Ruth G. Strickland

Criticism of American education, always vocal but not always well-reasoned, veers from one area to another, centering from time to time on American history, "frills" versus "fundamentals," or science and mathematics, stimulated by various currents in our national life. Some of the concern regarding education arises within the profession and some outside it. Regardless of the source, critical study of educational programs and problems can be of immense value to the schools and to society if pursued with sincerity, integrity, and impartiality. Such a spirit motivated the group of professional organizations which co-operated during 1958 and 1959 to study the teaching of English in our schools and to outline what seem to be the basic issues in the matter.[1]

From Ruth G. Strickland, "Some Basic Issues in the Teaching of English," *Phi Delta Kappan,* May, 1960, 41:332–335. Ruth G. Strickland, Professor of Education at Indiana University, Bloomington, was President of the National Council of Teachers of English when this article was published. Reprinted by permission of the *Phi Delta Kappan.*

[1] Twenty-eight teachers of English met for three three-day conferences under the auspices of the American Studies Association, the College English Association, the Modern Language Association of America, and the National Council of Teachers of English. The enterprise was supported by a grant from the Ford Foundation.

The study of the subject called "English," or more recently by some the "English language arts," is a part of the curriculum of every American student from the time he enters first grade until he is at least part way through college. To be sure, children learn to speak their native language at home, but proficiency in reading and writing it requires years of instruction and practice. No one questions the need for the study of English; neither does anyone feel that the results obtained through years of study are as satisfying as they should be. In a culture as highly verbal as ours, there are many vocations in which effective use of spoken and written language and the ability to understand difficult reading matter are essential. In some measure the rewards and penalties assigned by society are based on the extent to which individuals demonstrate these abilities.

The report of the Conference on Basic Issues states three reasons for studying English: for its *practical value,* for its *civilizing value,* and *for the love of it.* In the modern world everyone recognizes the practical value of the skills of communication, but the study of English includes subject matter as well as skills. The subject matter is the literature available in English — the cultural inheritance of the English-speaking people. This literature tells the story of man, "what he has dreamed and felt and thought — not only in the past, but in the present also." Literature is a source of vicarious experience which helps man to understand himself and the rest of mankind. Therein lies its civilizing value. Literature is also an art which utilizes a medium known and used by everyone. "The materials of a good liberal education are to be found in the paperback books, now available at newsstands everywhere in the country. But to profit from this opportunity, the habit of reading and a love of good literature are necessary."

The members of the Conference on Basic Issues as well as the entire profession are deeply concerned both with what is taught in the English classes at all grade levels and with the quality of the work in English. The demands of modern life and the influence of mass media have brought changes and additions to the curriculum at many points. Elementary schools have placed increasing emphasis on oral language — listening and speaking — and on the needs of all children for skill in letter writing, use of the telephone, language as it relates to good manners, and the like. Junior and senior high-school teachers have given increased attention to vocational guidance and language for vocational and social purposes. This is not to say that curricula in English have omitted the traditional emphasis on skills and literature but rather that new emphases have been added and time allotments modified.

Concern regarding the teaching of English centers about the question of whether or not all of these emphases, valuable though they may be, divert attention unduly from the major tasks of fostering in children a love and appreciation for good literature, together with the ability to read and comprehend it, and the equally important development of skill in writing. Public criticism as well as criticism within the profession have dealt mainly with these points.

It is wise to state at this point that the reactions expressed in this article are based upon experience in teaching all grades of the elementary school and in programs of teacher education, as well as considerable study of the development of language in children and some research which involves application of the work of specialists in descriptive linguistics. Teachers who approach the report on basic issues from other points of view may be expected to react somewhat differently at various points.

The Most Crucial Issue

Probably the most crucial issue raised by the conference is found in the question, "Can basic programs in English be devised that are sequential and cumulative from the kindergarten through the graduate school?"[2] Every other idea in the report to some extent hinges on it. Each level of the English program utilizes of necessity the competencies built at preceding levels and moves in the direction of succeeding expectancies. The question is asked whether agreement can be reached upon a body of knowledge and a set of skills as standard at certain points in the curriculum, allowing, of course, for flexibility of planning, individual differences, and patterns of growth. This writer has long advocated that curriculum makers seek to determine the natural and logical sequence in the development of skills in each aspect of the English program — listening, speaking, reading, and writing — as a guide to teachers at all levels. This is not for the purpose of setting definite standards of attainment for all children at any point, but for the guidance of teachers in caring for individual differences. With the help of such a chart, the teacher at any grade level could study a student, determine where he stood at any given time, and plan next steps for him in line with his need.

Developing a Background for Literature

The conference report expresses considerable concern regarding the development of a scholarly approach to literature and the requisite back-

[2] *The Basic Issues in the Teaching of English.* Supplement to *Elementary English, English Journal,* and *College English,* October, 1959.

ground for understanding and enjoying literature. It includes the questions of approach and timing: "When is it most appropriate to practice rigorous textual analysis? To employ the historical and sociological approach? To relate the work to the history of ideas?" (p. 7)

A major objective of the elementary school is to make readers of children. Teachers endeavor to select prose and poetry to read and tell to children through which to develop tastes and interests and make children hungry for more of what is wholesome and valuable. Today's children are bombarded outside of school by so much that is cheap and valueless that satisfying experience in school with more wholesome material appears the only antidote. A child builds himself as he builds his language. His attitude toward himself, toward others, toward life on the earth, and toward man's relationship with man is shaped and colored in large measure by the stories with which he lives.

Teachers seek to open to all children a wide range of reading possibilities and introduce them to many types of material that are well-written for their kind and the purpose they are designed to serve. The present emphasis on guided individual reading is means to that end. Among the stories which teachers present to children should be, at appropriate ages, the folk stories, myths, Biblical stories, and stories from history that form a part of literary allusion at later levels. But to confine the literary experience of modern children to these materials would be to lose sight of the major goal — to make readers of children.

Analysis and Didactic Approach Repel

Every teacher of elementary grade children is aware of children's aversion to analysis of stories and to a didactic approach to them. It is wiser in most instances to follow children's leads in discussion or to let a story speak for itself than to insist upon analysis which repels children. Suggested lists of material calling attention to the values to be sought through the use of content from certain categories would appear wiser than required lists. Elementary grade teachers have no choice but to take each child where he is and guide his development from that point — whether he comes with a rich background and wholesome interests or from no contact at all with literature and no interest on which to build.

Teachers of junior and senior high school groups need to be aware of the backgrounds young people possess and their psychological reactions to various approaches to literature. They need especially to study students' reactions to literary analysis, since even well-educated parents with high standards for their children report their children repelled at times by literary vivisection. How much textual analysis should be attempted with children of average ability and background would need to be determined by the results of such study.

The Need for Writing Improvement

Another area of major concern of the Conference on Basic Issues deals with writing. Several questions are asked regarding it. It is comforting to teachers to read the statement, "We have seen no reliable evidence that students are writing less well than comparable students wrote twenty, forty, or a hundred years ago." (p. 9) Nevertheless, neither teachers nor the general public is satisfied with the present quality of student writing. Undoubtedly, a part of the problem is traceable to the relatively small amount of writing demanded of children in many schools. Filling in blanks in workbooks and doing brief prescribed exercises is not enough writing for the development of skill in communicating ideas on paper. Children need to write for many purposes — both to convey facts and related ideas and to express their own creative imagination. Surely, some of what they write should be carefully studied for mechanics as well as for clear handling of content and should not be put aside until it has been corrected and put into the best form of which the child is capable. In writing of an imaginative sort, emphasis might better be placed on creative thinking with less attention to form.

General dissatisfaction is expressed by the conference report when it comes to the inevitable topic of grammar. "A knowledge of traditional English grammar is sometimes considered an intellectual discipline and a social necessity. Accordingly, over the past century, grammar has been taught in thousands of classrooms, but with little apparent effect upon the written or spoken language of many pupils. Perhaps it was naive to expect it, in terms of what we know today about the language learning process." (p. 13.) With what a sigh of relief many a conscientious elementary teacher will read this statement from a document produced by a scholarly group composed largely of teachers of English from colleges and high schools! The teaching of traditional English grammar in the elementary school has had to be followed, almost inevitably, by the reteaching of the same grammar in junior and senior high schools.

The report calls attention to the possibilities which may be found in the work of the descriptive linguists. Research now being carried on regarding the development of clarity and maturity in the structure of children's sentences indicates that there are real values here. Children enjoy playing with language. To take a simple sentence consisting of bare subject and predicate, the two essential slots, and add to it movables which denote time, place, manner, and the like, would be of real interest to children of elementary school age. They have learned by ear a great deal of grammar before they come to school at the age of five or six. To learn through study of their own oral sentences how one can modify emphasis and shades of meaning by placing movable elements in various positions in a sentence would help to tune their ears to correct forms and patterns. It is fairly safe to say that no elementary school child writes better than he talks. If he rarely twists his tongue or his mind around a well-constructed complex or compound sentence, he will read such a sentence orally with poor interpretation, and silently with inadequate comprehension of meaning. Growth in the maturity of a child's oral language appears the key to growth in all other aspects of language.

No One Can Create in a Vacuum

Undoubtedly, at least at the elementary school level, there is clear relationship between hearing and reading imaginative literature and learning to write. Until a child has first heard and later read and enjoyed well-written imaginative literature, he has little within himself to draw upon for his writing. No one can create in a vacuum. Children can think creatively and compose satisfactorily only out of fullness of experience. Whether this requires "studying" literary works at this period or "experiencing" them is another matter. The kind of experience in which a child loses himself in a story, feels and thinks with its characters, and enjoys real empathy, is perhaps of greater value than any program of "study" at this age.

A question is posed regarding the possibility of establishing national standards for student writing at the various levels and the value of such standards. It is true that teachers need help to teach writing more effectively. But poor teaching at the present time appears to be the result of too many pressures and too little time for individual guidance rather than lack of understanding of what ought to be done. The pressures take the form of emphasis on mechanics to the detriment of emphasis on content and style — and, surely, no sentence correctly punctuated, spelled, and set down on paper is of any real value unless what it says is worth reading. Teachers need help to understand how to guide children's thinking and how to enrich the content of their minds as well as help with how to teach children to write correctly. It is doubtful that national norms, even as suggestion and guidance, could serve the real needs of children and teachers.

How Enlist Aid Elsewhere?

How can teachers of English enlist the aid of everyone, teachers of other subjects, administrators, members of boards of education, and the public at large, to make the English program as effective as possible? The answer to this question requires a great deal of thought. A basic need is to study the factors that operate to tear down what is being done by the schools as well as to study what would improve the work of the schools. Mass media of all types, particularly television, could be made far more valuable to the life of the nation as a whole through improvement of the offering to children. Only in the realm of children's books has genuine progress toward high standards of quality been made. Here there is real richness for children, for which only ease of access and guidance are needed to bring about highly desirable results in child growth and the development of individual, personal standards regarding quality. The same values could be gained through other media if public interest could be built to the point that higher standards in offerings for children were demanded of all producers.

Necessary Research Studies

There are great values in the report of the Conference on Basic Issues, in the interest it has engendered, and in the study and discussion which have grown out of it. Fortunately, the report raises questions but lays down no demands and proposes no definite solutions. The solutions must come from further study and research in communities, schools, and individual classrooms. Reactions will differ widely, depending on the reader's philosophy of education, his personal experience, his interests, and his biases. As was stated at the beginning of this article, critical analysis of curriculum and of teaching may be the means to improvement and new values for students and for society. But the analysis, in order to be truly valuable, must be pursued with sincerity, integrity, and impartiality. It is hoped that many people will study this report and help, through their study, to add depth and concrete value to the teaching of English.

Looking beyond the elementary school, several research studies appear necessary if the questions of the report are to be answered in the light of the values for the teaching of English that are stated or implied in the report. Studies are needed to throw light on these questions: 1. What are the interests and capacities of young people at various grade and ability levels as they relate to English? 2. What are the results, in terms of student interest and *actual voluntary reading*, of rigorous textual analysis at junior and senior high-school levels? For whom can this analysis best be provided? When? How much? 3. Why do students decide to major in the field of English? What interests lead them to do so? At what levels do they make their decisions? 4. How adequate to demand is the supply of English teachers educated according to the standards of the conference? 5. Why does so small a proportion of college students elect courses in English after they have completed the required courses? 6. Where programs in English exist such as the conference appears to approve, what are the end results of such work — for example, is there wide voluntary reading of literature such as is advocated and a high quality of voluntary writing? With what proportion of students? Why? All of these questions *can be answered* with factual data if the profession sincerely wishes such answers. It appears that the questions will continue to perplex and irritate many people within and without the profession until these answers are made available.

5. Language Arts in the Curriculum

Helen F. Olson

The English language arts are concerned with communication, or the receiving and expression of ideas. They are concerned also with composition, which is thinking — the organization and composing of thought for speech and writing. Therefore, the language arts include both content and skills. Although the content may range as wide as the

From Helen F. Olson, "Language Arts in the Curriculum," *Educational Leadership*, February, 1962, 10:302–306. Helen F. Olson is Director of the English Language Arts, Seattle Public Schools. Her writings have appeared in many academic and professional journals and she is co-author of *Holt English Language Arts, Grades 7–12,* and *Experiences in Writing.* This article is reprinted by permission of the Association for Supervision and Curriculum Development and the author.

interests and purposes of students engaged in communication, the special content areas of the English language arts are: (a) the nature and development of language and (b) literature. The skills of language arts are: (a) observing and listening, (b) reading, (c) speaking, (d) writing, and (e) the related language skills.

An Effective Program

The place of the English language arts in the curriculum is fundamental, because these are the content and skills upon which most learning is based. A good language arts program does not just happen; it is planned, implemented and supported.

The English language arts program, in any school district, can be just as good as the school personnel and the citizens of the community wish it to be. For effective teaching and learning, the program must be so developed and implemented that it can be described as providing for (a) adequate coverage of the important content, (b) arrangement of content to meet the needs of all students, (c) use of appropriate teaching methods, (d) conditions which foster superior teaching and maximum learning, and (e) recognition of the importance of the work.

An effective program centers on a basic course of study. A good program ensures that high school graduates will have, in common, a certain background knowledge of English. They will not all have learned any aspect of the subject to the same extent or to the same depth. Yet each will have had the opportunity to learn, to the best of his abilities, those aspects of English which, in the twentieth century, a young person needs in order to succeed in useful work, to go to the college of his choice, and to take his place as a thinking individual and a worthy citizen.

What is to be taught must be allocated to the various grade levels, kindergarten through grade 12, in such ways that certain content and skills are introduced and emphasized at each grade level. For instance, the reading program begins with the prereading activities of kindergarten and continues through grade 12. An adequate reading program is four-faceted; it provides for basic reading skills instruction, functional reading, development of literary appreciation and development of independent-reading habits. To have adequate coverage of the subject, the course of study must include materials or information concerning sources of materials: language texts, spellers, readers, literary anthologies, literary works, records, film strips, films, magazines, newspapers.

Good literature, appropriate to the maturity of the pupils, should be taught at all grade levels, from the primary grades through grade 12.

An effective course of study is sufficiently specific and yet sufficiently flexible to meet the needs of all students. Since every teacher of each grade level has the complete course, he is able to use it to suit any particular classroom situation. For inadequately prepared pupils, he utilizes material from previous grades. With slow learners, he selects only the most fundamental parts of the course so that there will be time for thorough learning of these. With accelerated students, the teacher may move ahead to the work of the next grade or of succeeding grades. The only limitation is that materials — textbooks, readers, literary works — allocated for all-class or group work at a certain grade, should not be used in previous grades. A good program provides for enough sufficiently varied materials that selection for individual classroom situations is possible.

A good English language arts program makes additional provision for individual interests and abilities by offering numerous electives and special programs. Electives may include speech arts, journalism, writing laboratory, drama, senior writing, and advanced literature. Special programs are important at all grade levels. For instance, special classes in reading improvement should be offered for students whose potential reading ability is demonstrably greater than their current reading level.

An effective course of study frees the teacher by providing for diversity within unity. Diversity is encouraged through teaching procedures which utilize the creativity of the teacher and allow adaptation to the individual classroom situation. Unity is assured when each teacher covers what is to be taught at each grade level. Thus, the teacher following the basic course knows that he will cover content and skills to be taught and feels free to apply his energy and creativity to finding ways of inducing maximum learning in young persons. A section of the course of study might present numerous ways of teaching various phases of the work at different grade levels. Teachers manuals for approved textbooks and readers should be made available. Bulletins may be issued from time to time describing teaching procedures used successfully in the school system or in other school systems. The well-trained teacher studies these suggestions and adapts them to the needs of the individuals in his classroom.

An effective course of study is characterized by teaching conditions which foster superior teaching and maximum learning. However clear the course of study, however available the materials, however superior and well-trained the teacher, teaching and learning tend to be influenced by the conditions of the teaching.

The teacher's load must be reasonable. Ideally, a teacher in the elementary school should have 25 or fewer pupils. A teacher of English in the secondary school should have not more than five classes of 20 or fewer students. Where financial considerations make such class size impossible, other means should be used to reduce the load to one where adequate discussion of literature and handling of written work are possible. Such means include readers to help with paper correction, clerical assistance, and rearrangements of classes to vary the size of groups in accordance with specific content or skill being taught. For instance, several hundred high school students might be grouped together to see a Shakespeare film or to hear a lecture on theme writing.

An effective language arts program is characterized by general recognition of the importance of the content and skills being taught. The first responsibility is the English teacher's. Too many students move through school without ever being made aware of what the language arts program is all about. The teacher's first responsibility is to explain the goals to the students, to show them how the content and skills are related, to make clear, each step of the way, what the work is about, why it is important, and how they can gain satisfaction from their specific, individual accomplishment. Clearly stated listings of expected attainments in the course of study help the teacher to stimulate growth and achievement.

Developing the Program

Development of the program described involves considerable organization. Curricula are likely to be most successful when the participation in their development is extensive. Such participation is notably simpler in a small school system where all teachers concerned might gather in one room. In a large school system, participation must be gained through a system of representation, delegation and reporting. To develop a basic course of study in a large city system, for instance, the language arts director and staff must first achieve a climate favorable to the revision and reorganization of an established program. They must talk with teachers and department heads, counselors and principals, with individuals and with groups. They ask questions and listen to comments and gradually gain a fairly clear picture of desirable changes. Perhaps a questionnaire is used, with the findings tabulated and reported back to the teachers.

The first step is to form a steering committee to head the work of revision. Since the course of study is to outline what is to be taught in all areas of the language arts at all grade levels, there must be representatives of all grade levels on the steering committee. To insure that administration is actively involved in the program, principals of the three levels — elementary, junior high, and senior high — should be invited to serve.

The first work of the steering committee is to examine courses of study in cities of comparable size, to study available research, to assess what can be utilized from the previous course of study, and then to do some specific planning for a long-time job. Probably a year is required for this study and planning. During this time, too, through department heads in the secondary school and principals and teacher representatives in the elementary school, all teachers of language arts are led into discussions of what should be included in the new course.

The next step is making sequences and trying these out in the schools. The steering committee appoints a committee including a representative from each grade level and resource persons from the steering committee, for each of the six major divisions of language arts: reading, observing and listening, organizing thought, speaking, writing, and specific language skills. At the end of the year, each committee has decided tentatively what should be taught in its area of the language arts, and at what level it should be taught. Also, the sequences have been sent out to teachers for discussions in the buildings and for written reactions to be referred to the steering committee.

The next year, the steering committee reorganizes so that there are 13 horizontal committees, one for each grade level. Each of these committees studies the six sequences and develops a course outline for a particular grade level. The steering committee then edits the work and prepares the course in four mimeographed sections: for the primary grades, for the intermediate grades, for the junior high school and for the senior high school years.

Clarifying Emphases

The course is tried out for one year — each teacher being asked to submit suggestions for improvement. During this year of trying out the course, consultation, discussions in buildings, area meetings, talks before parent-teacher and other community organizations are even more extensive, if possible, than during the year of initial planning. Librarians, counselors, staff members — all are brought into the evaluation; all are kept in tune with the progress of the work.

At the end of the year, the steering committee goes over all the suggestions, edits the material, and prepares to have it published as a single book.

A course of study is effective only to the extent that it is accepted and put into practice. If the discussion, consultation, interpretation, and involvement of the years during the development of the course have been effective, staff members and citizens are asking to see the completed book before it is off the press. If such is the case, one big step toward implementing the course has already been taken. Thus, as soon as the copies of the book have been distributed, the work can center on clarifying the emphases of the course of study.

It is important to stress the value of achieving focus in the English language arts. Each teacher uses the outline of what is to be taught as a check list and makes his own plans for organizing the year's work into practicable teaching units. The elementary teacher must arrange for the timing of language arts in the daily schedule. He must schedule a regular time for the basic reading program, for the other facets of the reading program, for oral work, for written composition, for spelling, for handwriting, and for the other language skills.

Strengthening the Program

The secondary school teacher must plan to relate the various language arts as closely as possible, using one aspect, such as literary appreciation, to strengthen other aspects, such as oral discussion and written composition. This focus can be made through utilizing a basic, five-step process of composition: (a) reading and thinking together; (b) planning for writing; (c) writing the first drafts; (d) sharing, evaluating, revising and rewriting; and (e) studying some related language skills.

This process is open to many variations. It may require a day or two or several weeks, depending upon the extent of the activity required for each step. The value is that such a process combines all aspects of the language arts, gives them focus, and makes accomplishment easy to evaluate.

A program is either becoming continuously strengthened or it is losing, little by little, its effectiveness. This truth is particularly applicable to the English language arts because of the constant changes in language, the new developments in the field of grammar and linguistics, the growing interest in research into methods of teaching reading and listening, the nation-wide attempt to raise the level of written composition. Maintaining and strengthening the English program calls for at least five kinds of active leadership.

An effective in-service training program is essential. All needed materials for teaching — courses of study, bulletins, teachers manuals — should be made easily available to the teacher. Demonstrations at all grade levels should be encouraged, with consequent emphasis upon exchange of classroom visits by interested teachers. Building meetings, area meetings, small-group conferences are important. Workshops and professional classes should be available to teachers each year. Most important, over-all planning and the development of teacher leaders are essential to maintaining a high level in all in-service training. The good teacher is a creative thinker, and the best program is the result of the creativity and the constructively critical thinking of all staff members.

The preparation of new teachers must be improved. One who will teach writing to young persons must have some training in written composition other than that gained through "Freshman Composition" or through writing term papers for other college subjects. One who is to teach grammar and syntax should not only be thoroughly grounded in traditional grammar but should also know something of the history and development of the English language and have taken at least one course in one or more of the emerging "new grammars," such as structural linguistics. A secondary school English teacher can no longer afford to be ignorant of how to teach the basic reading skills, nor of the relation of phonics to reading and to spelling and to speech improvement. An elementary school teacher must have much more training in English than can be gained from a three-hour course in "Language Arts."

A constant search for new materials and improved methods is a must. Television is still in the experimental stage. What can be done through television better than through the traditional pupil-teacher-classroom approach? This possible avenue to improved teaching and learning requires further exploration. Are teaching machines just expensive gadgets promoted by commercial interests? Can useful programmed learning be developed? Is the Carnegie unit the ultimate answer to school organization or can other and more effective scheduling be devised? If 30 pupils are too many for effective teaching of written composition, may so small a group be a waste of teacher time when a film is to be shown or programmed learning is to be used? Accompanying the search for new ways of teaching must be continuous evaluation of the current program in terms of pupil growth and achievement. There must also be evaluation of each new method in terms of its usefulness in furthering the basic program.

The English language arts program holds a position of priority in the curriculum since the skills and content of English are the foundations upon which other learning is based. The program described in this article is being developed and implemented in the Seattle Public Schools.

6. Literature: The Reader's Role

Louise M. Rosenblatt

Having been assigned the general topic, "literature as communication," I am tempted to dwell on the wit, the wisdom, the beauty that imaginative literature can communicate: It brings to us the funded meanings of our whole way of life; it enables us to share the inmost lives of people distant in time and space; it leads us to join in the great visions of what human life has meant and of what humane life can become. But I shall resist the temptation to linger on *what* literature offers, and move on to ask *how* literature communicates. In the work of art, the "what" and the "how" are ultimately only aspects of one another, yet in current discussions about the literature curriculum, confusion and disagreements often arise from disregard of this latter question. Especially does there seem to be neglect of the reader's role in literary communication.

W. H. Auden's "In Memory of W. B. Yeats" describes, you recall, the "dark cold day" of Yeats' death, when "the current of his feeling failed: he became his admirers."

Now he is scattered among a hundred cities
And wholly given over to unfamiliar affections;
To find his happiness in another kind of wood
And be punished under a foreign code of conscience.
The words of a dead man
Are modified in the guts of the living.

From Louise M. Rosenblatt, "Literature: The Reader's Role," *The English Journal*, May, 1960, 49:304–310, 315. Louise M. Rosenblatt, author of the well-known *Literature as Exploration*, is Professor of English Education at New York University. Her articles have appeared in numerous scholarly and professional journals. This article is based on an address given at the 1959 convention of the National Council of Teachers of English. Reprinted by permission of the National Council of Teachers of English and Louise M. Rosenblatt.

"The words of a dead man/Are modified in the guts of the living." Auden perhaps can startle us into realization of the reader's active role in literary communication. The words of a poet remain merely black marks on the page until they are brought to life anew by his readers in the context of their own worlds. "He became his admirers."

Much discussion of literature seems to imply that communication is a one-way process. The author, we say, communicates to the reader. The reader is thought of as approaching the text like a blank photographic film awaiting exposure. Actually, the reader and the text are more analogous to a pianist and a musical score. But the instrument that the reader plays upon is — himself. His keyboard is the range of his own past experiences with life and literature, his own present concerns, anxieties, and aspirations. Under the stimulus and guidance of the text, the reader seeks to strike the appropriate keys, to bring the relevant responses into consciousness. Out of the particular sensations, images, feelings, and ideas which have become linked for him with the verbal symbols, he creates a new organization. This is for him the poem or play or story. Thus does he enter into communication with the author. Only through a recasting of his own experiences can he share the writer's mood, his vision of man or society or nature.

Moreover, literature provides a special form of communication. Perhaps "communion" would be a better word to apply to imaginative literature. For in reading a poem or novel, we are preoccupied with the experience we are living through in the actual reading. We are alert to the very sound and rhythm of the words conjured up in our inner ear. We are intimately involved in what we are recreating under the guidance of the text. *Othello* is for each of us what we see in imagination as we read, what we think and feel during our actual imaginative participation in the personalities, the situations, the sequence of events, the lyric moments, called up in us by Shakespeare's words. We live through the suspense, the foreboding, the ultimate resolution. The structure of the work for us is the structure of our experience while under its spell. Aristotle, after all, recognized this inwardness of literary experience when he made the nature of the spectator's response a test of tragedy; it is the reader who feels the pity and terror that are the marks of tragedy. No one else can read — i.e., experience — a literary work of art for us. That is why, also, we find that the *Antony and Cleopatra* read at fifteen is not the same work we evoke at thirty.

Recognizing Factors in Literary Experience

Hence, the quality of our literary experience depends not only on the text, on what the author offers, but also on the relevance of past experiences and present interests that the reader brings to it. We all know that there will be no active evocation of the literary work, no such experience lived-through, if the text offers little or no linkage with the past experiences and present interests, anxieties, and hopes of the reader. The work will not, we say, "come alive" for that reader, but, of course, we should phrase this actively, and say that he is not ready to bring it to life.

This fact of the need for "readiness" is now usually recognized at the beginning of the child's career as a reader. The child is first helped to link experiences to verbal symbols. Thus he becomes able through words to structure past experience and to emerge into new understandings. Without sufficient relevant experience, he can evoke nothing from the page. At best, he may be able to make the appropriate sounds and parrot the words, but there will not be organization of meaning. To phrase this simply as a matter of "vocabulary" is to miss the point. Probably Ernest Hemingway's vocabulary in "The Killers" and other of his stories is quite within the range of some fourth-graders. They would understand the individual words, yet be unable to organize them into a meaningful story. They would not bring to the text the experience that would enable them to recreate the story in all its complexity. This, of course, is another way of saying that we must postpone asking them to read this story until they develop sufficient awareness and maturity to interpret all that is implied or suggested by the text.

What, then, are some implications for curriculum of this briefly-sketched view of how literature communicates? The primary inference, of course, is that curriculum planning must take into account two elements: on the one hand, the great wealth of literature of which we are guardians, and, on the other hand, what the student-reader at any point brings to this cooperative enterprise of literary communication. We need to remember that always we seek to help particular students, at particular times and places, with their special past experiences and present concerns, to participate in literary works. Literature equals book plus reader. The danger is that we may neglect either one or the other factor in this equation.

Avoiding Overemphasis on the Work

We may fall into the error of concentrating mainly on books: As specialists, we naturally feel our responsibility toward transmitting the rich heritage of English and American literature, and we are increasingly being called upon to broaden our purview to include the whole range of world literature. Today, with all that threatens our system of values from within and without, literature can perform a crucial function. Surely, we are justified in reviewing our literature curricula, to make certain that they include works embodying the esthetic, social and moral sensitivities that constitute our living humane tradition. Yet we must guard against preoccupation simply with designating those works that we consider important from an historical, social, or esthetic point of view. We cannot afford merely to assume that the reader's contribution will be taken care of, or to imply that simple exposure to a sequence of works is sufficient.

Of course — whatever the practice may be in particular schools — there are very few today who would urge a return to, let us say, a set list of books which every high school student should read, or which even every college-bound student should read. The Advanced Placement program has demonstrated that the colleges certainly do not seek such uniformity. Nevertheless, a tendency to speak mainly of books alone emerges in current discussions of the literature curriculum. For example, the current — very laudable — concern with raising standards is often phrased simply in terms of names of authors or kinds of books, such as classics or certain genres, that should be included in the literature program, with perhaps only vague remarks about levels of comprehension taking the place of a real facing of the other factor in the literary equation.

At a conference of college and high school teachers of English, for example, I heard a college instructor complain that he could not count on his freshman students' being able to recognize various allusions to mythology or the Bible, nor could he count on knowledge of any particular literary masterpieces. He seemed to believe that high school teachers were wilfully thrusting inferior books upon their pupils in place of the great masterpieces. I fear that he was not alone in looking upon the high school years simply as preparation for *real* literary experience in college. Surely, entering college freshmen should have had experience with mythology, the Bible and Shakespeare. But when the pupil does read such works in high school, it should not be simply in order to be able *later* to recognize allusions or make comparisons, nor should it be for the purpose of later simplifying the college instructor's task. If the high school student reads the *Odyssey* or the Book of Job or *Romeo and Juliet,* it should be primarily because at this point in his life this particular work offers a significant and enjoyable experience for him, an experience that involves him personally and that he can assimilate into his ongoing intellectual and emotional development. *Potential present meaningfulness* should be the first criterion of selection. Without this, we have said, there will be no real literary experience. And that, of course, brings both the student and the book into the center of focus in curriculum planning.

Fortunately, a major advance in American education and in the teaching of English during the past twenty years has been the increasing provision for individual differences and for the interests and needs of the individual student. It is also more and more generally recognized that the immediate, deeply personal concerns, anxieties, and aspirations of the young reader — especially the adolescent — remain the major path for him into literature. It would indeed be unfortunate if those who are seeking to raise our cultural standards should defeat their own ends by encouraging a disregard for this still by no means universally-understood insight. Yet the implication often seems to be that concern with the personal or social approach to literature, or concern with the interests and needs of student readers has caused, and necessarily leads to, neglect of the classics or literature of high quality. Nothing is more contrary to the nature of literature itself than the notion of such an inherent contradiction.

To improve, not simply the quality of books studied, but rather the quality of literary experiences undergone: this should be the emphasis when we speak of raising standards. To lead the student to have literary experiences of higher and higher quality requires constant concern for what at any point he brings to his reading, what by background, temperament, and training he is ready to participate in. Literary sensitivity and literary maturity cannot be divorced from the individual's rhythm of growth and breadth of experience. Sometimes a lively and discriminating response, let us say, to Enid Bagnold's *National Velvet* may be a sounder rung in the ladder of literary maturation than a pale, confused perusal of, say, *A Tale of Two Cities* or *Pride and Prejudice.* Hence the need for a curriculum based on the idea of individual development rather than on a standard sequence of books.

A developmental curriculum would make personal involvement and immediacy of interest the basis for growth — growth in the capacities required for participation in good and great literature. Let us not, therefore, reject the plans for the study of literature that take into account the concerns and interests of youth, and that allow for individual differences in maturity, breadth of experience, and temperament. Our aim, after all, is to help students develop a lifetime habit of turning to good literature. Books are losing out at present in the competition for the American's attention; evidently even college graduates read very little. To blame this on failure to expose pupils to specific books, or types of books, is to oversimplify. A more realistic explanation, surely, is that the student in school and college has not been led again and again to literature as relevant to his ongoing life, offering him, here and now, esthetic pleasure in the actual reading and help in organizing his sense of himself and his world. Once such a feeling for literature is established, we need not fear neglect of the masterpieces of the past or present.

Avoiding Overemphasis on the Personal Factor

But we have said that neither of the elements in our two-pronged equation should be overemphasized. If to be concerned mainly with books does not insure a sound curriculum, so also are there dangers in too narrow a concern with the personal factor. One danger is that we shall be satisfied with lively response for its own sake. This reflects a very limited view of literature as communication. Tolstoy, it will be recalled, fell into such a fallacy in "What Is Art?" Insistence on the capacity to arouse emotion as the test of art can lead to the notion that that work is greatest which produces a response in the greatest number of readers. Tolstoy's attempt to define the kind of emotions he valued led only to didacticism. Emphasis on the intensity of response may come ultimately to justify "box office" and best-seller standards, or propagandist demands of a totalitarian state dictating the reactions to be elicited from readers. At fault, of course, is the conception of literary communication as a one-way process, with the passive reader being stimulated to respond emotionally, rather than to engage in an intellectually and emotionally active process, first, of literary recreation and, second, of critical reflection on that experience.

Concern for the personal factor may sometimes also lead to overconcentration on works dealing with the immediate world of the student, on the assumption that these are automatically closer to their interests. This, again, reflects too limited an understanding of the kinds of personal linkage possible between the reader and the literary work. If we think, not simply of the externals of setting and situations, but rather of the underlying emotional and social preoccupations of young people, we shall be able to find personally relevant experiences awaiting them throughout the whole range of literature. Too early or too remotely academic study of Shakespeare in the schools, for instance, has alienated many from his works. The solution sometimes will be to substitute modern plays about contemporary life. But often the solution will lie in looking at the works of Shakespeare from the point of view of the youthful reader. For example, the adolescent's sense of himself launched in a grim world of his elders' making may be the door through which he can find his way into *Romeo and Juliet.* Let the scholar not shudder at the thought that interest in "family relations" may serve as the bridge from the student's world into that starlit tragedy. The young reader, when personally involved, will be impelled to leap the hurdles of time and language and form, and will become caught up in an active recreation of the work itself. Wisdom may lie, too, in being content with what the student makes of a great classic, if he lives through it in his own terms without distortion, even if these do not include all the subtleties apparent to our more mature eyes. This will be sounder training than the glib echoings of sophisticated critical dicta that too often take the place of the young reader's organization of his own response.

Fortunately, to seek literary works that will first of all personally involve the student does not inevitably lead to emotionalism for its own sake. Irresponsible, irrelevant, impressionistic free associations, discussion of topics tangential to the text, simply are evidence of inadequate communication, an imperfect sharing with the writer. The text remains the writer's controlling contribution, the test of the relevance and adequacy of the reader's response. Here, surely, the teacher enters actively. He knows that a lively personal reaction is a necessary, but not a sufficient, condition of full literary communication. Once the live circuit has been set up between the book and the student, he can be helped to bring forth a more complete, a more balanced, a more discriminating experience from it. Indeed, it is precisely the linkages with the student's own intimate preoccupations that provide the challenge to cope with constantly more complex and more diffcult works.

Helping Students Reflect on Literature

Recalling that the literary work is something lived-through by the reader, we can recognize that "teaching the literary work" — teaching a novel or teaching *Romeo and Juliet* — means helping the student primarily to reflect on what he has made of the text. He needs to become aware of the points at which his own concerns have led to excessively emotional or biased reactions, or his lack of experience and knowledge have prevented adequate participation in the work. He needs to scrutinize his response to the various aspects of the work, in order to achieve a more unified patterning of it. He needs to inquire whether the literary experience has brought about a reshaping of what he brought to it. He needs to sense the difference between the shoddy and the genuine. He needs to fit the work into the context of his past encounters with literature and with life. The teacher's task is to help him better to carry out such responsibilities of the reader in the process of literary communication.

Given this view of literary communication, we can avoid the danger of putting one or another peripheral concern in place of the refinement of the student's power to enter into and to interpret literary experiences. We have already mentioned the danger of making literature simply an excuse for discussion of, say, teen-age problems. There is an equal danger, of course, of making the literary work merely the starting point for absorption in literary history, intellectual or social history, or the author's biography. Another such flight from the literary-work-as-experienced can be the study of technique and critical terminology as somehow an end in itself, leaving the amateur critic still incapable of handling his own emotional responses to the text.

Surely, we should be wary of any literature curriculum for the schools designed mainly to illustrate literary history, to demonstrate literary categories, or to inculcate critical terminology. The matter of readiness cannot be merely taken for granted or left to improvisation and compromise. Literary history, the history of ideas, biography, technical analysis, are all, of course, valid and essential subjects for study, when they provide a context for literature and illuminate the literary work — the literary experience — itself. When, for example, students came into a classroom recently exclaiming that they had felt Jane Eyre's troubles so much more intimately than David Copperfield's, the teacher made this the starting point for discussion of differences in style and method. Without such response, lecturing the students on narrative techniques or the use of imagery would simply build up a view of literature as something to be analyzed for academic purposes. Personal involvement, again, provides the impetus for meaningful study of technique, for acquiring a critical vocabulary, or for placing the work in its historical context.

Defining the Value of Literature

In the current upheaval in education, we shall undoubtedly be called upon often to defend the value of literature in the school and college curriculum. (Recently, I was told that the preoccupation with science is leading even writers of elementary reading texts to increase the amount of "scientific" material, and to reduce the amount of space given to narrative!) It is indeed important not only that we base our English curriculum on sound theoretical grounds, but also that any plans for the literature program be phrased to give evidence of due care for all of the factors.

We are justified in arguing the importance of literature, because of both *what* it communicates and *how* it communicates. As our little equation indicated, we can point both to the culture-bearing riches of books and to the reader's achievement of intellectual and imaginative powers through his active role in the literary process. Our age requires people capable of cooperating in the common tasks of a complex society and at the same time capable of living a truly free creative inner life as individuals. Literature — the good and great literature of the past and present — is at once an intensely social and an intensely personal kind of experience. Using the socially-produced system of symbols which is language, using "the words of the tribe," the poet, the novelist, the dramatist give utterance to their most personal and yet most broadly human visions of nature, man, and society. The reader, recreating these works, living through them intensely and personally, is freed to discover his own capacities for feeling, his own sense of the world, and his relation to it. Thus through literature, the business of self-discovery and self-organization can go hand-in-hand with imaginative participation in the cumulative experience, the keenest sensitivities, the highest aspirations of our culture. We can indeed claim an important place for literature in the curriculum; such imaginative liberation, such nourishing of a personal life is needed throughout the whole span of the student's growth. In these troubled days, we can echo Auden's words of 1939:

Follow, poet, follow right
To the bottom of the night,
With your unconstraining voice
Still persuade us to rejoice;
With the farming of a verse
Make a vineyard of the curse,
Sing of human unsuccess
In a rapture of distress;

In the deserts of the heart
Let the healing fountain start,
In the prison of his days
Teach the free man how to praise.

7. Grammar and Linguistics

Don M. Wolfe

For many years leaders in the National Council deplored the emphasis given to formal grammar throughout the nation. Almost every teacher knew grammar; very few teachers felt the competence or the enthusiasm or the energy to teach writing. The very schedule of English teachers, five or six classes daily, two hundred pupils a week, made writing assignments impossible to cope with. The fault with the teaching of grammar was the failure to apply grammatical knowledge to punctuation and style. Many critics felt, indeed, that no great amount of grammar teaching could be applied to style. Hence the teaching of grammar as such was discouraged. To such an extent as the leaders of the Council held to a party line, it was a hard position against formal grammar; indeed the teaching of any grammar was in the minds of many somewhat suspect. Grammar appealed to a small intellectual part of a student only; it did not take into account his need for letting his deep feelings and thoughts flow into language. When grammar flourished in the classroom, the sympathies of both teacher and students somehow dried up; before such a limited analysis of the power of language the student stood alien and hostile to the teacher's idea of English. The deep and violent emotional life of the high school student found in many if not most English classrooms no link to expressive reality as encouraged by the teacher. The more grammar, the less self-expression; it was grammar that defined the student's attitude toward English, not themes which opened the deep streams of his life and let them flow into burning images. Life

From Don M. Wolfe, "Grammar and Linguistics: A Contrast in Realities," *The English Journal,* February, 1964, 53:73–78, 100. Don M. Wolfe, Professor of English at Brooklyn College, is the author of numerous scholarly publications and textbooks in the field of English. He is General Editor of the *Complete Prose Works of John Milton* in preparation for the Yale University Press. This article is reprinted with the permission of the National Council of Teachers of English and Don M. Wolfe.

seldom invaded the classroom; it was a separate compartment of cars and girls and friends and midnight hours.

Nevertheless, many gifted teachers combined expert teaching of grammar with remarkable power to draw forth the student's deep thoughts. They saw that once a grammatical concept was taught, the student should immediately use his own prepositional phrases in a story, his own predicate adjectives to express his moods, his own participles, infinitives, and adverbial clauses. When thus taught, grammatical constructions became personal possessions that found continuing expression from theme to theme. Many teachers assigned grammatical autobiographies to combine mastery of grammatical concepts with self-expression.[1] Meanwhile they assigned themes from week to week which tapped the explosive powers of self-expression about those topics that the *student,* not the teacher, defined as experience with deepest meaning. In such a teacher's classroom, learning grammar was not inconsistent with the flow of original thoughts and feelings. To such a teacher the relation between the teaching of grammar and the teaching of writing was not one of mutual hostility and rejection; the student accepted both. Indeed the more personal became his weekly themes, the more grammar took on new and vital significance.

Then came linguistics, or a new zeal for linguistics, an interest in which was fostered by outstanding college professors and leaders within the National Council. To almost every enthusiast for linguistics, traditional grammar had failed to describe the language with those minute and accurate qualifications necessary to scientific analysis. Unlike the traditional grammar, the new science incorporated the sounds of language as well as the function of each element of structure. Instead of eight parts of speech, the linguists followed Fries in defining four parts of speech as Class 1, Class 2, Class 3, and Class 4 words and denominating fifteen to seventeen groups of structure words. In the midst of proliferating linguistic theory, Paul Roberts and others attempted in a series of books to bring linguistics within reach of the average classroom teacher. Lou La Brant in her exciting series, *Your Language,* adopted and expanded the new linguistic terminology. If the terminology of the old grammar was antiquated and inexact, the terminology of structural linguistics was so extensive and so difficult to define that even those teachers most eager to comprehend the new science found it impossible to adopt in the classroom or teach with any degree of assurance, especially in the midst of a new surge of the writing and usage assignments to college-bound students. When an eager

[1] See Don M. Wolfe, "A Grammatical Autobiography," *English Journal,* 49 (January 1960), pp. 16–21.

classroom teacher tried to teach linguistics to a class oriented in traditional grammar, he more often than not found the task baffling and fruitless. Indeed he was now taking a dozen-fold as much time to teach a new grammar as he had taken to teach the old, meanwhile neglecting his far more important task of assigning college essays and analyses of great books to those students preparing for college. If the old grammar brought lethargy and boredom to the classroom, the new grammar to some teachers brought sickness of spirit and a more colossal waste of precious time than the old grammar had ever mustered. Meanwhile, where was English? What new insight did linguistics bring to an appreciation of style, to the rhetoric of beautiful sentences? Where was the visualization of the incandescent moment from a great book, from the student's life — a moment of fear, hope, happiness, despair, discovery?

My own view is that those who believe in structural linguistics for the average classroom must show how the new science can be used to improve both punctuation and style: the same tests that they justly believed should be applied to the teaching of grammar. I believe that traditional grammar has a hundred times more potential for improving punctuation and style than has structural linguistics. I wish to present again some concrete principles by which formal grammar can be used by the average teacher. I am not defending grammar as a wholly economical resource; I am defending it as a resource of limited benefits that no person of professional training can afford to dispense with. Consider the five sentence patterns below and the classroom assignments based on them. Traditional grammar can help the student to understand these patterns. Creative imitation of these sentences can enhance the student's comprehension of grammar while improving his appreciation and command of literary diction.

Pattern 1. Introductory Prepositional Phrases for Background

> *On the pleasant shore* of the French Riviera, *about halfway* between Marseilles and the Italian border, stands a large, proud, rose-colored hotel.
>
> — *F. Scott Fitzgerald,* from *Tender Is the Night*

Assignment: Describe a building you know in a sentence constructed like the one above. Begin with a background image in a prepositional phrase naming state or country or town; then, as Fitzgerald does, use another prepositional phrase to identify the place more exactly. Finally, use the verb and subject of the sentence, with the subject at or near the end.

Example: Among the mountains of West Virginia, on a steep road between Elkins and Parsons, stands a lonely, roofless house of gray stone.

Pattern 2. An Adjective Following the Subject

> A half moon, *dusky-gold,* was sinking behind the black sycamore tree.
>
> — *D. H. Lawrence,* from *Sons and Lovers*

Assignment: Write a sentence like this one in construction and intensity of diction. In your imitation use two color adjectives following the subject, as Lawrence does; also use one other color in your sentence.

Example: A high sail, chalk white, was dipping toward the blue water.

Pattern 3. A Past Participle Following the Subject

> The lazy October afternoon, *bathed in a soft warmth of a reluctant sun,* held a hint of winter's coming chill.
>
> — *Ruth Firor*

Assignment: Describe an afternoon, a morning, a house, a yard. In your imitation try for personifying words such as *lazy* and *reluctant.*

Example: The raw December air, showered with gusts of swirling snow, swept down the long alley.

Pattern 4. Two Participles; Two Verbs; a Simile

> *Streaming* with perspiration, we *swarmed* up the rope, and coming into the blast of cold wind, *gasped like men plunged into icy water.*
>
> — *Joseph Conrad*

Assignment: Write a sentence with grammatical elements parallel to the one above, opening with a participle as Conrad does, using two verbs as visual and dynamic as *swarmed* and *gasped.* Conclude your sentence with a simile as intense in diction as Conrad's.

Example: Shivering with cold, I jumped into bed, and wrapping myself in the warmth of the blanket, drew my head under it like a turtle shrinking back into its shell.

Pattern 5. Adverbial Clause Followed by an Absolute Phrase

> Even as she was falling asleep, head bowed over the child, she was still aware of a strange wakeful happiness.
>
> — *Katherine Anne Porter,* from "Maria Concepcion"

Assignment: Opening with an *as* clause, as in the sentence above, use an absolute phrase to give an image of the person, as Katherine Porter does.

Example: As he stood before the class, head tilted toward the window, the sunlight brightened the brown of his freckles and the blue of his eyes.

By analyzing these five patterns and then writing sentences containing for each pattern the same sequence as in the original, the student is required to use grammatical elements in a way that makes them memorable. The principle of creative imitation, a highly neglected art of explosive possibilities, relies here upon a realistic knowledge of grammatical elements. They become memorable to him because they are combined with intense diction. In order to do well, the student must use a verb or an absolute phrase or a participle as electric as the original words. The teachers who have tried this method know that each sentence imitation instantly shows both the good taste and the grammatical knowledge of the pupil at work. Is there any element of structural linguistics that makes such a direct application of theory to style as is found in this application alone of traditional grammar?

The principle applied above to short sentences may be further extended to passages like the one below from Thomas Hardy:

SPHERES OF THISTLEDOWN

And in autumn airy spheres of thistledown floated into the same street, lodged upon the shop fronts, blew into drains; and innumerable tawny and yellow leaves skimmed along the pavement, and stole through people's doorways into their passages with a hesitating scratch on the floor, like the skirts of timid visitors.

— *Thomas Hardy, Mayor of Casterbridge*

Merely analyzing this passage for its remarkable resources, its use of background, middleground, and foreground images, its use of the blending elements of the spheres of thistledown and the flying leaves, its images of color and sound and touch, its simile at the end: all of this is not enough. The teacher must then ask the class to write a sentence similar step by step in grammatical construction to Thomas Hardy's original. Once a student has used his own diction, his own visualization, in constructing a sentence exactly like Hardy's in grammatical order, he has applied grammar to style in the most realistic way possible:

IN THE WINTER DUSK: IMITATION OF HARDY

And in the winter dusk, long gusts of wind whispered secrets to the windows, wailed under the door, sighed across the carpet to the fires; and delicate purple-white snowflakes danced around the treetops, pitted the roof, and trickled down the cottage with wistful resignation, like the tears of silent lovers.

— *Frances Dyller*

The student perforce extends his command of grammar for style in imitating this sentence: by the use of three parallel verbs in the first independent clause as electric as those of Hardy; by the use of parallel prepositional phrases in each clause. Meanwhile he tries in his own diction for a combination of consonant sounds as beautiful as the *l*'s, *m*'s, and *n*'s in "innumerable tawny and yellow leaves" or the use of the *s* sound in such words as *passages, scratch, skirts,* and *visitors.* The beginning of the achievement is the student's ability to imitate the structure of the sentence; the end is beauty of rhetoric and diction.

This approach to style we have described presupposes a long apprenticeship in the elements of grammar. This apprenticeship is often wasteful of time and energy that might be devoted to writing experiences without emphasis on variety of sentence structure or punctuation according to grammatical rules. However, for that increasing proportion of students who intend to go on to college, the knowledge of grammatical constructions for both style and punctuation is in the opinion of many college teachers indispensable. The more the student aspires to attend college or prepare for a profession, the more he needs a knowledge of elementary grammar in both speech and writing. If the student is not going on to college and does not expect to enter a profession, certainly he does not need a knowledge of grammar. He can get along perfectly well in conversation. Even though he punctuates incorrectly, he can write letters well enough to make himself understood. He can, indeed, make his meaning clear without punctuating sentences. The growing acceptance, however, of the necessity of some college work in addition to high school for the average student makes a knowledge of elementary grammar increasingly vital as the years pass.

Value of Traditional Grammar

For whatever purposes the teacher uses grammar, whether or not the time she spends on it is justified, she needs a stable and consistent description of the language. Traditional grammar provides such a classification, however weak and inconsistent much of its terminology and applications. Traditional grammar presents a crude and often inconsistent classification of word function. As Verna Newsome points out in *Structural Grammar in the Classroom,* the word *brother's* in such a phrase as "My brother's classmate" defies exact analysis in terms of formal grammar. Certainly fundamental grammar is a crude instrument. It depends for definition now upon meaning, as in definition of nouns, and now upon structure, as in definitions of adjectives and adverbs. Nevertheless, despite such weaknesses this grammar *does* function better than *any other* because it is simpler, it has fewer terms, it has a long history of pragmatic effectiveness. Moreover, its Latin-derived description of language is used not only by teachers of English, but also by teachers of French, German, Spanish, and Italian. Each of these languages has roughly the same formal classification of the parts of speech. So far there is no attempt in any of the European countries to make a new science of structural linguistics a substitute for formal grammar in the secondary schools. This fact alone should give pause on the American scene to those scholars now attempting to make structural linguistics a consistent system of language analysis to replace formal grammar on the high school level.

One of the curious deficiencies of some structural linguists is their refusal to recognize the intricate difficulties of descriptions of structure in which scholars of the new science take refuge. May I call attention, for example, to a sentence in one of the great works on structural linguistics, Fries' *The Structure of English* (p. 183):

> The subject itself is simply that Class 1 word that is bound to a Class 2 word to form the basic arrangement of the sentence, and it is identified and distinguished from other Class 1 words not by meaning but by certain contrastive arrangements.
>
> — *Charles Carpenter Fries, The Structure of English*

How anyone involved in a classroom situation could explain to the class such a sentence as this, or paraphrase the sentence in understandable diction, I cannot see. Fries, it is true, did not intend this sentence to be used in a high school classroom. He was writing for scholars who would, in turn, translate his principles into comprehensible terms. Nevertheless, the very nature of the principles involved in structural linguistics, of breaking down the old terminology and substituting new terms for old conceptions, makes it difficult for the scholar to devise a nomenclature as simple and easy to use as the old one.

Is there any teacher in a practical classroom situation who prefers the term, "Class 1 word," to the word *noun* or the word *pronoun*? Is there any teacher in a practical teaching situation who prefers the term, "Class 2 word," to the word *verb*? Whatever may be the deficiencies of such terms as *noun, pronoun, verb,* or *adverb,* are they more vague or difficult to teach than such terms as "Class 1 word," *determiner, in-*

tensifier? Each time the structural linguist adds a new term to his description of the language, he may be adding new knowledge to the world of subtle and sophisticated scholars. Necessarily, however, he is reducing the area of fundamental communication of language principles in the average classroom situation. Whereas structural linguistics shows the weaknesses of the simple classification of parts of speech, at the same time it provides a dramatization of the dangers of a complex, highly rarefied nomenclature which only a few scholars can be expected to understand fully.

Whatever the weaknesses of formal grammar, the terminology is at present to many teachers more consistent and stable than the terminology of structural linguistics. If it is uneconomical of time and energy to apply formal grammar to style, as many of its critics claim, then it is many times more uneconomical to apply structural linguistics to style. Indeed I have not found, among the many proponents of structural linguistics, any claim that it can be applied realistically to classroom writing for college-bound students. Every new book on structural linguistics presents the teacher with new terms, often new terms for old concepts, new terms which she is forced to translate into terms provided by traditional grammar. All the objections that the opponents of traditional grammar have made to a nomenclature barren of stylistic fruitfulness can be applied a hundred-fold to the nomenclature of structural linguistics in terms of the average high school classroom. One cannot find in the history of English teaching on the American scene so many conceptions on a high intellectual level set forth and described with so little effective application to classroom writing problems as in the many books written on structural linguistics. This does not mean that the study of structural linguistics is barren or fruitless for advanced students of language. Indeed this is where the study of linguistics belongs — in the comparative study of language on the graduate level.

Structural linguistics belongs to those scholars who have a profound knowledge of the roots of English in Anglo-Saxon and Norman French and Latin, to those teachers who have lived for years in each of several European countries, mastering the spoken tongue. Structural linguistics involves inherently a knowledge of phonetics which is virtually useless in the average high school classroom. It involves a comparative evaluation of speech sounds in various languages, an evaluation totally foreign to the problems of the average English teacher. Indeed there is no department of structural linguistics that the average high school teacher can take hold of and make practical in her own classroom.

Problem of Terminology

Those who have, like Mr. Roberts, applied structural linguistics to classroom teaching have been most successful in this effort when they have returned bluntly to traditional grammatical terms. They have been most unsuccessful when they have been drawn into strange terminology for old principles. Almost all the vocabulary of structural linguistics can be translated into the traditional vocabulary of grammar. Why, then, do we need a new vocabulary at all? We need rather to simplify the terminology of traditional grammar and agree upon nomenclature, as has been done in France. Instead of reducing the nomenclature, however, to a minimum number of terms agreed upon by publishers, scholars, and textbook writers, we are expanding grammatical nomenclature by leaps and bounds. The proliferate nomenclature of structural linguistics alone is sufficient reason why it cannot become an effective instrument of classroom teaching on the American scene. Only in the teaching of traditional English grammar is it possible to prepare the student for his increasing need to learn foreign languages. The nomenclature of structural linguistics has no counterpart in the teaching of French, Spanish, German, or Italian. This does not mean that structural linguistics is a useless pursuit. It is extremely useful, as I have suggested, for advanced scholars of comparative languages.

There is more waste of time and energy in the teaching of grammar than in any other aspect of American education. Our problem, however, is not to abolish traditional grammar in favor of a rarefied new science, but to devise new ways of dramatizing the parts of speech and the grammar of the simple sentence in daily lessons of *one year* or *one semester*. Let us have the help of a gifted cartoonist, an artist of the quality of Bill Mauldin, to help us dramatize grammar. Let us have dedicated teachers who *know* they can make grammar stick. Each of us can call back a time when *one* teacher and one classroom made grammar become a reality. Only one such teacher is needed. In some excellent New England high schools years ago, grammar was taught as a separate subject to those going on to college. The basic course should always be a separate subject. We have the resources to make traditional grammar a workable reality. Meanwhile, let those scholars who believe in structural linguistics continue their quest, not to make the new science a high school resource, but to trace on the postgraduate level a more complete and accurate description of the language, spoken and written, than any group of scholars has thus far created.

8. Linguistics and the Elementary Language Arts Program

Paul McKee

Linguistics is an extremely broad term. It is really the scientific study of all man's languages, just as medicine is the scientific study of his physical well-being or lack of it.

Within the broad scope of both medicine and linguistics are many fields of specialization and research. Not all the findings of medical research are necessary or pertinent to the school programs in physical fitness and hygiene, nor are all the findings of linguistic research applicable to the language arts program in the elementary school.

Linguistics is not a new science, but only recently have linguists and English teachers in elementary and secondary schools recognized that they have a common concern. *Linguistics* has emerged from the seclusion of the graduate school, and teachers are looking to the linguists for help in finding more efficient methods of teaching the language arts.

The linguist finds that our traditional teaching of English grammar has many shortcomings. He knows that each language has its own set of *sounds* (he may call them phonemes) which are used alone or in combination to form words. Words in any language are oral *symbols* for objects, actions, ideas, relationships, and many other things. The *system* by which words are formed, inflected, and put together to communicate facts and ideas is the grammar of the language and the grammar of one language is different from that of any other.

Traditional English grammar, says the linguist, is really Latin grammar, and the English language should not be expected to fit into it. What linguists have tried to do is develop a grammar which truly

From Paul McKee, "Linguistics and the Elementary Language Arts Program," *The Instructor,* March, 1966, 75: 19, 136. Paul McKee has been a recognized authority in reading and language arts for four decades. Author of many college textbooks, scholarly articles on reading and related areas, and reading series for elementary schools, he is currently serving as Consultant in Language Arts to the Denver Public Schools. His most recent book is *Reading: A Program of Instruction for the Elementary School.* This article is reprinted by permission of *The Instructor,* describes the English language as it is used today, not one which prescribes how it should be used.

Formulating an accurate descriptive grammar of English is an extremely difficult task. English has had a complicated history, starting with an Anglo-Saxon base, plus a Danish influence, plus the French overlay following the Norman invasion. For centuries English has been a living language, and any living language changes as people use it. New words are added, pronunciations change, and usage varies depending on locality and standards within social groups in a community. English has many nouns with irregular plurals and verbs with irregularities as well, which further complicate the problem of grammatical rules.

In the face of these obstacles, it is easy to understand why there is, as yet, no complete agreement on the so-called "new grammar." The linguists, however, are making us take a long hard look at traditional grammar teaching. When we do, we find that the hard and fast rules and definitions that we were taught and have taught to pupils just don't stand up. For example, in this sentence, *Mr. Brown sklued the president of the snergon,* you can tell that *sklued* is used as a verb — not because it shows action or expresses a state of being. In this context, it could do either. It has a typical verb ending, *ed,* and it comes in the right position in the sentence for a verb. You know that *snergon* must be used as a noun because it follows the word *the.* Linguists use sentences of this type to prove that typical endings, word order, and function are more reliable clues to the form class or part of speech, whichever term you prefer, than are the old definitions.

In general, people who are teaching the new kind of grammar use an inductive method of teaching so that the pupils discover generalizations for themselves instead of memorizing rules and definitions and then trying to apply them. Emphasis in this new type of teaching is also on building sentences rather than analyzing them. The linguist can help the elementary teacher of English to teach grammar and sentence construction more efficiently and with greater effect on all written work done by the pupils.

The linguist draws a very sharp line between grammar and usage. He says that *I seen him when he done it* is a sentence that conforms to English grammar, because the words are in the correct order and it communicates meaning. It is substandard English, of course, but the person who uses such a sentence is speaking English in a way that enables him to communicate with others. It is only the usage in that sentence which does not conform to the standards of English that we are expected to hold to in the classroom.

Many linguists speak of levels of usage. One level that is easily recognized is the substandard, but even in standard English, we all have different kinds of language that we use in different situations. In an informal conversation with friends, we are not so particular about our speech as we would be when conducting a meeting of the Teachers' Association. In talking with pupils in the classroom, we don't use the same level of language that we would use in a university seminar. We all have at least two levels of spoken English, formal and informal. In addition, we probably adapt each of them to the particular individual or group to whom we are speaking. In writing also, we write to a relative or close friend in informal English, but we write a formal letter when we are applying for a teaching position or a university fellowship.

What bearing does all this discussion of usage and levels of usage have on the teaching of English in the elementary school classroom? First of all, a teacher need not apologize to anyone for trying to bring the speech and writing of her pupils up to standard. Standard English is the language of the classroom in America, just as High German is the language of the classroom in Germany. However, teachers may need to be a little more realistic and philosophical about the language pupils use outside of school. If a child's family and neighbors use substandard English, that is what he will use outside school. If he never leaves that particular social stratum, he will never have any incentive to use standard English. Your responsibility is to see that he learns the standard forms, so that if he should find himself in a situation where he needs to use them, he will have them at his command. You should not be upset or discouraged at hearing pupils on the playground or street using wrong forms after all your hard work. The teacher in Germany is not surprised when pupils revert to their local dialect as soon as class is over.

The linguist, to sum it up, can help you to teach sensible, truthful grammar which will enable your pupils to understand the way English operates in order to communicate meaning. This should help them to listen to and read more efficiently the language of others, as well as to use language effectively themselves in speaking and writing. You can also learn from the linguist to take a more realistic view of the whole problem of good language usage.

Does this mean that linguistics will answer all your problems of teaching English? No, it doesn't. In fact, in the area of good usage, it may complicate things a little. It is much easier to be completely authoritarian than it is to recognize the fact that there are levels of usage and to adjust to this recognition. This requires much more subtlety than drawing a sharp right or wrong distinction on every item of usage.

What areas are still going to pose problems for you? Linguistic grammar will not help in teaching pupils to organize their thoughts for a report, to write an interesting letter to a friend, to write a good story, or to do better any of the composition jobs they must do. It will not help them to choose exactly the right word or to avoid cliches.

Linguistic grammar will probably be much more interesting to you and to your pupils than traditional grammar, but even the new grammar can be taught as a disembodied field of knowledge, and if it is, it will do little to improve your pupils' speaking or writing. Either traditional or new grammar can degenerate into verbalizing under the wrong teaching.

May I give you one caution which applies to the teaching of the new grammar as well as to all other school subjects? Don't try to teach too much too fast. It is much better to teach fewer items and to teach them well enough to insure understanding than to try to cover so many that the treatment is superficial. Remember, your pupils will be in school next year and probably for some years to come. Send them on with a solid foundation of knowledge and understanding upon which other teachers can build new learnings successfully.

9. The Field of Speech

Committee on the Nature of the Field of Speech,
Speech Association of America

I

Teachers and scholars identified with the academic field of speech label themselves in various ways: speech and linguistic scientists, speech clinician, rhetoricians, students of theatre, teachers of speech. As

From the Committee on the Nature of the Field of Speech, Speech Association of America, "The Field of Speech: Its Purposes and Scope in Education," *The Speech Teacher,* November, 1963, 12: 331–335. Members of the Committee which scientists they seek to understand and describe speech behavior, and the process of communication. As humanists they study the practical and artistic forms of discourse associated with the oral tradition of western civilization. As teachers they transmit the products of their study to students and help them develop effective, responsible, and artistic habits of communication.

The use of the term "speech" to identify an academic discipline emerged in the first two decades of this century. These decades were part of the half century of educational ferment from 1870 to 1920, when many contemporary branches of study were acquiring their current names; for example, English, psychology, political science, and sociology. The first M.A. degree in Speech was granted in 1902, and the first Ph.D. degree in 1922. By 1962 some 150 American universities had granted about 18,000 Master's degrees, and 40 universities had granted approximately 2,300 Doctor's degrees. The national professional society, The Speech Association of America, was founded in 1914 as The National Association of Academic Teachers of Public Speaking.

II

Although its name is a coinage of this century, speech as a field of study grew from an academic tradition as old as the history of western education. The study of the theory and practice of public discussion, under the name *rhetoric,* was a central concern of Greek, Roman, medieval, renaissance, and early modern education. Subjects allied to rhetoric also flourished in the western educational tradition: argumentative dialogue and logical inquiry, usually called *dialectic;* literature which was inseparably linked to rhetoric; and speculative inquiry into the nature and function of language.

Growing thus from a major educational tradition, the field of speech has shared in the unparalleled expansion of knowledge characteristic of this century, and in the specialization of research and instruction. The speech or voice scientist, whose area is sometimes identified as experimental phonetics, is primarily interested in the analysis of speech behavior, viewed as a physiological, acoustic, and linguistic phenomenon. He studies the structure and functioning of the mechanisms of

---

prepared this authoritative report were Karl R. Wallace, Professor of Speech and Head, Department of Speech and Theatre, University of Illinois; Donald K. Smith, Professor of Speech and Assistant Vice-President of the University of Minnesota; Andrew T. Weaver, Emeritus Professor of Speech, University of Wisconsin. Reprinted by permission of the Speech Association of America, William Work, Executive Secretary.

voice and hearing, analyzes vocal production in terms of its acoustic and linguistic structure, and develops instruments and methods of analysis to improve the reliability and objectivity of his data. The speech pathologist and the speech therapist center attention on defective speech, its description, etiology, and diagnosis, its personal and social impacts, methods of treatment, and the methods and instruments used in diagnosis and evaluation of therapy. The specialist in educational theatre is partly a creative artist, concerned with playwriting, acting, and directing, and with the visual and auditory aesthetics of theatre. He is partly a teacher and student of dramatic literature and its theory, and of theatre art and its theory. The teacher of interpretation analyzes literature from the point of view of its recreation in speech. He is concerned with the "sound and sight" implicit in the meaning of the literary text, in principles and styles of spoken presentation, and in the history and theory of delivery. The contemporary rhetorician focuses on the practical art of discourse as revealed in the variety of forms and functions evident in public discussion. He is concerned with the history and structure of rhetorical theory, with the history and criticism of public address, and with the relationship between the artifacts of public discourse and their cultural and institutional correlates. As an experimental rhetorician, he may subject hypotheses about the functioning of public discourse to scientific investigation, using experimental methods appropriate to the behavioral sciences. Teachers of radio, television, and the film see their field in terms of rhetorical and theatrical principles and methods as these are applied to, and shaped by, the media of mass communication. They study communication forms and structures as these interact with cultural values.

The field of speech reflects the thrust characteristic of contemporary academic disciplines — a moving out from its original center in expanding segments of specialized study. Speech also reveals, like other fields, increasing interaction with disciplines whose boundaries have widened to include aspects of speech behavior of particular interest to them. Thus today the specialist in speech may find his interests akin to those of the linguist who analyzes the structure of spoken language, the psychologist who studies verbal behavior, the sociologist who relates social structure to symbolic interaction, the anthropologist who studies the structure of speech and language as reflecting the structure of culture, the philosopher who investigates the problems of meaning in everyday language, and so on. The list of specialists in the contemporary world of learning who have become in part or almost wholly concerned with speech is long and growing. To students of the disciplines already mentioned could be added the scholars working in highly specialized aspects of history, literary theory and criticism, psycholinguistics, mass communication theory, biological and medical science, psychiatry, information theory, and the like. Both the dynamics of internal expansion and of increasing interplay with other disciplines emphasize the utility of restating the assumptions which bring together persons whose primary academic home is the field of speech.

III

Despite their manifest specializations, teachers and scholars in the field of speech share assumptions that are reflected in the nature of the courses they characteristically teach and in the nature of their scholarly research. The assumptions most common are these:

(a) Speech is man's most distinctive and significant behavior. Speech is learned, and it is learned from teachers. The "teachers" include all members of the social groups in which the child moves as well as the persons who give direct attention to speech instruction in formal educational settings. The learning of speech and the form and efficiency of the habits developed are matters of utmost consequence to the individual and his society. Speaking is prerequisite to the child's development of a sense of identity. It is a behavior inseparably linked to the processes of thought and communication. Speech habits mirror the form and quality of one's thought, the nature of his social identifications, and the form and quality of his interaction with his physical environment and with other persons. Speech habits are important to vocational success and effective citizenship. Speech is thus *central* to the nature of man, to the development of the person, and to the functioning of political, economic, and social institutions. It is the most important single feature of the environment within which every individual conducts his life. Behavior of such importance and complexity deserves disciplined study. No one can be said to be knowledgeable about himself and his environment unless he understands speech, its nature, structure, and functioning.

(b) An educated person needs more than an understanding of speech behavior. He should be capable of transmitting his meanings with accuracy, correctness, and clarity. He should be capable of speaking in ways that resolve misunderstanding, that express clear preferences and justify them, that advocate decisions in keeping with his personal integrity and the rights of others, and that aid in adjusting ideas to people and people to ideas. The man who has "the power of summoning thought quickly" and the habit of forceful and efficient expression serves himself well; he who enters effectively and responsibly into public discussion serves the public interest well. The field of speech is still committed to the ideal of the citizen-speaker first set up by the Roman schools, the ideal of the good man speaking well.

In the education of such a man, knowledge and skill meld inextricably. Teachers in their instruction and research recognize this fact. Characteristically, beginning courses in school and college involve students both in the study *of* speech behavior and in directed practice *in* speaking, knowledge serving to shape attitudes and judgment, practice serving to develop effectiveness. Curricula in the college and university respect creative activity, historical study, analysis of concepts and criteria, and critical evaluation of performance. Courses in public speaking, debate, and discussion are balanced by courses in the theory of exposition, argument, and persuasion, in the history and criticism of public address, and in rhetorical theory. Courses in acting, directing, spoken interpretation, and technical theatre are balanced by courses in theatre history, dramatic theory and literature, art and aesthetics. Courses in speech and hearing rehabilitation are balanced by courses in speech science, hearing science, the psychology of speech, and the pathologies of speech, together with their physiological and psychological correlates.

(c) Man cannot avoid being essentially and significantly a communicator. Hence instruction and research in speech focus on the major functions and forms of discourse important to the life of man as a human being, citizen, and artist. The forms characteristic of public discussion in western civilization — public speaking, group discussion, and debate — serve as centers for organizing the kinds of knowledge appropriate to understanding, appraisal, and participation. Behind the forms of public discussion lie the theory of rhetoric, the general theory of signs, symbolic behavior, and communication, and the ways these are related to the structure and function of social institutions. The forms and function of public discourse furnish a rationale for a curriculum in public address, but they limit neither the breadth nor depth of the studies they generate. Often they provide the focus and vitalizing force in a general or liberal education.

The concept of theatre as a significant cultural form provides the center for studies in dramatic literature and aesthetics, and in the theory of performance, direction, design, and visual presentation. The concept of creative activity as man's complete and full response to his problems is at the center of playwriting and play producing. Plays-as-produced offer recurring experiences that constitute for both scholars and participants the final act essential to full understanding and appreciation of theatre art. A similar rationale informs both instruction and participation in radio, television, and film, and in clinical performance in speech correction and audiology.

(d) The acts and arts of communication in speech and language are humanistic. The field of speech has always had a strong and traditionally humanistic point of view. Man's capability and need to symbolize and communicate; his acts of choice, judgment, and expression; his significant and telling acts of communication — these are taken to be the center of a humane study and the center from which the search and transmission of knowledge about man properly proceeds. The enterprise entails discipline, the discipline inherent in the structure of knowledge about speech behavior and the discipline achieved by any man who commands the power of appropriate communication.

IV

A field committed to humane and significant educational purposes has inevitably concerned itself with the nation's system of formal education from the elementary school to the graduate school. The learning of speech begins before formal education, and the development of knowledge about speech behavior and the development of skill in speaking are necessarily continuous processes. At every level of education the speech and language skills of the student both limit and are limited by the kind and extent, the breadth and depth, of the student's knowledge. The growth, refinement, and permanence of communication habits parallel the development of the knowledge built into the process. Hence continuity of instruction in speech is of primary concern in formal education.

The American educational system recognizes the importance of speech instruction, but it has not decided upon the amount and kind that should be generally provided for the common education of Americans. Despite massive evidence to the contrary, the assumption that speaking skill can be expected to develop as a by-product of instruction in reading and writing seems still to be prevalent. In too many schools, instruction in speech is represented only in extra-curricular endeavor.

The disorganized and erratic nature of education in speech has been a matter of deep concern to the Speech Association of America since its founding. The Association has sought to provide through its publications both theoretical guidance and practical curriculum materials for sound programs in speech education. The twelve-year school curriculum should provide explicit and systematic attention to the study of speech processes and forms, and to the development of speaking skills. For this task, teachers of speech in the elementary school should have specific college preparation. Teachers in the secondary school should have the equivalent of at least an undergraduate minor in the field of speech.

There are problems in staffing and conducting the current curriculum in the English language arts. Most secondary schools require five to six years of instruction in the English language arts in the junior high school and high school curriculum, or from three to four years of such instruction in the four-year senior high school. Since the early part of this century, it has generally been assumed that this sequence in the English language arts includes instruction in the skills of speaking and writing, reading and listening, instruction in the nature of language and in literature. Yet *as a rule* teachers prepared within college departments of English have received little instruction in speech and language behavior and the arts of public discussion. The result is an anomaly: a school curriculum in the language arts which assumes instruction in speech but which is taught for the most part by teachers with little or no preparation in speech. The situation has serious consequences. Innumerable graduates of the common schools have practically no knowledge of speech behavior and of the arts of communication, only the most superficial acquaintance with any of the "literature" of public address and discussion, and no experience at all in rhetorical analysis and appraisal. Large numbers of graduates face a variety of situations requiring ready speech with powers far under their abilities. Such an attenuated and unbalanced treatment of the study of language and the development of language skills is a most serious problem in American education. Teachers of speech and English must recognize their related problems in the curriculum in the English language arts and confront them cooperatively.

V

For the better part of 2,000 years, the education of western Europeans and Americans centered on the language studies of rhetoric, dialectic, and grammar, appropriately supported by the study of the history of public address and of creative literature. The field of speech, as it has come to be known in the twentieth century, is a lineal descendant of the linguistic tradition of classical learning. In a century of expanding knowledge and increasing specialization of study, the field seeks not only to encourage the education of young people in the arts and sciences of spoken discourse, but also to add appropriately to man's understanding of speech behavior and to promote the effective intercommunication of ever increasing knowledge.

For Further Reading

Allen, Harold B., (ed.), *Readings in Applied English Linguistics,* Second edition, Appleton-Century-Crofts, Inc., New York, 1964.

Bamman, Henry A., Ursula Hogan, and Charles S. Greene, *Reading Instruction in the Secondary Schools,* Longmans, Green and Company, New York, 1961.

Bassone, Richard M., "Let's Talk Sense About English," *The English Journal,* October, 1954, 43: 371–373.

Broenig, Angela M., "Development of Taste in Literature in the Senior High School," *The English Journal,* April, 1963, 52: 273–287.

DeBoer, John J., "Composition, Handwriting, and Spelling," *Review of Educational Research,* April, 1961, 31: 168.

Educational Leadership, February, 1962, 19: 281–352. (Theme of the issue, "Language Arts in the School," seven articles.)

The English Journal, May, 1963, 52: 317–370. (Entire issue deals with linguistics and linguistics teaching.)

Evans, Bertrand, and James J. Lynch, *Dialogues on the Teaching of Literature,* College and University Press, New Haven, Connecticut, 1962. (See Dialogue #1, "Why Should Literature Be Taught?")

Francis, W. N., "Linguistics and Composition, the Teacher's Theoretical Training," *Phi Delta Kappan,* May, 1960, 41: 336–341.

Frazier, Alexander, "Making the Most of Speaking and Listening Experiences," *The English Journal,* September, 1957, 46: 330–338.

Gleason, Henry Allen, Jr., *Linguistics and English Grammar,* Holt, Rinehart and Winston, New York, 1965.

Grady, Michael, "Structured Structuralism: Composition and Modern Linguistics," *The English Journal,* October, 1965, 54: 633–639.

Heinberg, Paul, "Phonetics, Linguistics, and Voice Science: Where To?" *The Speech Teacher,* January, 1965, 14: 7–13.

Henry, Nelson B., (ed.), *Development in and Through Reading,* Sixtieth Yearbook of the National Society for the Study of Education, Part I, University of Chicago Press, Chicago, 1961.

Hillocks, Geroge, Jr., "Approaches to Meaning: A Basis for a Literature Curriculum," *The English Journal,* September, 1964, 53: 413–421.

Hook, J. N., "Project English — A Progress Report," *School Life,* May, 1962, 8–9, Vol. 44, No. 7.

Hutton, Harry K., "Basic Troubles in Teaching Grammar," *The English Journal,* September, 1954, 43: 320–322.

Journal of Education, December, 1965, Vol. 148, No. 2 (Theme of the issue, "Correlation and the Teaching of English." Eleven articles dealing with correlation among subjects, specifically, between English and science, mathematics, social studies, art and music, and physical education. Bibliographies are suggested for seventh and eighth grade teachers.)

Leichty, V. E., *Discovering English,* Prentice-Hall, Englewood Cliffs, New Jersey, 1964.

Lehmann, Winfred P., *Historical Linguistics: An Introduction,* Holt, Rinehart and Winston, New York, 1962.

Massey, Will J., and Virginia D. Moore, *Helping High School Students Read Better,* Holt, Rinehart and Winston, New York, 1965.

Miles, Robert, "Literature for the Average Student," *The English Journal,* February, 1966, 55: 172–178.

Neville, Mark A., "English Language Arts — A Condition of Practicable Education," *Teachers College Journal,* October, 1962, 34: 14–16, 37.

Neville, Mark A., "English as a Condition of School Life," *Teachers College Journal,* January, 1961, 32: 102–111.

Pei, Mario, *The Story of English,* Fawcett Publications, Greenwich, Connecticut, 1965.

Pooley, Robert C., *Teaching English Grammar,* Appleton-Century-Crofts, Inc., New York, 1957.

Rinker, Floyd, "Priorities in the English Curriculum," *The English Journal,* May, 1962, 51: 309–312.

Squire, James R., "English at the Crossroads," *The English Journal,* September, 1962, 51: 381–392.

Strickland, Ruth, "Linguistics, a New Influence in Reading and Writing, *The Grade Teacher,* April, 1964, 81: 53, 100.

Weiss, M. Jerry, *An English Teacher's Reader: Grades Seven Through Twelve,* The Odyssey Press, New York, 1962.

Williams, Robert D., "Linguistics and Grammar," *The English Journal,* October, 1959, 48: 388–392.

Wolfe, Don M., *Creative Ways to Teach English,* Second edition, The Odyssey Press, New York, 1966.

Wyatt, Nita M., "Research in Creative Writing," *Educational Leadership,* February, 1962, 19: 307–310.

PART THREE

Social Studies and the Social Sciences

10. On History

President John F. Kennedy

There is little that is more important for an American citizen to know than the history and traditions of his country. Without such knowledge, he stands uncertain and defenseless before the world, knowing neither where he has come from nor where he is going. With such knowledge, he is no longer alone but draws a strength far greater than his own from the cumulative experience of the past and a cumulative vision of the future.

From John F. Kennedy, "On History," *American Heritage*, February, 1964, 3–4, Vol. 15, No. 2. This perceptive essay was written by President Kennedy at the request of the editors of *American Heritage* to serve as an introduction to *The American Heritage New Illustrated History of the United States*, published by the Dell Publishing Company. The editor of the present collection is deeply grateful to the Estate of President Kennedy for permission to reprint it here.

Knowledge of our history is, first of all, a pleasure for its own sake. The American past is a record of stirring achievement in the face of stubborn difficulty. It is a record filled with figures larger than life, with high drama and hard decision, with valor and with tragedy, with incidents both poignant and picturesque, and with the excitement and hope involved in the conquest of a wilderness and the settlement of a continent. For the true historian — and for the true student of history — history is an end in itself. It fulfills a deep human need for understanding, and the satisfaction it provides requires no further justification.

Yet, though no further justification is required for the study of history, it would not be correct to say that history serves no further use than the satisfaction of the historian. History, after all, is the memory of a nation. Just as memory enables the individual to learn, to choose goals and stick to them, to avoid making the same mistake twice — in short, to grow — so history is the means by which a nation establishes its sense of identity and purpose. The future arises out of the past, and a country's history is a statement of the values and hopes which, having forged what has gone before, will now forecast what is to come.

As a means of knowledge, history becomes a means of judgment. It offers an understanding of both the variety and unity of a nation whose motto is *E Pluribus Unum* — out of many, one. It reminds us of the diverse abundance of our people, coming from all races and all parts of the world, of our fields and mountain ranges, deserts and great rivers, our green farmlands and the thousand voices of our cities. No revolution in communication or transportation can destroy the fact that this continent is, as Walt Whitman said, "a nation of nations." Yet it also reminds us that, in spite of the diversity of ethnic origin, of geographic locale, of occupation, of social status, of religious creed, of political commitment, Americans are united by an ancient and encompassing faith in progress, justice, and freedom.

Our history thus tests our policy: Our past judges our present. Of all the disciplines, the study of the folly and achievements of man is best calculated to foster the critical sense of what is permanent and meaningful amid the mass of superficial and transient questions which make up the day-to-day clamor. The history of our nation tells us that every action taken *against* the freedoms of conscience and expression, *against* equality before the law and equality of opportunity, *against* the ordinary men and women of the country is an action taken *against* the American tradition. And it tells us that every action taken *for* a larger freedom and a more equal and spacious society is one more step toward realization of what Herbert Croly once called "the promise of American life."

A knowledge of history is more than a means of judgment: It is also a means of sympathy — a means of relating our own experience with the experience of other peoples and lands struggling for national fulfillment. We may sometimes forget, for example, that the United States began as an underdeveloped nation which seized its independence by carrying out a successful revolution against a colonial empire. We may forget that, in the first years of the new republic, George Washington laid down the principle of no "permanent alliances" and enjoined the United States to a course of neutralism in the face of the great-power conflicts then dividing the civilized world. We may forget that, in the first stages of our economic development, our national growth was stimulated to a considerable degree by "foreign aid" — that is, investment from abroad — and by public investment and direction on the part of our state and local as well as our national government. We may forget that our own process of economic change was often accompanied by the issue of wildcat paper money, by the repudiation of bonds, by disorder, fraud, and violence. If we recall the facts of our own past, we may better understand the problems and predicaments of contemporary "new nations" laboring for national development in circumstances far less favorable than our own — and we will, in consequence, become less liable to the self-righteousness which is both unworthy of our own traditions and a bane of international relations.

A knowledge of history is, in addition, a means of strength. "In times of change and danger," John Dos Passos wrote just before World War II, "when there is a quicksand of fear under men's reasoning, a sense of continuity with generations gone before can stretch like a life line across the scary present." Dos Passos called his book *The Ground We Stand On* — and the title concisely defines the role of the past in preparing us for the crisis of the present and the challenge of the future. When Americans fight for individual liberty, they have Thomas Jefferson and James Madison beside them; when they strive for social justice, they strive alongside Andrew Jackson and Franklin Rooselvelt; when they work for peace and a world community, they work with Woodrow Wilson; when they fight and die in wars to make men free, they fight and die with Abraham Lincoln. Historic continuity with the past, as Justice Oliver Wendell Holmes said, "is not a duty; it is only a necessity."

A knowledge of history is, above all, a means of responsibility — of responsibility to the past and of responsibility to the future . . . of responsibility to those who came before us and struggled and sacrificed to pass on to us our precious inheritance of freedom . . . and of responsibility to those who will come after us and to whom we must pass on that inheritance with what new strength and substance it is within our power to add. "Fellow citizens," Abraham Lincoln said, "we cannot escape history. . . . The fiery trial through which we pass will light us down, in honor or dishonor, to the latest generation." American history is not something dead and over. It is always alive, always growing, always unfinished — and every American today has his own contribution to make to the great fabric of tradition and hope which binds all Americans, dead and living and yet to be born, in a common faith and a common destiny.

11. History and the Social Sciences

Mark M. Krug

History is an imaginative reconstruction of the past. This reconstruction, while scientific in its methods and findings, is artistic in its presentation. History concerns itself with the story of human society and how it has come to be what it is today. The subject of history is men in action, what things happened, and why they happened. History is concerned with the totality of human experience. It is not, as Sir John Seeley said, "past politics." It is "past politics, past economics, past science, past society, past religion, past civilization — in short, past everything." History is concerned not only with the story of kings, rulers, wars and conquests, but also with how men grew wheat and corn, how they sold their wares, how they built their homes, how they worshipped God, and how they lived and how they died. It is because of this concern with the totality of human experience that history, unlike other social sciences, has loosely defined boundaries.

From Mark M. Krug, "History and the Social Sciences: The Narrowing Gap," *Social Education,* December, 1965, 29: 515–520. Mark M. Krug is Professor of Education in History and the Social Sciences at The University of Chicago. Noted for his many contributions in both history and education, Professor Krug's latest publication is *Lyman Trumbull: Conservative Radical.* This article is reprinted by permission of the author and of the National Council for the Social Studies.

The word *history* comes from the Greek word, *to inquire.* That is exactly the job of the historian — to inquire, to illuminate the past as best he can on the basis of the available evidence. Historians start their inquiries basically with three questions: "What happened? How did it happen? Why did it happen?"

The task of the historian is made easy because of a strong preoccupation with history by human beings in all times. Men have always paid great attention to the record and judgment of history. Kings, emperors, and common people have been concerned about what history will say about them. Even humble folk always worried, and still do, about leaving a "good name." In fact, the writing of history is one of the most important signs of progress and civilization.

From most ancient times primitive peoples, long before they possessed the art of writing, attempted to leave a record of their existence on earth by paintings of animals and hunters on the walls of their cave dwellings. They left rather strange stone structures like the Stonehenge in England. Egyptian Pharaohs, the kings of Moab and Persia, and rulers of ancient states wanted to make sure that posterity would know of their deeds and even of their misdeeds. They built pyramids and carved the record of their accomplishments on huge monuments. Rulers and nobles in medieval and more modern times had the same concern. Many of them employed writers and monks to write their personal chronicles. It must be concluded that history meets a deep human need — a strong curiosity about the past. This need undoubtedly has a strong connection with the realization of the terminal nature of human life.

It is of interest to note that recent United States Presidents have, like thc Pharaohs of old, made provisions during their terms of office for the erection of separate libraries which would house their official papers, proclamations, private letters, and even occasional doodlings. We have the Roosevelt Library in Hyde Park, New York; the Truman Library in Independence, Missouri; the Eisenhower Library in Abilene, Kansas; the Kennedy Library at Cambridge, Massachusetts; and will soon have the Lyndon Johnson library at the University of Texas.

Even our everyday language reflects the unique preoccupation of people with history. Politicians running for election, writers, debaters, and common people use such expressions as "the lesson of history," "the verdict of history," "history teaches us," "history will show," "history is on our side." It would be unthinkable and even ridiculous to have a candidate for political office exclaim from the platform: "Sociology teaches us," or "The lesson of anthropology is. . . ."

Why this deep concern with history? It may well be that historical continuity gives human beings some assurance of immortality. History makes it possible for puzzled, bewildered human beings to contemplate their relationships with the past and bear with greater ease the uncertain future. The study of the historical record, with its repeated, if not orderly patterns of successes and failures, progress and regression, periods of brilliance and of chaos and decline, contributes to the sense of unity and common fate for all mankind.

Lord Acton said that while history is a record of the past, it is also, strangely enough, "a record told of ourselves, the record of life which is our own, of efforts not yet abandoned to repose, of problems that still entangle the feet and vex hearts."[1] A great musician, Vladimir Horowitz, who came out from a self-imposed retirement, expressed a similar thought in these words: "To people I am a legend, but I am still alive. In a way, my future is my past and my past is my present." There is some consolation for mortal human beings in the realization that they are a link in the long chain of human generations. The English historian, George M. Trevelyan said: "At bottom the appeal of history is imaginative. Our imagination craves to behold our ancestors as they really were. . . . It is the detailed study of history that makes us feel that the past was as real as the present."[2]

It might be shocking for some to realize that as a matter of fact, history as such, does not exist. What we have are the fruits of an effort to recreate *segments* of past human experience on the basis of usually incomplete records. Since no eyewitness can be called upon to testify, each historian comes to his task of reconstructing the past with his own special cultural, national, and economic background and his own values and prejudices. Thus, what we have and what we read is what historians write *about* a particular period or event in history. That is why we have many histories of the American Revolution and of the Civil War and biographies of great men like Napoleon, Peter the Great, and Lenin. The authors of these volumes more often than not greatly differ in the interpretation of the events and the people they describe. This is an important fact to remember. Teachers and students alike must realize that *a history textbook is not history,* but an extended statement on American or world history by the author or the authors of the textbook. The same is true of all history books, including those written by great historians. Even views and interpretations of distinguished historians have been subject to criticism and disagreement. Not all historians, for instance, have agreed with the main thesis in Gibbon's book on the fall of Rome or with Parkman's hostility to French colonization efforts in

[1] Lord Acton, *The Study of History*. London: Macmillan, 1903, p. 19.

[2] "Clio Rediscovered." In Fritz Stone, editor, *The Varieties of History*. New York: 1956. p. 243.

North America. One only has to read an account of the American Revolution by American and English historians, or the story of Reformation written by Catholic and Protestant historians, or the history of British occupation of India written by English and Indian historians, to realize that while history is a story about the past or an investigation of the past, *it is not the past itself.* The past, the whole past can never be reconstructed.

Historians reconstruct only a small part or some fragments of the past which are of particular interest to them. It is disturbing that few of our students and even many of the social studies teachers do not realize this simple fact. Such a realization may well lead to an abandoning, or at least a weakening of the reliance on textbooks, and it might lead to more exciting teaching by making both the teachers and the students aware of the human qualities in the writing of history. The attempt to understand how a particular historian went about his work, how he interpreted his data, can be a useful and absorbing experience for students. Selected experiments with students acting like "minor league" historians and applying the historical method of inquiry to a particular event, may be a rewarding and effective teaching strategy in the social studies.

The Uses of History

The study of history has been required of school children from ancient times until today. Most of the states in our Union require the study of United States history by law. The reason lies in the wide-spread belief that the study of history, especially of national history, the study of the nation's heroes and of its heroic deeds, is useful as a creative and inspiring force in the molding of the minds of the younger generation. The study of the nation's past is considered by many, and with good reason, one of the best means of instilling love of country and patriotic devotion. There is little doubt that the dramatic, heroic story of the American Revolution, of the genius of the Founding Fathers, of the brilliance of Thomas Paine and of the patriotism of Patrick Henry, makes generations of young Americans proud of their heritage. The study of national history and of their glorious past and of their rich heritage has enabled the Jews, the Irish, the Poles, and many others to survive centuries of dispersion or many years of foreign occupation.

The most persistently claimed use of history concerns the assumption that the knowledge of the past helps in the understanding of the present. If one knows how men dealt with a problem or a crisis in history, he may be more able to cope successfully with a contemporary problem. To a limited extent, this seems to be a valid assumption.

The English deeply believed that history was the best school for statesmen. Many of their leaders and Prime Ministers, including the more recent one, Winston Churchill, were historians. During the era of their imperial greatness, the British maintained that the best training, for the governors and district commissioners in their far-flung possessions should include not courses in administration, but courses in history.

Lord Acton believed that history was "the most powerful ingredient in the formation of character and the training of talent."[3] Thomas Jefferson shared this view. When he formulated the Education Bill for his state of Virginia, he wrote that children in the elementary schools must be required to do a great deal of reading in history. "History," he wrote, "by apprising them of the past, will enable them to judge the future . . . it will qualify them as judges of the actions and designs of men."[4]

Many instances can be cited where the knowledge of history is indispensable to the understanding of a current event or political development. Only one who is knowledgeable about the territorial disputes and nationalist rivalries between Imperial China and Czarist Russia can fully understand the growing rift between Communist China and the Soviet Union. Only one who knows the complicated and often dismaying history of Reconstruction can understand the die-hard resistance to Negro voting rights by Mississippi and Alabama. There are also instances of historical events whose memory does not fade and which become traumatic experiences to the entire nation and influence its national policy and behavior. The foreign policy of the United States seems to have been permanently influenced by the rejection by the Senate of the Treaty of Versailles in 1919, and our domestic economic policies are never free of the specter of the economic disaster which threatened the nation during the Great Depression of 1929–1932.

But the lesson of history is more often neither so direct nor so obvious. It would be wiser to speak of lessons of history instead of a lesson of history, of uses of history instead of the use of history. History as the story of man's struggle to conquer the forces of nature and of his faltering attempts to attain the goal of better and happier existence does make men more sophisticated and better equipped to deal with problems of their own life. The knowledge of how men acted in the past, how they have striven to overcome diversity, may not always suggest an ingenious solution to present crises, but it undoubtedly makes the task easier by providing a background and a body of past experience. History is

[3] Lord Acton, *op. cit.*, p. 20.

[4] Allan Nevins. *The Gateway to History*. New York: 1962. p. 17.

indeed an inexhaustible source of examples and modes of life and "styles of life," and as such and to that extent, it is a school of wisdom.

A historian is usually unwilling to make predictions, he is even reluctant to make many broad generalizations. However, he does engage in predictions of the future, and he does present lessons of history by the mere fact that he analyzes and offers conclusions from his description of a past event or of a past crisis. Professor Carr gave a very apt answer to the question of whether history can serve as a guide to the present. He wrote:

> The historian . . . is bound to generalize; and in so doing, he provides general guides for future action, which, though not specific predictions, are both valid and useful. But he cannot predict specific events, because the specific is unique and because the element of accident enters into it. This distinction, which worries philosophers, is perfectly clear to ordinary men. If two or three children in school develop measles, you will conclude that the epidemic will spread; and this prediction, if you care to call it such, is based on a generalization from past experience, and is a valid and useful guide to action. But you cannot make the specific prediction that Charles or Mary will catch measles.[5]

The study of history is also an excellent tool for the achievement of the rather ephemeral objective in our civic education called "responsible citizenship," by which we mean the development of a desire and readiness to participate in community civic and political affairs. Knowledge and enjoyment of history can, and often does, bring about a lasting concern with politics.

It is rather easy to make a case for the study of history on the basis that it contains an intrinsic pleasure in and by itself. It is a fascinating and a pleasurable aesthetic experience to be able to peer behind the curtain of time, to try to reconstruct the scene of Pericles delivering the funeral oration for his fallen Athenians or the drama of the bare-foot Emperor Henry IV prostrating himself in less than sincere penance before Pope Gregory VII in the snow-covered courtyard of the Canossa Castle. There might not be any immediate practical use in getting our young to learn about the heroic defense of Thermopylae by three hundred young Greeks under the Spartan King Leonidas, or about the stoic suffering of the underfed and ill-clothed Revolutionary soldiers in Valley Forge kept in line by the valor and tenacity of General George Washington, but it is, or it can be, if taught well, a glorious and self-edifying experience.

[5] Edward Hallett Carr. *What Is History?* New York: Knopf, 1962. p. 87–88.

History and the Social Sciences

History belongs to the social sciences, but it also belongs to the humanities. In an important sense, history is both a science and an art. Historical scholarship has very important ties with the social science disciplines, with their methods and research insights. In fact, the objectives of history and of the social sciences are the same. English historian Carr put it this way: "Scientists, social scientists, and historians are all engaged in different branches of the same study: the study of man and his environment, of the effects of man on his environment and of his environment on man. The object of the study is the same: to increase man's understanding of, and mastery over, his environment."[6]

A historian is a social scientist because he uses the scientific method. He methodically collects his data, analyzes it systematically, looks for an inner logic in his accumulated evidence and subjects his data and evidence to thorough testing and scrutiny by comparing the evidence from source materials of many varieties. By the use of inductive logic, the historian then develops his hypotheses and provisional generalizations. After further tests and additional scrutiny of his evidence, the historian is ready to commit his findings to paper.

In these respects, history is a social science and the historian is a social scientist. But a historical work, if it is to survive and become a classic to be read by generations of school children and adults, must also be a work of great literature. The historical inquiry is based on the scientific approach and method, but the final conclusions are intuitive, highly individual; in a word, they belong to the world of art. When history is written in the grand tradition of a literary narrative, it becomes important not only as a scientific record of a segment of the past, but also as an artistic and aesthetic experience. Thus, history is also a branch of literature and belongs not only to the social sciences, but to the humanities. *The History of the Peloponnesian War* by Thucydides, *The Decline and Fall of the Roman Empire* by Edward Gibbon, or the *History of England* by Thomas Babington Macaulay are not only great history, but also masterpieces of literature. They are both artistic and scientific achievements.

The same is true of such great American historians as William Prescott, the author of *The Conquest of Mexico* and *The Conquest of Peru,* and Francis Parkman, the author of *The Jesuits in North America* and *Montcalm and Wolfe.* Consider, for instance, this brief excerpt from Parkman. It is written in the tradition of a great narrative history. It is

[6] *Ibid.,* p. 111.

scientific and accurate because Parkman was a hard-working historian who pored days and nights over first-hand documentary sources, but it is also an artistic accomplishment because it is great literature:

> The peace was broken, and the hounds of war turned loose. The contagion spread through all the Mohawk nation, the war-songs were sung, and the warriors took the path to Canada. The miserable colonists and their more miserable allies woke from their dream of peace to reality of fear and horror. Again Montreal and Three Rivers were beset under murdering savages, skulking in thickets and prowling under cover of night, yet when it came to blows, displaying a courage almost equal to the ferocity that inspired it.[7]

Or take this description of Emperor Constantine in *The Decline and Fall of the Roman Empire* by Edward Gibbon:

> The person, as well as the mind of Constantine, had been enriched by nature with her choicest endowments. His stature was lofty, his countenance majestic, his deportment graceful, his strength and activity were displayed in every manly exercise, and, from his earliest youth to a very advanced season of life, he preserved the vigor of his constitution by a strict adherence to the domestic virtues of chastity and temperance. He delighted in the social intercourse of familiar conversation, and though he might sometimes indulge his disposition to raillery with less reserve than was required by the severe dignity of his station, the courtesy and liberality of his manners gained the hearts of all who approached him. . . . In the dispatch of business his diligence was indefatigable; and the active powers of his mind were almost continually exercised in reading, writing, or meditating, in giving audience to ambassadors, and in examining the complaints of his subjects. In the field he infused his own intrepid spirit into troops, where he conducted with the talents of a consummate general; and to his abilities, rather than to his fortune, we may ascribe the signal victories which he obtained over the foreign and domestic foes of the republic. He loved glory as the reward, perhaps as the motive of his labors. The boundless ambition which, from the moment of his accepting the purple at York appears as the ruling passion of his soul, may be justified by the dangers of his own situation, by the character of his rivals, by the consciousness of superior merit, and by the prospect

[7] Francis Parkman. *The Jesuits in North America.* Boston: Little, Brown and Company, 1963. p. 404.

that his success *would* enable him to restore peace and order to the distracted empire.[8]

Who but a historian supremely endowed with literary gifts and with full knowledge of the complex psychological make-up of a great man could have written this paragraph?

In fact, history, if it is to be durable and reach many readers must be highly attractive in the power of its narrative. A volume of history written in the best scientific tradition, but lacking the felicity of style and the richness of language, will not be read and will not endure.

diff. from Soc. Sci.

In addition, history differs from social sciences in other important respects. While social scientists concentrate their efforts on the formulation of the general concepts and general rules and laws, historians, while not ignoring "lower" and "higher" generalizations are at least as interested in the *singular,* the *concrete* and the *unique.* The combination of the jingo-imperalist and the pacific President and recipient of the Nobel Peace Prize in the person of Theodore Roosevelt, is as important to a historian as the discovery of a sound generalization on the basic pattern of revolutions. The human drama involved in the dismissal of Chancellor Bismark by Kaiser Wilhelm is as important to a historian as the possible discovery of a plausible generalization explaining the recurrent economic depressions in Germany after World War I. In general, while history is interested in the study of the uniqueness of cultures and civilizations, the social sciences prefer to look for the common elements and for the common processes in all cultures. Professor A. L. Rowse explained this difference between history and the social sciences in a particularly felicitous way:

> The study of mankind does not resemble the study of the physical properties of atoms, or the life history of animals. If you find out about one atom, you have found out about all atoms and what is true of the habits of one robin is roughly true of the habits of all robins. But the life history of one man, or even of many individual men will not tell you the life history of other men. . . . Men are too complicated, too spiritual, too various for a scientific analysis.[9]

The historian keeps in mind that "fifty men do not make a centipede."

History, unlike the social sciences, is vitally interested in the realm of values, attitudes, moods, and motives. It is not only a scientific

[8] Edward Gibbon. *The Decline and Fall of the Roman Empire.* A One-Volume Abridgement, by D. M. Low. New York: Harcourt, Brace and Company, 1960. p. 266–67.

[9] Alfred Leslie Rowse. *The Use of History.* New York: Collier Books, 1963. p. 66.

enterprise, but also a moral one. In its study of human beings involved in the great story of human drama, it is directly related to moral values inherent in life in all its manifestations. The anthropologist who lives in an Indian or Mexican village or in a tribal village in Africa observing daily the mores and customs of the villagers, can and does abstain from any value judgment. He is not concerned whether a particular custom, however alien to his own scale of values, is "good" or "bad," "right" or "wrong." Not so a historian. He is constantly involved in value-judgment and in the assessment of motives. Thucydides expressed strong views and preferences between the Athenian and the Spartan modes of government, and Gibbon made no bones about his conviction that Christianity was the main cause of the downfall of the splendid ancient civilization. Historians have probed deeply and differed sharply on the question of whether Oliver Cromwell was a truly religious man or a hypocritical autocrat. Parkman made clear his conviction that English civilization was superior to the French and that the Protestant religion was more amenable to free institutions than the Catholic faith. Most American historians would agree with their distinguished colleague, Samuel E. Morison, who said in his Presidential Address to the American Historical Association in 1951: "Unless it be the dull pedantry of the average doctoral dissertation in history, there is no quality more repugnant to readers than chilly impartiality."

The historian, unlike his colleagues in the social sciences, doubts whether many important questions and problems in history can be understood by a quantitative empirical analysis which is the preferred method of inquiry of social scientists. The historian is increasingly impressed with the powerful role that fate and accident play in human history. Was it not an accident that brought about the emergence of Mahomet in the deserts of Hedjaz? Was it not an accident that gave Oliver Cromwell a weak son, Richard, who promptly lost the fruits of his father's revolution? A historian, who like Barbara Tuchman in her *The Guns of August* examines the causes of World War I, stands awed by the erratic nature of human beings, who placed by destiny in positions of great power, passively allowed themselves to be swept into an abyss by the tide of events.

Finally, history alone, among all other learned disciplines, tries to recapture how things were in the past, or in the words of a great German historian, Leopold Von Ranke, "things as they *really* were." Other social disciplines abstract from the past those phenomena or segments of man's experience which are of particular interest to them, but history alone attempts to give a full and true account of all of human experience.

While it is important to keep in mind how and why history and the social sciences differ, it is equally important to emphasize the ever growing flow of communication between the historians and the social scientists. Some historians have gratefully acknowledged that the application of concepts, approaches, and methods of inquiry from sociology, economics, political science, and anthropology has been very helpful to them in the study of the past. Many historians have borrowed from the social scientists more sophisticated sampling techniques and are not averse to using social science terminology and asking questions about social mobility, role-playing, social status, and model building. Anthropologists have taught historians to become more aware of the pitfalls of cultural ethnocentrism, and Richard Hofstadter, the foremost writer in American intellectual history, has gratefully acknowledged his debt to sociological insights and concepts which, in his view, greatly enhance "the speculative richness of history."

In his excellent volume, *The Age of Reform: From Bryan to F.D.R.* which won a Pulitzer Prize, Hofstadter applied the relevant aspects of the method of sociological research to the study of Populism and Progressivism. He found such sociological and psychological concepts as status anxiety, self-deceiving image, role-playing, and social mobility very useful in tracing the sources of social conflict in the latter part of the nineteenth century and in the fuller explanation of the character of the leaders of the Progressive Movement and of the leading Muckrakers. The Populists, Hofstadter suggested, failing to understand the true causes of the agricultural depression, projected their animosities and grievances on "alien" forces — Wall Street, New Yorkers, English capitalists, and Jewish bankers. The split personality, the paranoic tendencies of the Populists became clear when such leaders of the Peoples' Party as Thomas Watson and Ben Tillman became bitter Negro haters.

As to the Progressive leaders, most of whom came from the clergy, the law, and the universities, Hofstadter asserted that their reform crusades were an expression of their resentment against the loss of status to the newly rich industrialists and the politicians. Using a sociological term, Hofstadter spoke of "the status revolution."

William L. Langer and H. Stuart Hughes seem to be fascinated by the potential contribution of psychoanalysis to history and especially to the field of biography. They agree that historians have, on the whole, ignored, in the words of Erik Ericson, "the fateful function of childhood in the fabric of society." David Donald has acknowledged his indebtedness to frequent consultations with psychoanalysts in the process of writing the biography of Charles Sumner. Professor Hughes sees a great affinity between historians and psychoanalysts. "For the historian as for the psychoanalyst," he writes, "an interpretation ranks as satisfactory not by passing some formal scientific tests, but by conveying our inner conviction. For both plural explanations are second nature. . . . Indeed, for both of them the word 'cause' is admissable only if defined with extreme flexibility. . . . Both deal in complex configurations, searching for a thread of inner logic that will tie together an apparent chaos of random words and actions." Hughes has suggested that at least some Ph.D. candidates in history should go through the process of psychoanalysis to be prepared to use psychoanalytical insights in their historical investigations.[10]

There is another important factor which brings about a growing convergence of interests between the sciences, the social scientists, and the historians. The social scientists and even the natural scientists are not so sure as they were before that the laboratory method of direct observation of phenomena is the only or even the best way to learn the secrets of the human society and of nature. A distinguished Yale physicist, Henry Margenau, stated recently that "the scientist of the twentieth century had become exceedingly humble with respect to absolute truth . . . if you base your world picture only on direct experience — observations, immediate impressions, sensory data — you are going to get a chaotic world. There is going to be no cohesion whatever. . . . Facts have to be mapped against a whole network of ideas. . . . We must shift the emphasis from facts to ideas."[11] There is a great affinity between these views of an eminent scientist and the efforts of the historian to search for the "meaning" of an event or an action, or for a historical understanding of an epoch in history.

While good history is distinguished by an artistic narrative, by an analytical analysis of events and their causes, and is as exciting as the best dramatic plays presented by the best companies of actors, it is nevertheless true that for a variety of reasons history as taught in the schools is often a pedestrian fact-by-fact and date-by-date approach. The infusion of concepts, modes of inquiry, and types of questions asked by social scientists holds great promise in making the study of history in our elementary and secondary schools more meaningful, more dramatic, and more interesting. This infusion from the social sciences will also help to focus greater attention on contemporary problems of our society and thus give more relevance to the study of the past.

It is just because history has broad and not clearly defined frontiers

[10] H. Stuart Hughes. *History as Art and as a Science.* New York: Harper and Row, 1964. p. 47.

[11] *The New York Times.* March 18, 1965. p. 57.

and because it is a social science, a humanity, and an art, that it must remain the core of the social studies curriculum. Only history as a core discipline is in a position to accept and put to use the materials, the research findings, the concepts, and the modes of inquiry of the social sciences. Teachers of ancient history, for instance, cannot do justice to their subject and even more important to their students, if they do not include in their teaching units and their teaching strategies the wealth of research done by archeologists in Egypt, Israel, Jordan, and Iraq, or the concepts and the methods of inquiry of modern anthropology for a better understanding of the village and town organization in the ancient world.

The trend toward greater integration between history and the social sciences is becoming ever stronger. Historians now pay more and more attention to urban history, business history, and social history. It is a sign of the times that Allan Nevins donated half a million dollars to Columbia University for a chair in economic history. While narrative history is still the mainstay of historical writing, many historians use the methods of inquiry of sociology, economics, and of other social sciences.

Writing on the interrelationship between history and the social sciences, English historian Carr states that "the more sociological history becomes, and the more historical sociology becomes, the better for both. Let the frontier between them be kept wide open for two-way traffic." While most historians do see a great deal to be gained by close contacts with their colleagues in the social sciences, they wish to preserve the uniqueness of history as a separate discipline allied both to social sciences and to humanities. Most of them remain fascinated not only with the general, but with a particular event or a particular actor on the stage of history. Having dealt with the complexity of human nature as revealed in the actions of men of leadership and action, and having repeatedly been forced to give multicausal evaluations of periods of great stress and crisis, historians are doubtful whether some important historical problems are amenable to quantitative analysis.

However, most historians are gradually reaching a consensus that the rapid growth of the social sciences demands that historians make use of the ways of thinking and techniques of inquiry of the social sciences whenever and wherever this can prove to be beneficial. Thus, there is every reason to expect that the next decade will see a steadily narrowing gap and an increasingly fruitful collaboration between history and the social sciences.

12. American Studies, Social Studies, and the Process of Education

Donald G. Baker

Relate subject matter to people.

I

A specter is haunting the social studies. It is the specter of its own obsolescence. High School science and mathematics courses, in both scope and teaching methods, have undergone radical transformations in the past decade. The social sciences, meanwhile, have remained transfixed at a point which, in the estimation of some critics, is 50 years behind the times.

Bernard Berelson, in his introduction to *The Social Studies and the Social Sciences*,[1] complained that most high school social studies programs remain patterned after a 1916 National Education Association report which proposed, for that era, a curriculum that included civics or world geography in the ninth grade, world history in the tenth, United States history in the eleventh, and a problems of democracy or similar course in the twelfth grade.

This feeling of uneasiness has prompted reassessments of the social studies curriculum. For example, in 1957 and 1958, the National Council for the Social Studies published two reports; and, recently, other groups and foundations have turned their attention to the problem. The basic question being asked is: What type of social studies program is required to fit the needs of students living in a revolutionary world? An answer to this elicits a second question: What, therefore, should be the

From Donald G. Baker, "American Studies, Social Studies, and the Process of Education," *Social Education*, December, 1963, 27: 427–430, 455. Donald G. Baker is Director, Social Science Division, Southampton College of Long Island University, Southampton, New York, and Associate Professor of Political Science. He has contributed numerous articles and reviews to scholarly journals in the field of government. This article is reprinted by permission of the author and of the National Council for the Social Studies.

[1] Sponsored by the American Council of Learned Societies and The National Council for The Social Studies. New York: Harcourt, Brace & World, 1962.

scope and content of the specific courses that are given in the social studies program?

While these are, undeniably, crucial questions, there is perhaps a third, an even more fundamental one, that should be posed. It is: What is the process of learning, of education, and how does our knowledge of this affect the curricula and courses to be developed? Only when this question is first answered is it then possible to proceed to the shaping of a desired social studies program, for no course, however exciting or challenging it may appear in outline form, can be effective if it surreptitiously undermines the learning process. For this reason, Professor Jerome S. Bruner's provocative essay, *The Process of Education,*[2] merits close attention and serious consideration *prior* to the development of new programs.

Professor Bruner, although his major concern is the applicability of learning theory to mathematics and science, concedes its applicability to the social studies. There is, he argues, a fundamental structure to all fields of knowledge. That is, certain basic ideas, certain assumptions, if they are initially grasped by the student, facilitate subsequent learning of content. Simple as this point may appear, it is often disregarded in the development and teaching of courses. The structure is merely assumed, if even that, and the student is left to wander in a maze of facts, the interrelatedness of which are further obscured by the addition of more facts. Inevitably, the fundamental structure remains obscured or concealed; and, in terms of the old adage, the student misses the forest for the trees.

Any given field of knowledge has a basic structure which, in scientific terms, postulates a model of that particular universe of discourse. The structure, Bruner indicates, should be presented initially to the student, for:

> Grasping the structure of a subject is understanding it in a way that permits many other things to be related to it meaningfully. To learn structure, in short, is to learn how things are related.

Thus, "understanding fundamentals makes a subject more comprehensible. This is true not only in physics and mathematics, . . . but equally [true] in the social studies and literature." When this is recognized, it is thence possible to evaluate the process of learning as it pertains to the student's capability of grasping materials.

Bruner goes on to state that:

> We begin with the hypothesis that any subject can be taught effectively in some intellectually honest form to any [student] at any

[2] Cambridge, Mass.; Harvard University Press, 1961.

age of development. It is a bold hypothesis and an essential one in thinking about the nature of a curriculum. No evidence exists to contradict it; considerable evidence is being amassed that supports it.

Bruner's last point should be stressed: ". . . considerable evidence is being amassed that supports" this view. Moreover, the fundamental ideas, whether they be in science, math, or the social studies, are comprehensible even to a child, *providing* they are presented in a context that the child understands. Earlier education, of necessity, is on a simpler level, but its focus is still the basic structure. In subsequent years, education moves to the more difficult, the more sophisticated level where there is "the continual broadening and deepening of knowledge in terms of basic and general ideas."

In terms of learning, it is essential to begin with the fundamental structure of a subject. This provides meaning; it facilitates understanding; it promotes retention of materials learned; and, equally significant, it provides a context within which new materials are more readily comprehended. This last point is crucial for the learning and the retention of materials.

> Perhaps the most basic thing that can be said about human memory . . . is that unless detail is placed into a structured pattern, it is rapidly forgotten. . . . What learning general or fundamental principles does is to ensure that memory loss will not mean total loss, that what remains will permit us to reconstruct the details when needed. [Structure] . . . is the vehicle not only for understanding a phenomenon now but also for remembering it tomorrow.

It should be evident that "piece meal" or fact-oriented courses, whether they be in mathematics, science, or the social studies, are self-defeating unless they have structure. This, Bruner contends, should not be overlooked in the development of the curriculum:

> [The] curriculum of a subject should be determined by the most fundamental understanding that can be achieved of the underlying principles that give structure to that subject. Teaching specific topics or skills without making clear their context in the broader fundamental structure of a field of knowledge is uneconomical. . . . [S]uch teaching makes it exceedingly difficult for the student to generalize . . . [and such a course] has little reward in terms of intellectual excitement. . . . [K]nowledge one has acquired without sufficient structure to tie it together is knowledge that is likely to be forgotten.

II

As inferred previously, Bruner's concept of "structure" is similar to the term "model" employed in scientific thought. The applicability of the latter term is not limited to science, however, for man, be he scientist, historian, or layman, constructs from his experiences and observations certain conceptual models of the universe, i.e., of reality. It is on the basis of these models or conceptions that he grounds his behavior, makes his predictions, or interprets his society and its history. The model undergoes alteration as more data are collected and synthesized, until, finally, it is thought to approximate reality. But there is never a one-to-one relationship between the model and the universe, for man's observational techniques, be they the scientist's more precise instruments or man's sensory organs, have their limitations. What is strived for, nevertheless, is a closer approximation, or correspondence, between the model and reality.

Although the historian and the social scientist work with different types of data than the scientist, their task is similar. They, too, construct models, either of past or present societies, which enable them to better understand the world. The approach is similar to that of the scientist; and each, fashioning his tools to fit his particular type of data, nevertheless utilizes the hypothetico-deductive methods of scientific thought. The historian, be he a Marx, Toynbee, or Spengler, or a Beard, Turner, or Boorstin, postulates such models. The models of the former group encompass a broader sweep of history; of the latter group, a narrower scale — usually focusing on a specific country, period, or event. In a similar vein is the work of the social scientist, and here the economist and the sociologist have been most successful in developing highly sophisticated models.

So far, American Studies has been ignored, but it is precisely at this point that it is relevant to the discussion of new social studies programs. In particular, the approaches and models of American Studies deserve closer examination.

It is the goal of American Studies to build a model (or, if necessary, models) that more fully interpret American society. A model must encompass that concatenation of forces which have shaped the nation. The model's rationale, then, is that of providing a better explanation of American society, particularly of its behavior, actions, and history. There is still no fully accepted model, for American Studies is at that stage where agreement has not been reached. Rather, numerous individuals are engaged in building their own models. These studies, it is anticipated, as in science, will have a cumulative effect, and eventually there should emerge a model that receives wide acceptance from analysts. The need for eclecticism, particularly at this stage, prompts American Studies to reject rigidified methods or approaches to the study of society. Flexibility and diversity are its *modus operandi,* and it encourages new approaches, methods, and techniques. Even a cursory assessment of American Studies programs in existence will confirm this; and, as might be anticipated, this eclecticism would characterize any social studies program that modeled itself after American Studies.

The eclecticism of American Studies; indeed, the very nature of the discipline, suggests that models are essentially heuristic and functional. Such models provide explanations; but more important, they stimulate further research and exploration. In the process, the models undergo persistent examination and modification.

III

Basically, there are three fundamental goals for a social studies program. These are: (1) to develop the critical thinking abilities of the student; (2) to extend his knowledge and thereby his comprehension of the world; and (3) to promote what the National Council for the Social Studies has termed "desirable socio-civic behavior." There is little basis for the argument that the latter two are incompatible, that they are mutually exclusive. This, as Bernard Berelson has suggested, is "largely a spurious issue." It is not a question of developing *either* good citizens *or* knowledgeable students, for both goals may be realized in a properly developed social studies program.

None of these factors can be ignored in the building of a program. Basic to all of them, of course, is an understanding of the process of learning, for this becomes the very basis in the shaping of the program. While there would be some disagreement within American Studies, it can be assumed that there would be some consensus in what should be incorporated in a social studies curriculum. The broad outlines, perhaps, can be distinguished here; and a four-year program might include: for the first year, a course in "Area Studies"; in the second year, "American Values and Ideals"; third year, "American History"; and fourth year, "American Issues." A further explanation of each of these courses should clarify their function.

First Year: "Area Studies." The emphasis in this first year would be on the geography, culture, politics, and basic problems of major areas of the world; namely, Europe, Russia, Asia, the Middle East, South Africa, and South America. Similar basic problems and issues confront all societies. These include: how economic goods are to be produced and distributed; what type of political system is desired to achieve the particular goals of that society; and what type of social system will best fit the needs of that society. Each society answers these questions in a different manner; and it is the basic function of the course to show students these differences. Moreover, the course provides the student with the basis for drawing later comparisons with American society and the ways in which it resolves these issues.

Second Year: "American Values and Ideals." The second year course would focus on the interaction of beliefs and environment and illustrate how these have shaped American life and thought. Major attention would be devoted to the analysis of basic American values. The first semester centers on "The American Experience"; the second semester, using the first semester as a base, on the derivation of these values in "The European Heritage." This would not be a history course in the usual sense of the term.

Emphasis in the first semester is on basic American values. These include: (1) a belief in the dignity and worth of the individual; (2) a belief that man, by nature, is neither good nor bad, but is endowed with the ability, through education and experience, to correct his mistakes and thereby better himself; (3) a belief in equality of opportunity for all people; (4) a belief in freedom of conscience, which includes freedom in religious and intellectual spheres; and (5) a belief in a free political system, one that allows for the maximum realization of these basic beliefs.

The first semester would focus on major American figures; namely, Franklin, Jefferson, Madison, Emerson, Whitman, William James, and Dewey, and show how they applied these beliefs to the problems and issues of their times (other figures, of course, could be used). An analysis of these individuals illustrates how deeply ingrained these beliefs are in the American experience.

The second semester would trace the source of these values in Greek, Roman, humanist, protestant, rationalist, and Enlightenment thought and practice. Some of these values enjoyed a long heritage; others were only written about but never practiced. Still others were unique to America. As Ernst Cassirer has suggested, the achievement, in practice, of some of these values was first realized in America. The semester terminates with an analysis of these values as they converged on the American scene in the latter half of the eighteenth century, where they became, in the estimation of Jefferson, "an expression of the American mind."

Third Year: "American History." There is increasing criticism of the value of a general survey course that tends to be little more than a repetition of the seventh- or eighth-grade American history course. One recent proposal for change is for development of a course that focuses, in depth, on major periods or events that have shaped the nation. Under a grant from the Wemyss Foundation, a group of scholars has been working at Amherst College for the past two years on the development of this type of course. This is precisely the type needed for the third year of this suggested social studies curriculum.

Fourth Year: "American Issues." Either one or two semesters, dependent upon the time allotted, this course would probe the major issues confronting American society. Four such issues might be suggested. These are: (1) contemporary America, the political-economic transformations since 1900, and the implications of these changes for contemporary society; (2) problems resulting from revolutionary changes occurring in the world, particularly in underdeveloped countries, and the implications of this for American foreign policy; (3) the Communist challenge to the free world, with emphasis on the cold war conflict and American foreign policy; and (4) the political responsibilities of the individual in a free and democratic society.

IV

This, it should be remembered, is only a brief sketch of a proposed social studies curriculum that utilizes the American Studies approach. Its value is primarily as a model to test the extent to which it fulfills the major criteria set down as necessary for a well-developed program. These, it will be recalled, include: (1) consideration of the process of learning; (2) a program with broad scope; (3) a program with emphasis upon content; (4) development of the student's critical thinking abilities: and (5) the development of socio-civic values. These are commented upon individually below.

Process of Education. Bruner maintains that there is a structure to all fields of knowledge. If this structure is made clear, learning, memory, and comprehension all benefit. The program outlined above is based on this, and it has a basic, underlying structure. It moves from Area Studies, to American Values and Ideals, to American History, to American Issues. Together, they constitute a tightly-knit program. There is continuity and an underlying theme or rationale. As a citizen, the student, if he is to fulfill his role in a democratic society, must know something about the world and its problems and his own society and its problems and values. Only then can he make wise choices and fulfill his responsibilities as a citizen. Moreover, each course, independent of the others, has its own structure. This is reflected in the basic assumptions of the Area Studies course, in the fundamental assumptions in the American Values and Ideals course, in the emphasis on key historical periods in American History, and, finally, in the assumptions of the American Issues course.

Scope. Within the time allotted to social studies, it is the intent of the program to present as extensive a view as conceivable. Area studies represent an integrative effort at utilizing materials from all applicable disciplines. There is questionable validity, especially at the high school level, to the argument that courses in each of the social science disciplines should be given. The effort at this level should be towards the integration of materials from the disciplines; and their interrelatedness should be emphasized. Specialization should be left to the college; but even there the growing criticisms suggest the apprehension precipitated by over-emphasis on specialization at the undergraduate level.

Content. A current criticism of incoming college students is that they are poorly equipped despite their high school social studies courses. As compensation for this, it is advocated that students be given courses in each of the social science disciplines. The criticism is valid; the suggested solutions are questionable. The basic problems appear to arise from the unstructured and fact-oriented courses given students, courses that emphasize facts the student will need to know to pass state and college board examinations. These materials, as Professor Bruner suggests, are retained only for short periods of time. The need, therefore, is for better structured courses rather than courses in each discipline. When there is structure, the materials are better retained. The proposed curriculum, because of its structure, should lead to increased understanding and retention of learned materials.

Critical Thinking. Each of the proposed courses aims at developing the critical thinking abilities of the student. He is expected to evaluate similarities and differences of societies, including his own; and, in the American History course, as a result of his intensive study of specific periods and events, the student is expected to draw his own conclusions. Finally, in the American Issues course, the student is expected, on the basis of his earlier studies to consider alternative solutions or methods of confronting and resolving the problems facing American society.

Socio-Civic Values. Because of the emphasis in the proposed program on values, issues, problems, and the student's role in society, it is anticipated that the curriculum will definitely lead to an understanding and acceptance of the desired socio-civic values. The student has the opportunity to compare and evaluate the values of his society with those of others; he is taught why his participation is significant in the preservation of a democratic society; and, in coming to recognize the complexity of issues and problems, he is less likely to fall prey to future demagogues who often achieve an uncritical following through the espousal of simplistic solutions to complex problems.

In brief, then, the above proposed social studies program is patterned after the American Studies approach. It has its weaknesses, for it is doubtful that any program can fully achieve the desired results in the time allotted social studies programs. Nevertheless, a critical reassessment of such programs is needed. In the development of new curricula, Professor Bruner's suggestion should be carefully heeded:

> If the hypothesis . . . is true — that any subject can be taught to any [student] in some honest form — then it should follow that a curriculum ought to be built around the great issues, principles, and values that a society deems worthy of the continual concern of its members.

13. Geography

James High

Geography has been traditionally an elementary school subject. Formerly this was universally true, but recently, possibly resulting from the tendency to fuse many subjects into one social study, even elementary geography at the lowest level of sophistication — place name drill — has been neglected. Not meaning to be merely nostalgic, one regrets the passing of a systematic review in elementary school of the physical elements and place-name knowledge traditionally assigned to geogra-

From James High, "Geography: Coordinating Element in Secondary Social Studies," *The Journal of Geography*, September, 1960, 59: 270–278. James High is Associate Professor of History, San Jose State College, San Jose, California. He has published many articles in history, sociology, geography, technology, and education in professional journals in the United States, India, and Holland. A college textbook, *Teaching Secondary School Social Studies*, was published in 1962. This article is reprinted by permission of the author and of the National Council for Geographic Education.

phy. In many places during the last few years there has been a renewed emphasis on this sort of thing, but the content usually has a distinctly local orientation. Texans in elementary school usually learn about Texas, and Californians find out about the distinctions of California; but worldwide coverage of principles and places is only rarely attempted.

In Junior High School

Basic geography, when it appears in the curriculum at all, seems to fall usually in the junior high school, but rarely as a separate subject. Judging by the junior high school social studies textbooks, geography now shows up, and will probably continue, as a strong component of study but ordinarily as a part of the specialized setting of a much more general theme in history or culture.[1] Even so, it might be quite desirable to make sure, in an orderly survey of geography as such, that all students acquire a basic knowledge in elementary school of the place names of the world, the chief world regions, and the primary principles that make our relatively unchanging environment possible.

As geography appears in the junior high school it is generally in support of a historical or social subject placed in a particular region. For example, in certain grades there may very well be an inclusion of Latin American life as the year-long theme of social studies. In the course of this work students may become quite familiar with places, climate and economic production in Latin America — but not with the rest of the world.

In junior high there is usually no coverage of world history, and consequently there is no examination of world geography. The most to be expected from an integrated or fusion approach to geographic study is treatment of those areas that make up the central theme of whatever course is under consideration.

In Senior High School

As students enter senior high school it might be expected that the same fusion approach to history-geography-culture would be followed. The usual first course in high school social studies is world history; if this were accompanied by world geography, then there would be no need for this sort of comment. Such is not ordinarily the case. World

[1] Louis M. Vanaria, "Bibliography of Textbooks in the Social Studies, 1958–1959," *Social Education* (December, 1959), 384 ff., is the eleventh annual supplement to a bulletin published by the National Council for the Social Studies. These lists incidentally show an increase in elementary geography, but none in high school texts.

history is a tremendous subject and it takes all of a teacher's ingenuity to get through it with a respectable feeling of "coverage" in one year. Usually the teacher is not a geographer and he often feels reluctant to undertake a whole course in geography when he is supposed to be teaching history.

This is incidentally a commentary on the disparate characters of the two divisions of American education — elementary and secondary. High schools are inhabited, not by young children, but by people who are suddenly growing up, and their teachers are properly concerned that they learn as broadly and quickly as possible in the specialized fields of knowledge. It is expected that high school students come equipped with the fundamental skills needed to encounter the liberal arts subjects. In certain fields it has been recognized that this cannot always be true. In mathematics, for example, it has become a commonplace to offer elementary or remedial arithmetic in high school; writing, composition, spelling and grammar — even reading — are skills that are being given fundamental remedial attention in high school. Geography, an equally important skill, has not received the same recognition.

High school social studies teachers usually and quite properly teach history. Unfortunately there are not many high school geography teachers, and there are not many courses in geography in high schools. In a survey of 107 school systems made in 1953, only eight required geography and this was usually in grade nine. (Most often grade nine is in junior high school.)[2] If more teachers were trained in geography, then social studies teachers might properly and usually teach geography.

Current Curricular Trends

Out of 15 curricular suggestions made for the social studies in 1939, only one included a specific course in world geography in the tenth grade. Two included the same thing in the ninth grade. The rest either neglected geography altogether or else vaguely specified it as a part of the integrated study of problems or units mainly concerned with social adjustment.[3]

Twenty years later, in 1959, the consensus among social studies specialists as well as among the growing number of geographers interested in general education has changed remarkably. Now it is felt that at least careful consideration *ought* to be given to geography in relation to the social studies. It is now recognized that man's enivronment is a

[2] Emlyn Jones, "Analysis of Social Studies Requirements," *Social Education* (October, 1954), 257–258.

[3] *The Future of the Social Studies,* edited by James A. Michener, National Council for the Social Studies, Washington, D.C., 1939.

complex and important set of relationships among man and his physica setting and that there is a mutual change constantly operating therein Climatology, landforms, population and demography, economic production, conservation and place-name knowledge *must* form an essential part of any serious study of man, his social and political organization, and his history. How this is to be translated into learning in school and what curricular pattern is to be developed still are moot questions, but at least the purpose and function of geographic study have been assessed.[4]

If it is assumed that geography is essential in social studies, that it is primarily a social science, and that it is not exclusively an elementary school subject, then there are two sharp implications for general education. First, a respectable established place must be made for geographic study in secondary schools, and second, teacher training must take this into account. Neither has been adequately considered, say, in the terms that history occupies interest in the public school curricula and in the process of teacher training.

Meaning and Scope of Geography

Possibly the first consideration is to establish the meaning and scope of geographic study. It is primarily a coordinating study, having practically no exclusive body of source materials, such as might be the case for nuclear physics or organic chemistry. On the other hand, geography is, above all, studied empirically and therefore is a science insofar as methodology is concerned. No geographic formulation can be made without impeccable evidence. The meaning of geography is implicit in the relationships that nature bears to man, and it must be remembered that man is part of nature, both affecting and being affected by his environment. In fact man is part of his own environment. Geography cannot, therefore, arbitrarily exclude any part of the environment from its scope of study; the geographer cannot say "such and such a subject has no meaning for me; it is the field of the climatologist, the historian, and biologist." All knowledge relates to all other knowledge, and it all bears on man's occupance of the earth; therefore geography is both a social and a natural science. Fundamentally it is socially oriented because knowledge of man's setting is of no significance without man and it is not entirely subject to exact measurement. Geography must be viewed as an orderly and as nearly scientific as possible coordination of the fields of knowledge most pertinent to man's understanding of himself as a social being in a physical setting. Professor Hartshorne has per-

[4] Lorrin Kennamer, Jr., "The Place of Physical Geography in the Curriculum," *New Viewpoints in Geography,* edited by Preston E. James, National Council for the Social Studies, Washington, D.C., 1959, 211–228.

haps stated the matter as thoughtfully and succinctly as anyone in America. He says that "geography is concerned to provide accurate, orderly, and rational description and interpretation of the variable character of the earth surface."[5]

Without quibbling about the exact limits that might be placed on geographic study, and there must be some in order to make possible any individual's mastery of the subject, it is obvious that it is not a discrete science such as geology, for example, nor at the same time is it a traditional social science such as sociology or political science, dealing only with human relationships. Neither does geography partake of the humanistic artistry of good history, dealing as it does with man's image of himself. On the other hand, it is equally easy to see that geology, sociology, political science and history have little meaning without reference to the nature of the environment on earth, and that the geographer cannot refuse to consider the findings and interpretations of any of those fields as well as many others. Geography is truly the bridge between natural and social science and as such should certainly be included in general secondary education.

At the lower levels of education, geographic relations are first represented by simple, worldwide place-name knowledge. Small childern are quite capable of and much interested in learning the designations of nations, cities, rivers, mountains and the like, along with their vital statistics, such as items of production, governmental significance, climate, communication activities, elevation, population, distances — all the things that constitute the elements of geographic relationship. Next, the basic principles of the solar system, isostacy, the earth's declination, seasonal change, the effect of elevation on temperature, polar and mountain variations from mid-latitude plains, ocean currents, winds and weather — all of the relatively unchanging superficial environment can be of interest to young children if properly presented, and such knowledge can then form the basis for more complicated and sophisticated consideration of relationships at a secondary level of general education.

No subject of consequence can be learned completely and in all its ramifications by passing over the material once. A repetitive or spiral approach to social studies learning has long been a principle, with successive grade level offerings in the same subject. In United States history, for example, the usual experience of school children is to encounter the subject some three or four times between the third grade and graduation from high school, with the expectation of yet another survey during the first two years of college. It is therefore safe to assume

[5] Richard Hartshorne, *Perspective on the Nature of Geography,* Rand McNally, Chicago, 1959, p. 21.

that geography on a world scale cannot be mastered in only the elementary review possible before entering high school. The junior high school fusion of geography into a total social study in some measure recognizes this principle, but such treatment is neither universal nor consistent. At best, if geography is substantially covered in the ninth grade, for most students — three-fourths of high school graduates — it is the last time they will ever be required to study relationships from this special point of view. For those who go to college, a vast majority of them never having had even the ninth grade treatment, geography will be a new experience and they will usually discover with dismay that their ignorance is appalling.[6]

From these things it may be inferred that geography could have — should have — a place in secondary school social studies. It does have, regardless of whether it is recognized in the curriculum or not, since geography is a study of relationships among the environmental factors. Its neglect can only reflect a degree of ignorance, and high school teachers are far from being an ignorant lot. Good students and good teachers have always paid some attention to the elements of geography. It is only argued and advocated here that the obvious be recognized and that geography be included in curricular offerings on the same grounds as other components of liberal, general education.

One of the forces working against the acceptance and extension of geography in education at all levels is the dearth of educators and administrators with geographic training themselves. This tends to minimize emphasis on geography as an important part of the curriculum. In opposition to this is the obvious effect of the great social changes which have taken place in recent years that make geographic study imperative. Two world wars, the Korean conflict and the Cold War, not to mention tremendous population increase and great mobility of people over the whole world, have forcefully called to human attention the need for widespread geographic knowledge. The most easily observed result of this pressure is the rapid increase of collegiate departments of geography both in the United States and abroad. This has been most marked in Great Britain where candidates for secondary teacher certification in geography have increased three to four times faster than in any other field.[7]

[6] Not over five per cent of the students in my introductory course in geography at the University of California, Santa Barbara (approximately one hundred each semester) have ever had any organized course in geography at either elementary or secondary levels, and of those who have had any very few can remember anything from the remote elementary school days.

[7] Earl B. Shaw, "Forces Contributing to Changes in Geographic Education," *Professional Paper No. 16,* National Council for Geographic Education, March, 1958, pp. 55–62.

A second consideration of major importance after the acceptance of geography into the high school curriculum has to do with the way it is to be handled. Actual technique of instruction is one element of this consideration, but not the first one. Of first importance is the decision as to whether geography is to be handled as a discrete subject, allocated to a specific course in high school or as a fused part of other courses such as United States history, world history or general problems. There is a cogent argument for either method, and in either case basic educational philosophy is involved and teacher training has to be considered.

If, on the one hand, social studies teachers are well enough equipped to integrate the knowledge of geography and history so that students are left with a rounded and full view of both subjects in their multiplex relationship, then the approach to human experience in its complete setting is infinitely preferable. It is, however, doubtful that most social studies teachers are expert in both geography and history; therefore it is probably best to teach them as separate subjects and hope for an integrated result in general education in much the same way that it is hoped that students will develop a balanced knowledge of their roles in life through the study of English, mathematics, history, natural science and foreign languages.

Assuming that geography is to be taught as a separate subject in high school, if world history is given in the tenth grade, world geography should also be given at the same time. The teachers of the two courses, in addition to being somewhat specialized in their respective fields, are essentially teachers and interested in the art and process of teaching. They, therefore, should and could confer with each other, plan their work toward the same goal — the student's resultant learning — and thus help greatly in the expected process of integration of two bodies of knowledge in the student's mind.

If geography is to be incorporated into other social studies courses, then naturally the instructor will have to adopt a basically different philosophy from that of the specialist. He will also have to have a much broader specialized knowledge in order to be able to supply the necessary information at the appropriate points. He will first of all need to give up any rigid adherence to coverage of material specifically included in only one discipline, such as history. He must make room for the geographic study, and this means that some other subject will have to be replaced at least in part. Next, the instructor will have to develop techniques to allow him to incorporate geographic relationships. Just to indicate one such procedure, the history teacher can use several different kinds of maps to illustrate his lessons in history which may be accompanied by some introduction to the way in which maps are made, their specialized uses and general function in geographic study. Many student exercises are available to achieve familiarity with maps, such as problems to work out on outline maps, or particular embellishment of a large wall map with place name postmarks or other items obtained from the places in question.[8] The technique is unimportant so long as the objective is clear and the result is achieved.

Content of Instruction

Whether geographic study is to be pursued separately or in conjunction with some other subject, it is necessary to decide what ought to be incorporated into the body of learning to be achieved. From the outset of geographic study, whether it is to be on a very restricted local level or of worldwide scope, there are two major categories to consider: physical and cultural. They are not mutually independent of each other, but for purposes of study they must be broken down into component parts or the student may be confused by their complexity. Starting with the lower grades the purely physical elements are perhaps easiest to envisage, and as the student progresses through the grades and high school he may gradually advance to a position of understanding geography as a whole just as he is expected to do with history, or his language, or the general body of scientific knowledge that he must have in order to function usefully as a citizen.

Following a widely used college textbook one can lay out a generalized outline of the two groups of areal characteristics to organize study of either a small region or the whole world.[9]

Physical

A. Atmosphere (Air)
   1. Weather
   2. Climate
B. Lithosphere (Earth)
   1. Earth materials
      a. Bedrock
      b. Regolith, especially soils
      c. Minerals

[8] See James K. Anthony, "Geography: Suggested Activities," *Social Education* (March, 1956), 115.

[9] H. Kendall, Glendinning, R., and MacFadden, G. H., *Introduction to Geography,* Harcourt, Brace, New York, 1958, second edition, p. 5, discussed and quoted in *New Viewpoints in Geography,* Twenty-Ninth Yearbook of the National Council for the Social Studies, p. 212.

    2. Surface configuration
        a. Continents and islands
        b. Major landforms
        c. Minor landforms
C. Hydrosphere (Water)
    1. Oceans and seas
    2. Waters of the land
        a. Surface water
        b. Ground water
    3. Glaciers and icecaps
D. Biosphere (Life)
    1. Native plants
    2. Native animals

Cultural

A. Man
    1. Population
        a. Numbers
        b. Distribution over the earth
        c. Density
    2. Cultural groups
        a. Major groups
        b. Other groups
    3. Cultural institutions
        a. Languages
        b. Religions
        c. Political units
B. Works of Man
    1. Settlements
        a. Rural
        b. Urban
    2. Forms resulting from economies or ways of life
        a. Hunting, fishing, and gathering
        b. Pastoralism
        c. Agriculture
        d. Exploitation of earth resources, i.e., lumbering, mining, etc.
        e. Manufacture
    3. Routes of communication and transportation

The cultural side would seem at first glance to be the more interesting and useful, but on more mature consideration neither list can really be considered separately. They add up to one body of knowledge and in turn must be added to all of the other knowledge available to allow a total understanding of man. Truth is unitary, but we have access only to a part of it and certainly only to a small part of it at a time. In regard to cultural geography one may consider the changing emphasis on study and significance centering around the sources of power for the economic machine of today. With the advent of nuclear power the whole outlook on power consumption has had to change. This alters the human view of the significance of the physical elements of geography. A like thing may be said concerning human occupance of polar or desert lands by reason of technological development that makes it possible. The frigid or arid lands remained frigid or arid, but their significance to man is altered tremendously by his ability to occupy them.

Referring to the comments on integration or fusion of geography and history in school subjects, one is struck by the closely corresponding purposes and techniques of historical and human geographical study. Geography is concerned mainly with space, its organization and relationships as they affect people. History is concerned with the story of man as he occupies space in a sequence of time. Both studies aim at the same thing by using different means — an understanding of man. It is impossible, therefore, to think of geography and history as mutually exclusive either in content or purpose. It is only necessary to learn about them in separate segments — either as parts of the same course or as different courses, in terms of school curricula.[10]

As to the actual choices of content for secondary school geography, if it could be relied upon that students had previously, in elementary and junior high schools, been given an introduction to the physical elements of geography and some specialization in at least one of the world's major regions, it would be reasonable to require a recapitulation of basic physical geography along with a survey of the whole world at the same time as the course in world history is given. The best approach to such coverage is by regions, dividing the world rather arbitrarily into eight or nine areas, all with something in common so that a few large generalizations can be made.

Geographic Regions

One of the most important concepts in geographic study is the region. A region is an area with defined limits within which there are identifiable common characteristics. The more numerous the characteristics, naturally, the smaller must be the region. If one is speaking only of common occupance of a major land mass, a region may be coterminous

[10] John Wesley Coulter, "Human Geography and History," *Social Education* (November, 1954), 307–308.

with a continent or even two continents, for example, the Americas. As soon as common cultural components are specified, then we must have Anglo-America and Latin America as regions. For other purposes the national state may be considered as a region, but if one were to compare Great Britain and the United States it would be much more profitable to sub-regionalize the United States, and thus, for most comparative purposes a great deal of the United States could be eliminated. Such areas as the Great Plains or the sub-tropical Gulf Coast or Southern California, as regions, have nothing which can be compared with any part of the British Isles.

Any basis may be selected for the purpose of marking out regions to be studied. There may be climatic or land form regions; economic production; religious practices; political party alignment — innumerable items or ideas might be used. In conjunction with the study of history usually a political region is the most useful, but it is also the most arbitrary and great care should be exercised to ascertain that in the minds of students there are not identical definitions for the national state and the geographic region. Nationalism is a strong and important force, but it is not necessarily the function of geography to foster and support any ideology. On the other hand, a national feeling may be one of the strongest common bonds over an entire region, strong enough to predicate other common characteristics which may well serve to identify the region. The Soviet Union may thus be called a major world region despite the many variations within Soviet boundaries.

One suggestion for regionalizing the world might be as follows: Anglo-America, Latin America, Western Europe, Middle East, Soviet Realm, Africa, the Far East, the Pacific World, and the Polar Lands. (The last region is noncontiguous and could be left out without disturbing a unified view of world geography.)

If sufficient elementary work has not been done in the field of geography to warrant a worldwide study in high school, then it is the responsibility of the high school to start at the beginning and repair the flaws in knowledge just as is the case in mathematics and English. This might mean the expenditure of as much as two years principally spent in geographic study, but social studies requirements in most high schools only take up about two years, leaving an elective year which could very profitably be spent studying geography. In Washington State a few years ago the Board of Education instituted a requirement in World Problems and Geography to be met by all students who did not have a year-long course in the history of civilization. In a good many schools both requirements were adopted.[11]

[11] James High, "An Experiment in the World Problems Approach," *Washington Education* (February, 1956), 14.

Geography in Teacher Training

If geography is to become anything like the coordinating factor in secondary social studies instruction — regardless of discrete courses in geography — it is obvious that what has been said must bear a direct relationship to teacher training. In the education of the teacher there are at least three segments of learning with three different yet closely related purposes: general education or that which all educated persons know in order to function within the limits of their group in society; the specialized body of knowledge that any professional person must have in order to distinguish him from laymen; and the actual professional equipment distinctive of education, that is, the methodology and philosophy of instruction. College level geography, building on the general education foundation of secondary school, must be a part of the general liberal sophistication of everyone and most particularly of teachers. Teachers of geography, that is, of those whose main effort is to be in that field, should naturally have a collegiate major in geography equivalent to the accepted entrance requirements of most graduate schools for master's or doctoral study in geography. Incidentally, the number of such majors is growing in the United States as is the group of colleges and universities offering the work.

For most social studies teachers probably a major in geography is not desirable; their training will be likely to continue to emphasize history, but it is not too much to believe that "a secondary school teacher expecting to teach history, both world and American can hardly expect to do the job well without having taken the customary survey courses in world geography, plus the course in the geography of the United States and that of any other political areas with which the history course or courses are concerned. As a basic policy, it is recommended that the history teacher be well grounded in the geography of the political divisions which he presents." For the teacher "presenting the social studies, including geographic concepts, to children and youth, the minimum geography preparation should be 12 to 15 college semester hours." No specific prescription of college units will insure knowledge, but certainly without the required courses generalized ignorance has a more persistent chance. "Adequate preparation for teaching social studies courses in the junior and senior high schools must include a substantial knowledge of world geography as well as comparable preparation in the several related social studies areas."[12]

[12] Frank E. Sorenson, "The Role of Geography in the Training of the Social Studies Teacher," *New Viewpoints in Geography,* p. 230.

Conclusion

How fascinating is the study of man's story as he passes through time, his relationships with individuals and in groups, as a social, political, economic or biological being. How varied and colorful are the dimensions of human behavior, but without reference to the physical facts of the universe — seasonal change, energy consumption, natural resources, location, size and shape of the earth's landforms — how much less interesting is man's story. By continual reference to the setting and to the cultural changes wrought thereon, the historian, sociologist or economist can liven his work and come just a little closer to the truth that all of them seek. For example, just to take one facet of geography in connection with China, about 1900 China had a population of approximately 400,000,000. Now, in Red China, using their own figures, there is a population of 625,000,000. It has been said for years that excess Chinese must die of famine. What is the limit of population that China can support? Or in all the world? Some of the answer may be in history and sociology, but still more lies in the study of geographic elements in conjunction with other factors. At least the picture becomes more complex and fascinating with the added probing from the standpoint of geography and its special view of man and the land.[13]

It has been shown that geography has a place in secondary as well as in elementary school, and that frequently it has been neglected in both. Geography is both a discrete subject and at the same time it is essential to a proper understanding of the most commonly taught secondary social study: history. Geography can perform the coordinating or bridging function between natural and social sciences at all levels of general education and in at least two aspects of social studies teacher training: general education and professional specialization of subject matter. Geography as a subject of study is increasing, not only at collegiate level and in the field of teacher training, but also in secondary schools throughout the world and especially in the United States and Canada.[14]

[13] *The Determinants and Consequences of Population Trends,* United Nations Population Studies, No. 17 (New York, 1953), is an interesting set of conclusions drawn from worldwide population data. In regard to "overpopulation" the point is made that population limits are directly proportional to technological developments that may make possible the subsistence of tremendously larger numbers of people than is presently the case (p. 159, paragraph 34; p. 170, paragraph 45–46).

[14] Thomas R. Weir and William J. Russell, "The Status of Geography in the Social Studies Curricula of Canadian Schools," *The Journal of Geography* (September, 1959), 280–285.

14. Anthropology

Joseph A. Francello

Within the social sciences, probably no one discipline has received the attention of late as has the field of anthropology. This attention has come from educators, students, and the public in general. The latest pronouncements of Margaret Mead on American teen-age problems, anthropological field work in New Guinea, East Africa, and the Near East, are reported speedily and voluminously in the mass media. On college campuses throughout the entire United States, courses in anthropology attract greater and greater numbers.

It is not surprising, therefore, that among educators the question of how anthropology could be incorporated into the public school curriculum receives more and more attention. Does the anthropological approach promise a new and better understanding of man's long and difficult path through the ages? Can the public schools profit by the addition into the curriculum of courses utilizing the insights and techniques of the anthropologist?

Before attempting to answer these questions, it would be advisable to arrive at some understanding as to what anthropology is about.

By simple definition, anthropology is the study of man in accordance with the recognized principles and techniques of the scientific method. It is *both* a natural and social science in that the anthropologist is interested in man as a physical being as well as man as a social being. Man, the physical specimen, is the primary interest of the physical anthropologist while man, the social animal, is of primary interest to the cultural anthropologist.

The main concern of the cultural anthropologist is the behavior of man as he responds to those values and attitudes which his culture makes known to him. With the exception of those basic drives which

From Joseph A. Francello, "Anthropology for Public Schools: Profits and Pitfalls," *The Social Studies,* December, 1965, 56: 272–275. Joseph A. Francello is Professor of Social Science, Edinboro State College, Edinboro, Pennsylvania. Reprinted by permission of *The Social Studies.*

originate out of man's needs as an organism, all of man's behavior is learned. Behavior traits taken as an integrated whole and identified with a specific group of people form what the anthropologist refers to as culture.

In what way can the public schools profit by the work of the anthropologist? I believe there are both profits and pitfalls in attempting to relate this to the social studies curriculum of the public schools.

Among the profits, I see seven worthwhile contributions which anthropology can make:

1. Clearing up the concept of race — one has only to pick up a newspaper to see the timeliness of such a contribution. Race is something about which Americans can well stand clarification.

Anthropology offers scientific evidence that race is a valid *biological concept* but is invalid as a *socio-cultural concept.* Heredity bestows certain physical characteristics such as skin pigmentation, body type, hair covering, facial features, and stature which are used as criteria for classification into racial categories. The racial concept is not a valid one when applied to cultural considerations, however, because all races have the potential to develop any set of behavior patterns. All races are equal in their capacity to learn and to profit from this learning — if they so choose. There is no scientific proof that any race is superior to another.

2. Repudiation of "instinctive behavior" and "human nature" as explanations for human behavior.

The anthropologist rejects the concept of instincts, believes instead that man has three basic biological drives to satisfy his need for food, protection, and reproduction. How man goes about satisfying these drives comes as a result of learned behavior. It is through learned behavior that we know what to eat, what clothing we should wear, the kind of shelter we wish to live in, what kind of marriage our society considers desirable, proper behavior toward other mortals and correct behavior toward the gods or god. Man's behavior is not a result of "human nature" which is the same the world over and which we must passively accept as inevitable. Rather, man's behavior is the result of what his particular culture defines as "human."

3. The rejection of the concept of superior and inferior cultures.

In the eyes of the anthropologist, all cultures are equal. They are different due to the fact that man has learned to meet his problems in different ways. He may have chosen to emphasize certain aspects of cultural development and others not so much. For this reason some cultures, such as ours, may be advanced in the area of technology but may be experiencing a culture lag in other areas such as law, property concepts, and spiritual matters. Leaders of so-called underdeveloped areas of the world, of which Nehru would be a good example, have made it clear they want our technology but do not want our materialism, alcoholism, juvenile delinquency, high crime, and divorce rate.

4. The concept of cultural variability — this says that values, ethics, and morality are defined by the culture one lives in.

There is no absolute set of values which applies equally to all peoples in all cultures at any given time. What is considered proper behavior toward your fellow man in one culture may be highly improper in another. That which is considered immoral in one culture may scarcely raise interest in another. The actions of man must be weighed in terms of the culture within which the individual involved has been molded and which provides the basis for his behavior. The Comanche brave, who was raised in a society that looked upon horse stealing as a means of proving one's manhood, was most bewildered by the white man's determination to "hang the hoss thief" when the horse was located tied behind his tipi. There definitely was a lack of understanding of the other fellow's values in this case.

5. Greater tolerance toward other people and other ways of life — this means more than tolerance as verbalized in the American slogan.

When we say "regardless of race, creed, or color," we are usually referring to fellow Americans who have slightly different backgrounds but who nevertheless are a part of our total culture. Anthropology goes beyond this because it advances the cause of tolerance toward all peoples of the world — even those who do not want to change their way of life. That is a more profound test of tolerance than the usual American experience of dealing with various ethnic groups within our own country.

6. Better understanding of ourselves — we see that man has basically the same problems and needs and that he tries to solve them as best he can.

This can give us a better insight into why we do certain things and why we refrain from other modes of action. Our great confidence in overcoming obstacles to the production of goods causes us to leap into urban renewal projects — undertakings designed to improve the physical environment of the city. When it comes to improving the social aspect of life in the city, say in breaking the ghetto restrictions on Negro housing, we don't quite have the confidence and verve. Our culture does a much better job in providing good housing than in providing good neighbors. This has been our conditioning regarding peoples who appear "different" whether they be Negro, Oriental, Jew, or just plain foreigner.

7. Increased consistency with our role as a world leader — where we hope to inspire confidence among peoples of many different cultures.

When the United States was developing the West, it could afford to concentrate on history and especially the greatness of American history. Now that we have reached our present position of development and power, we must make a departure from our traditional approach toward other cultures. It must no longer be only a matter of pride in how we developed our greatness, but also a recognition that other peoples and cultures have equally worthy accomplishments, even though some aspects of their cultures might be primitive by our standards.

The benefits to be derived from the use of anthropological insights and techniques in the public school curriculum should not lull us into thinking, however, that we have discovered a panacea which will take care of all the ills which afflict the social studies program. I feel there are a number of serious hazards and pitfalls which raise questions that must be thought out carefully before attempted implementation of such a program.

Five major pitfalls which could bring about disastrous consequences if not anticipated properly and if steps are not taken to ameliorate their effect are:

1. Others are strange; too bad that they are missing so much not being more like us — an easy attitude to acquire and one which is evident in social studies classrooms in too many instances already.

The introduction of anthropological subject matter could make this condition worse unless competent and skillful guidance on the part of the teacher kept this within bounds.

2. We are more complex, hence we must be superior — an understandable conclusion for an American to arrive at in view of the emphasis we place on things being "bigger and better."

The concept of proceeding from a simple stage to a complex one may be interpreted by the student as going from the inferior to the superior. The values of our culture place greater worth on the complex in comparison to the simple. The industrial revolution has conditioned us to regard items which include many operations in their manufacture as having greater value than those which have only one or a few operations connected with their production.

3. They are technologically backward; therefore they are backward in everything.

This was an error made by the early anthropologists of 19th century Europe who considered non-Europeans as basically inferior due to their lack of industrialization. This is also an error made by American tourists today who judge the worth of a country by how close it comes to our own standards. The teacher who attempts to reverse this trend will have his work cut out for him as the students will reflect the emphasis which American culture places on technology and material goods.

4. This is a "snap" course — students think anyone can pass it and administrators think anyone can teach it.

Only teachers with a good background in the social sciences and course work in sociology and anthropology should teach courses utilizing the anthropological approach. This will help safeguard against the abuses of the easy-to-pass course taught by whatever teacher had that hour open on the schedule.

5. Community taboos regarding certain areas of human behavior — sensitivity toward certain topics which could inflame public opinion and bring down the wrath of the good citizenry upon the teacher. From a realistic standpoint, will it be possible then to cover certain aspects of human relationships which are an integral part of anthropological study? One had better know his community!

The community in which you teach may be reacting to some specific social problem which has spread alarm and anxiety among the citizenry. For example, there may be great concern about contemporary morality and, as is always the case, it is supposed to be degenerating. How will you handle such topics as Samoan pre-marital sexual relations or Eskimo wife-borrowing? If the community is extra-sensitive to the dangers and challenges of the cold war, how will you handle collective ownership of property as it exists among many primitive peoples? In the face of problems connected with juvenile delinquency, how will you handle the acceptance of private law with its emphasis on individual revenge which is the concept of law in many primitive societies?

As is true in so many problems in education, there is no simple solution. Anthropology all by itself cannot save the world or even social studies. Anyone grasping at it as an all-purpose cure-all is due for disappointment. Its advantages must be carefully appraised, caution observed regarding potential dangers and limitations, and highly qualified and motivated people given a chance to test its potentialities in the classroom. All by itself, no, — but as one important facet contributing to a better understanding and tolerance of other people and other cultures, anthropology can be a mother lode of opportunity.

15. Sociology

Marvin R. Koller

Sociology is a scientific discipline which focuses upon human groupings, their intricate systems of relationships, and the behavioral patterns that occur in the midst of social systems. Of course, like many definitions, this one may be found wanting by professional sociologists who are engaged in healthy academic exchanges concerning the nature of sociology, its goals, its procedures, and its appropriate place in intellectual inquiry.[1]

There are persons who view sociology as capable of bringing a constructive perspective to bear upon a wide variety of social problems. For others, sociology is essentially one of the social sciences which seeks constantly to refine its methods and findings concerning human inter-

From Marvin R. Koller, "Sociology in the Curriculum," *Educational Leadership*, February, 1965, 22:310–312. Marvin R. Koller is Professor of Sociology, Kent State University, Kent, Ohio. He is the author of *Modern Sociology* and co-author of *Sociology of Childhood*. A forthcoming book is *Social Gerontology*. Reprinted by permission of the Association for Supervision and Curriculum Development and the author. Copyright, 1965, by the Association for Supervision and Curriculum Development.

[1] For a brief and stimulating discussion of the nature of sociology, see *What Is Sociology?* by Alex Inkeles, Foundations of Modern Sociology Series, Englewood Cliffs, New Jersey: Prentice-Hall, Inc., 1964.

action. Sociology's practical applications, from the latter point of view, are outside the province of sociologists, but remain the appropriate responsibility of all persons. Obviously, this dichotomy is a matter of legitimate emphasis and occurs also in other fields in which there are pressures for immediate solutions to social difficulties or in which there is stress as well as insistence upon cautious, slow, painstaking investigation and analysis or basic or fundamental research unhurried by extraneous or disconcerting demands.

Educators, however, are conscious of the steady march of oncoming generations, who will live under societal conditions not of their own making, but who will, nevertheless, be affected by these conditions. Because these generations will, in turn, affect social circumstances, there must be thoughtful appraisal of curriculum content.

There has been a long-standing dictum that school systems should not divorce themselves from current trends and changes in the society which activates them. In the past, the social upheavals of waves of immigrants entering an almost totally new world, the distress stemming from the deepening Depression of the thirties, and the impacts of global wars provoked a reexamination of educational content. In coping with the ramifications brought about by the acceleration of social changes in more recent times, educational leadership again is challenged.

To name only a few matters of momentous significance, educators need to weigh carefully the civil rights movement, adult and juvenile crime, urban development and renewal, the proliferation and appeal of mass media, family disorganization, discovery of new sources of energy, mental health, challenges from foreign regimes and technology, emerging nations, vocational guidance in an age of specialization, greater visibility of the aged, pockets of poverty, and school "dropouts." Every social science, including sociology, offers useful data and insights about these phenomena and should not be discarded, neglected or overlooked.

A New Threshold

There are numerous "straws in the wind" which indicate that sociology is on the threshold of taking its place among its sister social sciences in the curriculum of the nation's schools. Sociology originated as a formal discipline at the highest graduate levels in colleges and universities, and it has rapidly spread to undergraduate courses. In 1962, the U. S. Office of Education reported that 8,183 bachelor degrees in sociology were awarded by over 640 colleges and universities. The entry of sociology into secondary schools is evident in the U.S. Office of Education report for 1960–1961, which noted that approximately 290,000 students were enrolled in sociology or social problems courses.

Out of the 22,833 high schools in the United States, 4,461 offered courses in sociology or social problems.

Sociology is chiefly offered at the eleventh and twelfth grade levels, with a preference for the twelfth grade. Approximately 17 percent of twelfth grade students were studying sociology in 1960–1961. There seems to be a further preference for sociology to be taught as a half-year course. About 178 thousand students studied sociology as a half-year or semester course, whereas the remaining 112 thousand studied sociology for a full academic year. The largest enrollments in the half-year course in sociology were found in California, Indiana, Ohio, Michigan, Illinois, and North Carolina.

At the elementary level, sociology is rarely identified as a separate and distinct field, but is incorporated into the study of history, geography, and citizenship. Yet, under the "expanding environment" theme, elementary schools are, indeed, drawing upon sociological data and theory as they examine family life, the local community, the region, the nation, and international affairs. If it is true that social ferment requires the utilization of the best intellectual resources available, then the earliest grounding in fundamentals is needed. Far too often, elementary exposure to selected, traditional or favored areas of study has led to the neglect of those fields which have remained unexplored territory when mature choices are made. Every citizen draws upon his grasp of societal knowledge and the harvest of neglect is reaped by everyone.

Need for Sociology

While students must be treated in harmony with their respective capacities, there is little doubt that the goal of dealing with social complexities calls for a graduated preparatory program starting at the elementary grades and moving through the secondary schools. By this preparatory work, much wasteful "unlearning" at higher educational levels can be minimized and entry into colleges and universities can truly become "higher" education. Basic sociological concepts such as status, role, prediction, categories, social stratification, objectivity, and norms become familiar analytical tools instead of strange, useless jargon to the uninitiated. If an illustrative parallel might be cited, the current conditions in sociological instruction in many, but not all, school systems, would be similar to attempting to teach trigonometry and calculus without first grounding students in basic numbers.

The American Sociological Association has taken note of the need for a legitimate place for sociology in the curriculum of secondary schools. Supported initially by a grant from the course content improvement section of the National Science Foundation and led by a selected

American Sociological Association committee, a Center for Sociological Resources for Secondary Schools was established in the summer of 1964 at Dartmouth College, Hanover, New Hampshire. A series of materials is being developed for use in the senior high school sociology course consisting of major units developed from the sociological perspective. A second series of materials will consist of self-contained units designed by teams of sociologists and social studies teachers for supplementary use in other secondary school social studies courses. Both series should be available by September 1965 for classroom trial.

In similar fashion, the Society for the Study of Social Problems has created a division dealing with sociology instruction in the schools. One can predict that this work, too, will result in increased liaison between sociologists at the university level and social studies instructors at the secondary and elementary levels.

The development of sociology in the curricula of the nation's schools rests solidly upon interested lay and professional leadership. Both texts and teachers are in short supply. Currently, there are relatively few teachers either grounding themselves in sociology or including sociology in their preparation for teaching. Alert schools of education are, of course, remedying this situation. Only three textbooks are currently on the market in high school sociology. A fourth text will be published this academic year and will utilize the teamwork of a university professor and a concerned high school instructor.[2]

Finally, it should be noted that, in the midst of the general upgrading of all curriculum content, many secondary schools throughout the country are raising the required number of Carnegie units in the social sciences and social studies for graduation. This trend mirrors our need for the best possible use of our educational resources in the face of the social ferment in our times.

REFERENCES

Robert H. Bohlke. "The Teaching of Sociology in Secondary Schools: Problems and Prospects." *Social Forces* 42: 363–74; March 1964.

Stanley E. Grupp. "High School Sociology: A Challenge," *High School Journal* 46: 170–74; February 1963.

Stanley E. Grupp. "The Status of Teaching Sociology in High Schools." *Sociology and Social Research* 45: 327–31; April 1961.

Durlyn E. Wade. "Case for Political Science and Sociology in the Elementary Social Studies Program." *Instructor* 72: 79–80; March 1963.

[2] These texts are: *Social Living*, Third Edition, Paul H. Landis, Boston: Ginn and Company, 1958; *High School Sociology,* William E. Cole and Charles S. Montgomery, Boston: Allyn and Bacon, 1959; and *Living in Social Groups,* James A. Quinn, Philadelphia: J. B. Lippincott Company, 1962. The new text will be *Modern Sociology,* Marvin R. Koller and Harold C. Couse, New York: Holt, Rinehart and Winston.

16. Political Science

Peter Woll

To what extent is the study of political science appropriate for elementary and secondary school curriculum? This is an extraordinarily difficult question to answer. It leads to an examination of the importance of transmitting democratic values to students. The discipline of political science at one level tends to exclude value judgments and concentrates upon finding the factors that shape and define political systems. But political science cannot, as it moves to different levels of analysis and purpose, reject values.

Throughout the history of political science in this country numerous prominent scholars have concentrated upon proving the usefulness of democracy, and indicating the places where improvement can be made in our system. Political scientists writing under the guise of objectivity usually put forth a number of value-laden statements, for it is virtually impossible to be entirely objective when dealing with political matters. After examining "facts," scholars often state goals. Woodrow Wilson, for example, in his famous book, *Congressional Government* (1885), after objectively discussing the organization and operation of Congress, went on to point out that the legislature needed far more leadership, organization, and information than it possessed at that time in order to perform its "proper" role in a democratic government by discussion. It was not sufficient, Wilson stated, for the legislature to be involved only in drafting legislation. It must also act as a continual critic of administration and of the affairs of government. He hoped that his study would be helpful in solving the problems of Congress.

More recently, Harold Lasswell, in *The Future of Political Science* (New York: Atherton Press, 1963), suggested that political scientists should use their knowledge to help solve public problems. Lasswell is

From Peter Woll, "Recent Developments in Political Science," *Social Education*, March, 1966, 30: 168–172. Peter Woll is Associate Professor of Politics, Brandeis University, Waltham, Massachusetts. He is the author of several books in law and government, the latest of which is *Public Administration and Policy*. This article is reprinted by permission of the author and of the National Council for the Social Studies.

implying that it is not enough for political science merely to deal with facts, for it must also evaluate the ends of government. This, interestingly, differs somewhat from his earlier statement in the famous book *Politics: Who Gets What, When, How* (New York: McGraw-Hill, 1936): "The study of politics is the study of influence and the influential. The science of politics states conditions; the philosophy of politics justifies preferences." His book, he went on to state, deals with political science and not philosophy. The implication was that the study of philosophy should properly be left to philosophers, not political scientists.

The Place of Political Science in Secondary and Elementary Curriculums

There is undoubtedly widespread agreement that when politics is taught to secondary and elementary students some inculcation of values is necessary. Often courses dealing with political science are described as courses in citizenship, implying that it is necessary to teach youngsters the importance of democracy and their responsibilities as democratic citizens. This attitude is well reflected in a recent statement made by two professors of education:

> The word *idiot* is derived from the Greek *idiotes,* which meant "those citizens who do not take part in public voting." Although in ancient Greece the *idiotes* failed to vote because they were not *permitted* to, and although the word has taken on a different meaning today, when one considers the large number of Americans who *choose* not to participate in local, state, and national elections, the word (with its 20th-century connotation) may not after all be an entirely inappropriate political adjective. . . .
>
> It is important that American youth emerge from their schooling with solid understandings of and attachments to democratic tenets, processes, and procedures as a way of adult political life. Education for young people in a democracy *is* different from education for children and youth in a totalitarian state.[1]

Here we see clearly reflected the idea that one of the purposes of political education at the lower levels is to "indoctrinate" in the tenets of democracy.

The idea that political science courses must give attention to "citizenship education" poses a dilemma, and also illustrates the difference in approach often taken at the university level on the one hand, and at the secondary and elementary levels on the other. At the university level,

[1] Francis J. Sorauf. *Political Science: An Informal Overview.* Columbus, Ohio: Charles E. Merrill Books, 1965. pp. 75–76. The statement is taken from a concluding chapter by Raymond H. Muessig and Vincent R. Rogers.

citizenship education is generally not considered to be the central core of most political science courses, but rather a more objective approach is taken. True, in many universities, by state law, it is necessary to teach American government and citizenship, as well as state and local government. Nevertheless, the university approach tends to let the validity of democracy as a system of government emerge from an examination of the facts, rather than from any specific indoctrination. Many disturbing conclusions about the viability of the democratic process can be and are presented to college students.

Below the college level, citizenship education is vital, but it is undertaken differently. It is not appropriate to present elementary and even secondary school children with all of the "facts" of political science as they have been recently developed. Students at these levels cannot be expected to analyze the complex facets of the subject. We might not want to suggest to certain groups of students, for example, that nonvoters may perform a very important function in a democracy, a conclusion that is tenable but difficult to understand. At lower educational levels we have to explain the democratic process, and recognize the importance of teaching patriotism and loyalty, stemming from a need for what has been called "political socialization" (transmitting the values of the political system to citizens).

Philosophers from Plato and Aristotle to the present have been concerned with the role of education in a political system, and have supported the idea that it is necessary for any political system to inculcate its values in young people if it is to survive. This is an entirely proper and necessary undertaking with which there would be little disagreement. *How* this is to take place may be a matter of debate, but all would support the notion that young people must be taught or somehow given respect for the institutions of our constitutional democracy. At the university and college level, once such an inculcation of values has succeeded, we must then move on to analyze more candidly some of the deficiencies and problems of democracy with a view to improving it. At this higher level, it is entirely appropriate to study communism, totalitarian systems, and many other forms of government with a far more objective eye than at the secondary and elementary levels.

All of these considerations are important in any attempt to analyze the relevance of recent developments in political science to elementary and secondary education. We can treat political science in two ways in this regard. First, we can note what information has been gained from recent research, and this may be used as an aid to teachers. On the other hand, there may be developments of use to students. How to use information, of course, will have to be left to the discretion of those who are actually engaged in teaching.

It should always be kept in mind that political science is a fairly sophisticated discipline and deals realistically with matters that might better be treated less candidly at lower levels. This will depend upon the caliber of students with which one is dealing, whether or not they are going on to university and graduate levels of education, and a variety of other factors. Political science has not conclusively been able to explain the nature and success or lack of it of our political system or of other systems, and it is important that both teachers and students recognize that studies in political science suggest only tentative conclusions for the most part. This is particularly difficult, of course, for the indiscriminate student to realize.

Recent Developments and Research

Political science today roams very widely. Scholars study all aspects of American government — the workings of the legislative, executive, and judicial branches; the role of political parties, elections, and the nature of voting behavior; state and local government, problems of federalism, and so forth. Apart from this, attention is focused upon the international arena with international relations, defense policies, international organization and law being at the center of attention. Comparative government deals with such problems as the factors determining stability or instability in emerging states, as well as with problems of supranational authority such as the European Coal and Steel Community and other aspects of foreign governments. Political theory includes large doses of sociology, psychology, and related disciplines. Because of space limitations, the best way to cover some of the more important recent developments in political science is to discuss generally a few key books that present significant research findings or contain new ideas.

The nature of "political socialization" — that is, the way in which attitudes towards the political system are developed and transferred — is the subject of several recent and important studies. How do people learn political attitudes? What effect does the learning process have upon their support of a democratic or other political system? In other words, how is "political socialization" connected with the political system? In the well-known book by Gabriel A. Almond and Sidney Verba, *The Civic Culture* (Princeton: Princeton University Press, 1963; Boston: Little, Brown and Company, 1965, paperback edition), it is suggested that there is a direct connection between the way in which attitudes are learned and the support of democracy.

The Civic Culture contains an analysis of the attitudes of a cross section of the people of five countries — the United States, Great Britain, Germany, Italy, and Mexico. The purpose of this study was to find out the connection between political and social attitudes on the one hand, and the effectiveness and stability of the democratic process on the other. Questions were designed to determine exactly how citizens felt about their government, and the political system generally. Did they think that they could influence local and national government? Did they actually attempt to exert influence upon government officials and governmental policies? Did they view partisan activities favorably? Did they feel a sense of participation in national affairs? Did they feel that they would be treated fairly by the governmental bureaucracy? These and many other questions were designed to determine whether or not there was a "civic culture," — that is, a culture which supports the democratic process by fostering favorable attitudes towards political participation, trust in the government, in political elites, and in people generally.

In this cross-cultural review of attitudes it was found, for example, that individuals in the United States consistently feel they have had more influence in family decisions, more freedom to participate in school discussions and debate, and that they have been consulted about job decisions more frequently than people in countries such as Italy, Germany, and Mexico. Somewhat surprisingly, respondents in the United States felt a greater sense of identification with school, job, and family than did those interviewed in Great Britain. This comparative study comes to a tentative conclusion that those who are socialized toward greater participation in the nonpolitical areas of life are more likely to feel that they are able to participate in politics and influence governmental decision-making.

The final conclusions of this important study, although they cannot be stated fully here, bear very directly upon secondary and elementary school political science courses. The authors point out that:

> The civic culture is not the political culture that one finds described in civics textbooks, which prescribe the way in which citizens ought to act in a democracy. The norms of citizen behavior found in these texts stress the participant aspect of political culture. The democratic citizen is expected to be active in politics and to be involved. Furthermore, he is supposed to be rational in his approach to politics, guided by reason, not by emotion. He is supposed to be well informed and to make decisions — for instance, his decision on how to vote — on the basis of careful calculation as to the interests and the principles he would like to see furthered. This culture, with its stress on rational participation within the input structures of politics, we can label the "rationality-activist" model of poltical culture. The civic culture shares much with this rationality-activist model; it is in fact such a culture *plus something*

else. It does stress the participation of individuals in the political input process.[2]

What must be added to political participation in order to enable a civic culture — that is, one which supports the democratic process — to exist? There are many things, but one of the most important is a division of labor, a recognition that government must in many important respects be left to a circulating elite, but at the same time there must also exist a feeling that influence can be exerted, and that those in the government can ultimately be held to account for their actions. Another important ingredient of the civic culture, according to Almond and Verba, is trust of the elite. There must be a feeling that the government will deal fairly with citizens, and generally handle political matters well in terms of the interests of the community. It is important that the myth of participation be maintained and that people feel they can influence political events, even though this may not in fact be entirely the case. The information contained in *The Civic Culture* should provide a very good basis for class discussion at a very advanced level among discriminating students. It is, however, of primary value for teachers to gain a perspective on the subject of political science and new approaches of systematic comparative analysis.

A book of particular interest to teachers will be *Children and Politics,* by Fred I. Greenstein (New Haven: Yale University Press, 1965). This book attempts to analyze the way in which children learn about politics, and the way in which early "political socialization" occurs. The study is based upon an analysis of New Haven school children in grades 4–8, representing different socio-economic backgrounds and reflecting a cross section of the population. Among the conclusions reached, teachers and school principals will be interested to find that when asked what role is "most important," 80 percent of the fourth-grade children interviewed picked the President of the United States, whereas "school teacher" was listed by 35 percent of the sample, and 22 percent selected the role of school principal. This reflects the very benign attitude that, not only fourth-grade, but other grades of children held toward the great institution of the American Presidency.

In many respects the conclusions of the study are not surprising, pointing out that children of these ages have a very limited knowledge of the political system. Their awareness extends to the Presidency, the mayor of their city, and local more than state government. Knowledge of partisan politics tends to be totally absent. What feelings are expressed more often than not reflect the family attitude, and depend upon the

[2] *The Civic Culture,* paperback edition, pp. 29–30.

extent to which there is political discussion at home. The differences in political participation that show up later in life between those of higher and lower socio-economic status are not apparent by the eighth grade, for roughly the same number of children from these two groups reflected a desire to participate in politics. This book will certainly provide interesting insights into the political attitudes of fourth- through eighth-grade students, and may give teachers some new ideas on how to enliven the subject of political science in the classroom at these levels. The questionnaire that was used is included in an appendix of the book.

One of the most interesting developments of the last decade in political science has been the expansion of the Survey Research Center of the University of Michigan, which has conducted a series of systematic surveys of electoral behavior from which new conclusions have been reached regarding the role of voters and the significance of elections within the democratic political process. The results of many of these surveys are analyzed in V. O. Key's book, *Public Opinion and American Democracy* (New York: Alfred A. Knopf, 1961).[3] This is a book that should be read by all who are concerned with American government and the relationship between public opinion and policy formation. Key goes into the question of the extent to which pressure groups, political parties, and other organs of public opinion actually influence the decision-making process. He also discusses the way in which public opinion is formed dealing with the mass media and the educational system, as well as the impact upon the public of pressure groups and political parties.

Key's conclusions generally support Almond's thesis that democratic process cannot rely completely upon active voters. Excessive activism is an unnatural situation which tends often to produce or reflect tension rather than a healthy political environment. Public opinion in relation to public policy is more often than not very vague, and the interaction of pressure groups and parties with the governmental process often revolves around the elites of interest groups along with the elites of the bureaucracy and other decision-entities of "the people" on the one hand, and "the government" on the other. The power of elites does not mean that the democratic process is not healthy, but only reflects the nature of electoral and political behavior about which very little can be done.

Unlike Almond, who was concerned with a broad "civic culture," Key deals more with the governmental process and agencies that directly or indirectly influence it. He demonstrates that the relationship between

[3] See also Angus Campbell, Philip E. Converse, Warren E. Miller, and Donald E. Stokes. *The American Voter.* New York: John Wiley and Sons, 1960.

public opinion and government is very nebulous indeed, and results in a tremendous amount of discretion being left in the hands of political decision makers. Governmental perception of public opinion may actually be more important than public opinion itself, although it is often difficult for Congressmen or bureaucrats to perceive a general public opinion, regardless of their frequent statements to the contrary. General popular mandates simply do not exist in most areas of public policy, and, as Key points out, "Even if mass opinion assumes forms incompatible with a national interest, the articulation between government and mass opinion is so loose that politicians enjoy a considerable range of discretion within which to exercise prudence and good sense." The opposite proposition is also true: If governmental decision-makers assume attitudes incompatible with the national interest (whatever this may be), they will, within boundaries, be able to act regardless of a public expression of opinion to the contrary. This means that we must place great trust in our government, which in fact we do (according to Almond), and that the future of the democratic process depends upon *responsible leadership* which must exist without the guidance of a clearly articulated public opinion.

Discussions of leadership lead to another interesting book, which reflects an important school of thought in American political science. This group holds that the separation-of-powers and checks-and-balances system has produced a "deadlock of democracy," which prevents effective democratic leadership. This thesis is well articulated in James M. Burns, *The Deadlock of Democracy* (Englewood Cliffs, N. J.: Prentice Hall, 1963). The separation of powers gives to the President and Congress separate constituencies, so that the dependency of each upon the other is reduced to a minimum. The President is not always able to act as the focal point of leadership for his party in Congress. Voters who have selected a liberal Democratic President, for example, may find him frustrated by a conservative congressional majority, just as more conservative Republicans voting for the President may find, if he is elected, a Democratic and more liberal majority in the Congress. This entire system, it is held, essentially nullifies the choice of the people.

Burns, and others of this school of thought, feel that something has to be done to strengthen the nature of our party system and make it more disciplined and able to transmit public opinion into policy through the leadership of the Presidency. Where public opinion does not exist and provide a mandate, it is necessary for the President to act as leader if our democracy is to survive. How can changes be brought about in the system? Essentially, the proposals relate to bringing the constituencies of Congress and the President closer together, and breaking the conservative grip of the machinery of Congress. Various constitutional devices can be employed for this purpose, such as electing Congress and the President every four years rather than on the basis of staggered terms as it is now done.

One of the central problems of Burns' thesis is that the very factors that give to the President an independent position in relation to Congress have actually strengthened his leadership rather than diminished it, because of the conflicting interests in the community. In other words, in the absence of the separation of powers, we would more likely have a multi-party system which would increase the present diversity of our national government. We cannot have unity at a national level unless it exists within society, and with a diversified and geographically dispersed country such as ours an independent Presidency can provide leadership in times of crisis that otherwise would be absent. General de Gaulle recognized this in France when he sought to imitate at least parts of the presidential system in the Fifth Republic to create an independent institution that could provide leadership in a very dispersed political community.

Recent political science, in addition to these general and important studies, has also provided insights into other aspects of American government. It would be impossible here to list all of the recent literature, but perhaps a few key books will serve to provide a basis for further reading. Beginning with the Presidency, there is very little that has been said that adds to the material of Clinton Rossiter, *The American Presidency* (New York: Harcourt, Brace, 1960) and Richard Neustadt, *Presidential Power* (New York: John Wiley, 1960), but a different dimension is discussed in Aaron Wildavsky, *The Politics of the Budgetary Process* (Boston: Little, Brown, 1964), which deals with the Presidency and the Bureau of the Budget along with other elements in the budgetary process, including congressional committees. Because of the highly personal nature of the Presidency, much of the scholarship in the area has been historical, for the institution does not lend itself to the kind of survey research analysis done on voters and other groups.

Turning to Congress, one of the most important recent works is that of Charles L. Clapp, *The Congressman: His Work as He Sees It* (Washington, D.C.: The Brookings Institution, 1963). Clapp presents an insider's view of the workings of Congress, and covers the attitudes of Congressmen concerning their role in government, and the way in which they formulate legislation and deal with constituent grievances. Much direct quotation from the Congressmen themselves is included, and there is even a section on the wives of Congressmen and the difficulties and problems that they face. Another work on Congress is that of Lewis

Froman, *Congressmen and Their Constituencies* (Chicago: Rand McNally, 1963). This is a book that deals, as the title implies, with constituency influence upon Congress and the nature of congressional constituencies generally. It presents the results of a variety of behavioral surveys. A more general work on Congress that contains the views of many is that of Robert L. Peabody and Nelson W. Polsby, *New Perspectives on the House of Representatives* (Chicago: Rand McNally, 1963). This book consists of articles and selections dealing with Congress, and is particularly useful for an understanding of the literature of the field.

With respect to the judicial process, readers might take particular note of John P. Roche, *Courts and Rights* (New York: Random House, 1961; second edition, 1966), which is both a general analysis of the nature of the judicial process and an examination of the important areas of civil liberties and civil rights. The current controversy over the activism of the Supreme Court stems from its opinions in many fields, including legislative apportionment. These are summarized in Howard E. Hamilton, *Legislative Apportionment* (New York: Harper and Row, 1964), which also contains a general analysis of the area of apportionment.

Finally, the effects of the emergence of the federal bureaucracy upon our constitutional democracy are analyzed in my own book entitled, *American Bureaucracy* (New York: W. W. Norton, 1963), and a variety of selections from important current research relating to all fields of American government are included in my *American Government: Readings and Cases* (second edition, Little, Brown, 1965). Much of the current research has been published in article form in scholarly journals, and these are included in the latter work.

Hopefully, the preceding remarks and suggestions for reading will be helpful to teachers in their attempts to relate the discipline of political science to the classroom. Nothing is more important than that the future citizen understand and appreciate our political system, even though he may not wholly participate in it. Of course, participation should always be encouraged, and citizens should always feel that they can potentially influence the course of government. This is a necessity for a healthy democratic process.

17. Economics

John E. Maher

A commuter to Manhattan pays his fare and boards the 7:10 train from Chappaqua, a 90-minute ride to Grand Central. To the sociologist, this little event may symbolize the great removal of people to residences far from their places of work, and a profound change in cosmopolitan culture. The political scientist, on the other hand, may view this event as representing the shift of political influence from rural regions and from urban centers to the new suburban communities where redistricting is giving increasing political weight to these growing areas. Again, the traffic engineer may see the commuter on railroads and on rapid transit systems as the answer to the cities' problem of motor vehicle congestion. The economist may be struck by the special importance of maintaining passenger rail service in the face of relatively declining passenger revenues and rising costs and the severe competition between rail transportation, busses, and private passenger automobiles.

In reciting the different inferences that may be drawn from what appears to be the same behavior, we underscore the fact that different areas of learning are fruitfully depicted as different perspectives on the same phenomena. Just as we may say that a human being is a composition of chemicals, a soulful creature, and a psyche, so we recognize that chemistry, theology, and psychology are among the appropriate modes for understanding him. Thus, it can rarely be *what* a discipline concerns itself with, but rather *how* it views its material and how it analyzes that distinguishes it from other disciplines.

From John E. Maher, "Economics: Conceptions and Misconceptions," *Social Education,* April, 1966, 30: 229–231, 235. John E. Maher is Senior Economist at the Joint Council of Economic Education and Director of its Developmental Economic Education Program. Dr. Maher has written extensively on economics and specific economic problems for scholarly and professional journals. He is the author of a text on labor economics, *Labor and the Economy.* A forthcoming book seeks to make the process of thinking in economics more meaningful to teachers and students. This article is reprinted by permission of the author and of the National Council for the Social Studies.

The economic view of reality sees in human behavior the need to cope with the problem of resources that are scarce in relation to the objectives that they may be used to attain. Whether these objectives are the limited wants of a hermit or a Robinson Crusoe or the more varied wants of a modern industrial worker or an affluent executive — the means of satisfying our wants are scarce relative to the extent to which we should like those wants satisfied. Thus arises the economic problem: how to allocate our scarce resources as best to satisfy our wants. Whether we are studying primitive man or the economy of a modern Western state, a monastic order or a business enterprise, an individual or a nation, the fact of scarcity pervades and conditions human behavior.

To grasp better the nature of the problem of scarcity, we must understand the system of relationships that leads from resources to the satisfaction of human wants. This kind of system is highly general and, we may hope, generally useful to analysis. It is useful whether we consider a child's attempt to use scissors and paste to make valentines, a grocery store's effort to schedule the hours of its cashiers, the steel industry's program to compete successfully in foreign markets, or the nation's plan to achieve full employment. All of these forms of behavior have fundamental, economic features in common.

The features that are common to virtually every economic activity include, principally, *resources* used in a process we call *production.* From production we get *outputs* (valentines, groceries, steel, national income) that are transformed through a process called *consumption* (use by consumers). The consuming of outputs satisfies *wants;* this satisfaction is the objective of the system.

Now this simplification of economic activity does not pretend to do justice to the plurality of processes and objectives that are included in most economic analyses. Yet it serves as a generalization that makes systematic analysis easier to approach. Moreover, it leads to the important notion of efficiency. If the achievement of the objective of any system is to be rationally pursued, then the system must be governed by an appropriate criterion of efficiency. Roughly stated, this criterion is: Getting the most satisfaction from the employment of resources.

The diagram that follows is a schematic representation of those features common to virtually every economic system, using "system" in a broad sense. Those familiar with the textbooks of a few years ago will recognize the way in which the figure draws upon earlier ways of thinking about economics. Reading upward from the box at the bottom, we see that economic activity includes resources, which are transformed by a process we call production, into outputs. In turn, the outputs are transformed, through a process we call consumption, into the satisfaction of human wants. And these five steps or stages are all held together by relationships which make of them a system. This is true whether we speak of the gross national product of the entire economy or the rendering of haircuts by the local barber. The relationships are principally a set of prices, a set of technical production combinations (the ways in which steel, glass, rubber, and other materials are combined, say, in the making of automobiles), and relationships guiding the consumer in the uses to which he puts the goods and services he wants. If this entire system, running from resources to satisfactions, is to operate efficiently, a standard of performance, earlier alluded to, is essential. Usually, we express this as maximizing satisfaction.

DIAGRAM OF ECONOMIC ACTIVITY

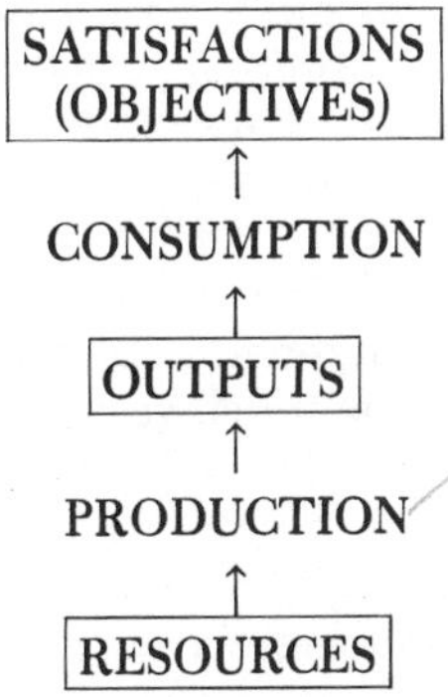

In a properly balanced social studies curriculum, economics makes an important contribution to education. Its wide applicability and its coherence as a body of knowledge makes of the discipline a powerful mode of inquiry.

As an appreciation of the kind of thinking toward which economic understanding should strive, we may refer to Whitehead's definition of style which he called the "ultimate morality of the mind":

> Finally there should grow the most austere of all mental qualities. I mean the sense for style. It is an esthetic sense based on admiration for the direct attainment of a foreseen end, simply and without waste. . . .
>
> The administrator with a sense for style hates waste; the engineer with a sense for style economizes his material; the artisan with a

sense for style prefers good work. Style is the ultimate morality of the mind.[1]

The mind exposed to economic inquiry, we may hope, will achieve a sense of style. There can, of course, be no pretension that all children should be turned into economists, but it is equally true that no civilized mind should be without the ability to assess the economic dimension of human life.

We have defined economics in the most general terms as a perspective, a mode of inquiry, a special appreciation of human behavior. Other disciplines may similarly be thought of as various perspectives, differing from one another according to the principles upon which the perspectives are organized. If we base our economic understanding upon this view of economic learning, then we avoid some of the worst pitfalls that confront those in education. Three of these pitfalls are worth more detailed consideration. I call these three misconceptions of economic science the "nuts and bolts" approach, "that's what *you* say," and "the worrybird." Let us take these up in order.

"*Nuts and Bolts*"

If you lay out the component parts of an automobile, you will have an engine, carburetor, distributor, wheels, crankshaft, and a lot of nuts and bolts. But these parts from which you could make a vehicle are not an automobile; rather, instead of an automobile, you have a pile of nuts and bolts.

The same is true of economics. Too often, many teachers and their students are misled into thinking that economics consists of the component parts of study; i.e., the table of contents of a typical text in the subject. In this way economics may come to be thought of as international trade, money and banking, business cycles, labor relations, and a host of other areas of applications. But this, of course, is not economics. This is not what makes it a peculiar mode of inquiry of the discipline, nor does it reveal its essential structure.

Carried further, the nuts-and-bolts interpretation of economics sees the discipline not only as areas of application, but even as specific, detailed, and superficial symbols of economic behavior. Along these lines, economics becomes the operation of a cash register, writing a money order, answering the telephone, and going out to lunch.

Just as chemistry is not beakers, test tubes, and Bunsen burners; physics is not cyclotrons and cloud chambers; so, economics is neither the things it uses, nor the things it studies.

[1] Alfred North Whitehead. *The Aims of Education,* New York: The Macmillan Company, 1929. p. 24.

Our illustration of the commuter boarding a train shows that human behavior exhibits simultaneously economic, political, sociological, and other aspects. It is not an event or a fact that is peculiarly economic, but the angle from which this fact or event is viewed. Economics is a way of organizing observations. This notion carried with it the implication that there are generally not such things as economic institutions or organizations, but rather there are institutions and organizations which, when viewed from a certain angle, display an economic aspect. Thus, neither the AFL-CIO nor the National Association of Manufacturers is solely a political, economic, or social organization, but all of these things together.

"That's what you say!"

Equally dangerous to sound thinking in economics is the view that economics is a matter of opinion. Some would defend this spurious notion by saying that if economics were not a matter of opinion, all economists would agree among themselves and there would be no dispute over economic policy.

Disputes, of course, do not signify the extent or nature of agreement on basic principles. Medicine, for example, is usually considered both an art and a science. No one would think of arguing that the scientific basis of medicine is questionable because different doctors are sometimes required to consult on a given case. Consultation and disagreement may arise in economics, as in medicine, because different interpretations are placed on facts, because different objectives are sought by practitioners, or because, while there is agreement on facts and on objectives, there remains contention over the appropriate methods to be used for achieving the best results. Furthermore, differences of opinion over methods may arise, not because of any disagreement on principles, but rather because certain methods entail consequences that one group finds acceptable and another finds objectionable.

The view of economics as a matter of opinion is largely fostered by those who are ignorant of the subject. Their reasons for promoting this view may be innocent or, on the contrary, may be an attempt to persuade the public of political views that are, in fact, without economic foundation. Critics of economics from both the far right and the far left are often discovered persuading their constituents that economics is a matter of opinion. The reason is usually pretty obvious. If you wish in simplistic fashion to argue for the abolition of private property, or the banking system, or the public schools, then you will, indeed, require an unscientific argument. If the simplistic argument is largely based upon economics, it will have to be bad economics. And the only time a bad economic argument can be successfully advanced among any but the most economically illiterate is when it is forcefully coupled with the spurious notion that, after all, economics is only a matter of opinion.

Of course, economics is not a matter of opinion. The wide consensus on the nature of the subject is clearly shown in economics textbooks. No matter what the topic under consideration, it will be found that the same general principles are applied to each. Similarly, the economist, whether hired by business, labor, or the colleges and universities, will have been exposed to the same orthodox training and will bring the same professional standards to bear, no matter in whose employ. Of course, it is true that economic "rationalization" may be offered by economists according to their own interests. But this is no different from the behavior of engineers, chemists, and others who bespeak different philosophies depending, in part, upon their outlook and position in society. In no case, however, need one call into question the underlying principles that unify each of the sciences.

"*The Worrybird*"

In recent years, both the natural and the social sciences have enjoyed great stimulation from the development of a "problem-solving" approach to teaching and learning. No one can doubt the benefits derived from applying general principles to concrete situations. The student and teacher engaged in common enterprise find that the hope for solution is a powerful inducement to study, and that problems that can capture the imagination serve to enliven and enrich the process of education.

Despite the value that derives from solving problems, there are difficulties that can be encountered in using the problem-solving approach in teaching and learning. One difficulty in particular is that a method of solving problems will be confused with the discipline itself. For example, consider the following rough outline of how a problem in the social sciences might be attacked. In descriptive fashion, the student might be urged to follow these steps:

1. Identify the problem.
2. Gather pertinent facts about the problem.
3. Analyze the alternative solutions to the problem.
4. Introduce the objective toward which a solution should point.
5. Determine which alternative solution approaches most closely the objective.
6. Arrive at a judgment as to the best solution.

I have deliberately avoided attempting to work out in detail the logic that underlies this approach and have not taken care to spell out some intermediate steps that might intervene. Yet I think this readily suggests the kind of method that has gained acceptance in the social sciences. But if we ask ourselves, "Has this method of problem solving anything special to do with economics?" the answer must be, "No, it has not." The same steps may be indifferently applied to political science or sociology or chemistry, physics, astronomy.

The fact is that logical reasoning plays an important role in all disciplined inquiry. But logic itself is not a definition of these disciplines, nor is the use of logic in problem solution peculiar to any particular field of inquiry. Therefore, we must guard against the danger of substituting a particular chain of reasoning for the special mode of inquiry that is economics.

The learning of economics is advanced when the particular aspect of human behavior that is *economic* is understood. There is a body of economic principles underlying the perception that we call economics, and certainly, when these principles are understood, and when, in addition, the use of logic is brought to bear, the students' appreciation of economics is greatly enhanced.

There are, of course, other misconceptions as to the nature of economics that would be worth noticing in a more extensive treatment of the subject. One of these which plagues economists themselves is the odd idea that economics is a branch of applied mathematics. We cannot here take up this more complex problem, nor another; namely, that economics is in some fashion especially concerned with "material wants" or "material satisfactions." This latter myth was exploded some 30 years ago by Lionel Robbins,[2] and yet we often encounter the deviant and, indeed, sometimes self-contradictory notion that economics has a special preoccupation with the material world.

In conclusion, we may re-emphasize the fact that economics is essentially a way of organizing special observations upon human behavior. The principle underlying the method of organization is the condition of scarcity which shows itself to us in the fact that typically the resources at mankind's disposal are not adequate to meet all its wants and that, therefore, people must choose between alternative uses to which these resources may be committed. Economic man, depicted historically as a creature of unlimited wants and voracious appetite, was never a real person nor a really typical person. And economics does not depend upon assumptions about this historical fiction. For the "economic problem" confronts all people both within and without their forms of social organization. Economics is not the topics of which it consists, nor is it a

[2] *An Essay on the Nature and Significance of Economic Science.* Third edition. Washington, D.C.: The Brookings Institution, 1962.

matter of public or private opinion, nor a general method of solving problems.

To the extent that we can convey the meaning and usefulness of economic science, to that extent shall we be able to contribute to the advancement of the education of the student toward the attainment of that ultimate morality of mind which Whitehead calls style.

18. Curriculum Trends in the Social Studies

Willis D. Moreland

The urgencies of the times place great responsibility on the social studies curriculum. The rapid changes in social, political, and economic forces should be reflected in a constantly changing secondary school social studies program. The continual assessment of the offerings in the social studies is necessary to provide information as to the adequacy of these changes. To ascertain the present status of the social studies offerings, a study was conducted to survey nationally the offerings, patterns of required and elective courses, and current trends and emphases in the social studies program for grades seven through twelve.

The procedures of this study were to select at random from *Patterson's American Education*[1] five hundred secondary schools which would be a representative cross section of the schools of the nation. A question-

From Willis D. Moreland, "Curriculum Trends in the Social Studies," *Social Education,* February, 1962, 26: 73–76, 102. Willis D. Moreland is Professor of Secondary Education at the University of Nebraska. His latest book, with Harry Bard, is *Government and Citizenship in North America.* This article is reprinted by permission of the author and of the National Council for the Social Studies.

[1] *Patterson's American Education.* North Chicago, Ill.: Educational Directories Inc., Vol. LVI, 1959.

naire was constructed and sent to each of these five hundred schools seeking information regarding the social studies offerings in each school. A total of 281, or 56 percent, of the school systems responded with a completed questionnaire. Of this total, 154 school systems reported all grades from seven through twelve; 60 included only the senior high school; while 67 school systems included only junior high school grades. The survey included school systems in all 50 states. The schools represented ranged from systems with enrollments of less than 50 students to large metropolitan secondary schools of over 1,000 enrollment.

Requirements in Social Studies

One aspect of this study was to determine the extent to which the social studies are required of all secondary school students. It is also important to note at which grade levels these courses are most frequently required of all students, since this determines to a large degree the courses or emphases in the social studies that the schools feel are most important. The information on these two questions may be summarized as follows:

1. Of the 179 school systems which included both junior and senior high schools, 87 percent require four or more years of social studies, and 32 percent require a full six-year program for all students. A total of 173 schools, or 96 percent, prescribe more than two years of social studies in the junior and senior high school. Only five school systems require as little as two years, and one school two and one-half years in the six-year program.

2. In the school systems reporting only the junior high school grades, 27 schools, or 55 percent, require a student to take a social studies course in each of grades seven, eight, and nine. Nineteen junior high schools, or 40 percent, make mandatory a social studies program in two of the three junior high school grades, while only one school has a minimun of one year.

3. In the senior high grades, the situation is similar to that of the junior high program. Ninety-three percent, or 32 schools, require at least two years of social studies, while 43 percent prescribe a full three-year course.

4. The grade levels most frequently required are indicative of what subjects are considered of paramount importance in the social studies curriculum. In the junior high school grades 217 of a possible 221 schools require seventh-grade social studies; 212 also prescribe eighth-grade social studies; and only 182 require it in the ninth grade.

In the senior high levels, social studies is most frequently required in the eleventh grade as indicated by 209 of a possible 214 schools. The twelfth grade required it in 166 schools, while the tenth year social studies is required in only 134 schools.

Required Social Studies Courses for Grades Seven, Eight, and Nine

The pattern of subjects listed as being the most frequently required social studies courses for the junior high school level are presented in Table No. I. The program of required studies in the seventh grade is unique in that no one course combination predominates. Rather, there are three different offerings which have been mentioned with almost the same degree of frequency: world geography is the required subject in 28 school systems, a combination of American history and geography in 28 schools, and American history is reported as required in 27 schools. A total of 39 different course organizations are reported for the seventh grade.

TABLE I

MOST FREQUENTLY REQUIRED SOCIAL STUDIES COURSES IN GRADES SEVEN, EIGHT, AND NINE

Subject	No.
Grade 7	
World geography	28
American history-geography	28
American history	27
Geography	21
State history-geography	21
Social studies	14
State history	13
Grade 8	
American history	105
American history-state history	19
American history-civics	17
American history-geography	16
World geography	10
Grade 9	
Civics	66
World geography	24
World history	17
State history-civics	17
Social studies	15

A study of these programs for this grade level, however, reveals that the study of geography is most frequently required of students in the first year of the junior high school. Geography taught separately or in combination with other subjects is required in the programs of 121 school systems. However, in most of these schools, it is offered as a one-semester course. Within the field of geography, the primary emphasis appears to be on the study of world or global geography. The study of American history is the next most popular course for seventh grade. A total of 59 school systems list American history as a required subject of study in the seventh grade, with 27 of these requiring it for a full year. American history as a one-semester course is required in 32 school systems, appearing in combination with geography, state history, and world history.

American history is the most commonly required course for the eighth grade. The extent to which this subject prevails at this level can be seen by the fact that it is required as a full-year course in 105 schools, and in combination with other courses in an additional 59 schools. Thus slightly more than 77 percent of the systems in the survey make the study of American history mandatory at the eighth grade level. As a combined course, it appears most frequently with geography, civics, and state history. Certainly the predominance of American history at this level reflects, to a large degree, the fact that many states require by law the teaching of American history before the completion of the eighth grade.

The study of civics is the most frequently required course for the ninth grade, being listed by 98 school systems. It appears as a full-year requirement in 66 of these schools and as a subject combination in an additional 32 schools. Although it is most often a combined offering with state history, it is also frequently combined with orientation, geography, and other history courses.

Second in frequency for the ninth grade is the study of geography. While world geography is offered as a full-year course in 24 school systems, it also appears in combination with other subjects in an additional 15 schools. Most of the emphasis in geography is upon world geography.

The extent of the requirement for world history at the ninth grade is a relatively substantial one. Some 27 schools require world history as a single subject, in combination with other subjects, or emphasize a particular phase of world history. This degree of importance in the study of world history at this level is particularly important in the light of the concern expressed over the ability of even sophomores to adequately comprehend the complexities of a world history course.

Required Social Studies Courses for Grades Ten, Eleven, and Twelve

The senior high school program seems to be more definitely established than that of the junior high school. In two of the three senior high years, there is almost a uniform course requirement, while the senior year shows some degree of flexibility. The courses most commonly required for the senior high school are presented in Table No. II.

The sophomore level has been traditionally devoted to the study of world history, and the results of this survey indicate very little change in the nature of the offerings for the tenth grade. In 97 schools, the required course is a full-year program in world history. Thus, approximately 72 percent of the schools that require some social studies in the tenth grade make this requirement a year course in world history. However, an additional 18 schools provide for world history in combination with some other subject, with world geography being the most frequently mentioned. Thus, some 85 percent of the school systems provide for some study of world history at this grade level.

The eleventh grade has the fewest number of required offerings of any grade level. It should be noted that junior social studies is more frequently required of all students than any other senior high grades. The emphasis in the eleventh grade is almost solely on the study of American history as can be seen in Table No. II.

A total of 165 school systems require a full-year course in American history, and an additional 22 systems combine the study of American history with some other course offering. The degree of dominance of American history at this grade level may be seen by the fact that approximately 90 percent of all schools requiring junior social studies focus on American history.

The extent of the world history offered at the eleventh grade closely approximates the number of school systems offering American history in the sophomore year. This may be indicative of a trend in some schools to change the sequential relationship of world and American history.

The most popular required offering at the twelfth grade is the full-year course entitled "problems of democracy."[2] Next in frequency of mention is American government. American history is also an important requirement at the twelfth grade which can be partially explained by the two-year requirement in American history which has been established in several states.

[2] Since titles for this course vary somewhat in individual schools, they have been grouped together and reported under the single heading of "problems of democracy" course.

TABLE II

Most Frequently Required Social Studies Courses in Grades Ten, Eleven, and Twelve

Subject	No.
Grade 10	
World history	98
American history	10
World history-geography	6
Social studies	3
Modern world history	2
World geography	2
World history-driver education	2
Civics	2
Civics-world history	2
Grade 11	
American history	165
American history-government	13
World history	13
American history-economics	3
American government	3
Problems of democracy	3
American history-state history	3
Grade 12	
Problems of democracy	46
American government	36
American history	19
Problems of democracy-American government	12
American history-American government	4
Problems of democracy-economics	4
American government-economics	3
American history-problems of democracy	3
American government-sociology	3
Sociology-economics	3
Social studies	2
American history-economics	2
Psychology-economics	2

Probably the most significant aspect of the required sequence in the senior year is the number of combined semester courses which are reported. Although the problems of democracy course is a full-year requirement in 46 schools, an additional 18 systems combine this course with some other area. A course in American government is required most often in combination with a semester offering in problems of democracy.

Although the American government course is required in 61 school systems, a full-year course in government is required in only 36 schools. Problems of democracy is the subject most frequently reported in combination with American government.

One important aspect of the required senior program is the extent of requirements in the nonhistorical social sciences. The study of economics, sociology, and psychology as separate courses seems to be increasing. Although only one school reports a full year of economics at the twelfth-grade level, an additional 26 combine economics with some other subject matter area as a requirement for seniors. The combination of economics with the problems of democracy course, American government, or sociology seems to be the most common arrangement. No system reports a full year of sociology or psychology in the senior year but the twelfth-grade program in 17 schools includes some work in sociology, and psychology is listed as a senior subject in five schools.

Elective Courses in the Social Studies

Very little in the way of elective offerings is reported for grades seven and eight. Only seven schools permit students to elect a social studies course at the seventh grade with six different course titles listed. A similar situation occurs at the eighth grade in which four schools offer three different course offerings.

The ninth grade is generally the level at which the schools begin to permit some freedom of choice for students. Civics is the most popular elective for the ninth grade followed by world geography which is similar to the required program. The remainder of the elective program at the ninth grade reveals very few trends with a total of 17 different course combinations reported. Some attention is given to world history as an elective, with a variety of other offerings representing different areas.

A total of 22 different course combinations are reported as electives in the sophomore year. The most common electives for the senior high grades are presented in Table No. III. World history is listed as a full-year elective offering in 63 schools with an additional 17 schools offering some aspect of world history or world history in combination with other courses. The second most frequently mentioned area at the tenth grade is geography with emphasis upon world geography. Some economics and sociology is also being offered as elective for this year. One inter-

TABLE III

MOST FREQUENTLY ELECTED SOCIAL STUDIES COURSES
GRADES TEN THROUGH TWELVE

Subject	No.
Grade 10	
World history	63
World geography	20
Modern history	6
Economic geography	4
State history	4
World history, geography	4
European history	4
Sociology	4
Geography	3
Ancient Medieval history	3
Economics	2
Bible	2
Grade 11	
Economics	21
Sociology	15
World history	14
World geography	12
Problems of democracy	8
Psychology	7
Current history	4
Business law	4
State history	3
International relations	3
Consumer economics	3
American government	3
Modern history	3
Advanced geography	2
Civics	2
Grade 12	
Problems of democracy	38
Sociology	32
Economics	31
Psychology	18
American government	13
World history	11
International relations	9

TABLE III (*Continued*)

World geography	9
Business law	6
State history	5
Latin American history	4
Consumer economics	4
Current history	4
Family living	3
Modern history	3
Contemporary issues	2
Law	2
Civics	2
Bible	2

esting course is the one entitled "Bible" which is reported by two schools. No description was given of this course which would indicate the exact nature of this offering.

Economics is the most frequently offered elective at the junior level with sociology, world history, and world geography also receiving considerable attention. The major characteristic of the eleventh grade elective program is its emphasis upon the non-historical social sciences. Although world history is reported as an elective offering in 14 schools, most of the courses at this grade level are concerned with such subjects as economics, sociology, geography, psychology, and topics generally included in the various types of problems courses. Economics is offered in 24 schools, and geography in 18. The degree of emphasis upon psychology as an elective offering may be indicative of a new trend in course offerings.

The greatest variety of electives are available at the senior year. The elective subjects for the junior and senior level are, in many respects, quite similar. The wide range of offerings at both levels, and the emphasis upon economics, psychology, sociology, and world history appear to characterize both the eleventh- and twelfth-grade elective program. However, the most common elective for seniors is the full-year course in problems of democracy. Sociology and economics are next in frequency of mention. A total of 30 school systems make available some work in history at the senior level with the most emphasis being upon world history or some related phase of history. Again, geography has some substantial emphasis at the twelfth grade as indicated by the elective program in 14 schools. It should be noted that the elective program for grades seven through twelve parallels almost exactly the sequence of required courses.

The only differences are at the eleventh grade and, of course, the variety of offerings which are available at all levels from grades nine to twelve.

Conclusions

From an analysis of the programs of the school systems included in this study, the following conclusions may be stated:

1. The pattern of required courses in today's schools strongly reflects the influence of previous national commissions, particularly the Committee on the Social Studies in 1916. This would seem to indicate that a re-examination of the social studies sequence in the secondary schools is of utmost importance.

2. The social studies program is still primarily oriented to the more traditionally organized subject matter courses. The criticism that the social studies concept has meant a decline in courses in history, geography, and other standard offerings seems unjustified on the basis of data from the school systems in this study.

3. There is a great need to limit the scope of most course offerings in the social studies curriculum. It is apparent that a discernment of trends in the social studies indicates that the social studies program is a haven for many new emphases which, in many instances, are only tangentially related to the more traditional pattern of courses.

4. The general practice of curriculum revision in the social studies is more of changing emphases of subject matter within courses than in the reorganization of basic course titles. The major changes in emphases have been generally that of greater attention to modern history, developing concern for international understanding and cultures of newer areas of the world, and relating social studies more closely to current events.

5. The social studies program has been significantly broadened by utilization of a greater variety of elective offerings. Generally, the scope of the elective offerings has tended to encompass more of the areas normally considered as non-historical social sciences. Many newer courses and emphases have had difficulty in finding a proper place in the schools.

6. There are certain trends in the sequence of course offerings which give indication of some revisions in the social studies curriculum. Certainly the predominance of the modern problems course at the senior level is not as pronounced as might have been expected. The most predominant type of offering for the senior year appears to be that of a combination of two semester courses as a replacement for the full-year modern problems course.

It would also seem that there is some experimentation in the schools to alter the sequential relationship of tenth-grade world history and eleventh-grade American history. Although the preponderant majority of the schools follow the traditional sequence, there is indication that the two courses may be revised in sequence placing the world history at the eleventh grade and American history at the tenth grade.

Although it may seem paradoxical, there are a significant number of schools which offer American history also at the senior level. This, in many instances, may be explained by a number of schools which are experimenting with a two-year sequence in American history at the junior and senior level.

One of the most significant changes in the social studies curriculum is the extent of the geography offerings. Formerly reserved for the junior high school, it would seem that there is growing recognition for an emphasis on this area at the senior high school level. It should be noted, however, that geography in the senior high school is an elective rather than a required offering.

Finally, the ninth-grade program gives indication of the greatest amount of indecision as to the proper course content for that level. Civics and world geography predominate at the ninth-grade level although the number of courses related to state history, occupations, and guidance seem to suggest that many schools feel that this is the proper emphasis for the ninth grade. It is apparent that there is need for some reorientation as to the purposes and functions of the ninth-grade program.

For Further Reading

Alilunas, Leo J., "An Analysis of Social Studies Content in the Middle Grades," *Social Studies,* November, 1961, 52: 210–218.

Anderson, C. Arnold, "A New Frame for the Social Studies," *The School Review,* Winter, 1964, 72: 415–436.

Anderson, Howard R., (ed.), *Approaches to an Understanding of World Affairs,* Twenty-fifth Yearbook of the National Council for the Social Studies, The Council, Washington, D.C., 1954.

Association for Supervision and Curriculum Development, *Educating for Economic Competence,* The Association, Washington, D.C., 1960.

Becker, James M., "Emerging Trends in the Social Studies," *Educational Leadership,* February, 1965, 22: 317–322.

Bohlke, Robert H., "Teaching of Sociology in the Secondary School," *Social Forces,* March, 1964, 42: 363–374.

The *Bulletin* of the National Association of Secondary School Principals, November, 1965, Vol. 49, No. 304. (Theme of the issue, "Economic Understanding." Seven articles plus descriptions of six economics programs in specific high schools.)

Cartwright, William H., "The Future of the Social Studies," *Social Education,* February, 1966, 30: 79–82, 100.

Cartwright, William H., and Richard L. Watson (eds.), *Interpreting and Teaching American History,* Thirty-first Yearbook of the National Council for the Social Studies, The Council, Washington, D.C., 1961.

Dunlap, Robert, "Teaching Anthropology in High School," *The Education Digest,* April, 1961, 26: 52–53.

Education, February, 1966, Vol. 86, No. 6. (Six articles on the social studies.)

Educational Leadership, February, 1965, 22: 290–372. (Theme of the issue: "Social Ferment and the Social Sciences." Eight articles dealing with this theme.)

Erickson, Edgar L., "A Case for English History," *Social Education,* March, 1965, 29: 164–168.

Frankel, M. L., *Economic Education,* The Center for Applied Research in Education, Inc., New York, 1965. (See "Rationale for Economic Understanding," pp. 13–17, and "Economics as a Discipline," Chapter V.)

Franzen, Carl G. F., "Why Geography?" The *Bulletin* of the National Association of Secondary School Principals, February, 1961, 45: 127–131.

The Instructor, April, 1966, Vol. 75, No. 8. (Geography Feature. Five articles explaining geography and its applications in elementary education.)

Jarolimek, John, "Curriculum Content and the Child in the Elementary School," *Social Education,* February, 1962, 26: 58–62, 117–120.

Johnson, Earl S., "The Social Studies Versus the Social Sciences," *The School Review,* Winter, 1963, 71: 389–403.

Keller, Charles R., "Needed: Revolution in the Social Studies," *Saturday Review,* September, 1961, 44: 60–62.

Mercedes, Sister M., "Sociology in Elementary Social Studies," *The Instructor,* March, 1966, 47, 148, Vol. 75.

Meyer, Alfred H., "The Stature of Geography: Stake and Status," *The Journal of Geography,* October, 1961, 60: 301–309.

National Task Force on Economic Education, *Economic Education in the Schools,* Council for Economic Development, New York, 1961.

Perucci, Robert, "What Sociology Is," *The Instructor,* March, 1966, 47, 148, Vol. 75.

Powell, Thomas F., "Teaching American Values," *Social Education,* May, 1965, 29: 272–274.

Rundell, Walter, Jr., "History Teaching: A Legitimate Concern," *Social Education,* December, 1965, 29: 521–524, 528.

Scarfe, N. V., "Geography Across the Curriculum," *School and Society,* February 13, 1960, 88: 61–64.

Scoville, Warren C., "Economics in the High School," *The Balance Sheet,* March, 1962, 43: 292–296, 336.

Sheldon, Kenneth, "An American Desert — Economic Education," *Journal of Education,* April, 1966, 50–55, Vol. 148.

Smith, Gerald R., "Project Social Studies — A Report," *School Life,* July, 1963, 45: 25–27.

Social Education, April, 1966, 30: 227–307. (Theme of the issue, "Economic Education." Thirteen articles, seven of which deal with economics in the school curriculum. Economics as a separate course, correlation with history and twelfth-grade problems and the incorporation of economics at various grade levels are treated.)

Travers, John F., "Let's Teach Geography," *The American School Board Journal,* July, 1963, 15–16, Vol. 146–147.

Trump, J. Lloyd, "Focus on Change: Organizing for Teaching the Social Studies," *Social Education,* March, 1966, 30: 163–167.

PART FOUR

Science

19. Science and Education

E. W. R. Steacie

As science has become more important in our lives there has been a great deal of interest in the relation between science and education. Unfortunately, however, far too many people seem to have taken extreme stands, the arguments ranging all the way from the idea that it is a waste of time and effort to do anything but train everyone to be a scientist or engineer, to the opposite extreme that all scientists and

From E. W. R. Steacie, "Science and Education," Chapter I, pp. 17–21, in *Science in Canada*, The University of Toronto Press, Toronto, Ontario, Canada, 1965. E. W. R. Steacie was one of Canada's foremost scientists. In 1944–1946 he was Deputy Director of the British-Canadian Atomic Energy Project. From 1958–1961 he was Canadian Representative, NATO Science Committee. In 1961 he was President, International Council of Scientific Unions. At the time of his death in 1963 he had been President of the National Research Council of Canada for the previous decade. He held more than 17 honorary degrees and numerous international honors. He wrote more than 200 papers and three books dealing with photochemistry, the kinetics of gas reactions, and free radical reactions. *Science in Canada* is a collection of his speeches and thoughts in science. This extract presents the case for science in education in the broadest human and philosophical terms. Permission to reprint was granted by the National Research Council of Canada.

engineers are of necessity uncouth, ignorant, and essentially uneducated. I hasten to say that I am going to take a middle position.

There are really two quite separate aspects of the problem. First, what is the place of science in a general education? In other words, how much science should be taught to an intelligent person who is not going to become a scientist? The second question is to what extent should a scientist be educated in other things? The ideal situation, of course, would be to teach everybody everything, but life is too short. Essentially, therefore, what we have to decide is what compromise to make, and the virtues of breadth *versus* specialization.

The Place of the School

First, there is the question of how the school comes into all this, and here one can obtain some guidance from history. There has always been a tendency for the university curriculum to move with the times. The original universities, 700 years ago or so, taught people to read and write and not much more. (Their education perhaps looked more dignified because it was Latin that they were taught to read and write.) At a time when almost no one *could* read or write this appropriately constituted higher education. As general education has increased in depth and become more widespread over the past seven centuries, the universities have continually sloughed off the more routine items to the schools. A junior clerk now requires much more education than was possessed by many university graduates a few centuries ago. In this connection the word "continually" should be used with some reservations because there have been periods of decline and decay in the universities. It is essential that this process of sloughing off continue if the universities are really to deal with *higher* education. With the changing demands of society for educated people it is vital that the curricula of both the schools and the universities move forward.

The Importance of Science

As science has become more important to society as the basis of technology, of defence, and perhaps of survival or the reverse, it might have been expected that the sharing of education between the school and the university would have been modified so that more and more science and mathematics were included in the schools. This would mean that the universities could raise their sights in science and start their teaching at a more advanced level. At the same time an increase in the teaching of science in schools would ensure that the general public of the coming generation would have some appreciation of the objectives and the method of operation of science.

In reality, however, a great deal of the worry over present-day education is due to the fact that exactly the reverse is happening. In many cases, as science has become more important to society the schools have given it less attention, and the university curriculum is obliged to move backward rather than forward.

Science and a Broad Education

In discussing the foundations of a general education it is impossible to avoid some reference to the unfortunate debate which has been going on as to the relative merits of the humanities and of science as part of the process of creating a "broadly" educated man. There is often the suggestion that the humanities are intrinsically broader, and that a narrow education in, say, the classics will produce a broader man than an equally narrow education in biology. It is perhaps worth pointing out that this argument that one part of knowledge is superior to another is of a relatively recent date.

The revival of classical learning at the time of the Renaissance was not an attempt to push one part of learning rather than another. It was merely the attempt to go back from a state of barbarism to a much higher level of learning which had prevailed ten or more centuries previously, and to rediscover the knowledge and learning of classical times.

This was soon followed by a revival of interest in learning in all fields and the new "science" was vigorously pursued in the sixteenth and seventeenth century by poets, philosophers, theologians, and classical scholars. By the eighteenth century science had become a fashionable pursuit of educated men, but the universities were in an almost total decline as far as real scholarship was concerned in any field. After the revival of the universities in the nineteenth century, science became a part of university education in a real way, but it was about this time that the idea of the superiority of the classics began to be a rallying point for conservatism.

There were, of course, good reasons for the type of education offered by the universities in earlier days. The *Oxford Dictionary* (compiled mainly from 1900 to 1920) defines a liberal education as education fit for a gentleman. Ashby remarks that this is still an acceptable definition: it is the idea of a gentleman which has changed. To quote Sir Eric Ashby,

> A century ago, when Britain awoke to the need for technological education, a gentleman belonged to what was called the leisured class. The occupations of his leisure did not require any knowledge of science or technology. Modern gentlemen do not belong to the leisured class — and more and more of them are finding that their business requires expert knowledge. Even members of the

House of Lords are called upon to make decisions about radioactive fall-out, overheating during supersonic flight, and the strontium content of bones. Even such a gentlemanly subject as the state of the river Thames cannot be understood without some knowledge of oxidation and reduction, detergents, and the biochemistry of sewage.[1]

This raises the very important question of the status of science in a broad education. The change in man's civilization, outlook, and knowledge in the last 300 years constitutes a revolution as great as that of the Golden Age of Greece. Can one ignore all this and still have sufficient breadth of education to decide where society is heading? The major new factor today is man's ability to exercise control over his environment. It is difficult to see how a man can express contempt for his environment and all knowledge of it and still claim to be educated. In short can you deal with the "whole man" while neglecting his environment altogether? These arguments have particular force in Canada because, as an animal, man is here very far north of his "range" and can live here only because he does possess control over his environment. It is necessary in Canada to have some appreciation of the facts of life.

These questions pose a serious problem for education. Somehow it is necessary to give future leaders of society some general idea of the aims and methods of science, the frequent lack of which is a great complication in present society. Some understanding of science is necessary not only in order to make appropriate decisions for the welfare of science, but also as self-protection against scientists who might be putting something over. When our whole technology is based on science it is certainly as important that it be generally understood as it is to have economics generally understood. The problem, however, is not easy, and is not to be solved by cramming elementary chemistry or physics down the throats of first-year Arts students. What are necessary are not the efforts of the popularizers of science who write semi-fictional articles about its wonders, or try to explain the whole of nuclear physics in one easy lesson. The effort must rather be to give some idea of what science is and how it works, of its philosophy and methods. If possible, the ideal situation would be to try to give everyone a knowledge of one science in some depth, rather than the more usual method of trying to give a smattering of everything. Another method of attack is through history. There has been a highly desirable trend in the study of history away from too many wars and dates and towards more social history.

[1] *Technology and the Academics; An Essay on Universities and Scientific Revolution* (London: Macmillan, 1958), p. 81.

It is peculiar in this connection how little attention has been paid to the history of science and technology which could well give greater insight into the real workings of science than more formal courses of the Physics I type. Certainly the school as well as the university could do much along these lines. . . .

20. Improving Science Education

J. Darrell Barnard

More man-hours have gone into projects to improve science education in the past 10 years than in any 50 years in our history. The primary motivation for such a phenomenal effort is to increase the quantity and quality of our scientific manpower. Although the evidence is substantial that this effort is beginning to pay off, the task is far from done — if it will ever be. Because of the multiple variables in the educational process, we will never completely solve the problem of improving educational practice. To complicate the problem further, these variables interact between two dynamic enterprises — science and a free society. We must not complacently assume that new science courses and intensive effort to improve the science teacher's background have raised or will raise

From J. Darrell Barnard, "Improving Science Education," *School Life,* October, 1962, 33–36, Vol. 45. J. Darrell Barnard is Professor and Chairman, Division of Science and Mathematics Education, New York University, School of Education. He has made extensive contributions to the field of science teaching and has conducted and supervised numerous research investigations in the teaching of science. His research has focused on studies related to teaching of inquiry or problem solving. He was Chairman of the Yearbook Committee for the 59th yearbook of the National Society for the Study of Education, Part I, *Rethinking Science Education.* He is currently associate director of COPES (Conceptually Oriented Program in Elementary Science), a development project funded by a grant from the United States Office of Education being conducted at New York University. This article is reprinted by permission of Professor Barnard.

science teaching to the level we want. Science teaching will improve only as we persistently work at improving it. There will never come a time when we can say "the job is done."

Before anything of significance will come from a commitment to the principle that curriculums must be *sequential* and *developmental* from the elementary school through the secondary school, for all students, we must look hard at our points of view toward *objectives*, the *learning process*, and *evaluation in science teaching*.

We have developed a laissez-faire attitude toward certain practices which we, as educational leaders, should vigorously challenge. The most critical of these practices is the manner in which curriculum workers, course-of-study makers, and teachers have dealt with the objectives of science teaching. Nearly every curriculum or course of study has a well-formulated list of objectives in its preamble reflecting the objectives that have appeared in professional literature for 30 years. Yet many who develop these courses have little intention of letting objectives get in the way of developing a course or curriculum according to conventional patterns. Nor do curriculum makers seem to have much predisposition to follow through with teachers to make certain that they understand the objectives and reflect them in teaching.

"Critical thinking" and "understanding of basic concepts" are objectives common to these lists. Yet in some courses, the range of content is such that to cover it and develop reasonable understanding is impossible and the suggested learning activities do not clearly identify "critical thinking" as an outcome. Moreover, investigators such as Beauchamp, Obourn, and Powers have found that teachers either do not accept these objectives or do not comprehend them — and, consequently, do not provide for them in teaching.[1] Too many educators view the learning process as only a matter of filling the mind with facts, a no longer tenable idea. Their attitude toward evaluation is no better. As long as they judge achievement in science learning primarily by verbalization of definitions and factual material, discussion of or planning for more significant objectives will be largely a waste of time and effort.

A good science program gives the student an understanding of basic concepts and the processes of science or methods of critical thinking, and through it he learns that concept and process are inextricably related.

[1] Wilbur L. Beauchamp, Instruction in Science, U. S. Office of Education, Bulletin No. 17 (Monograph No. 22), Washington, Government Printing Office, 1932. 63 pp. Ellsworth S. Obourn, Assumptions in Ninth Grade General Science, unpublished doctoral dissertation, New York University, 1950. S. R. Powers, "The Correlation Between Measures of Mental Ability and Measures of Achievement in Chemistry," *School Science and Mathematics*, 28 (December 1928), pp. 981–986.

It teaches him that scientific concepts are not made known by supernatural authority but are wrested from nature through the persistent application of man's intelligence.

Insofar as the concept-process purposes relate to teaching and learning science, correspondence with the scientific enterprise is striking. Research on learning shows clearly that no one can give another person an idea — a concept. He must think his way to it. It is his when it becomes part of his conceptual schemes and patterns through a critical thinking process. He learns by getting meaning out of what he is taught, and meaning develops from experiences that involve him in critical thinking.

Powers found that chemistry students can verbalize concepts without understanding them. He found that a relatively small proportion of the good verbalizers understood chemistry as it was conventionally taught. His research seems to indicate that much of what has gone on in science classes has been a tragic waste of time and effort.[2] Tyler found that science students taught with emphasis on verbalism in 1 year forgot about 80 percent of what they had learned. On the other hand, he found that the retention curve of students taught to think their way to an understanding of selected principles of science went up during the year after completion of the course.[3]

If we specialists in science education believe that decisions about what to teach in science and how to teach it should be based on experimental evidence, then we are morally committed to work for a major reconstruction of science curriculums and drastic reorientation of classroom practices. If we take the evidence seriously, we will make radical changes in science teaching.

We need to reconsider the objectives of science teaching in terms of their validity and the methods by which they may be applied more effectively in helping students to acquire a better understanding of the basic concepts of science. We need to reexamine the conceptual structure of science and to identify the basic concepts. We need to design and use evaluation instruments that measure achievement in understanding science concepts and in using the processes of scientific thinking. We need to be more concerned about the way in which young people are going to be different because of their experiences with the science curriculum we build. Through these experiences they should attain not only a better comprehension of the conceptual schemes that

[2] S. R. Powers, "The Correlation Between Measures of Mental Ability and Measures of Achievement in Chemistry," *School Science and Mathematics,* 28 (December 1928), pp. 981–986.

[3] Ralph W. Tyler, "What High School Pupils Forget," Ohio State University, *Education Research Bulletin* 9 (November 19, 1930), pp. 490–492.

explain natural phenomena, but a better understanding of how these concepts affect the personal, social, economic, and political lives of people. They should develop not only a better understanding of the processes of inquiry as used by scientists, but greater competence in using the processes and, consequently, in becoming more self-directive in their learning. We should motivate more of them than we do to sustain intellectual interests after formal schooling is completed. It is imperative that science — and other subjects — in our schools fulfill the demand of a free society for citizens who possess the essential skills and motivation to continue their intellectual development. Our progress toward this goal as a central purpose of education has been less clearly demonstrated than has our progress toward meeting the needs for scientific manpower.

I recommend the reexamination of the points of view and recommendations of such science improvement projects as those of the Bureau of Educational Research in Science and the 8-Year Study. These projects were more clearly directed toward the personal-social meaning of science than appears to be the case in most of the current science improvement projects. The earlier projects sought ways in which science could be used to change the behavior of young people in personally satisfying and socially desirable ways and were concerned with the scientific literacy of all young people.

Of recent projects to improve science teaching, the best known are being conducted at the University of Illinois, University of California (Berkeley), University of Colorado (Biological Science Curriculum Study), Harvey Mudd College (Chemical Education Material Study), Earlham College (Chemical Bond Approach Project), and Educational Services, Inc. (Physical Science Study Committee). The first two projects are on elementary science; the last four on secondary school science. The elementary studies were motivated by the feeling that present courses of study, textbooks, and other materials in elementary science do not adequately reveal the methods and goals of basic science. The secondary school studies have sprung from concern over the fragmentary, descriptive, and technological nature of the conventional high school courses in biology, chemistry, and physics. The studies are designed to reduce each science to its basic structural concepts and to develop materials for teachers and students.

These projects represent breakthroughs in the development of materials and courses. Rather than merely revising present courses or working over classical learning activities, each project is taking a fresh look at what should be taught and how it should be taught from a scientist's point of view. Rather than merely developing point-of-view statements, lists of objectives, and generalized guidelines for curriculum workers and teachers, each project is developing specific learning experiences for teachers to use with students. Rather than assuming that these learning experiences are suitable, the projects have extensive programs for trying them out and using the evidence obtained as bases for revisions. Rather than assuming that the dated and variable subject-matter preparation of teachers and the teaching methods which they learned can see them through new courses, the projects are developing intensive programs for the reeducation of teachers.

These projects also represent other worthy breakthroughs. To the fact-happy, ground-covering teacher and test maker they clearly demonstrate the significance of science facts and major scientific concepts in teaching for understanding and of pupil participation in processes leading to concept formation and an understanding of the methods of scientific inquiry.

I am, however, concerned about three matters connected with these projects: Their exclusive commitment to basic science; the extent to which the new secondary school courses are adaptable to the ability, interests, and needs of all high school students; and how the results will be incorporated into a K-12 development sequence.

Many proponents of the projects are more strongly antitechnology than probasic in their passion to be "pure," perhaps as a natural reaction to science courses that had become almost exclusively applied science, in both elementary and secondary schools. My thinking about science teaching has been stimulated and challenged by these reactionary or radical purists, and I'm not about to write them off. Neither am I about to write off a belief that science should make a difference in the lives of young people; nor the convincing evidence that the man-made environment of spaceships is in many ways more challenging to young people than phenomena categorized as natural environment. To teach science unrelated to or insulated from the lives of young people would leave much to be desired. But to deal with science only from a consumer's point of view would be equally disastrous. We must have both — pure and applied. We should not, however, give the impression that technology and science are synonymous.

The answer to the question of the extent to which the new secondary courses are adaptable to the ability, interests, and needs of all students should be coming through soon from field tests in schools.

There are many unanswered questions on what should be the nature of science courses for the student who is not planning a career in science. Some of us foolishly assumed we had the answers 30 years ago. I hope those working on the answers now will not make the same assumption.

Neither of the two elementary science projects I have mentioned have developed an overall elementary science curriculum. The materials they have developed, however, are being tried at several grade levels to determine grade placement. None of the new high school science courses has been conceived within a developmental sequence. Nor has there been a major study of what the nature of the sequence should be in junior high school.

Several proposals for studies of sequence have been made. Studies on sequence will be charting relatively unexplored territory. It is probable they will chart several routes. It is important that a clearly defined purpose be identified and that plans be made early in the studies to evaluate relative progress toward their achievement.

We have reached the place where the "cut-and-fit" method of curriculum development in science needs a pattern to follow. We need to design and try out several K-12 curriculum patterns so that the old patterns and the new ones can be fitted into a rational whole. Some may believe that the basic design should be uniform for all schools. Others may contend that a minimum uniform basic design should be developed, one that local communities and the States can modify as they see fit. Still others believe that several "good" patterns should be developed and tested and their relative success evaluated. On such evidence, schools could adopt whichever pattern best fits their needs. It is imperative that we develop some rational designs and test them under conditions which permit objective comparisons.

Those of you who have built curriculums know what an accomplishment it is to get ideas on paper. Consider how difficult the job becomes when teachers must be persuaded to try a new curriculum and submit reactions. It will be a monumental undertaking to develop evaluation instruments and design a study to determine objectively the relative success of several K-12 curriculum patterns, but it must be done before we can make defensible decisions based on experimental evidence.

The great national interest in science and the improvement of our scientific effort has two primary implications for us: To get on with the job of building K-12 science curriculums with scientifically rational sequences that are developmental in terms of concepts and process goals and are based on the needs, interests, and abilities of all students at each grade level; and to prepare teachers to do the job demanded by the new curriculums.

The preparation of science teachers begins in the high school with science teachers who zealously recruit their best students for science teaching. It continues in college, where the convert's zeal is fed and fanned by experiences tailormade for the future science teacher. It continues once he is teaching — both the college and the school must work together to help the teacher continue his education.

Hurd is highly critical of the conglomerate college programs of science study for science teachers and questions the effectiveness of general courses in methods of teaching as preparation for science teaching. He recommends that colleges wanting to improve their science teacher education programs follow, as a beginning point, the eight guidelines set forth in the joint report of the American Association for the Advancement of Science and the National Association of State Directors of Teacher Education and Certification.[4]

Until colleges and universities redesign or overhaul their teacher education programs, science teachers will need inservice education. The inservice preparation of teachers is a major part of the course improvement projects I have mentioned. To date, institutes sponsored by the National Science Foundation to upgrade and update the science backgrounds of teachers have enrolled more than 30,000 science teachers. Many teachers have attended several institutes. There is little question that these institutes have an influence on science teaching, but the extent of the influence is yet to be evaluated.

Gruber, from a study of 55 high school science and mathematics teachers who attended an academic year institute at the University of Colorado, found that the program's main weakness is that it transmits attitudes and information relevant to teaching science as a body of knowledge, not as a way of thinking.[5]

The planning of institutes for science teachers has largely been the responsibility of college scientists who have planned on limited knowledge of what high school science teachers need. It seems to me that it would be more appropriate for people from the schools and the colleges to plan institutes cooperatively. The effectiveness of the institutes thus developed could be evaluated in terms of measured changes that take place in the schools. I believe that a cooperative attack on the problem at the State level would pay high dividends.

The problems involved in the improvement of science teaching are numerous, as are the variables involved in their solution. The success of this conference will be determined by the extent to which it will help each of us to more clearly define the problems, establish priorities, and point the way to promising solutions.

[4] Paul DeH. Hurd, "The Education of Secondary School Biology Teachers," *BSCS Newsletter 13*, Biological Science Curriculum Study, University of Colorado, Boulder, May 1962, pp. 7–10.

[5] Howard E. Gruber, "Science Teachers and the Scientific Attitude: An Appraisal of an Academic Year Institute," *Science* 132 (19 August 1960), pp. 467–468.

21. Programs of the National Science Foundation

Staff, Division of Pre-College Education in Science

The prime objective of the Course Content Improvement Programs of the National Science Foundation has been to encourage the development of improved teaching materials in mathematics, science, and engineering through the collaboration of scientists, teachers, and educators. The programs began with small exploratory planning projects in the middle of the last decade and have grown now to a dollar level for the fiscal year 1966 of $16,000,000, a total which includes the support of both pre-college and undergraduate projects. Studies concerned with course content improvement have taken varied approaches, but commonly fit one or more of the following patterns: (1) committee and conference studies designed to identify problems in a given field and to formulate guidelines for the evolution of modern instructional programs; (2) planning and coordination projects designed to develop basic guidelines for course improvement, to stimulate the initiation of appropriate projects, to correlate independent developmental projects, and to facilitate wide dissemination of the results of such efforts; (3) small-scale experimental projects, typically limited in subject-matter scope and academic level, whose primary purpose is the investigation of innovative approaches to science and mathematics teaching; (4) projects for the development of instructional components dealing with new subject-matter presentations through written materials, film, television, laboratory experiments and equipment, and programed approaches; and (5) comprehensive projects, such as the BSCS, to develop complete model courses or course sequences, using many types of learning and teaching aids.

From the Staff, Division of Pre-College Education in Science, National Science Foundation, "The Course Content Improvement Programs of the National Science Foundation," *BSCS Newsletter*, #28, April, 1966, 14–15, 18. This concise and authoritative summary of the programs of the National Science Foundation is reprinted by permission of the Biological Sciences Curriculum Study and the National Science Foundation.

The first major projects supported by the Foundation belong in the last category of this list, and were aimed at the development of an integrated set of course materials for use in the conventional spots in the high school curriculum. The Physical Science Study Committee, organized in the fall of 1956, was the first of these to receive support from the Foundation. Soon thereafter the School Mathematics Study Group was initiated, followed by the Chemical Bond Approach Project, Biological Sciences Curriculum Study, and Chemical Education Material Study. By 1963, commercial versions were available from all of these projects except SMSG, whose books were published in paperback format through a university press, rather than through a book publishing company. The wide acceptance of these materials and their favorable impact on school science and mathematics instruction led the Foundation to extend support to elementary levels, on the one hand, and to college and university curricula on the other. Curriculum reform is now seen as a continuing effort requiring periodic revision and recasting as new approaches and materials are introduced at the various levels.

The status of the principal study groups supported at the pre-college level under the Course Content Improvement Program is summarized in the accompanying chart. It should be noted that this chart shows neither the time span required for the development of project materials nor the variety and detailed nature of the materials produced. The grade span shown for a particular project thus has no definite correspondence with the level of effort and support involved.

At the undergraduate level a corresponding variety of projects in each of the five categories listed earlier are supported under the Science Curriculum Improvement Program. No attempt will be made here to describe these in detail. However, mention should be made of the college commissions, which function at the undergraduate level as indicated in the second category above. At the present time, the following groups are receiving support: Committee on the Undergraduate Program in Mathematics, Advisory Council on College Chemistry, Commission on Undergraduate Education in the Biological Sciences, Commission on Engineering Education, Commission on College Geography, Council on Education in the Geological Sciences, Commission on College Physics, and Commission on Education in Agriculture and Natural Resources.

The NSF publication, *Science Course Improvement Projects* (NSF 64–8), includes reports of course content improvement projects supported up to July 1, 1964, with the exception of (1) some preliminary conferences and (2) projects under the Science Teaching Equipment Development Program which are described in a companion publication, *Science Course Improvements Projects 2, Science Teaching Equipment* (NSF 63–15). Each project description includes an address where further information can be obtained upon request. These booklets are now being revised and brought up-to-date and will be issued as a single publication (E66-P-20) in the near future.

Looking to the future from the present state of affairs, it seems clear that the explosive rate of increase of scientific knowledge makes it both more difficult and more important to continue to bring up-to-date the content of instructional curricula. Hence the Foundation sees curriculum reform as a continuing and increasingly important area of national concern, and one requiring the active participation of the best talent available. It is quite clear, however, that there are distinct limits to the speed with which reform can be implemented. The preparation of the necessary materials is an exceedingly difficult and exacting task and the number of individuals competent and available to perform this task at any one time is finite. Beyond that necessary to support such individuals, additional funds cannot be used with maximum effectiveness. Furthermore, it is useless to develop new materials for wide usage which are too far in advance of teachers' ability to handle them. Course content and teacher competence must go hand in hand. Lastly, the curriculum and its teachers must be able to mesh with the available time, space, and facilities of contemporary schools. In all these senses, curriculum reform must be governed by both need and feasibility.

The present conception of the Foundation's role for the future in course content activity can be analyzed in terms of long-range and short-range prospects.

Long-Range Prospect

The National Science Foundation has played a significant role in course content and curricular improvement, and regards these as among the most significant of all its activities. This role has been made possible by a happy concordance of circumstances: enabling legislation that gives latitude for pioneering new approaches to education in the sciences; the cooperation, support, and participation of the scientific and educational community; and the financial support of these programs by the Congress. Without any of these, the educational reform now going on throughout the nation in all subjects would have been much slower and quite possibly not have begun at all.

It is a fact, however, that the reform is under way and its support outside the Foundation is a growing likelihood. The extent to which the Foundation should be involved in this movement, say ten years hence, will depend upon a number of factors: progress achieved at any given time; the activities of other agencies, both public and private; and,

PRINCIPAL CURRICULUM STUDY GROUPS • PRE-COLLEGE EDUCATION IN SCIENCE

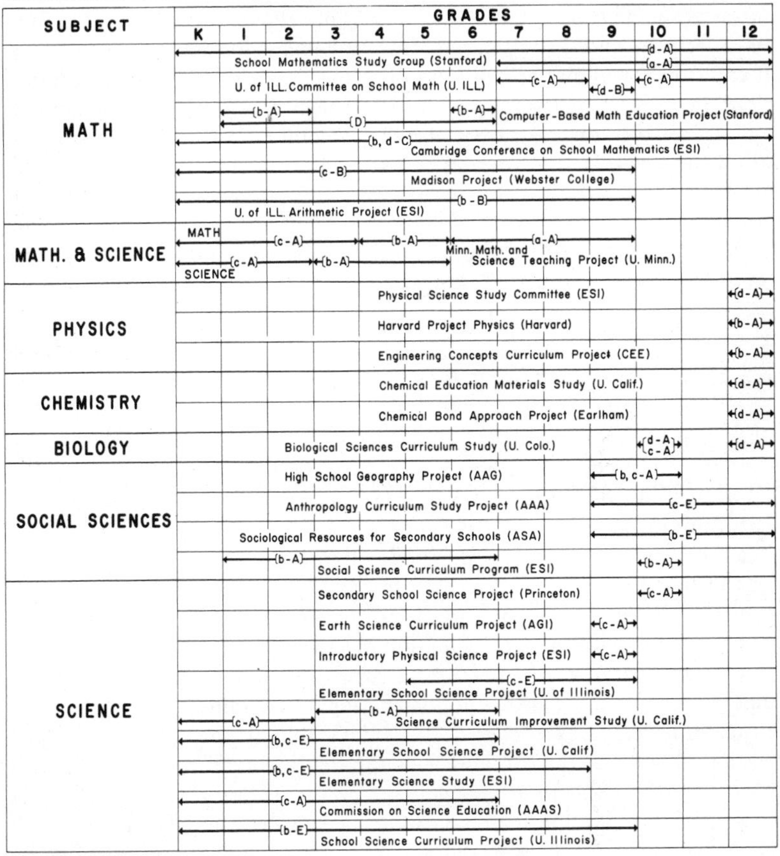

SUBJECT
GRADES
K 1 2 3 4 5 6 7 8 9 10 11 12
MATH
(d - A)
(a - A)
School Mathematics Study Group (Stanford)
U. of ILL. Committee on School Math (U. ILL.)
(c - A)
(d - B)
(c - A)
(b - A)
(b - A)
(D)
Computer-Based Math Education Project (Stanford)
(b, d - C)
Cambridge Conference on School Mathematics (ESI)
(c - B)
Madison Project (Webster College)
(b - B)
U. of ILL. Arithmetic Project (ESI)
MATH. & SCIENCE
MATH
SCIENCE
(c - A)
(b - A)
(a - A)
Minn. Math. and Science Teaching Project (U. Minn.)
PHYSICS
Physical Science Study Committee (ESI)
(d - A)
Harvard Project Physics (Harvard)
(b - A)
Engineering Concepts Curriculum Project (CEE)
(b - A)
CHEMISTRY
Chemical Education Materials Study (U. Calif.)
(d - A)
Chemical Bond Approach Project (Earlham)
(d - A)
BIOLOGY
Biological Sciences Curriculum Study (U. Colo.)
(d - A)
(c - A)
(d - A)
SOCIAL SCIENCES
High School Geography Project (AAG)
(b, c - A)
Anthropology Curriculum Study Project (AAA)
(c - E)
Sociological Resources for Secondary Schools (ASA)
(b - E)
(b - A)
Social Science Curriculum Program (ESI)
(b - A)
SCIENCE
Secondary School Science Project (Princeton)
(c - A)
Earth Science Curriculum Project (AGI)
(c - A)
Introductory Physical Science Project (ESI)
(c - A)
(c - E)
Elementary School Science Project (U. of Illinois)
(c - A)
(b - A)
Science Curriculum Improvement Study (U. Calif.)
(b, c - E)
Elementary School Science Project (U. Calif)
(b, c - E)
Elementary Science Study (ESI)
(c - A)
Commission on Science Education (AAAS)
(b - E)
School Science Curriculum Project (U. Illinois)

KEY TO SYMBOLS:

a. Planned or projected
b. Preliminary version
c. Extended trial version
d. Released for general use
A. Text and Supplementary Materials
B. Teacher Training Films and Course Materials
C. Guidelines for Curriculum & Course Development
D. Research in Learning
E. Unsequenced Units and Source Materials

CEE Commission on Engineering Education
ESI Educational Services Incorporated
AAG American Association of Geographers
AAA American Anthropological Association
ASA American Sociological Association
AGI American Geological Institute
AAAS American Association for the Advancement of Science

viewed against that background, the ability of the Foundation to assist the development of new and imaginative ideas.

In the field of education the Foundation's preferred role is furthering innovation. The usefulness of Foundation activities in course content improvement over a long period of time depends on the extent to which it can foster imaginative thinking in creative programs. The Foundation does not envisage its role to be that of the Government's exclusive agency for the administration of large-scale, long-term, massive support of educational activity, even in the sciences.

Short-Range Prospect

For the next few years Foundation plans for conducting its course content activity follow these lines:

1. Support of course content improvement will be directed in such a way as to bring to a successful conclusion a variety of projects at each level of education and in all the major scientific disciplines. Support of large new projects will be undertaken only if they are of high quality and fit into an over-all pattern of disciplines and levels of education. The rate at which additional projects will be taken on depends in part on availability of funds but also, more importantly, on the quality and nature of projects proposed for support.
2. Among the projects supported will be some based on conventional and also some based on unconventional approaches. Given the opportunity, at least one of each kind will be supported at each level and, where appropriate, in each scientific discipline.
3. Excessively specialized or narrowly delimited materials that are inconsistent with a reasonable instructional program at a given level of education will be avoided. In elementary school, for instance, subject matter should be broad and general, while more narrowly defined topics may be appropriate for college level work.
4. The Foundation will continue to devote some funds to small experimental projects that place emphasis both on increasing understanding of how scientific subjects are learned and on materials for such learning. Such projects need not produce results that fit into typical curricular patterns, although it is hoped that the results will be useful and significant in future curriculum development.
5. Finally, the Foundation intends to utilize to the maximum its close relationships with the scientific and educational communities in order to detect and foster new and promising ideas. The Foundation will seek to support those judged to be the most significant and innovative.

22. A Rationale for the Teaching of Biology

W. C. Van Deventer

A. The High School Biology Problem

The present high school biology offering is an outgrowth of earlier course types which have formed a part of secondary education since the days of the earliest American high schools more than a century ago. The curriculum of these schools included courses in natural history, which, although they were taught from the viewpoint of nature study and natural philosophy, occupied much the same position in the curriculum as the high school biology course of today. These gave way to separate botany and zoology courses, influenced by the introduction of laboratory methods at the college level by Louis Agassiz and Asa Gray in the 1870's. Such high school courses emphasized taxonomy, dissection, morphology and, to a lesser extent, physiology. Finally, in the 1920's and later, integrated general biology courses were introduced, and replaced the older kinds.[1]

Little has been done, however, in the forty years since the introduction of general biology courses in high schools, to evaluate the offering or arrive at a workable definition of its function. At present, there are three general kinds of biology courses offered at the high school level: (1) the "types" course, utilizing mainly the taxonomic approach; (2) the "principles" course, which attempts to integrate biological materials around the functioning and behavior of living things, with

From W. C. Van Deventer, "A Rationale for the Teaching of Biology," *School Science and Mathematics,* February, 1960, 60: 113–121. W. C. Van Deventer is Professor of Biology at Western Michigan University, Kalamazoo. He has contributed more than sixty articles in science education and ecology to professional and scholarly journals, is a Past President of the National Association for Research in Science Teaching, and is Editor of the Michigan Science Teachers Bulletin. This article is reprinted by permission of *School Science and Mathematics,* George H. Mallinson, Editor.

[1] Rosen, Sidney, "The Origins of High School Biology," *School Science and Mathematics,* LIX (June 1959), 473–489.

emphasis on the physiology of cells, organs and organ systems; and (3) the "consumers" course, which involves an attempted organization on the basis of the needs of students, real or presumed.

The first two kinds are mainly watered-down versions of freshman college courses, perpetuated largely by the tendency of high school teachers to follow the easy road of teaching biological materials as they have learned them in their college courses. This is in turn the result of failure on the part of college curriculum-makers to recognize the needs of prospective high school teachers in terms of the needs of their future students. As a consequence, prospective teachers are placed in the same courses as premedical students and those planning on going into biological research. In many institutions which lack a well-developed general education program, various non-biological groups, such as English, history and economics majors, are placed in the same beginning biology course as are prospective teachers, premedics and research majors. The beginning biology course involving one of the first two listed approaches, or some combination of them, is presumed to be the answer for everybody, with little or no thought being given to the diverse needs of those taking it. It is this course, then, which is, consciously or otherwise, copied at the high school level.

The third listed approach, the "consumers" course, is an amorphous category not widely represented among college courses. It is supposed to "meet the needs" of high school students, especially the non-college-oriented and terminal ones. Perhaps the best that can be said for it is that it does show the result of thinking and original planning on the part of its instigators, and constitutes a serious attempt to get away from the unquestioned following of established patterns, regardless of the needs involved. It breaks down, however, in that there is a general lack of agreement as to what the needs of high school students are, and even as to how to determine them. The same may be said of "consumers" courses in the few cases where they have been tried at the general education college level.

Textbooks are generally written to fit one of the three listed kinds of courses, or a combination of two or even all three of them. Although each kind of course or textbook generally makes a bow toward one or both of the other kinds, such that it is difficult to find a course or book of "pure" type, the result is that there are widely differing bases for the presentation of high school biology. The situation is made more diverse by varying degrees of laboratory emphasis, depending usually on availability of equipment and room, and size of classes. A further reason for diversity lies in differences in extent and kind of teacher preparation, and the ability of the individual teacher to extend and repair his own background, utilize new techniques and materials, and devise new class experiences for his students.

The result of this wide variation is that it is not possible to find any dependable basis for judgment of students' knowledge and understanding at the beginning of a freshman college course in biology, following their completion of high school biology. Based upon thirty years' experience in the teaching of biology at the freshman-sophomore college level, the writer has come to the position of assuming *no* difference between freshman students who have had, and those who have not had high school biology, because, with rare exceptions, no difference can be detected after the first three weeks of the college course. Actually, those who have not had high school biology often rate higher at the end of the course than those who have had it. All of this is in the face of the fact that most high school biology courses are simply watered-down copies of college courses.

Mallinson, in a provocative article in *The American Biology Teacher,*[2] has pointed out that while two-thirds of all high school students in the United States take biology, in a typical group of forty students, only four will ever take another course in biology, and of these only one will go beyond the introductory college course. He expresses the opinion that the present typical course in high school biology serves adequately neither the terminal student nor the college entrance student. It is inadequately adapted to the needs of the former of these two groups, and has little carry-over value for the latter, in that it is taught at a grade level when their intelligence is still immature from the standpoint of the subject matter which is included in it. Furthermore, he raises the questions of (1) whether much attention is paid to the problem of the functions which the high school biology course is expected to fulfill, other than meeting a laboratory science requirement for graduation, and (2) whether, even if consideration is given to the matter of function, the course is actually organized and taught in such a way that this is recognizable.

B. A Re-Thinking of General Biology

In the light of the problem which has been stated, it might appear that the answer would lie in an attempt to attain uniformity of content and presentation for one or more courses in biology at the high school level. It has been proposed[3] that one biology course for all

[2] Mallinson, George G., "Biology — An Anomaly," *The American Biology Teacher,* XX (November 1958), 248–250.

[3] Mallinson, *op. cit.*

students be offered at the 9th grade level, and an additional elective course for advanced students be offered at the 12th grade level. Others have suggested separate courses for terminal and college-entrance students (a two-track system).

It is the belief of the writer, however, that regardless of the level at which biology is taught, uniformity of subject matter and presentation, even if it were possible in so broad a field, is not necessarily desirable. What is necessary, rather, is to develop a common basis for understanding in all students, whether they are college-entrance students or not. In order to do this we need to re-think what "general biology" is from the teaching standpoint, and particularly what *ideas* we want our students to come out with.

This is not a problem of the high school alone. It is a problem common to the teaching of biological materials at all levels K-14 (kindergarten through junior college). All biology taught K-14 is general biology. At elementary levels (early, middle and later) it is integrated into elementary science. At the junior high school level it begins to emerge as a segment of general science. At the senior high school level it emerges full-blown as "general biology." It retains this status through the junior college level.

At the senior college and graduate levels, biology takes the form of specialized "area" courses which constitute tools for advanced study, professional study and research. These include courses in taxonomy, physiology, anatomy, histology, embryology, ecology, genetics, parasitology, entomology and other specialized sub-disciplines. They may be further sub-divided into plant and animal branches, branches related to certain taxonomic groups within these major categories, and elementary and advanced levels.

The need is to find a common basis of understandings that can be developed in all students (including high school), who are taught under the general biology approach. If this can be done, they will carry these understandings into out-of-school living, if they are terminal students, and/or into advanced, professional and graduate study, if they are so bound, using them in any case as a basis for integrating their later experiences.

Such common understandings must not be dependent on the selection of particular areas of subject matter, or particular methods of presentation. They must be in the form of *ideas* common to all biological subject matter by virtue of its biological nature. They must therefore be approachable and teachable through the medium of *any* reasonably large selection of biological subject matter, or in terms of any biological area. Furthermore, they must be approachable and teachable at *any* educational level where general biological material is used.

It may appear that the location of such ideas is too large an order; but if such is true, then perhaps it is time that we raised the question of whether there is such a thing as "general biology," or even whether biology is a unified science at all, rather than a family of related sciences. The writer believes that it is possible to locate such pervading ideas, and that in order to find them we have only to delve deeply enough into life science and ask ourselves what its unique characteristics are.[4]

What may constitute the basis for these common understandings which we can legitimately hope that all "general biology" students, at whatever level, will attain? One idea is primary: *Life is a matter of dynamic interrelationships, ever changing, never standing still, understandable only in terms of its totality as a constantly shifting picture.* This is the unique characteristic of life, and of biology as the science of life. It is that which differentiates life science clearly and unequivocally from its sister sciences.

This idea furnishes an avenue through which all major biological areas can be successfully approached for teaching. This is simply another way of saying that it is a unifying fabric which runs through all of them, or that it constitutes a major portion of the basis on which they rest. The following are brief outlines of four such areas which are commonly taught in general biology courses, indicating the subtopics under each where the pervading idea of dynamic interrelationships applies:

1. The balance of nature (including)
   a. Energy and chemical relationships within any plant-animal community
   b. Relationship of all plant-animal communities to changing physical environmental factors
   c. Operation of environmental gradients, thresholds and the law of the minimum
   d. Plant-animal-human relationships in the total world of life
2. Heredity (including)
   a. The necessary interaction of heredity and environment in the expression of any particular trait
   b. The gene as a "place where" rather than a "thing which" on a macromolecule of desoxyribonucleic acid (DNA)

[4] Van Deventer, W. C., "The Use of Subject Matter Principles and Generalizations in Teaching," *School Science and Mathematics,* LVI (June 1956), 466–474.

   c. The gene as the initiator of a chain of enzyme actions culminating in a specific characteristic or process — the total organism as a "bundle of enzymes" at work
   d. The probable origin of life through biochemical evolution, and the development of the present autotroph-heterotroph balance in the world of life through accumulation of balanced "loss mutations."
3. Evolution (including)
   a. Variation and natural selection within any taxonomic group
   b. The continuous adjustment of all living things to the demands of a changing environment
   c. The interaction of challenge and response in the history of evolutionary development of any group
   d. The relationship of the evolution of man to the attainment of the upright posture, the freeing of the hands for use as grasping organs, and the development and use of tools.
4. The human body in health and disease (including)
   a. The body as a community of cells, tissues and organs
   b. Functional and parasitic diseases as responses to unbalances and invasions of the body community
   c. The relationship of faulty body functioning and inadequate body defenses to lethal and partial lethal genes, and consequently imperfect enzyme chains.
   d. Study of the body in terms of interrelated functional areas, rather than traditional organ systems.

This concept of dynamic interrelationships, while well-adapted to laboratory treatment, does not depend heavily on laboratory experience for its comprehension. A few well-planned and carefully timed laboratory or field experiences, preferably of the open-ended sort — possibly one such broad experience to each unit — are sufficient. The collection of laboratory experiences which has been prepared by the project sponsored jointly by the National Academy of Sciences and the National Research Council, centering at Michigan State University, is an excellent source for some of these.[5] Others might consist of modifications or adaptations of traditional laboratory experiences, or those which might be originated by any imaginative teacher to take advantage of local opportunities and conditions.[6]

[5] Lawson, Chester A., editor, *Laboratory and Field Studies in Biology: A Sourcebook for Secondary Schools,* Committee on Educational Policies, Division of Biology and Agriculture, National Academy of Sciences-National Research Council, Washington, D.C., 1957.

[6] Van Deventer, W. C. and Staff, *Laboratory Experiences in Biological Science,* Western Michigan University, 1959.

Extensive equipment is not necessary for teaching a course of this type. What is necessary is the kind of thinking on the part of both teacher and students which is involved in problem-solving operations. Elaborate audio-visual and other classroom equipment may sometimes constitute an actual barrier to this kind of thinking, through the temptation which it presents to both teacher and students to rely on ready-made, cut-and-dried presentation of subject matter. While the kind of thinking desired is that which is involved in the better types of laboratory and field experiences, it is by no means limited to them. It can take place equally well in connection with discussions and library investigations.[7] The student must be trained to think, to analyze and synthesize, independently. This is the opposite of rote learning. It involves the use of facts, but as tools to arrive at understandings, rather than as ends in themselves.

The concept of dynamic interrelationships can be taught at any educational level, and by utilizing any, or almost any biological materials. It is only necessary to select materials which are meaningful to pupils (i.e., within their range of comprehension), and to use vocabulary which they either understand or can be led to understand. Schultz[8] demonstrated the effectiveness of this approach in teaching 2nd and 6th grade pupils, utilizing a unit involving the study of an aquatic plant-animal community.

The biological materials utilized by different teachers in corresponding courses at the same level (e.g., high school biology courses) do not necessarily need to be the same, or to be taught in the same way. All that is necessary is that the basic idea be "gotten across" in terms of whatever materials and methods are used. The idea of dynamic interrelationships is a kind of "least common denominator" for all biology.

It also makes no difference if the same materials (e.g., the biology of insects, change of leaf coloration in the fall, man in space, or what happens to food in the human digestive tract) are used at different levels (i.e., repeated) in the pupil's experience. The idea of dynamic interrelationships is broad enough and deep enough that it bears repetition in terms of the same materials in a progressively sophisticated form at advancing levels.

Finally, while this approach to biology makes constant use of concepts native to the fields of physics and chemistry (e.g., the atomic-molecular theory of matter, the kinetic theory of heat, chemical bonds,

[7] Van Deventer, W. C., "Laboratory Teaching in College Basic Science Courses," *Science Education*, XXXVII (April 1953), 159–172.

[8] Schultz, Ida Beth, *A Way of Developing Children's Understanding of Ecology*. (Unpublished doctoral dissertation), University of Florida, 1955 (microfilm).

catalytic and enzyme action), there are none of these that cannot be explained in simple and readily understandable terms for purposes of biological understanding. Physical and chemical knowledge in the form of prior courses taken is not a necessary prerequisite for a biology course of this type.

While physical and chemical tools and mathematical analyses must necessarily play an increasing role in certain avenues of biological research, the value of holistic, organismal and other typically biological approaches and methods of analysis must not be lost sight of, particularly at the general education level. Unless these broad understandings are built into the foundation of the future teacher, professional man or research worker, as well as the general citizen, a proper balancing and evaluation of the results of combined chemo-physico-biological research is impossible. Without this he "cannot see the forest for the trees."

C. Where Do We Go from Here?

Unless biology teachers of all levels get together and train themselves and their students of all ages in the basic understandings of biology and the nature of life phenomena, the results may well be tragic. Present emphasis on the teaching of science at all levels is principally in the area of the physical sciences. This is good and necessary, because this area had been badly neglected. If the time were ever to come, however, when the only approach to biology at the general level lay through the physical sciences, we would lose heavily in an understanding of the unique characteristics of the world of life and of ourselves as living organisms. To prevent this, as well as to increase the efficiency of our teaching and improve its end-product, we need a re-vamping of our approach to general biology.

Physical scientists have dealt with a similar problem in connection with presenting physics at the high school level. Their problem was occasioned by the fact that modern developments in physics have outrun the content and methodology of the traditional high school physics course. This is a related but somewhat less complicated situation than that which we have outlined for biology. The Physical Science Study Committee, which operated at Massachusetts Institute of Technology, utilized the concepts involved in wave motion as an approach to the teaching of high school physics.[9] The laboratory equip-

[9] Little, Elbert P., Friedman, Francis L., Zacharias, Jerrold R., and Finlay, Gilbert, "The Physical Science Study," *The Science Teacher,* XXIV (November 1957), 316–330.

ment which they suggest can be largely locally-made or easily obtained, and is not particularly complex.

The chemists are conducting a similar study, attempting to integrate beginning chemistry teaching around the ideas involved in an understanding of the electro-chemical bond. Groups of mathematicians at the University of Illinois, University of Maryland and Yale University are re-studying mathematics curricula and re-building beginning mathematics courses around similar broad understandings. Some preliminary experimental work in the physical sciences and mathematics indicates that this teaching of broad concepts can be carried into the elementary levels with success.[10]

In the area of the biological sciences, a development is in progress which may prove equally helpful. The Biological Sciences Curriculum Study, under the directorship of Dr. Arnold B. Grobman of the University of Colorado, and under the sponsorship of the American Institute of Biological Sciences, financed by the National Science Foundation, is carrying on a study of offerings in the life sciences at all educational levels (elementary, secondary, college and professional) and is considering problems of coordination among them. This project is described in detail in the April, 1959, issue of the *A.I.B.S. Bulletin,* in an article by Dr. Grobman.[11]

As a part of this study "a special committee will attempt to answer the general question, what should a student graduating from high school know about the biological sciences? The committee will attempt to determine what knowledge a citizen should have who has completed twelve years in our public schools. In conjunction with these studies it will be necessary to investigate the proper sequential arrangement of the new biology in the high school in line with other sciences and mathematics. It will also be an important concern to determine whether additional courses, perhaps at the twelfth grade, would be desirable for superior students, college preparatory students and other special categories of students."[12]

From this study could come the basis for a solution to our problem. It should be remembered, however, that no one person's or one com-

[10] Atkin, J. Myron, *An Analysis of the Development of Elementary School Children in Certain Selected Aspects of Problem-Solving Ability* (Unpublished doctoral dissertation), New York University, 1956.

[11] Grobman, Arnold B., "The Biological Sciences Curriculum Study," *A.I.B.S. Bulletin,* IX (April 1959), 21–23.

[12] Grobman, *op. cit.*

mittee's answer can be another person's panacea. Any program, no matter how well-planned, can degenerate into a deadly and monotonous repetition of factual learnings in the classroom and even in the laboratory. The best-conceived program will break down unless the individual teacher is trained to be alive and concerned with the use of facts as tools for getting at understandings, which in turn become the inspiration for the acquisition of additional facts to serve as tools to attain further understandings. Russian science education, so frequently alluded to in this country by critics of our own science teaching, has been criticized recently by a Russian educational writer for exactly this kind of shortcoming.[13]

It is necessary to point out, furthermore, that there is a danger inherent in any over-all biology program which aspires to general or uniform applicability. The peculiar genius of biology as a teaching discipline lies partly in its diversity. This makes for adaptability to the special needs of individuals and groups, and to local teaching situations which frequently offer unique and valuable opportunities for learning important principles and relationships. Too much uniformity is deadening. The behavior of a falling object in a physics laboratory, or of a particular acid and base when combined in a chemistry laboratory is the same no matter where you observe it, but the behavior of a crayfish of a particular species in a stream in Illinois may differ from that of one of the same species in a stream in Michigan, because of the operation of environmental factors, few if any of which we can control, many of which we do not completely understand, and some of which we probably are not even aware of.[14]

It would apparently be better in planning a biology program, possibly in contrast to one in the physical sciences, to agree upon a limited number of basic understandings, and then to allow for the working out of the specifics of subject matter and methodology in any particular course at any particular level within the broad framework thus provided. In the 13th and 14th grade biology course of which the writer is chairman, the staff has agreed upon a set of broad principles and ideas to be included, but within this framework each teacher is free in a very large measure to vary subject matter and method. This makes for a maximum of originality and initiative on the part of the individual teacher, and allows for a maximum of adaptability of the course to the needs of

[13] Evronin, G. P. (translated by Ivan D. London), "On the State of Physics Teaching in the Russian Republic," *Science Education,* XLIII (April 1959), 270–274.

[14] Van Deventer, W. C., "Studies on the Biology of the Crayfish, *Cambarus propinquus* Girard," *Illinois Biological Monographs,* XXXIV (August 13, 1937), No. 100.

particular groups of students.[15] A similar curricular philosophy could be made to apply to all teaching of biological materials at all levels.

[15] Van Deventer, W. C. and Staff, *Basic Ideas, Generalizations and Subject Matter Principles Included in the Biological Science Course,* Western Michigan University, 1959.

23. BSCS Biology

William J. Brett

In 1959 the American Institute of Biological Sciences set up the Biological Sciences Curriculum Study (BSCS) under the chairmanship of Dr. Bentley Glass, Professor of Biology at Johns Hopkins University. A steering committee consisting of university and college research workers and teachers, high school biology teachers, administrators, and writers of textbooks was formed to determine the major policies. These persons recognized the fact that inadequacies may exist in our biology training program at all levels but decided that the high school level is a more critical level than the elementary or college. The basis for this decision lies in the reasoning that students receive further science training after their elementary training but many individuals receive no further formal training after high school. Those high school students going on to college often determine their college areas on the basis of high school courses which often stifle rather than create interest. For

From William J. Brett, "BSCS Biology," *The Teachers College Journal,* March, 1962, 33: 116–118, 138–139. William J. Brett is Professor and Chairman, Department of Life Sciences, Indiana State University, Terre Haute. Reprinted by permission of Professor Brett and *The Teachers College Journal.*

these reasons, the steering committee decided to concentrate their efforts on the high school biology program. At what grade level the BSCS course should be aimed was a question of immediate concern. Most teachers of biology agree that an understanding of physics and chemistry is necessary for an understanding of modern biology, but to require these courses as prerequisites would place biology in the senior year of high school and deny biology to the majority of high school students. For this reason it was agreed that biology should remain at the tenth grade level where it is presently taught in most schools. In many of the schools in Indiana, biology is taught at the ninth grade level and recently some schools have moved it to the eighth grade level. Dr. Arnold Grobman, director of the BSCS, points out some of the differences in a high school biology course as compared to a chemistry or physics course:

> In America, today, eight out of every ten high school sophomores take biology; these students run the gamut in intelligence, aptitude and interest. Only three in ten high school students take chemistry and two in ten take physics — and these are generally the college preparatory students at the higher ability levels. Thus, tenth grade biology has a broad range of students where high school chemistry and physics have relatively homogeneous groups of students. Furthermore, of the students taking tenth grade biology, about half never again take another science course — they take no more school science and they do not want to go on to college. Tenth grade biology is their last formal contact with science in the school system. This gives high school biology the added responsibility of interpreting our scientific society to these students and of preparing them for living in a civilization that will be characterized by revolutionary scientific changes throughout their lives.[1]

In the summer of 1960 a writing conference was held at the University of Colorado and preliminary experimental editions of three versions of BSCS high school biology were prepared. These preliminary editions were tested by 105 teachers with 14,000 students during the 1960–61 school year. These teachers were carefully selected on the basis of their training and many attended a BSCS briefing session. Continuous evaluation of these courses during the 1960–61 academic year was obtained by teacher and student reports, visits of steering committee members and results of newly developed tests.

[1] Grobman, Arnold B., "The BSCS: A Challenge to the Colleges," (*AIBS Bulletin*, Dec., 1961. Vol. XI, No. 6, pp. 17–20), p. 17.

In the summer of 1961, a second writing conference, utilizing the previous year's evaluations, prepared revised editions which are now being tested by over 500 teachers and 50,000 students in schools in 37 states and four foreign countries.

The three versions are distinct courses each consisting of textbook, lab manual and teacher's guide. The three courses are called the Blue, Green and Yellow versions. In the traditional high school biology course, emphasis is placed on the tissue, organ and organismic level. The Green version places emphasis on the community and world biome level; the Yellow version places major emphasis on the cellular level; and the Blue version concentrates on the molecular and cellular level. In other words the BSCS courses attempt to deal with broad biological concepts whereas standard courses deal largely with individual and often unconnected facts. The time is long since past when it was possible to teach all the biological facts or even the more significant ones in a single course or even in a series of courses. At the present time biological data is being doubled every ten years and this rate will probably increase in the future: and yet many high school biology courses consist largely of fact memorization.

Although the three versions differ in the level at which they place their emphasis, certain basic concepts are stressed in all. Dr. Grobman lists these basic concepts under nine headings.

1) change of living things through time — evolution
2) diversity of type and unit of pattern of living things
3) genetic continuity of life
4) complementarity of organism and environment
5) the biological roots of behavior
6) complementarity of structure and function
7) regulation and homeostasis: the maintenance of life in the face of change
8) science as inquiry
9) the intellectual history of biological concepts[2]

All three versions place emphasis on laboratory work. Teachers using the BSCS courses report spending twice as much time in lab as they previously had. And one must bear in mind that these teachers participating in the testing of these courses can hardly be called the average high school biology teacher.

[2] *Ibid.*, p. 18.

Most teachers of science include the learning of the "scientific method of thinking" as one of the main objectives of any science course. Yet too seldom do we provide opportunity for the type of experience leading to this acquisition. To observe, record, hypothesize and test — these are the essentials of the scientific method and they are most easily pursued under laboratory conditions, but even here we have often stereotyped the lab exercise so that it becomes a technique learning process rather than an experimental procedure. It is easier to "dry lab" than perform the experiments; in fact one is surer of success by doing so. Dr. Glass in answering how the BSCS program differs from past efforts to improve the secondary school science curricula states:

> This may well be the first time that education in the natural sciences, at least in the elementary school, has placed the acquisition of scientific knowledge below the value of understanding the nature of scientific inquiry and of the scientific enterprise in which modern man is engaged. If we are successful, students of the new biology should acquire not only an intellectual and esthetic appreciation for the complexities of living things and their interrelationships in nature, but also for the ways in which new knowledge is gained and tested, old errors eliminated, and an ever closer approximation to truth attained.[3]

Another innovation by BSCS has been the preparation and issuance of a volume of one hundred research prospectuses of unsolved biological problems suitable for gifted high school students. These research problems were obtained from biologists throughout the country. This is an effort to place the high school student in actual contact with the frontiers of scientific knowledge. This is not busy work, or make-believe problems, but true scientific investigation. The student must devise means, test results, and perhaps the most satisfying facet, become a contributing scientist. The Science Fairs have been very successful in achieving these same results on a more limited scope. For as the foreword of the BSCS lab manual put it:

> No matter how much you learn about the facts of science, you will never quite understand what makes science the force it is in human history, or the scientists the sorts of people they are, until you have shared with them such an experience. The laboratory and the field are the scientists' workshops. Much reading and dis-

[3] Glass, Bentley. "A New High School Biology Program," (*American Scientist*, Dec., 1961. Vol. 49, No. 4, pp. 524–531), pp. 530–531.

cussion are necessary in scientific work, but it is in the laboratory and field that hypotheses are tested.

There should be little disagreement upon the desirability of the goals or objectives of the BSCS, but one immediately wonders if the courses as they are now designed achieve these goals. The BSCS has set up an evaluation committee with the sole purpose of determining this. During the 1960–61 year four tests were administered to all BSCS students irrespective of the version. It might be well to mention at this time, that all BSCS students were administered the School and College Ability Test early in the school year and students of all three versions scored somewhat higher than the national average. The problem of evaluating course materials using new testing instruments is at best somewhat hazardous and therefore only broad generalizations were attempted. These generalizations are: (1) Each version of the course is indeed teachable to the "typical" high school biology student and (2) in certain instances, test results were unsatisfactory. The unsatisfactory test results may have been due to defective test questions, inadequacies in the course materials or unsatisfactory teaching. A much more elaborate testing program is being administered during the 1961–62 academic year. The BSCS program was conducted mainly at the tenth grade level although there were some ninth grade classes involved. The 1961–62 testing program will make a comparison between the ninth and tenth graders; the 1960–61 testing was not evaluated on this basis therefore we may find that the courses are not as suitable for younger students.

With this as a brief description of the BSCS goals and some of the methods for achievement of these goals, let's consider the question of whether these goals are not already being achieved in our high schools. In other words, are the BSCS courses desirable or necessary? One has but to walk into the biology room of some of our schools to realize that true scientific investigation is going on outside the auspices of BSCS. I might cite one of our local schools — Garfield — as a prime example and there are certainly many others. But even the most optimistic but informed individual would be forced to admit that these schools are in the minority. For the most part the teaching of biology consists of a verbal force feeding, the results of which are tested by a factual regurgitation each Friday. Regurgitation is the proper word for as anyone familiar with nutrition knows, this usually precludes any digestion of material and certainly any assimilation or use of the material. The teacher often stands before the class asking questions directly from the textbook and the students obediently find the answer in the text and read it back to him. The class at its worst is an exercise in page turning and sight reading and at its best a parrot like memorization of facts. In many schools, biology classes are never exposed to laboratory work, and in many others the laboratory work consists solely of the drawing and labelling of specimens and structures. Neither student nor instructor finds science even interesting, never mind exciting, and little wonder for this is not science. My answer to the question "Are the BSCS courses desirable or necessary?" is a definite and most emphatic YES!

Certainly the objectives in the training of biology students can be accomplished outside the BSCS courses and, as was mentioned, are being accomplished in some schools, but the BSCS courses will ease the way by serving as a guide. I think that we should all realize that there are many changes required if we desire the brand of science proposed by BSCS. An attempt will be made in the remainder of this article to list some of these changes and how they might be accomplished. Like most problems in education it is difficult if not impossible to say what must occur first; therefore, there will be no attempt made to present these changes in any sequence.

An important factor is the role school administrators must play in any change that is to be initiated. The administrators must recognize the necessity for lab time and lab facilities. This is going to involve certain budgetary considerations. In the BSCS Newsletter #9, observations on laboratory facilities and equipment for BSCS high school biology were presented. They suggest a budget of $500 per year per biology teacher for perishable items which is far in excess of most budgets for the entire biology division in many of our high schools. But the recognition of the importance of laboratory work involves more than providing time and facilities; it has to be evidenced in the credit we give students and teachers for lab work. Even at the college level it is a common practice to consider two hours or even three hours of lab work to be the equivalent of only one hour of lecture both to teaching and student load. The philosophy seems to be that not much is accomplished in lab. This idea, which may be justifiable, must be corrected if labs are to be given their due importance by teacher and student alike.

Regardless of space and equipment the major constituent in a successful biology course is the teacher himself. Many of our teachers in biology are teaching in their minor or restricted field. This almost always means that they have had few if any courses in biology where research or true problem solving was performed or required. They are therefore faced with the problem of teaching science and training scientists when they have had very little scientific training themselves. One does not become a scientist by simply learning facts. No one denies that one must master tools before one can do a job, but tool mastery (fact learning) is only the first step towards the more important step of problem solving. Here again the administrator could exert his influence for improvement by being more critical and demanding of individuals hired to teach high school biology. This is not to say that a major or comprehensive in biology assures the production of a true scientist. This suggests that changes may have to be made in our teacher training program at the college level, and this has been suggested by BSCS.

The BSCS high school biology courses offer a twofold challenge to the colleges and universities:

1) The new high school courses are at a higher level and of more significance than many of the beginning biology courses in college.
2) It is the job of the colleges and universities to prepare high school biology teachers to present this type of course.

It is estimated that about 20,000 freshmen, who have had BSCS courses and perhaps the newly developed physics and mathematics courses as well, will enter college in the fall of 1965. We may assume the numbers will increase in future years. This means the colleges have about three years to prepare suitable courses, courses which will not plateau the interest and development of these students but continue to nourish the curiosity and intellect and direct the activities and energies of these potential scholars. In the competitive academic world of today, it is a certainty that those institutions which do not prepare for these desirable students, will soon be bypassed by the students themselves.

The biology teaching methods courses in colleges should certainly make available to potential biology teachers the materials and philosophies of the BSCS program. Some of the efforts, such as National Science Foundation Science Institutes, Grants in Aid, etc., being made to better prepare our high school teachers are covered in other articles in this issue. It should be mentioned here that during the summer of 1961, 26 National Science Foundation summer institutes elected to emphasize BSCS high school biology in their institute work.

I feel that all high school biology teachers should be required to take some hours in special problems or original research. If this is not possible at the undergraduate level, it should certainly be incorporated into the Master's program. You often hear the statement made that research training doesn't make a better teacher. If we accept problem solving as one of the desirable qualities of a scientist, then experience in research becomes an essential part of any biology teacher's training. The true scientist learns to distinguish between evidence and authority; therefore the science teacher must emphasize to his students that a textbook is an aid to learning, not the end of learning. Both teacher and student must become cognizant of the fact that textbooks contain the results and evidences of research and observation and do not supersede them. This could be partially accomplished if teachers would stop using the textbook verbatim.

A third change, already suggested, is a revision of our textbooks and of our use of textbooks. Many of the high school biology textbooks are twenty years or more behind the times. Perhaps we should do away with standard texts and rely upon current publications as source materials. This might help get the idea across to students that no single source can answer all questions.

An important change must be brought about in the public's idea of what constitutes a scientist. Most laymen believe that an ability to recite scientific jargon is the best indicator of scientific accomplishment. They indirectly, and sometimes directly, place pressure upon administrators and teachers to produce this type of training in our biology classes. A student who can name all the bones of the human body or list 25 families of insects must be a good student and what's more must have a "real teacher." They forget that given enough time a parrot or mynah bird can be taught to memorize these same terms.

At the present time it is fair to say that teachers, administrators and parents need further preparation for BSCS courses in biology; the courses need further revision; methods of evaluating the results of these courses need refining; in fact the only ingredient ready for BSCS brand biology is the *high school student himself.*

24. Chemistry

Frank X. Sutman

I should like to preface my remarks by making the assumption that expectations from high school chemistry are not unique to chemistry alone, but in general, also describe the objectives of all the sciences taught at the high school level. For even the valid objective or expectation, to develop interest in chemistry as a profession, is no longer limited to the chemistry class but extends to all of the sciences including certain phases of high school mathematics. The reasons for making this assumption will be borne out in what follows.

To consider the problem of expectations from high school chemistry it will be helpful first to examine some projected data about our future citizenry, and also to consider some of the needs of this country during the next ten to twenty years or so. For the high school chemistry (or science) student will be among those making the contributions, and more important the decisions, during these crucial years. To be useful our expectations must be governed by these predictions. The President's Council on Vocational Education [1] tells us that even by 1970 only twenty per cent of the students graduating from high school will complete college. This figure will rise somewhat; but even by 1980 most people in this country will be non-college graduates. For that matter there still will be a large sample of the population during the 70's that will not have completed high school — perhaps one third of those who enter. And yet it is true that we will need more and more scientists. We will continue to need technicians: (those scientific workers who are *not* primarily concerned with abstractions or the basic conceptual

From Frank X. Sutman, "What Should We Expect From High School Chemistry?" *Science Education,* April, 1965, 49: 290–293. Frank X. Sutman is Professor of Science Education in the College of Education, Temple University, Philadelphia. He is co-author of a high school chemistry text, *Concepts in Chemistry*, and author of *A Career for You as a Science Teacher,* the National Science Teachers Association. This article was presented before the Akron, Ohio, Section of the American Chemical Society, September 28, 1964. Reprinted by permission of *Science Education.*

schemes of science). Instead these people are concerned with solving the day-to-day practical problems of the scientific industry. There will be increased demands also for the (scientific) chemical research oriented person who does deal in abstractions, and for the development of the scientist who looks for and finds applications of the laws of science. The greatest need in quantity tomorrow, as today, however will be for the "scientist" who has only slight use for the abstract. This is in some ways a very fortunate situation since, from experience, it seems safe to say that only a small percentage of adults (much less high school students) can think abstractly and relate what is to them intangible. What percentage of our high school population, for example, are able to mentally develop a model of the processes that occur when energy of different forms is added to a solid system of geometrically perfect design? Experience with Chemical Bond Approach Chemistry [2] which is in itself a model in abstractions, shows that relatively few students grasp the "significant" abstractions of chemistry today.

The research scientist, development scientist, and technician, together still make up only a very small per cent of our population: it amounts to about two per cent today. Perhaps by 1975 or 1980 this will be 3 or 4 per cent. But what of the other 96 per cent of our population? What expectations do we have for this tremendous majority of our citizenry? If we can use the last 50 years of educational experience as data, we can conclude that many of these people will never become a member of a chemistry class or laboratory; for in most high schools where chemistry is offered it is not a required subject. Presently about 28 per cent of the high school population elect to take chemistry. But nearly all high school students take, and will continue to take, some science course before they complete the twelfth grade.

Personal experience in several areas of the United States and in Puerto Rico has indicated to me that technical high schools do train adequately school age youngsters to begin work as technicians in the chemical and other related industries, but that the type of school, generally referred to as the comprehensive high school, does an *in*adequate job in training for technician work as well as for work in "pure" abstract science. Comprehensive high school graduates are better risks than drop-outs simply because they have shown they can complete a job once started. There is less chance that these high school graduates will leave the projects they start before they have completed them. However, even with this insurance, in most instances, industry must train or retrain in one of several ways the average comprehensive high school graduate who is to fill a technician's position.

There is a large group today that believe high school chemistry (and science teaching in general at all levels) should be concerned chiefly with the process of scientific inquiry. It is too early yet to be certain; but evidence so far indicates the introduction of the two new chemistry curricula (CHEMS and CBA) [2–3] seem *not* to be changing to any great extent the inadequacy mentioned above. The data so far collected shows only a few more high school students who have passed through the CHEMS program go on to college to become chemists or other scientists, (and at the same time since the introduction of PSSC [4] in physics, percentage-wise enrollments in high school physics have *not* increased, but instead continue to become significantly *less*). *There is little evidence then that emphasis on the processes of science with its abstractions is having the profound effects expected.* There are undoubtedly a number of reasons for this: including the inability of the teacher to handle a discovery approach, the lack of laboratory facilities and time, and the varied additional activities of the youngsters during their high school years. But of prime importance simply is the nature of the school age youngster: the *inability* of the vast majority of them to *think abstractly*. None of the new physical science courses have been willing to accept this difficulty.

As Cyril Bibby points out in a recent issue of the *Saturday Review* [5]: "Children already accept too many abstractions too docilely and mouth them too readily, in unconscious imitation of their elders" (an approach exactly opposite to what we would like to expect). "At every point, the important thing is that the abstractions be never allowed to achieve primacy over that from which they have been abstracted."

This same point of view is presented in the publication *The NSTA* (National Science Teachers Association) *Position on Curriculum* [6] in a somewhat different way. The publication states that "All aspects of the scientific enterprise must be a part of the science curriculum:

> "Descriptive science or natural history because it provides the basis for scientific inquiry and plays so prominent a role in the child's conventional experience.
>
> "Science proper, because of its intellectual challenge which should be a goal of scientific education (this area includes the development and utilization of abstract ideas); and technology, because it serves so well to illustrate the practical application of scientific principles, and because of its impact on modern society."

To carry this point one step further, consider a quotation from the preface to a "conventional" chemistry textbook written sixteen or so years ago. (By conventional I mean it follows generally the approach of chemistry texts that has been followed for the last thirty or forty years.) The book is aged by the position of the first reference to subatomic structure and electron theory appearing on page 202. The book *Chemistry for the New Age,* by Carleton and Carpenter [7], in its preface, states in part, "The high school chemistry course of today must serve a twofold purpose in order to keep pace with the demands of the new age in education and the new age in science. The first purpose is to contribute generously and effectively to the general education of all the students. The second purpose is to help lay the foundation needed by some of the students for later specialization in science. . . . There is reason to believe that 'scientific problem solving' must be analyzed into its elements. . . . Reading or hearing about scientific methods and attitudes is not enough, and rote memorization in this case defeats its own ends." This quotation could very well have been taken from the CHEM study or CBA literature. Similar examples are possible to find in chemistry textbooks of even earlier vintage.

High school textbook writers of a generation ago, as well as today, believed their approach, at least in part, to be of an inquiring nature. Yet neither the older curriculum materials nor the newer National Science Foundation sponsored curriculum improvement projects in chemistry are able to solve the difficulties related to teaching the scientific process with their concomitant abstractions.

Then what *do* we expect from high school chemistry? We must not expect too much of a working knowledge of chemistry and of the abstract chemical theories, especially if developed mathematically, as only relatively few able students can understand the abstract ideas resulting from chemical and scientific history. But, all who take high school chemistry (or any other science) can leave the course understanding the importance of scientific honesty and understanding the time, persistence, care, and neatness that is required today in pursuing scientific or chemical truths. We must be certain they have had the opportunity to understand the reasons *why* chemists, as well as scientists in general, continually question and doubt. The students should learn enough about chemistry as a science, and about chemists as scientists, to gain the understanding needed to prevent a controlling faction of what has been referred to as a "scientific elite" from arising in this country. If chemistry, as well as all sciences taught at the high school level, can accomplish these things, we will maintain not only the kind of scientific stability essential to the survival of our society but we should also assure qualitatively the pool of resources from which can come the quantity of chemists and other scientists who will be needed to maintain our society.

REFERENCES

1. Report of the President's Council on Vocational Education, 1963.
2. Chemical Bond Approach Chemistry (A National Science Foundation supported course content improvement project in chemistry. Texts and other materials are printed and distributed by McGraw-Hill Book Company, New York.)
3. Chemical Education Materials Study Chemistry (A National Science Foundation supported course content improvement project in chemistry. Texts and other materials are printed and distributed by W. H. Freeman and Company, San Francisco, California. Films are distributed by Modern Learning Aids.)
4. Physical Science Study Committee Physics. (A National Science Foundation supported course content improvement project in physics. Texts are printed by and distributed by D. C. Heath, Boston, Massachusetts, 1960.)
5. Bibby, C. "Science A Tool of Culture," *Saturday Review,* June 6, 1964, pp. 51–53.
6. *The NSTA Position on Curriculum:* a resolution growing out of concern, by members, of the status of science teaching in grades K-12.
7. Carleton, R. and Carpenter, F. *Chemistry for the New Age.* New York: J. B. Lippincott, 1949 (preface).

25. Physics

Oscar L. Brauer

The teaching of High School Science is in a crisis now. University research scientists at the top of the educational ladder are looking down at the teaching of science in the high schools and are concluding that everything is being done wrong. So now they are trying to correct

From Oscar L. Brauer, "Attempts to Improve High School Physics Education," *Science Education,* October, 1963, 47: 372–376. Oscar L. Brauer is Professor of Chemistry and Physics, Emeritus, San Jose State College, California. The author of textbooks in chemistry and organic chemistry for both high-school and college use, Professor Brauer has contributed several articles to professional journals evaluating recent trends in physics instruction and curriculum. Reprinted by permission of *Science Education.*

everything with a new approach. Only the new approach to physics teaching has been completed so only in this case do we know exactly what is being attempted.

In this article we are developing four points: (1) That 100 per cent of high school students need the subject matter of physics. (2) That at the latest report, we have been reaching only 5 per cent of the students. (3) That the text book embodying the new approach omits half of the needed subject matter of physics. (4) That after the "tumult and the shouting dies," the new text, being too long and extremely hard, will frighten away a large part of the 5 per cent of the students, who now have courage enough to take the subject.

First, who needs high school physics? From July 28–August 4, 1960, one hundred delegates from 29 nations met in the Unesco House in Paris to consider the teaching of physics to pre-college students[1]. We quote from the committee's report.[2]

"Our own discussions have been upon our strong belief that physics, the most exact and fundamental of the sciences, is a vital part of modern culture, and, as such, a necessary element in the education of all children.

"So far as this is educationally feasible, our concern is with *every* child. The needs of those children who will not specialize later in science must therefore be preeminent, since these children are the overwhelming majority.

"The purpose of school education is to prepare children for the adult world in which they live. The principal years of school education should be devoted to this aim of acquiring broad understanding; the preparations of specialists should be regarded at this stage as a secondary purpose.

"Children who leave school at the age of sixteen should not be automatically restricted only to a partial course devised with the needs of a specialist in mind."

The same point of view is expressed by two educational specialists in our government. Kenneth E. Brown, Specialist for Mathematics, and Ellsworth S. Obourn, Specialist for Science, in the United States Department of Health, Education, and Welfare have the following to say.[3]

"On still another front, the impact of science and technology has a -nstantly increasing influence on the lives of average citizens who will ...ome scientists or mathematicians. They will, however, need to ... increasingly complex concepts in order to read intelligently ...ss and the periodicals, which constantly allude to new ... applications of science. For another thing automation is affecting labor in most industries. Thus, it seems almost imperative that more and more young people should be studying science and mathematics in order to provide the level of scientific literacy to be demanded of an informed citizenry."

For some idea as to how many students are now taking physics, we turn to the same government report of 1958.[4]

A record of the percentage of students taking physics in the last four grades of high school has been kept from 1890 to 1958. In 1890, 22.8 per cent of all high school students studied physics. The number increased slightly until 1895 then steadily declined to 4.4 per cent in 1956 and then went up to 5 per cent in 1958. Chemistry started 10.1 per cent in 1890 and decreased steadily to 7.3 per cent in 1954 and rose to 8.9 per cent in 1958. Biology started in 1910 at 1.1 per cent and has increased steadily to 21.3 per cent in 1958. General Science started in 1922 with 18.3 per cent, then dropped in the next few years to 17.5 per cent and gradually rose to 21.2 per cent in 1958.

The Paris Convention advocated the study of physics by *all* students, and the report by the Government Educational specialists pointed out that all citizens need this knowledge. How close are we coming to this goal? The statistically supported 5 per cent is a long ways from the desired 100 per cent. Starting from 22.8 per cent in 1890 and shrinking to 5 per cent in 1958 shows that we are headed in the wrong direction. Any change in our approach to the subject must be one that will get more into physics. Either we must prescribe the subject to more students or we must teach it in such a way as to attract more students.

On the other hand, what profit would there be in forcing more students into physics and then neglecting to teach the parts of the subject that they most need. This is the predicament of the PSSC text. Now let us go back to the purpose of a high school physics course. Is it not to enable the student to understand the complex civilization in which he finds himself? Suppose we review some of the things conventional physics teaches but which the PSSC text omits, and see if conventional physics doesn't come nearer the goal than the PSSC course.

Let us begin with sound, which is left out entirely. The cause of sound, how sound travels, sound waves, sound obeys the inverse square law, reflection of sound, interference, architectural acoustics, resonators, sympathetic vibrations, how complex sounds are analyzed, measuring speed of sound, measuring wave lengths, variation of speed of sound in air, speed of sound in other substances, the ear, music and scales, recording voice, talking pictures, laws of strings, laws of open and closed pipes, Doppler's Principle, and the phonograph.

Which is more a part of the adult world, sound or the geocentr confusion of early astronomy? Which is more important to students in general. Dr. William W. Cooley of Harvard says:[5]

"We won't get anywhere until we begin to get more specific in our critiques."

This we are now attempting to do. If we are to raise our boys up in a practical world to deal with cars, boats, etc. we need to teach them the elementary practical things of mechanics such as: The principle of moments, principle of work, torque, mechanical advantage, wheel and axle, geared wheels, inclined plane, balancing effort, working effort, levers, law of parallel forces, pulleys, definition of inertia, dyne, poundal, slug, center of gravity, kinds of equilibrium, nature of sliding and rolling friction, law of friction, axiom of friction, efficiency, rotational inertia, angular momentum, gyroscope, gyroscopic principle, uses of gyroscope, bridge and roof trusses, vectors applied to kite, airplane and sail boat, tensile strength, and factor of safety. These topics are all omitted from the PSSC text.

The young people need some understanding of the physics of liquids such as capalarity, surface tension, homogenized milk, flotation of minerals, osmosis, viscosity, hydraulic lift, hydraulic press, methods of getting specific gravity, Archimedes' Principle, density and compressibility of liquids, and hydrometers. Believe it or not, these subjects are not directly discussed in the PSSC text.

A student to be well prepared for the vocations, avocations and hobbies that he may choose should know something about the properties of matter such as rigidity, hardness, ductility, malleability, cohesion and adhesion. A certain amount of knowledge of the physics of gases as applied to the following topics is needed by every student: structure and composition of the air, uses of air pressure, lift pump, centrifugal pump, anercid barometer, altimeter, force pump, turbine, siphon, air drill, air brakes, Bernoulli's Principle, cause of a baseball curving, principle of flying an airplane. Again these topics are all missing from the PSSC text.

Although the PSSC text takes up some of the theoretical phases of the study of heat, the practical side, that which is necessary to understand everyday life has been omitted from the PSSC text. These topics are household thermometers, changing Fahrenheit readings to centigrade and vice versa, the clinical thermometer, maximum and minimum thermometers, the hydrogen thermometer, coefficients of linear expan- ... coefficients of cubical expansion, compensated pendulums, com- ... balance wheel of the watch, metallic expansion thermometer, ... in the expansion of water and its significance, Charles ... onductor of heat, convection currents, causes of con- ... ntilation, laws of radiation, Stefan's Law, absorbers and radiators, radiometer, and hot house. These subjects are all omitted from the PSSC text.

Change of state is practically omitted from the PSSC text. There is hardly anything of more importance in understanding weather, and how nature so efficiently uses the unusual properties of water to help us live comfortably. The following omitted topics are needed by the student: Specific heat, how to measure it, melting point, heat of fusion, the importance of the high heat of fusion of water, melting point of ice as related to pressure, nature of boiling, boiling point, how pressure effects boiling points, nature of distillation, distillation at reduced pressures, how dissolved substances affect boiling point, measuring the heat of vaporization, cooling by evaporation, and heat from condensation.

All students need the fundamentals of meteorology. Very few of them will have a chance to get them later. The following topics are needed: Weather and climate, dependence of climate on latitude, the relationship of mountain ranges, trade winds, moisture holding capacity of air as dependent on temperature, relative and absolute humidity, dew point, wet and dry-bulb thermometers, climate and ocean currents, origin of cyclonic movements of air, rain in relation to cyclonic movements of air, tornadoes.

In the PSSC text the treatment of light is more like that in the conventional text than any other subject, yet there are several important topics missing: naming lenses, Galilean telescope, the meaning of magnification in the telescope and how it is expressed, the terrestrial telescope, prism binoculars, spherical aberration, distortion, astigmatism, curvature of the field.

The treatment of the spectra is spotted and not well done. The spectroscope is hardly more than hinted at. The subject of color is mostly implied. Nowhere is there any unified and complete discussion of it. The following are left out: explanation of natural colors, the additive primaries, the subtractive primaries, complementary colors, mixing pigments, color transparencies, color prints, spectral lines and star motion, photometers, polarized light, polarimeter, double refraction, nicol prism, and uses of polarized light.

In the subjects of magnetism and electricity the PSSC text has gone wild. It would require an entire article to point out the impracticability of this part of the text for high school students. In the first place the authors try to do away with magnetic poles, but in explaining electromagnetic induction they use magnetic poles without explanation or apology. The behavior of the compass needle on the surface of the earth is not made clear. The fields between like poles and unlike poles are not studied, nor the field about a bar magnet.

Other necessary conceptions omitted by the PSSC text are: magnetic substances, strength of a magnet, magnetic lines do not cross, making a magnet, methods of weakening a magnet, definition of unit pole, definition of gauss, theory of a magnet, magnetic permeability, location of the earth's poles, magnetic variation.

The PSSC text makes one exaggerated statement regarding the earth's magnetic field. It says that south of the Arctic Circle the compass needle points approximately geographic north. What would a surveyor in a district where the declination is 20° think of this statement? A bright student might wonder why the compass needle does not point north, north of the Arctic Circle. The reason for these omissions is that the PSSC authors do not admit the existence of such a thing as a magnetic pole.

In the part dealing with static electricity the PSSC text lists only about one third of what the ancients knew about electricity. Other things omitted are: charges tend to concentrate at points, lightning rod, induced charge equals the inducing charge, Faraday's icepail experiment, stat-coulomb, Leyden Jar, capacitor, capacitance, farad, Coulomb's Law in which $K = 1$. In the PSSC equation

$$k = 2.4 \times 10^{-18} \frac{\text{newton-m}^2}{(\text{elem. ch.})^2}.$$

Imagine the perplexity in a high school student's mind when he runs up against an expression like this. This is just a sample of the perplexities that the authors bring into electricity. Much of their discussion is so abstract and rambling that the average high school student never could get the point.

The subjects omitted from current electricity are: How the cell was discovered, simple cell, right hand rule for electromagnets, galvanometers, dry cell, polarization of cells, non-polarizing cells, storage cell, electric bell, ohms, measuring ohms, Wheatstone bridge, slidewire bridge, formula for resistances in parallel, internal resistance of cells, applying Ohm's law to cell circuits, electrolytes, Faraday's law of electrolysis, electrolysis of water, power transmission, why alternating currents, why 220,000 volts, why 3 power wires, danger from electricity, circuit breakers, arc-lights, incandescent lights, gas-filled globes, fluorescent lighting, induction coil. A.C. ammeters, DC generators, magneto, transformer, motor with brushes, induction motor, Counter EMF, three phase system.

In electrical communication the PSSC text omits: Morse telegraph, long distance telegraph, duplex telegraph, submarine telegraph, Bell and the telephone, wireless telegraphy, coherer, crystal detector, radio transmitters, triode vacuum tube, vacuum tube as a detector, vacuum tube as an amplifier, vacuum tube as an oscillator, carrier wave, multiple element tube, and television.

A story writer would be criticized if he had an anti-climax to his story, but what would you think if he quit his story before he reached the climax? Or if instead of going on to the climax he turned aside and bogged down in irrelevant matters?

This is just what the authors of the PSSC text did. From their position in the "ivory tower" they ignore the most significant events that have happened in the world since 1930. They totally ignore the most dramatic events in the earth's history, and the most portentous developments in physics. Anyone who thinks for a moment will realize that the atomic bomb is the peak of significance in all science, and that the future of mankind rests largely on how man uses the atomic and hydrogen bombs and the intercontinental ballistic missiles. These with artificial satellites largely dominate the news. The artificial satellites were casually mentioned in the text, but the rest of the significant things were not.

What we have given so far is enough to indicate that the PSSC text has omitted most of the physics that all students need to know to enable them to understand our civilization. We maintain that college physics is soon enough for specialization in the deep and abstract theories and conceptions of the subject.

Our point of view is that we ought to be studying how to dispel the mistaken view in the high schools that physics is necessarily harder than biology and chemistry. Now chemistry is getting nearly twice as many students as physics and biology four times as many. We hope that the new planners for chemistry and biology do not make the same mistake that the PSSC did; that is, making a text too hard for the average students; one designed for the specialist and not for the regular citizen.

In face of the fact that the PSSC text omits half of the subject matter covered in conventional texts, one could hardly believe that their text is the largest high school physics text ever published. It has 634 two-column pages of text material on a page-size 7.5 inches by 10 inches. There are 6 lines per inch and an average of 9 words per line in one column of the two-column page. Net of the illustrations there are 6788 running inches of text material. This makes 40,700 lines and 366,500 words. The illustrations are large so this text weighs nearly 4 pounds. Other texts are far below it in length. The physical size is not the main objection to the book. Many teachers who have tried to use the text say that they cannot get through it in one year. Some of them did not get to electricity and magnetism at all.

Why has physics attracted so few students compared to chemistry, biology, and general science? The reason is mostly because physics has the reputation of being harder than the other science subjects. Very often students choose subjects that the former students say are not too hard. If conventional texts keep away students because they are supposed to be hard what will be the effect of the PSSC text?

This text is much harder and more mathematical than the other texts. Its problems are comparable to the problems in a college text, and beyond the ability of 60 per cent of the students. Instead of correcting the present trouble with high school texts the new approach will aggravate the situation many times. It will greatly reduce the number of students who take the subject of physics at a time when the need for people trained in the subject is greater than ever before.

The new approach in physics has had a tremendous amount of publicity. This has caused many school administrators and teachers to rush into it without comprehending what they were getting into. When they really learn what it is like they will gradually drift back to the old course. Much of the damage done will be irreparable. The reputation of high school physics will then be so bad that only a few students can be persuaded to take it. The 5 per cent will show a perceptible decrease.

REFERENCES

1. Physics Education: An Account of the Paris Conference. J. W. Buchta, *Physics Today*. January, 1961, pp. 28–29.

2. The Teaching of Physics in Schools. (A report to the Paris Conference by a committee of six.) *Physics Today,* January, 1961, pp. 30–38.

3. Kenneth E. Brown and Ellsworth S. Obourn, Offerings and Enrollments in Science and Mathematics in Public High Schools. 1958. U. S. Department of Health, Education, and Welfare, p. 1.

4. *Ibid.,* p. 22.

5. William W. Cooley. Challenges to the Improvement of Science Education. *Science Education,* December, 1961, p. 387.

26. Earth Sciences

Gates Willard

It might be interesting to conduct a poll which would request a vote on the relative importance of two scientific fields such as geology and chemistry. The results would vary widely according to who was replying. Understandably, the views of chemists and geologists could be expected to be somewhat prejudiced! On the other hand, a geochemist might have a mental breakdown while trying to weigh separately two sciences which he imagines to be mutually supporting. After all, virtually every "chemical" studied by man comes from the crust of the earth. The science teacher might cast his vote according to the kinds of experiences he has had. If, for example, his college geology course was uninspiring, he may favor chemistry. Yet he surely is aware that the earth is important to him. Literally, where would he be without it? Eventually, the high degree of inconsistency in the replies would probably cause the poll to be abandoned.

Which is the more important part of an automobile engine — the carburetor or the fuel pump? The question is absurd; the absence or failure of any of a number of components would prevent the engine from running. The scientific enterprise includes many interrelated and interdependent areas. Is it any more logical to vote upon whether some fields of science are more important than others?

In this era of constantly changing school curriculum there is mounting pressure to include more and more science. The schools, however, can hope to include only morsels of the vast fields of science which are expanding far more rapidly than curriculum. Is there really justification for adding geology, astronomy, meteorology, and related sciences to an already overcrowded school program? Are any of these areas *important* enough to *replace* something that is presently included?

From Gates Willard, "The Importance of Earth Sciences in the Curriculum," *The Science Teacher,* April, 1961, 22, 25, 27, Vol. 28. Gates Willard is a science teacher at Manhasset Junior-Senior High School, Manhasset, New York. He is New York Area Coordinator, Secondary School Science Project, Princeton University. Reprinted by permission of the National Science Teachers Association.

The Curriculum Problem

How is school science subject matter chosen? Decisions are frequently made about what should and what should not be part of the program. Most persons involved in science curriculum planning are specialists in biology, chemistry, physics, or combinations of these. If there were no room in their professional training for courses in geology, astronomy, or meteorology, would these people attach importance to the teaching of earth science areas?

In many schools, the earth sciences have been treated to some extent as a minor portion of general science. However, there are a number of more sophisticated principles and concepts which might better be developed at a higher level. Why are high school students deprived of experience with these? The traditional high school science courses continue to be biology, chemistry, and physics. Usually there is a syllabus which effectively keeps the teacher on a straight but narrow path. Teachers often claim that there is more than enough material in their own subject areas. Why should they even consider introducing fields which are unfamiliar to them? Perhaps these teachers are unaware of the strong relationship of the earth sciences to biology, chemistry, and physics.

What the Earth Sciences Can Do for the School Science Program

The subject matter of any science course should not be considered apart from the methods by which it is taught. *Any* science may be presented in a descriptive, and unchallenging manner. The earth sciences can be dynamic and vitally interesting, and problem-solving techniques may be used at least as readily as in other science courses. Moreover, some unimaginative teachers have presented earth science as a glorified story about the landscape with a little practice in rock identification from a key. Perhaps some constellations were memorized, and students learned how to read a weather map. Many a teacher has been unable to transfer depth of understanding to his students because his own formal training in the earth sciences has been lacking or incomplete. This is not an uncommon malady among chemistry, physics, biology, and general science teachers, but because earth science is a relative newcomer to the schools, the problem is particularly acute.

Since there appears to be a lack of awareness of the potentialities in earth science teaching, the balance of this article is devoted to a discussion of what the earth sciences can do for the school science program. A few specific examples are listed below:

1. The earth sciences are environmental in scope. The student can

develop greater understandings and appreciations of his natural surroundings. Local field trips can yield important information about the geologic history of an area and man's use and misuse of his natural resources. Brief trips to the schoolyard itself can reveal weathering and erosion at work. Students can see that natural forces are changing the earth today as in the past.

2. Interest in the principles of light and optics can be aroused when they lead into a study of the heavens by means of a telescope. Students are intrigued to discover how radiant energy from outside the earth is practically the only source of information about the universe.

3. Depending upon the location of the school, certain ecological projects may be undertaken. For example, the relationship of ancient as well as modern marine life to the physical environment may be studied in fossils or marine forms found on the beach.

4. In an introduction to minerals and rocks, many important chemical concepts can be emphasized. Students learn the value of determining physical and chemical properties with accuracy in identifying minerals. By studying and growing crystals similar to those found in rocks, students can learn far more about the behavior of atoms, molecules, and ions than a mere discussion could impart.

5. Earth science is of strong current interest. The impact of the International Geophysical Year is only beginning to be felt, and it is not necessary to elaborate here upon the need for space education. Strontium 90 in the atmosphere, the oceans as mineral resources, conservation of natural substances, and searching for new material are topics of vital concern.

6. There are numerous opportunities for club and hobby activities. Students can build their own weather instruments to record data on atmospheric changes. Those who are ambitious may want to construct telescopes, grinding and polishing their own mirrors. Mineral, rock, and fossil collecting are hobbies that can be maintained throughout life, and an inexpensive lapidary unit provides a source of pleasure for those who want to polish stones and make their own jewelry. This activity is enjoyed equally by boys and girls.

7. Earth science draws heavily upon biology, chemistry, and physics. An excellent medium is provided for demonstrating the *interdependence* of science fields. There is hardly a principle of physics that cannot be applied to the dynamic earth and other bodies of the universe. Virtually every substance used by man comes from the earth. The theory of evolution is based upon fossil evidence. It is interesting to note that most geology majors are required in college to take at least one year each of chemistry, biology, and physics in addition to their geological training.

8. There are excellent opportunities for integration with other courses. The tie to geography is obvious. Natural resources, the effects of climate upon the world's inhabitants, the dangers of atomic radiation, and the impact of new earth science discoveries upon society are topics which are treated in social studies as well as in science classes. Various types of models and visual-aid material may be constructed in art and shop classes.

9. With increasing emphasis upon laboratory experiences, the earth sciences have a great deal to offer. In addition to the outdoor laboratory, much can be accomplished in the classroom. A few subjects which may be investigated are listed below:

1. Reflection and refraction of light.
2. Determination of chemical and physical properties in minerals.
3. Identification of minerals by means of specific gravity.
4. Properties of water.
5. Principles of crystal growth.
6. Nature of solutions.
7. Evidence of evolution in fossils.
8. Gravity.
9. Map making.
10. Bernoulli's principle.
11. Transfer of heat.
12. Soil chemistry.
13. Construction of weather maps.
14. Acceleration.
15. Action-reaction.
16. Centrifugal-centripetal forces.
17. Determination of weight of air.

Finding a Place for Earth Science

If an earth science course could be a worthwhile part of the curriculum, what would be replaced? If earth science is put in, something will have to go. General science seems ripe for change. There are several reasons for disillusionment with it — particularly at the ninth-grade level.

1. Students become bored with "general" science year after year. This is particularly apparent in schools having a successful elementary science program. In the ninth grade, specialization in mathematics and language is common. Aren't students ready for a less "general" science course?

2. General science is usually a hodgepodge of unrelated information taken from too many areas to permit study of anything in depth. Today

students are learning about insects, and next week they will study atomic energy. How will they ever discover the interrelationships of scientific disciplines? What is general science? It defies definition! What guides are used to decide the areas that should be included?

3. There is a decided tendency for repetition of subject matter from year to year since general science usually skims lightly along the surface, barely touching upon a multitude of units and never treating any of them in detail.

4. Where can teachers be found who have a broad knowledge of many growing science fields? Some general science teachers are trained only in biology, chemistry, or physics. Many general science teachers are not well trained in any science field. What *is* the best training for a "general" science teacher?

5. How is it possible to plan what is to be taught at the various grade levels considering the diverse training, experiences, and abilities of teachers? What happens to the program when teachers leave the school system?

In some states such as Pennsylvania and New York, ninth-grade earth science is replacing general science in an attempt to solve problems such as those listed above. In the new course, it is possible to relate the earth to its atmosphere and the universe. With this unifying thread it offers a distinct advantage over the usually conglomerate "general" science. A small number of science areas are explored in depth so that students have a better opportunity of finding out what science is really about. Repetition and duplication are avoided. The course is unlike what is being taught at higher as well as lower levels. With depth of study, laboratory experiences are particularly important. Students can develop skills in handling basic equipment needed also in biology, chemistry, and physics. The course provides excellent training for students who will take other science courses. Teacher education is simplified. The ninth-grade earth science teacher has definite goals for which to train. He can become a specialist in a few areas rather than knowing too little about too many subjects.

The Status of Earth Science

Pennsylvania and New York have large-scale, rapidly growing earth science programs, although much of the teaching is being done by under-trained but enthusiastic personnel. In New York where the course has been offered for many years, earth science is being recommended for gifted ninth graders, but much of the course can readily be adapted to the needs of most students. Some New York high schools offer earth science as an alternative to biology, chemistry, or physics, thus creating a fourth science elective. Several other states have initiated or are contemplating earth science programs.

In anticipation of the growth in earth science teaching, the National Science Foundation is supporting the American Geological Institute in the development of earth science teaching resources. During the summer of 1959, twenty geoscientists and ten teachers assembled at the University of Minnesota in Duluth for the purpose of considering concepts of course content and cataloguing, evaluating, and developing teaching materials. Since the Duluth conference, preliminary copies of the sourcebook have been undergoing testing by 100 teachers in selected areas throughout the United States. At present the materials are being revised and edited in preparation for publication in 1961.

Three earth science textbooks are on the market. A fourth will enter the field early in 1961, and at least one more publisher is planning a text.

Someday, earth science may well achieve a status in the schools equivalent to that of biology, chemistry, and physics. As a new kind of course, it does not have to fit a traditional pattern. Any school that is searching for a *different* kind of science course would do well to investigate the advantages of instituting earth science.

For Further Reading

Abegg, Gerald, and Glenn H. Crumb, "Why Not High School Physics?" *School Science and Mathematics,* February, 1966, 66: 211–215.

Brauer, Oscar L., "Conventional Physics Against PSSC Physics," *Science Education,* March, 1965, 49: 170–171.

Educational Leadership, January, 1962, 19: 209–280. (Theme of the issue, "Science in the School," eight articles.)

Garrett, Alfred B., "The New Chemistry," *The Science Teacher,* April, 1961, 15–16, 19, 21, Vol. 28.

Heathers, Glen, "A Process-Centered Elementary Science Sequence," *Science Education,* April, 1961, 45: 201–206.

Heimler, Charles H., "General Science in a State of Flux," *School Science and Mathematics,* December, 1964, 64: 755–764.

Henry, Nelson B., (ed.), *Rethinking Science Education,* The Fifty-ninth Yearbook of the National Society for the Study of Education, Part I., The University of Chicago Press, Chicago, 1960.

Holton, Gerald, "Physics and Culture: Definition of Goals and Proposals for Science Instruction," *The Superior Student,* September–October, 1963, (21 page insert), Vol. 5, No. 6.

Journal of Education, February, 1966, Vol. 148, No. 3. (The entire issue consists of an annotated bibliography for elementary school science.)

Libby, W. F., "Importance of the Physical Sciences in the Curriculum," *Teachers College Journal,* December, 1963, 35: 109–110.

Mayer, William V., "Biology: Retrospect and Prospect," *BSCS Newsletter,* #28, April, 1966, 1–2.

Moe, David, "What Is Science?" *School Science and Mathematics,* June, 1964, 64: 453–458.

Nelson, Pearl A., and Gaylen B. Kelley, "Science in the Elementary School," *Journal of Education,* April, 1963, 7–11, Vol. 145.

Rainey, Robert G., "A Comparison of the CHEM Study Curriculum and a Conventional Approach in Teaching High School Chemistry," *School Science and Mathematics,* June, 1964, 64: 539–544.

Read, John G., "A Bold Design for Science Education," *Journal of Education,* April, 1966, 41–49, Vol. 148.

Richardson, John A., "Evaluating a High School Science Program," *The North Central Association Quarterly,* Fall, 1966, 41: 192–203.

Roucek, Joseph S., (ed.), *The Challenge of Science Education,* Philosophical Library, New York, 1959.

Sawyer, R. A., "Reflections on the High School Curriculum," *School Science and Mathematics,* May, 1965, 65: 389–400.

School Life, October, 1962, Vol. 44–45. (Theme of the issue, "Education in Science." Ten articles, covering instruction in biology, chemistry, physics, earth science, and general developments.)

The School Review, Spring, 1962, Vol. 70, No. 1. (Seven articles on science and mathematics, centering on curricula proposals of the National Science Foundation. Additional articles on testing and educational policy in relation to these projects.)

Schwab, Joseph A., and Paul F. Brandwein, *The Teaching of Science,* The Englis and Burton Lectures for 1961, Harvard University Press, Cambridge, Massachusetts, 1962.

Shea, James H., "The Earth Science Curriculum Project: A Progress Report," *The Science Teacher,* February, 1965, 32: 43, 45.

Strong, Laurence E., "Chemistry as a Science in the High School," *The School Review,* Spring, 1962, 70: 44–50.

Trowbridge, Leslie W., "A Comparison of the Objectives and Instructional Materials in Two Types of High School Physics Course," *Science Education,* March, 1965, 49: 117–122.

Van Deventer, W. C., "BSCS Biology," *School Science and Mathematics,* February, 1963, 63: 89–94.

PART FIVE

Mathematics

27. Mathematics Today and Tomorrow

Committee on the Undergraduate Program in Mathematics,
Mathematical Association of America

Mathematical ability and mathematical training are commodities in greatest demand today. Science is the new American frontier, and mathematics is the language of science. New pioneers in all fields of science, engineering, and technology will need to be experts in this language.

At the same time, the nature of mathematics has changed drastically. A broader conception of the subject today has stimulated amazing new

From the Committee on the Undergraduate Program in Mathematics, Mathematical Association of America, "Mathematics Today and Tomorrow," 3–4, *Recommendations for the Training of Teachers of Mathematics,* The Committee, P.O. Box 1024, Berkeley, California, January, 1961. Although these *Recommendations* are not copyrighted, the editor is happy to acknowledge the cooperation of Lincoln K. Durst, Director, Committee on the Undergraduate Program in Mathematics, whose suggestions for improving and updating the original writing were incorporated into the present manuscript.

theoretical developments, and in turn has led to new possibilities of application in the physical, biological, and social sciences. The number of research mathematicians alive today exceeds the total number in all previous generations, despite the several thousand-year history of the subject.

Our colleges are being called upon to fill an endless need for professional mathematicians, for mathematically trained scientists, and for a variety of mathematically skilled personnel in hundreds of activities. Our business schools often demand the very newest techniques developed by the mathematician. Medical research may soon require mathematical training comparable to that required of the nuclear physicist. Our engineers must be prepared to meet the needs of the rapidly changing American technology. The new industrial revolution — automation — each year demands many thousands of mathematically trained men and women to command our "giant brains."

Such topics as operations research, linear programming, theory of games, stochastic processes, and machine-simulation were unheard of a generation or so ago. Today government, industry, and our universities are clamoring for more experts in these fields.

Vast sums of money are being spent by the United States government — through the National Science Foundation, the Department of Health, Education, and Welfare, and the research arms of the various military services — to increase the amount of new mathematics produced and to interest more students in a scientific career.

It is fair to say that mathematics will play a central role in the American culture of tomorrow. We must train our young men and women to be able to attack and solve problems that did not exist when they attended school: problems which require the ability to think mathematically. This requires an educational system that teaches not only fundamental mathematical techniques, but stresses understanding and originality of thought in its mathematics courses. It is this new emphasis on the role of mathematics, the new demands made upon mathematical education, and the broader view of the nature of mathematics itself which motivates these recommendations.

The rate of development in mathematics since 1900 has been truly amazing. There are hundreds of journals all over the world reporting on the most recent discoveries in both pure mathematics and in its ever increasing applications. Our educational system has until recently not responded to these developments. We find thousands of people who now regret their failure to appreciate earlier the significance of mathematics in the modern world and who must return to college later in life to learn techniques demanded by their professions.

Our teachers on all levels, in primary and secondary schools as well as in colleges, must be competent to teach mathematics with an understanding of traditional mathematics and an appreciation of the modern point of view; and they must be able to convey to our students a new insight into the nature of mathematical thought and of its role in our culture. The training of these teachers should be one of the primary concerns of our civilization.

28. Progress in Mathematics

G. Baley Price

The Revolution in Mathematics

The changes in mathematics in progress at the present time are so extensive, so far-reaching in their implications, and so profound that they they can be described only as a revolution.

First Cause: Research in Mathematics. Let us examine the causes of this revolution. It has been caused in the first place by the tremendous advances made by mathematical research. Many members of the general public are surprised to learn that mathematics is a live, active, and

From G. Baley Price, "Progress in Mathematics and Its Implications for the Schools," Chapter I in *The Revolution in School Mathematics,* National Council of Teachers of Mathematics, Washington, D.C., 1961. G. Baley Price is Chairman of the Department of Mathematics at The University of Kansas. The publication in which this reading is a chapter summarizes the proceedings of eight Regional Orientation Conferences in Mathematics held in various parts of the United States during the fall of 1960. The conferences were conducted by the National Council of Teachers of Mathematics with financial support from the National Science Foundation. Professor Price, who served as executive secretary of the Conference Board of the Mathematical Sciences, presents the reasons why change was, and is, needed in school mathematics. Reprinted by permission of the author and of the National Council of Teachers of Mathematics.

growing subject. They seem to feel that mathematics was completed by Newton, and that undergraduate, and even graduate, courses in the subject never change — indeed, that there is no opportunity, need, or occasion for them to change. It is true that if a theorem is once true, it is always true. But theorems, like airplanes, become obsolete because new and better ones are discovered.

The twentieth century has been the golden age of mathematics, since more mathematics, and more profound mathematics, has been created in this period than during all the rest of history. *Mathematical Reviews* is an international abstracting journal that publishes brief reviews of research papers and books; the typical review is about two or three inches long in one column. In spite of the brevity of the reviews, the volume of *Mathematical Reviews* for 1960 contains 1,652 large, double-column pages; and it is estimated that the volume for 1961 will contain 2,400 such pages. The present century has seen the introduction and extensive development of subjects in pure mathematics such as abstract algebra, topology, measure theory, general theories of integration, and functional analysis, including the theory of Hilbert space. These subjects were not extensively taught in even the best graduate departments of mathematics until after 1930; as a result, many members of the older generation of mathematicians in the United States did not have courses in these new subjects when they were in graduate school. Since it is impossible to be a mathematician today without a knowledge of these new subjects and their continuing developments, the university mathematician has been forced to continue his "in-service training" throughout his entire career. It would be out of place here to enter into a discussion of the details of the new subjects I have named; it is sufficient to say that the changes made in mathematics by modern research are equally as profound as those in chemistry, physics, and biology.

There has been rapid development in certain other fields of mathematics which are more closely related to important applications than those already named. Probability and statistics are studied not only for their own sake, but also because of their extensive and important applications in the physical and engineering sciences, in the biological sciences, and in the social sciences. The recent development of this field is indicated by the fact that the Institute of Mathematical Statistics was not organized until 1935. The theory of games is a mathematical theory of games of strategy; the history of the subject dates essentially from 1944, when John von Neumann and Oskar Morgenstern published their *Theory of Games and Economic Behavior*. As the title of the book indicates, the theory of games was developed not only for its mathematical interest, but also as a mathematical model in terms of which economic forces and behavior could be explained and understood. Linear programming is usually dated from 1948; it has provided an important tool for the more efficient management of large-scale industrial and governmental operations. Operations research was introduced by England and by the United States to support their war efforts during World War II; after the war, many industrial firms employed operations research methods in an effort to make their operations more efficient and more productive. Operations research employs many mathematical and statistical techniques. The Operations Research Society of America was organized after World War II, and it holds several large national meetings each year. Quality control is concerned with techniques for the efficient control of quality in large-scale manufacturing processes. For example, millions of light bulbs are made by automatic machines; what steps can the manufacturer take to insure that the quality remains at specified levels? There are so many lamp bulbs (and similarly for many other items) that it is not economically feasible to test all of them. Furthermore, a complete test of a lamp bulb (and similarly of other items also) is a destructive test, and only those bulbs that are not tested can be sold. Quality control employs a variety of statistical techniques. The history of the subject dates from 1929 when Walter A. Shewart, of the Bell Telephone Laboratories, published a book entitled *Economic Control of Quality of Manufactured Product,* but quality control methods and techniques were not widely employed until they were demanded by the necessities of World War II. The field now has its own professional organization, the American Society for Quality Control, which was organized soon after World War II, and now has more than 12,000 members.

Second Cause: Automation. Let us return to our original question, namely, what caused the revolution in mathematics? I have said that this revolution was caused first of all by the advances resulting from mathematical research. In the second place, the revolution in mathematics was caused by the automation revolution.

The automation revolution consists of the introduction of machines that control machines, and of the consequences of the use of such machines. Examples of automation abound everywhere. Long distance telephone dialing is a simple but impressive example of automation that is so commonplace that it often passes unappreciated. The automatic pilot that flies our jet airplane is another example of automation. Guided missiles provide still another example. Complicated computers and control mechanisms are required to lift a missile from its launching pad and to place it in orbit. A final example is provided by the computing machines that are programmed to control milling machines for cutting complicated three-dimensional shapes from wood or metal.

The automation revolution has influenced the revolution in mathematics in two ways. First, it has made possible the construction and operation of machines of enormous size, complexity, and cost; and it has thereby created the necessity for the design and development of such machines. Until fairly recent years, most of the design and development problems could be solved by simple experimental procedures. I once heard the late Charles F. Kettering, Director of Research for the General Motors Corporation, explain how to design a better piston ring. He prescribed a simple experimental procedure as follows: "Make several hundred piston rings," he said, "using different combinations of design, metal, finish, and heat treatment. Then put them all in engines and try them out. The piston ring that gives the best performance has the design you want."

I am sure that Mr. Kettering was fully aware of the importance of mathematical and other analytical procedures, but the simple experimental procedures he suggested would undoubtedly be quite successful in the design and development of an item as small and simple as a piston ring. But the typical problem of today does not concern the piston ring, but rather something of the size, complexity, and cost of the B-70 airplane. This plane will be made of stainless steel, and it will be somewhat less than 200 feet long. Its range will be 7,000 miles, and it will fly at 2,000 miles per hour at an altitude of 70,000 feet. It will be capable of carrying in its thirty-foot bays enough nuclear bombs to blow a small nation off the map. Originally, the B-70 program called for 162 planes at a cost of $10 billion, a figure the Senate Preparedness sub-committee said was unrealistically low.[1] The experimental approach outlined by Mr. Kettering would suggest that we build a hundred of the proposed planes, using different combinations of wing types, fuselage designs, engine types and mounts, and control systems. This approach to the problem would be absurd. No test pilot would fly a plane that had been built in this fashion. Everyone knows the design and development of a plane of this type requires that the analysis — much of it mathematical — be carried to such a point that the first one built flies and performs essentially according to specification.

But the automation revolution has influenced the revolution in mathe-

[1] An article entitled "Program for B-70 at Mock-Up Stage" in the *New York Times* for February 12, 1961, contains the following statement: "Wonder or blunder, more than $797,300,000 has been spent on it so far, and the only tangible product is a wood-metal-plastic contrivance that looks like a cross between a plane and a spaceship."

matics in another way. Not only has it created the necessity for solving complicated design and development problems, but it has contributed an important tool for their solution. This tool is so important that I would list it as the third cause of the revolution in mathematics.

Third Cause: Automatic Digital Computing Machines. The introduction of the large-scale, high-speed, automatic digital computing machine is the third cause of the revolution in mathematics. This computer has made it possible for mathematical theory to be teamed with the computing machine to produce answers that are required by physicists, engineers, and others.

One example will illustrate the change in our ability to compute. About one hundred years ago an Englishman named William Shanks computed π to 707 decimal places. Working with pencil and paper, he devoted 20 years to this undertaking. In 1949, however, the computing machine known as the ENIAC computed π to more than 2,000 decimal places in 70 hours. Furthermore, the modern calculations of π have shown that Shanks made a mistake in the 528th decimal place. Some time after 1949, another machine computed π to more than 3,000 decimal places in 13 minutes. Still later, a smaller machine computed π to 10,000 decimal places; after the result was published in 1957, it was discovered that the machine had made a mistake in the 7,480th decimal place. By 1960, π had been computed correctly to 10,000 decimal places so many times that history does not record all of them.

The importance of the electronic digital computing machine arises not from the fact that certain calculations can be carried out more quickly than heretofore, but rather from the fact that computations which were formerly completely impossible can now be made quickly and efficiently. Consider again the launching of a guided missile. The computing machine remains on the ground, but radar supplies information to it about the flight of the missile. The computing machine makes the necessary calculations and, through a radar connection, sets the controls in the missile. The flight of the missile can be influenced only during the period the engine is in operation, a period which is usually not more than two or three minutes. No group of human computers could possibly receive the data, make the necessary calculations, and transmit the results back to the missile in so few seconds. The electronic digital computer handles the problem with ease.

Mathematics and the Technological Revolution

The technological revolution now in progress requires that new mathematics be taught in our schools, that the emphasis be shifted in the teaching of many subjects already included in our mathematics courses, and that we increase the production of mathematicians and mathematics teachers.

New Mathematics Required. Several examples will illustrate the changes in the nation's need for mathematics and in the nature of the mathematics courses taught in our schools. In 1850 almost no one was engaged in research. The members of the general public needed to know how to keep simple accounts and how to solve simple problems in measurement. Bookkeeping requires a knowledge of the four operations of arithmetic: addition, subtraction, multiplication, and division. The problems of measurement encountered in 1850 included the determination of the number of acres of land in a field, of the number of cords in a stack of wood, and of the number of bushels of grain in a bin. The public school courses in arithmetic included a treatment of all of these topics.

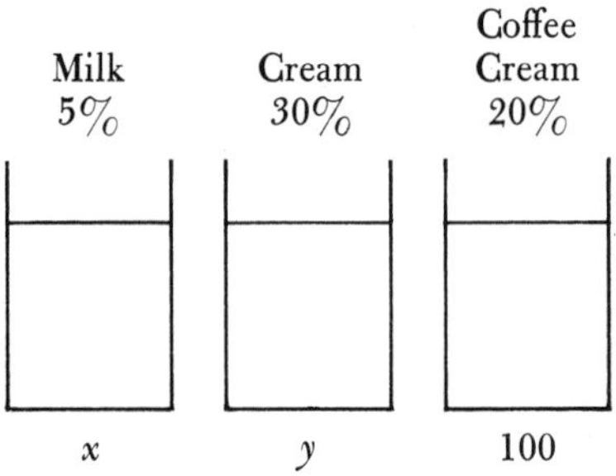

By the early years of the twentieth century, new needs for mathematics had arisen. I shall now describe one which resulted from two advances in dairy technology. The first advance was the invention and widespread introduction of the cream separator, a machine which separates milk into cream and skim milk; and the second was the development of a simple test for determining the percentage of butterfat in a sample of milk or cream. Given the cream separator and the butterfat test, a common problem for the dairyman is illustrated by the following: How many pounds of milk, testing 5 percent butterfat, and how many pounds of cream, testing 30 percent butterfat, must be mixed to give 100 pounds of coffee cream, which tests 20 percent butterfat? Let x and y denote respectively the number of pounds required. Then

$$\begin{aligned} x + y &= 100, \\ .05x + .30y &= 20. \end{aligned}$$

The solution of the problem has led to the solution of two linear equations in two unknowns. For many years high school algebra has included the treatment of the solution of systems of this type.

Next, consider a simple problem in linear programming. A certain manufacturer has warehouses W_1, W_2, and W_3 which contain 100, 200, and 100 tons, respectively, of his product. The manufacturer receives an order for 125 tons of his product from market M_1 and an order for 225 tons from market M_2. The freight rates from the warehouses W_1, W_2 and W_3 to market M_1 are respectively 1, 2, and 3 dollars per ton; and the freight rates from W_1, W_2, and W_3 to M_2 are respectively 6, 5, and 4 dollars per ton. How many tons should the manufacturer ship from each warehouse to each market to fill the two orders?

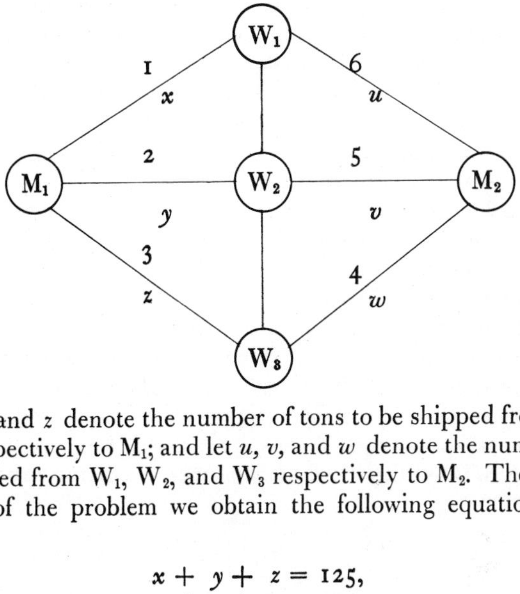

Let x, y, and z denote the number of tons to be shipped from W_1, W_2, and W_3 respectively to M_1; and let u, v, and w denote the number of tons to be shipped from W_1, W_2, and W_3 respectively to M_2. Then from the statement of the problem we obtain the following equations and inequalities:

$$\begin{aligned} x + y + z &= 125, \\ u + v + w &= 225, \\ x + u &\leqq 100, \\ y + v &\leqq 200, \\ x + w &\leqq 100. \end{aligned}$$

Finally, if C denotes the total freight charges for making the shipments, then

$$C = x + 2y + 3z + 6u + 5v + 4w.$$

The solution of the problem is obtained by finding the values of x, y, z, u, v, and w which satisfy the five equations and inequalities and which give C its minimum value.

Problems of this type are of great practical importance to business, industry, and government. Many examples arise in the oil industry. A given oil company will usually have several sources of crude oil, several refineries, many storage facilities, and widely scattered markets. The problems encountered involve many unknowns, and methods must be devised for solving them on large computing machines.

This problem in linear programming involves considerations which have not been taught in our high school mathematics courses heretofore. These courses have treated linear equations but not linear inequalities. A study of inequalities of all kinds is one of the new topics included in the new mathematics programs for high schools.

Consider the following problem. A certain manufacturer receives an order for 100,000 rods of a certain kind, each of which is to have a diameter of two inches. The buyer knows, however, that it is not economically feasible to produce rods whose diameters are exactly 2.000 inches; accordingly, his order states that rods whose diameters lie between 1.995 inches and 2.005 inches are acceptable. The manufacturer finds that although he cannot manufacture rods whose diameters are exactly 2.000 inches on an automatic lathe, he can successfully make rods whose diameters lie between 1.995 and 2.005 inches on this lathe. When the cutting tool is dull or when the lathe is out of adjustment, however, the lathe produces rods whose diameters fall outside the specified tolerances. The manufacturer finds that he must institute a quality control procedure to assist him. In a typical procedure a random sample of five rods will be drawn each hour. The diameters of the five rods will be measured and their average will be computed and plotted on a quality control chart. If the average falls within certain limits that have been established for the lathe, the manufacturing process is con-

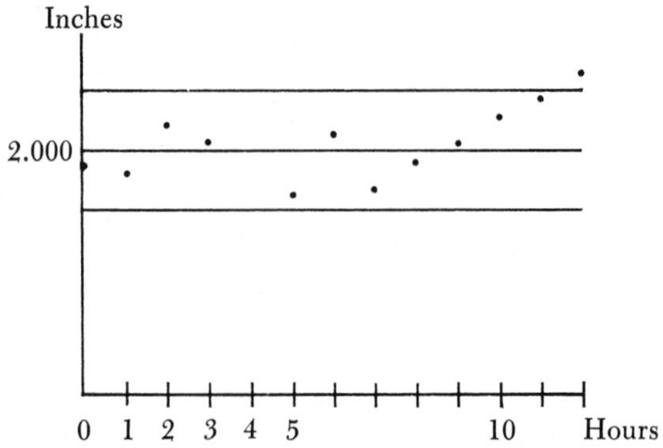

tinued; if it falls outside these limits, the lathe is stopped and put back in proper working order.

The operation of the quality control procedure described is extremely simple, but the mathematics involved in establishing the limits and justifying the procedure includes very deep results in the theory of probability. In the past, probability and statistical inference have not been included in our high school mathematics courses. The Commission on Mathematics, however, considered the subject so important that it wrote a textbook on probability and statistical inference for a course in the second semester of the twelfth grade. Furthermore, the second semester of Contemporary Mathematics, the mathematics course on Continental Classroom, will be devoted to probability and statistical inference, partly because of the importance of this subject for high school teachers, but even more because of its importance for many members of the general public.

Another example will illustrate further the importance of probability and statistics in the everyday affairs of the nation. As mentioned earlier, accounting in the past employed the four fundamental operations of arithmetic; there are strong indications, however, that accounting in the future will involve important applications of probability and statistics.

Consider the telephone companies. A long distance telephone call from New York to San Francisco will use the lines of several different companies, and each of them must receive its share of the revenue. There are undoubtedly millions of such calls each month. The determination of the exact amount of revenue due each telephone company requires only the four operations of arithmetic, but the amount of work involved is enormous. The telephone companies are now investigating the possibility of employing sampling theory in the solution of this problem; the Ohio Public Utilities Commission heard testimony in September 1960 regarding sampling to split revenues between Ohio Bell and the General Telephone Company, which operates in many areas of Ohio. Clearly the total amount of work involved in the accounting will be greatly reduced if the total revenue is divided in the same ratio as that in a small sample of the calls. Important mathematical and legal questions are involved, however. How large should the sample be to insure that the total revenue is divided fairly within certain limits? Will the stockholders accept dividends based on revenues divided by sampling theory methods; will the Bureau of Internal Revenue accept taxes based on income obtained by such methods?

It is freely predicted that sampling theory methods, based on probability and statistical inference, will be widely introduced into accounting procedures in the near future. These developments emphasize once more the importance of probability and statistics for the general public, and the importance of introducing a course on these subjects into the high school curriculum.

Changed Emphasis in Old Mathematics Required. Thus far I have emphasized the importance of new developments in mathematics. It would be a mistake to believe, however, that the only important parts of mathematics are those which have been discovered and developed recently. Many old subjects are still highly important and we must continue to teach them. Frequently, however, the emphasis must be placed on a different aspect of the subject, and an effort must be made to teach the subject so that the student gains a deeper understanding of it. The teaching of trigonometry and logarithms provides two examples. Trigonometry became a part of the college curriculum in mathematics about 300 years ago when the American colonies were located on the Atlantic seaboard. In the large majority of cases a college graduate became a sea captain, a surveyor, or a minister. A sea captain needed trigonometry for navigation; a surveyor needed it to lay out the farms and cities of the new continent; and the minister needed trigonometry for astronomy and the calculation of the date of Easter. Trigonometry was the all-important applied mathematics of this earlier period, and the solution of triangles was its important aspect.

Today, the important part of trigonometry is the study of the properties of the trigonometric functions rather than the solution of triangles. Radio beams and radar aids have made navigation easy; the new country has been staked out, and only a few, even among the engineers, study surveying; and our observatories now compute the date of Easter. The trigonometric functions, however, have many important applications, for example, in electrical engineering; and trigonometry is still an important subject in applied mathematics if the emphasis is placed on analytic trigonometry rather than on the solution of triangles.

Logarithms were introduced about 300 years ago, and they have been widely taught as an important tool for calculation. But logarithms are no longer important for calculations; small calculations are performed on desk calculators, and large calculations are performed on electronic digital computers. Shall we stop teaching logarithms? Not at all, but the emphasis should be shifted from logarithms as a tool for calculation to a study of the properties of the logarithm function.

Consider a final example. The study of the flow of heat and the distribution of temperatures in a solid body is a problem of great importance at the present time; it was first studied extensively by the French mathematician Jean Fourier early in the nineteenth century. His discoveries had few practical applications at the time, but they have many applications of the highest importance today. Many problems related to the flow of heat occur in the design of every steam power plant, of every air conditioning system, and of every nuclear power plant. The study of the flow of heat, begun by Fourier, and of the mathematical problems which have arisen from this original problem, have had a profound influence on the development of modern mathematics. Some of the changes that are being made in high school mathematics are designed to provide a better foundation for the study of some of the old problems in mathematics and their modern developments. The study of the flow of heat is an advanced problem which cannot be studied in high school. Nevertheless, it is important to develop the points of view and to lay the foundation that will permit the student to understand the old problems and the new methods which have been developed to solve these old problems.

More Mathematicians Required. As a result of the revolution in mathematics, there is an unprecedented demand for mathematicians and mathematics teachers; it is impossible to foresee a time when there will be an adequate supply. This demand for mathematicians is part of a larger demand for highly trained personnel in all fields. This demand represents a long-term development in our civilization — a civilization which is increasingly dependent on scientific and technological advances. This long-term increase in the demand for highly trained personnel was obscured first by the depression of the 1930's and second by the dislocations caused by World War II. The realization of the true situation burst upon the nation with startling suddenness in the 1950's, long after efforts should have been initiated to deal with it.

The Rockefeller Report on Education, entitled *The Pursuit of Excellence,* contains an account of the automation revolution, the accompanying long-term increase in the demand for highly educated personnel, and the crisis that confronts the nation. The following table[2] shows that the percent of the labor force in selected skills and occupations increased from 32.8 percent in 1910 to 47.6 percent in 1957.

The Rockefeller Report on Education stresses the crisis in science and mathematics education in the following paragraphs:[3]

> Though we cannot discuss in detail each of the fields of study, it is worthwhile to say a few words about education in science and mathematics. The public reactions to this subject have been so

[2] From: *The Pursuit of Excellence: Education and the Future of America.* © 1958, by the Rockefeller Brothers Fund, Inc. (as it appears in *Prospect for America,* p. 346. © 1961). Reprinted by permission of Doubleday & Company.

[3] *Ibid.,* p. 368.

OCCUPATIONAL DISTRIBUTION OF LABOR FORCE
(Selected skills and occupations as percent of labor force)

	1910	*1957*
Professional and technical workers	4.4%	9.9%
Proprietors, managers and officials, excluding farm	6.5	10.3
Clerical workers	10.2	14.1
Skilled workers and foremen	11.7	13.3
Total selected skills and occupations	32.8%	47.6%

intense and so diverse that it has not been easy for the informed citizen to appraise the issues. The simplest way to avoid confusion is to keep a few basic ideas firmly in mind.

First, the crisis in our science education is not an invention of the newspapers, or scientists, or the Pentagon. It is a real crisis.

Second, the USSR is not the "cause" of the crisis. The cause of the crisis is our breath-taking movement into a new technological era. The USSR has served as a rude stimulus to awaken us to that reality.

The heart of the matter is that we are moving with headlong speed into a new phase of man's long struggle to control his environment, a phase beside which the industrial revolution may appear a modest alteration of human affairs. . . .

How well is our educational system meeting the demands placed upon us? The Rockefeller Report on Education answers as follows:[4]

The fateful question is not whether we have done well, or whether we are doing better than we have done in the past, but whether we are meeting the stern demands and unparalleled opportunities of the times. And the answer is that we are *not.*

A Mathematics Education Adequate For Our Times

The implications of this crisis for our schools are clear. We must put forth whatever effort may be required to insure that the education provided by our schools — and in particular, the mathematics education provided by our schools — is adequate for the needs of our times. I shall now indicate some of the components of the mathematics education that is adequate for our times.

Appropriate Course Content. The first component consists of mathematics courses with the proper mathematical content. Many of the topics

[4] *Ibid.* p. 362.

in such courses are old mathematics, but they are presented in such a way that the student gains greatly increased understanding and insight into the subject. Algebra, an old subject, is one of the central topics in the new courses. Algebra has usually been presented as a collection of rules, which if followed, produce the answer; proofs were reserved entirely for geometry. Algebra in the new courses will now be taught so that its structure — its deductive character — is apparent. Many of the topics in courses with the proper mathematical content concern subjects which are entirely new in the high school curriculum. For example, a chapter on vectors is now available in a mathematics course for the eleventh grade. Vectors form a proper subject for study, not only because they form an interesting new mathematical structure, but also because they have important applications in physics and engineering. Another new topic in the high school curriculum is probability and statistics. I have already mentioned the textbook for a semester course on this subject in the twelfth grade. The course has already been taught in a number of high schools and it has been an immediate success everywhere. The engineers, among others, are demanding that their students know more and more about probability, statistics, and their applications. The theory of matrices is a final example of a new mathematical topic in the high school curriculum. Matrices are relatively new in mathematics, being only about a century old; they provide an example of an important new type of algebraic structure, and their study yields a tool of great significance and power in many fields in which mathematics is applied.

Qualified Teachers. The second component in mathematics education adequate for our times consists of well-qualified teachers. A teacher must know a great deal of mathematics in order to be a satisfactory teacher of school mathematics. Superintendents and principals should now realize that the day has passed when any teacher who happens to have an otherwise free period can be assigned to teach mathematics. Many of our high school students must now reach a level of attainment expected of college sophomores only 15 or 20 years ago.

The well-qualified teacher must know mathematics, and in addition he must teach the subject with interest and enthusiasm. The high school mathematics teacher must present the elements of algebra, geometry, and trigonometry, but in addition he must preserve and strengthen the student's native interest in and enthusiasm for mathematics. He must make the subject interesting and appealing, so that his pupils will continue to study it with enthusiasm. A teacher who fears and dislikes mathematics will not teach very much mathematics to his students, but he will readily convey his fear and dislike of the subject to many of them. Such a teacher will often build up in his students a permanent fear and dislike of mathematics, and they will abandon the study of the subject at the first opportunity. One of the best ways to attract students to the study of mathematics is to know and like mathematics, and then to teach good, significant courses.

Counselors. The third component in mathematics education adequate for our times consists of counselors who will make certain that those students who have mathematical interests and abilities take at least four years of good mathematics in high school, and that all of those who have the ability to do college work take at least three years of high school mathematics. A student who does not take at least three years of high school mathematics is so handicapped that many fields of study are permanently closed to him when he reaches college. The best courses and the finest teachers are to no avail if students do not take the courses. For this reason, there must be counselors to help students plan their high school programs.

Four Requirements

I shall now describe four requirements which must be met if our schools are to provide the mathematics education I have described.

In-Service Retraining of Teachers. Many high school mathematics teachers must undertake retraining immediately. Although many teachers had an excellent education originally, they need re-education because of the changes that have taken place in mathematics. Fortunately, excellent opportunities exist. The mathematics course entitled Contemporary Mathematics on NBC's Continental Classroom provides an opportunity for in-service training which is available to most of the teachers in the United States.[5] In addition, many teachers have organized seminars to study the new mathematics in their own schools and thereby gained valuable in-service training. Finally, the National Science Foundation has provided many opportunities for in-service training. Often a teacher can attend an in-service institute operated by a nearby college or university with NSF support. Also, there are many summer and academic-year institutes supported by the National Science Foundation.

Better Pre-Service Training of Teachers. A second requirement concerns the training of new teachers. Schools must encourage and help colleges and universities that train teachers to revise their teacher-

[5] The National Broadcasting Company announced on June 28, 1961, that Contemporary Mathematics will be repeated from 6 to 6:30 a.m., local time, during 1961–1962.

training programs so that their graduates are adequately prepared to teach the new courses. A vigorous program to modernize teacher-training programs has been launched by the Panel on Teacher Training of the MAA's Committee on the Undergraduate Program in Mathematics. The recommendations of this Panel have been published in the journals of the National Council of Teachers of Mathematics and of the Mathematical Association of America.[6]

Improved Teaching Techniques. Next, high school mathematics teachers must re-examine their teaching techniques. Some highly effective new techniques have been introduced by those who have developed the new courses. For example, many teachers have used, with much success, the "discovery technique" of teaching mathematics. Again the School Mathematics Study Group has emphasized the importance of learning mathematics by reading the textbook. SMSG has made an important contribution by providing sample textbooks which contain full explanation so that the student can learn by reading his book. It is clear that the introduction of new mathematics into the courses and the development of new teaching techniques have proceeded hand-in-hand.

Sufficiently Large High Schools. A final requirement for the mathematics education which I have described as adequate for our times is that the high school itself be sufficiently large. A small high school cannot provide the mathematics courses and the teachers I have described above as necessary; James B. Conant has suggested that a high school with a graduating class of 100 is the minimum size. Students in a smaller school almost certainly are denied proper mathematics courses. The nation cannot waste its limited supply of good mathematics teachers by placing them in schools where they teach their specialty to less than full capacity. The nation cannot afford the waste of talent that results from sending gifted students (they occur also in small schools!) to schools with poor mathematics programs and poor teachers. Fortunately, many states are solving the problem of the small high school by consolidating small schools into large schools.

• • •

In conclusion, I must emphasize that the elementary school, the junior high school, and the senior high school lay the foundation. I

[6] See "The Training of Elementary School Mathematics Teachers," *The Arithmetic Teacher* 7: 421–25; December 1960. See also "Recommendations of the Mathematical Association of America for the Training of Teachers of Mathematics," *The Mathematics Teacher* 8: 632–38, 643; December 1960; and *American Mathematical Monthly* 67: 982–91; December 1960.

must emphasize that the elementary school teacher, the junior high school teacher, and the senior high school teacher are absolutely essential to the success of our program to provide better mathematics; for these teachers must teach mathematics; and these teachers must teach with enthusiasm so that their students continue the study of mathematics.

29. The Old Mathematics in the New Curriculum

Max Beberman

The publicity that has accompanied many of the recent developments in mathematics education has been received with mixed feelings by teachers, administrators and school patrons. School people [and parents] who recall unhappy times in the mathematics classroom may believe that a new era is being prepared for students because the old incomprehensible mathematics is going to be replaced by new and useful mathematics — high school algebra which was so puzzling is now going to give way to something called 'Boolean Algebra' which is up-to-date twentieth century stuff.

The mathematics teacher of the "old school" is very uneasy because

From Max Beberman, "The Old Mathematics in the New Curriculum," *Educational Leadership,* March, 1962, 19: 373–375. Max Beberman is Professor of Mathematics and Director of the Mathematics Project of the University of Illinois Committee on School Mathematics. He is co-author of *High School Mathematics* and of *Mathematics Workshop, Levels A-F,* textbooks resulting from the UICSM project. Reprinted by permission of the Association for Supervision and Curriculum Development and of the author.

it is likely that he has not studied the "new mathematics." And, even if he takes a summer institute course bearing the title 'Modern Algebra,' he may be all the more concerned because he probably feels, and with some justice, that he would have a very difficult time teaching subject matter which he barely understood. Finally, some parents view the situation with either joy or misgivings because they feel that they shall no longer be able to conduct tutorial sessions around the dining room table.

It is my contention that too much has been made of the allegedly new mathematics in the new curriculum. In looking at the content of the new programs for grades 9–12, I am impressed more by the attempt to organize the traditional subject matter along logical lines than by the inclusion of new subject matter.

Elementary Algebra

This attempt is most striking in the elementary algebra portion of the curriculum. What has heretofore been a year spent on learning an assortment of isolated rules and techniques which are quickly forgotton or confused is now a year devoted to learning (preferably discovering) a few basic principles and considering some of the logical consequences of these principles. These logical consequences amount to the same old rules and techniques as before, but the students' reaction to them is vastly different.

Let us consider an example. Consider the pedagogical problem of teaching a student to solve a system of equations "algebraically." Suppose that the student faces the problem of solving the system of equations:

$$(1)\ 3x + 4y = 18$$
$$(2)\ 2x - 5y = -11$$

In the conventional curriculum, he is *told* that the thing to do is to multiply the sides of each equation by certain numbers so that the resulting equations will have either the x-terms or the y-terms alike. Multiply (1) by 5 and (2) by 4:

$$(1)\ (3\cdot 5)x + (4\cdot 5)y = 18\cdot 5$$
$$(2)\ (2\cdot 4)x - (5\cdot 4)y = -11\cdot 4$$

Then, add the equations. This will eliminate one of the unknowns.

$$(3\cdot 5 + 2\cdot 4)x = 18\cdot 5 - 11\cdot 4$$

Solve the resulting equation:

$$23x = 46$$
$$x = 2$$

Substitute in either of the given equations to find the other unknown. By dint of a tremendous amount of practice, the student finally masters the technique. But, it remains pretty much of a mystery to him. The justification for the steps involved is that they produce the right answer or that "this is the way the book does it."

Now, let us see how this problem is handled in one of the new programs. For one thing, the problem usually appears as an application of some more general idea. In this case, the general idea is that an equation in two variables defines a set of pairs of numbers. [For example, some of the pairs in the set defined by the first equation are (0, 4.5), (1, 3.75), (2, 3), (4, 1.5) and (5, 0.75).] So, solving this system of equations amounts to finding the pair of numbers which is common to the two sets of pairs.

One way to do this is to graph the two equations. The point of intersection of the two graphs gives you the sought-for pair. [The conventional curriculum may not have taught graphing prior to this topic.] The student graphs these equations and sees the common solution. Now, the student is asked to "add" the equations and graph the result. He gets:

$$(3)\quad (3 + 2)x + (4 - 5)y = 18 - 11$$

and, when he graphs this equation, he *discovers* that its graph passes through the point of intersection of the graphs of the original equations. This is moderately surprising and he may wonder whether this is just an isolated event, or whether it would happen with any two equations of the type he is considering. He has the basic principles to enable him to prove that it would always happen. Next, the student is asked to take equation (1), multiply both sides by some nonzero number, and graph the resulting equation. Say he multiplies by 7:

$$(1')\quad (3 \cdot 7)x + (4 \cdot 7)y = 18 \cdot 7$$

He knows from previous experience that the graph of (1′) is the same as the graph of (1). [Moreover, he can prove this.] Take equation (2); multiply both sides by, say 6:

$$(2')\quad (2 \cdot 6)x - (5 \cdot 6)y = -11 \cdot 6,$$

and graph. Once again, the graph of (2′) is the same as the graph of (2). Now, add equations (1′) and (2′):

$$(3')\quad (3 \cdot 7 + 2 \cdot 6)x + (4 \cdot 7 - 5 \cdot 6)y = 18 \cdot 7 - 11 \cdot 6$$

and graph the result. As before, the graph of (3′) will pass through the common point of the graphs of (1) and (2). We now have an important general result. Suppose that r and s are nonzero numbers, and the sides of (1) are multiplied by r and those of (2) are multiplied by s. If the resulting equations are added:

$$(*)\quad (3r + 2s)x + (4r - 5s)y = 18r - 11s$$

the graph of this equation will pass through the common point of the graphs of (1) and (2). Moreover, the values of 'r' and 's' determine the "tilt" of the graph of this equation. If this graph were a vertical line, all of its points would have the same first number as the common point. So, the problem now becomes one of finding those values of 'r' and 's' for which the graph of equation (*) is a vertical line. The student knows that any equation for which the y-term is missing has a vertical line as its graph. So, he seeks numbers r and s such that $4r - 5s$ is 0. The numbers 5 and 4 will do nicely. [So will 10 and 8.] Then, (*) becomes:

$$(3 \cdot 5 + 2 \cdot 4)x = 18 \cdot 5 - 11 \cdot 4$$

or:

$$x = 2$$

Hence, each point on this vertical line has first number 2. Since the common point is also on the vertical, its first number is 2. The second number for the common point can be found either by substitution or by choosing values of 'r' and 's' which convert (*) into an equation whose x-term is missing.

The student is now permitted to develop the most efficient technique he can out of this explanation. It is pretty clear that he does not have to think about the graphs. The whole job boils down to choosing the correct multipliers, r and s.

An Understanding Approach

Objections to the new programs should not center on questions concerning new subject matter. The real question is whether or not students should *understand* the skills which are taught in both the conventional and the new programs. This is not a trivial issue. If you decide on an understanding approach, the implications of this commitment are far-reaching. For example, the question of time becomes important. It requires only a few minutes in a conventional program to *tell* students how to solve systems of equations. It will take the better part of a class hour to use the other approach. Moreover, the other approach requires a consistency of treatment prior to this point in the curriculum in order to develop in the student a taste for and a delight in logical explanations. And, once this taste is cultivated, your later courses should be modified to keep students from rebelling at inconsistencies. An understanding approach requires much more of the teacher in terms of preparation, especially if the textbook has not been written in the same spirit.

Finally, there is the terrible hazard of thinking that any approach which emphasizes logical explanations leads to understanding. If such were the case, logical mathematics courses for high school would be plentiful, for mathematicians do know all the correct explanations. High school mathematics holds no mysteries for mathematicians. However, the trick is to build a curriculum in which the mathematics is logically developed and to match this curriculum both to the present interests, needs and capacities of the learners, and to their future interests and needs. For example, it would not require much to take the conventional approach to the system-of-equations technique described above and give a brief but sound mathematical explanation which did not refer to graphs. But, such an explanation would not call for the discoveries inherent in the graphing approach and would not appeal as much to students with strong geometric intuition.

The recent developments in high school mathematics education have not been concerned with replacing old subject matter with new subject matter. The primary task has been that of finding a matching between sound mathematics and sound pedagogy. The job has just begun.

30. What's New About the New Math?

Allen F. Strehler

Writing about the *new* mathematics these days is a safe and popular venture: everybody is talking about it and no one really knows exactly what it is.

The widespread self-consciousness about education in the United States, as Sputnik I orbited the Earth in 1957, focused national attention on the importance of mathematics. Though mathematicians were pleased to find that their traditionally "dull" subject had become the object of public concern and support and even catapulted to editorial pages, the sudden glare of the limelight took them by surprise. A sense of urgency

From Allen F. Strehler, "What's New About the New Math?" *Saturday Review,* March 21, 1964, 68–69, 84, Vol. 47. Allen F. Strehler is Associate Dean of Graduate Studies and Senior Lecturer in Mathematics, Carnegie Institute of Technology. He is a member of the Board of Governors, the Mathematical Association of America. He is indebted for editorial assistance during the preparation of this article to Miss Amity Doering, Department of Public Relations, Carnegie Institute of Technology. Reprinted by permission of the *Saturday Review* and of the author.

surrounded the ever-present task of revising curricula and courses; and, for the past five years, mathematics teachers have found themselves beset by new proposals to do this and do that and by a vast array of definitions, sometimes contradictory, of just what new educational problems need to be solved. The controversy and confusion that now surround the *new* mathematics is due in part to the haste with which this reappraisal was undertaken.

There are, of course, a number of other reasons for the controversy; and it is hardly necessary to comment that any attempt to bring order out of the present confusion must trace the causes of it. As mathematics teachers are painfully aware, the definition of a problem is a major part of its solution.

As I see it, the sources of the arguments surrounding the *new* mathematics are the following: the problem of semantics, which, for example, finds different writers attaching to the same word quite different meanings; an honest difference of opinion as to what the content of the *new* mathematics should be; and a failure to give the *new* mathematics its proper historical perspective (for example, when did it begin, how "new" is it really, and where is it going), with the result that its importance and innovations are often exaggerated.

Any attempt to treat these three extensive problems in an intensive manner is really quite difficult, since they have been widely misunderstood, but I shall comment on each of them briefly and in the order in which they are stated. Since almost all of the present debate has concerned itself with secondary school mathematics, my remarks shall be confined, for the most part, to mathematics at that level.

With regard to the problem of semantics, the first error here is in the use of the word *new* in connection with mathematics at the secondary school level. I presume that this use of the word would imply to the layman that the mathematics now being taught has just been discovered; whereas nothing could be farther from the truth. Professor W. W. Sawyer, a noted mathematics scholar and author, in a recent denunciation of the use of the word *new* in this connection, commented, after noting that most of the mathematics now being introduced into high school curricula was known by the nineteenth century at the latest, "We do not serve the cause of education, of mathematics, or of honesty by calling old things new, by making simple ideas appear imposing." What is *new* is the emphasis being given to topics that were not previously treated; and I shall discuss these further in connection with the content of the present secondary school curriculum.

To press the semantic problem somewhat further, since it is the basis of so much of the present debate, I would like to cite several other instances of words in mathematics that have come to have widely divergent connotations:

To high school students the word *algebra* denotes a subject (probably epitomized by quadratic equations) that is studied in the ninth grade and, more often than not, over again in eleventh grade; whereas to professional mathematicians algebra denotes an extensive area of higher mathematics that is presently alive with research and new results. Little wonder that freshmen become confused when a professor tells them that he has written his Ph.D. thesis in algebra.

With increasing frequency, high schools designate their college preparatory courses as *analysis*, but to students at Ohio State University, for example, analysis means the first really high-powered graduate course in functions of a real variable. And now, just recently, the department of mathematics at Carnegie has chosen to re-label its freshman and sophomore analytical geometry and calculus sequence simply analysis.

For the first time in the public schools, children are taught about sets, sometimes as early as in the fourth grade, and they are told that the word *sets* refers to such collections of things as the children in their classroom or the states of some union. But to graduate students in mathematics the word *sets* suggests such things as, perhaps, a geometric manifold with strange topological properties.

To mathematicians the word *topology* refers to a fairly abstract area of higher mathematics that students are really not mature enough to deal with until after they have finished their undergraduate work. And yet several months ago, as a judge at an essay contest for high school students, I heard a tenth-grader read a ten-minute paper on topology, in which he felt that he had dealt with the whole subject quite adequately.

It is really very paradoxical, and indeed quite embarrassing, that mathematics, which presumably is the academic discipline in which words and concepts are precisely and unambiguously defined, should find itself for the moment in such a semantic spin. And there is little wonder that various writers and editors find themselves sparring with each other as to what the *new* mathematics is all about. The University of Illinois Committee on School Mathematics (UICSM), in addition to its many notable achievements, is trying to straighten out the semantic problem, at least at the high school level, by substituting brand new words for ones whose meanings have become clouded; but I think that the question as to whether this dispels the confusion or compounds it is also matter for debate.

With regard to the content of the *new* mathematics, I have already commented that the first thing that can be said is that it is not *new*! What, then, does distinguish it from the mathematics that was taught almost everywhere until five years ago? The answer lies in the emphasis and selectivity of the topics in the various new curricula, and while there are differences here from program to program, I think that certain common features are beginning to emerge that are fairly easy to delineate. In my own best judgment these characterizing features of the *new* mathematics are the following:

1. *It eliminates those topics that are relatively unimportant.* Probably the two best examples of topics that are, or were, overworked in high school are trigonometry and solid geometry. In trigonometry, which previously occupied a full semester, the students spent much of their time computing the widths of imaginary rivers that they could not cross, or computing the height of some flagpole at different times of day — correct to more and more decimal places — using logarithms. This work is now being trimmed down to one-half or two-thirds of a semester, and the emphasis is being placed on the analytic aspects of the subject. In this connection it is interesting to note that in a course at Margaret Morrison Carnegie College, the women's college of Carnegie Tech, we treat all of trigonometry in four weeks, and we have found that there is no significant difference between the performance of those students who have had a whole semester's previous work in trigonometry and those who have had none. Similarly, much of solid geometry had consisted of theorems that were of no abiding interest even to professional mathematicians. For this reason, Carnegie Tech in 1957 dropped the subject from its entrance requirements and thus became one of the first colleges to do so.

2. *It integrates those topics that are important.* What remains of solid geometry is being combined into a one-year course with plane geometry. This has been found to be a reasonable combination in terms of time, and there are obvious pedagogical advantages to treating a given problem in two dimensions and three dimensions simultaneously. Furthermore, plane geometry had been taught in such a stereotyped manner that students all over the country, from Bangor to Berkeley, arrived at the same theorem at Christmas time and then at another theorem at Easter. One purpose of high school geometry is to teach deductive reasoning, and the School Mathematics Study Group (SMSG), in one of its new experimental textbooks, feels that it has achieved this purpose by introducing a shorter "deductive chain" that takes only ten weeks of study.

3. *It introduces recent and important developments in mathematics.* For

example, probability and statistics, with which almost everyone is confronted daily in the printed media and on television, was scarcely touched upon in the classroom until five years ago when the Commission on Mathematics of the College Entrance Examination Board came forth with its highly successful experimental textbook, *Probability and Statistical Inference for Secondary Schools.* Professor Frederick Mosteller of Harvard was invited to deal with the same subject in his lecture series on NBC's Continental Classroom for the spring semester of 1960–61, the first year that a mathematics course was offered for college credit over network television.

4. *It emphasizes the structure of mathematics, rather than isolated topics.* For example, algebra and geometry had been treated as though they were disjoint disciplines, separated by a long summer and taught by different teachers who had become specialists only within their own subjects. "Theorems" were unique to geometry, whereas "equations" were unique to algebra. Now students are led to understand that these two subjects have their counterparts in each other; that real numbers are useful in proving geometric theorems; and that such underlying principles as the associative and commutative laws, far from being limited to algebra, have important interpretations and applications in other branches of mathematics. Unfortunately and unbelievably, these strong algebraic laws had often been dismissed by even algebra teachers as being unimportant or else too intricate to bother with, even though they had appeared in bold-face type in the textbooks.

5. *It introduces subject matter to students earlier than was previously thought possible.* For example, the notion of a set, which previously was not mentioned even in high school, is now sometimes introduced in grade school. Group theory, which previously had its "corner" in the junior year in college at the earliest, is now being introduced in high school. And calculus, of all things, which the colleges previously guarded jealously, is being taught very successfully in some high schools that can supply the happy combination of able students and well-prepared calculus teachers. While these trends appear off-hand to hold nothing but advantages for student and teacher alike, I should hasten to add that some mathematicians have real fears about the dangers inherent in giving superficial treatment to profound and intricate mathematical concepts. They feel that an inevitable effect will be to train some youngsters to be simply pseudo-sophisticates in mathematics. The tenth-grader and his paper fell short of a real understanding of topology. Perhaps it is this development over the last five years, the introduction of concepts to students much sooner, that has led to the widespread and

mistaken notion that sets, binary numbers, and group theory are *new*, in spite of the fact that all of them are at least a century old.

Finally, I would like to comment about the history of the *new* mathematics. There is no doubt that the *new* mathematics as it is perceived by the layman was swept into the public mind shortly after the successful launching of Sputnik I. A certain evolution in the pedagogy of mathematics was in progress slowly but unremittingly at that time, both on the secondary school and college levels, receiving its greatest impetus from the Commission on Mathematics that was established by the College Entrance Examination Board in 1955. But it was that historic satellite which blew the whole problem wide open. All of a sudden it made the competitive position of America clear, forced the country to re-examine its scientific resources, and focused attention on the fierce shortage of personnel, especially in mathematics, the discipline on which so many other sciences depend. I do not mean for a moment to underestimate the contribution which the vast interplay of political, social, and technological events has forever made to the growth of mathematics. I am simply commenting on the explosive appearance of the *new* mathematics on the secondary school scene in 1958.

I recall attending a meeting of mathematicians in Washington, D.C., several months after the launching of Sputnik I, and the atmosphere of the conference was vibrant with the new importance that people everywhere were attaching to mathematics. A distinguished professor exclaimed to some of us in the hotel lobby one day, "Sputnik I has done more for the cause of mathematics and mathematicians in this country than we have been able to do for ourselves in the past two hundred years." It was as though we were poor cousins whose great aunt had just died and left us a fortune; or as though we had just been given membership cards to some elite club and did not yet have the proper formal clothes to wear.

One unfortunate consequence of that surprise attack, and the one which is still causing confusion as to what the *new* mathematics is, or what it should be, was the fact that it caught the forces of mathematicians in almost complete disarray, with the result that we didn't know which way to run and hence have found ourselves running in every direction at once. The *new* mathematics has become a controversy that has pitted old friends, and even old office mates, against each other; and I think that no one is really certain as to what the final outcome of this stimulating debate will be. Certainly to indicate that the matter is resolved, as some authors have chosen to do, is an incorrect statement of fact.

What final form the *new* mathematics takes — and it is bound to take a more stable form, since the whole evolution is inevitable — is only a matter for time to decide. Or perhaps I should say for the mathematicians to decide — as they regroup their forces. At the moment, the *new* mathematics is essentially a renewed mathematics — renewed in the attention it has attracted from many interested participants and observers; in the searching re-examination that has been forced upon its pedagogical intricacies; and in its increased importance in an age and society deeply involved in technology.

31. Evaluating a School Mathematics Program

David C. Johnson and Donovan A. Johnson

In a dynamic society such as ours, many persons accept as natural the idea that school mathematics programs — like others — should change. Yet this seems to come as a surprise to most people who think of mathematics as a subject which deals with ideas that never change.

Although the mathematics of the ancients is still true and important, many factors beyond those common to all subjects are causing changes in school mathematics:

From David C. Johnson and Donovan A. Johnson, "Evaluating a School Mathematics Program," *The North Central Association Quarterly,* Fall, 1966, 41: 184–191. David C. Johnson is Assistant Professor of Education and Chairman of the Mathematics Department, University of Minnesota High School. Donovan A. Johnson, Professor of Mathematics Education at the University of Minnesota, is President of the National Council of Teachers of Mathematics, 1966–1968. He is author or coauthor of a number of well known texts in mathematics and the teaching of mathematics. Reprinted by permission of the North Central Association of Colleges and Secondary Schools and of the authors.

. . . New mathematics such as game theory, linear programming, and computer science has been created during the past generation.

. . . New uses for mathematics have been found not only in the sciences but also in the humanities, the arts, and psychology.

. . . The electronic computer and automation which are creating such a revolution in our society are both based on mathematical ideas and logic.

. . . Our scientific and technologically oriented society needs an increasing proportion of its citizens with higher mathematical competence than ever before.

Partly as a result of these pressures, mathematics education has changed dramatically during the last 16 years. Experimental projects, such as the University of Illinois Committee on School Mathematics (UICSM), the Commission on Mathematics of the College Entrance Examination Board and the School Mathematics Study Group (SMSG) have developed new and independent programs. These programs largely supported both by private foundations and federal funds differ markedly from traditional programs in content, language, and emphasis. At the present time UICSM, SMSG, MINNEMATH (The Minnesota Mathematics Study Center), and ESI (Educational Services Incorporated) are continuing to develop even "newer" programs.

These experimental projects have been marked by some strong similarities as well as unique features. Each of the projects has sought to change the mathematics curriculum to reflect new knowledge and an improved treatment of selected traditional topics. All have given strong emphasis to structure and key concepts.

> "The emphasis in mathematics programs today is upon mathematical structures learned in an atmosphere of active inquiry. The student is encouraged to think for himself and to realize that there are often many ways to reach a solution. He meets many basic mathematical ideas very early, and he broadens and deepens these concepts as long as he continues in the mathematical sequence.
>
> "One of the important new ideas in the teaching of mathematics is that learning is not made more difficult when instruction includes complete, mathematically correct, and more sophisticated explanations. Master teachers have always known this and have acted upon it in their classes. The stress upon more adequate understanding enables the schools to teach more mathematics in the same time and it makes the experience of learning mathematics more rewarding for the student. Mathematics is presented as a way of thinking. In

the very process of learning the concepts, skills and uses of mathematics, the student has a valuable experience. Even when some facts are forgotten, the student will retain ideas and skills concerning proof, correct language, and inferential thinking.

"Teachers report that pupils at all levels of achievement can learn mathematics when appropriate explanations are given. The structure approach is effective with slow-moving classes as well as with honors classes."[1]

Current Criticism of New School Mathematics

New school mathematics programs have been criticized both by scholars and laymen. They say the new programs give too little emphasis to computation, application, and intuition, and that too much emphasis is given to rigor, precision, logic, and structure. The criticism is also made that little or no attention is given to the slow learner or the objectives of general education.

Frequently these criticisms are justified because poor judgment has been used in the classroom! New topics are frequently taught while omitting important traditional topics! Often, teachers are not aware of the goals of the new presentation and hence are unable to give proper emphasis. An example may be useful here: Some teachers spend a great deal of time teaching students to compute with numerals in base 5 as if this in itself were an appropriate goal. Rather, the purpose of studying a new numeration system, such as base 5, is to build an understanding of numeration in general. It is not to build skill in computing in this base.

As a result of these criticisms, the new programs are continuing to take a new look at unresolved issues in mathematics education. This examination will undoubtedly result in further extensive change in the so-called modern mathematics curriculum. The end does not yet appear to be in sight.

The First Steps in Self-Evaluation

A particular school system needs to be aware of the current developments in school mathematics, but this is not enough. The school system must use this information to improve its own program. In organizing faculty and staff to engage in an effective program of curriculum evaluation and revision, the following suggestions are pertinent:

1. The principal of the school, or the superintendent of the school system, must be a prime advocator of curriculum evaluation and revision.

[1] American Association of School Administrators and others, *Administrative Responsibility for Improving Mathematics Programs,* August 1965, p. 7.

He must assist and encourage those staff members responsible for the initiation of the self-study, and must make the necessary provisions for its conduct.

2. The study should involve active participation by teachers, administrators, counselors, librarians, students, and parents. Each member of the group should have a desire to participate and should assume responsibility for contributing ideas and services according to his interests and abilities. Voluntary participation by interested persons is essential for success.

3. Qualified leadership for such an undertaking is essential. It can usually be provided by some competent, enthusiastic member of the teaching staff or administration. Such a person should furnish the leadership to get the group to recognize the need for an evaluative self-study and instill in them a desire to work on the problem. The leader should be well-informed in mathematics, methods, curriculum, and guidance.

4. How much up-to-date information can be gathered will depend on what resources in time, materials, and consultants are made available to the group. Time is needed for committee meetings, for visiting schools with superior programs, and for attending conferences. Curriculum guides, periodicals, books, and other reading materials should be available for study. Consultations should be arranged with business men, teachers, scientists, mathematicians, and educators who can speak on recent applications and developments in mathematics.

5. The mechanics of organization usually require a chairman or supervisor and small study groups or committees. Participants should have the privilege of choosing the topic or groups on which they wish to specialize.

6. Although interested persons will usually be willing to give extra hours to such a project, the program will be most effective if provision is made for doing much of the work on school time. A committee chairman can be released from classroom assignments for a semester or a year; other teachers may be given reduced teaching loads; substitute teachers may be provided so that committees can meet during the school day; needed clerical help is a "must." In some situations, teachers might be employed to work on the study during the summer.

7. The key to the success of this self-study is the leader. He should have a strong background in mathematics, be well informed about current trends in curriculum and method, and have superior leadership qualities. This person should be able to work with teachers, administrators, counselors, and parents. He should have an understanding of the classroom situation from kindergarten through grade twelve.

This person especially should be given time and resources to carry out his responsibilities. For maximum effectiveness in the evaluation of the current program and initiation of innovations, the leader should coordinate the entire mathematics sequence of the school, teach demonstration lessons, assist in purchasing materials, and plan in-service programs for mathematics teachers. He should coordinate testing and evaluation, and should teach the new program. He should be involved in hiring new teachers for mathematics vacancies and assist in making teacher assignments.

Examination of the Existing Program

Before the study group can make specific suggestions for revision or curriculum development in the particular school or school system, it needs to survey the current situation in mathematics, seeking answers to such questions as the following:

1. What are the goals and objectives of mathematics instruction?
2. What are the needs of students?
3. What ideas and skills are now being taught at each grade level?
4. What resources in the form of instructional materials are now available?
5. What level of competence are students now attaining?
6. How do the students differ and what provision is made for individual differences?
7. What special methods of instruction have been found effective?
8. What provision is made for improving mathematics instruction?
9. How is mathematics achievement being measured and evaluated?

Objectives Have Top Priority

In evaluating a school's mathematics program, the curriculum must be viewed as much more than a course outline or the selection of a new text. A course of study is developed only on the basis of an established set of objectives. The course of study is built on accepted principles of learning and these determine which methods and materials of instruction are most pertinent. An effective course of study also includes provision for the needs of students of varied interests and abilities and selects the ideas and skills to be taught, as well as the grade level at which they are taught. Such a course of study considers the topics and activities for enriching instruction and the correlation of topics with other fields. It establishes an evaluation program which includes evaluation achievement, the evaluation of instruction, and the evaluation of the total mathematics program.

Thus, to develop a new course of study and subsequently to evaluate this program, it is necessary to place major emphasis upon the objectives of mathematics instruction. Each school system must select objectives which are valid and appropriate in its own environment. However, care must also be taken to select objectives which reflect the best thinking of persons concerned with mathematics education and this often means that a particular school will go beyond its own faculty to obtain the opinion of experts in the field.

When teachers are asked to state the specific objectives of mathematics instruction, they usually list items such as the following:

1. The student has a *knowledge* and *understanding* of mathematical processes, facts, and concepts.
2. The student has *skill* in computing with understanding, accuracy, and efficiency.
3. The student has the ability to utilize a general *problem solving* technique.
4. The student understands the logical *structure of mathematics* and the nature of proof.
5. The student associates mathematical understandings and processes with *everyday situations.*
6. The student recognizes and appreciates the role of *mathematics in society.*
7. The student develops *study habits* essential for independent progress in mathematics.
8. The student develops *communication skill* so that he can read, write and speak correctly about mathematical ideas.
9. The student develops *interest* and *curiosity* about mathematical ideas.
10. The student develops *attitudes* which lead to appreciation, confidence, respect, initiative, and independence.

After objectives have been selected as being appropriate for a school, it is then necessary to translate each of them into desired student behaviors, thereby to determine whether a particular student has actually attained each objective. This task is extremely difficult but it provides the only valid means by which we can evaluate student outcomes. The parallel listing of objectives and specific behaviors which illustrate their attainment should be part of the school mathematics curriculum outline.

The Content of the Mathematics Program

The objectives of mathematics are attained by means of learning mathematical concepts, procedures, and structure. The content should be selected in terms of criteria such as the following:

1. The content should be suitable to attain the objectives sought. (Note that a single given textbook seldom satisfies this criterion.) The content should not be selected just because it represents either modern or classical mathematics.
2. The content should emphasize broad principles, key concepts, and structures rather than minor facts and skills. It should provide experiences in applications and should also present the aesthetic aspect of mathematics.
3. The mathematics must be correct. It should maintain a degree of rigor that is appropriate for the maturity of the students involved.
4. The program should form a continuous, coherent, cumulative sequence for students from kindergarten through grade twelve. The content for a given grade should be selected on the basis of its difficulty, and sequence. Particular attention should be given to the readiness of the pupils at each level.
5. The content should be sufficiently varied so that it can provide for students of different ability, interests, and needs.

When these criteria are applied, one notes that the new school mathematics can include almost all the topics of traditional courses. To these topics new ones have been added such as sets, numeration systems, probability, inequalities, number systems, vectors, and symbolic logic. Thus, content is used to emphasize structure and many traditional topics are introduced at an earlier age than in the past.

The Setting for a New Mathematics Program

With the availability of federal funds for the purchase of instructional aids, a tremendous increase has been noted in the production of useful devices and equipment for the mathematics classroom. The teacher who places emphasis on discovery and independent investigation, will need to have available a considerable variety of materials. However, these materials need to be selected for a specific purpose and should be used only when they increase the effectiveness of learning and instruction. The following types of learning aids will be found helpful:

1. Reading materials such as library books, pamphlets, supplementary texts, and programmed texts.

2. Audio-visual materials such as over-head projectors, overlays, films, filmstrips, stereoptican views, bulletin boards, chalkboards, and kinescopes.

3. Demonstration materials such as models and charts.

4. Manipulative materials for laboratory work such as models, kits, and calculators.

5. Measuring instruments such as a transit, ranging pole, and tapes.

6. Construction materials and tools for building exhibits, projects, and models.

7. Computing devices such as a calculator, slide rule, and possibly a computer trainer, computer terminal, or electronic computer.

All of these materials will of necessity require adequate space for storage. Since teacher use of materials is inversely proportional to their distance from the classroom, they should be readily available to every mathematics classroom. To provide for laboratory activities, the classroom itself needs furniture and equipment which are different from that of the traditional mathematics classroom.

The Staff

The key to a successful school program is the teacher. What is done in the classroom is of fundamental importance. A new program, which is taught in a routine, rigid, unenthusiastic fashion, will be a weak program. Thus, a school system and community that want a superior program should select and keep good teachers and give them the resources, the encouragement, and the supervision they need.

A first requirement for success in teaching mathematics is competence in the subject itself. However, competence in subject matter is not enough. Teachers need instruction on how to teach. This is even more difficult to learn than the subject matter. It means supervision, demonstration classes, and in-service education, including training in the proper use of new instructional materials. To remain up-to-date in the subject, teachers need in-service education or continued study at a university or college. Schools should give credit for any appropriate course work done by a teacher to increase his level of competence whether or not this work is graduate level. Because of the rapid change in mathematics education, the background of many of today's teachers is inadequate and considerably below that of new teachers. The needs of these people may be readily met in the undergraduate programs of our colleges and universities. Support should also be provided for attendance at professional conferences.

The instructional staff also needs to have adequate time for the preparation of lessons and materials. This requires reasonable teaching assignments, adequate instructional materials, and clerical assistance. The latter should include typing service, duplication of materials, correction of objective tests, and the keeping of routine records. Instructional materials include supplementary texts, professional texts, and published tests. A teaching load of four classes and not more than 100 students would almost certainly increase the effectiveness of every teacher and might well serve as an appropriate goal for a school which seeks to develop and maintain an excellent program in mathematics.

Instruction in Mathematics

All new school mathematics programs recommend the use of the *discovery approach*. This method requires extremely capable teachers for the teacher must be an expert interrogator, secure in his knowledge of mathematics, capable of making repeated adjustments in his teaching to utilize student suggestions and able to exercise patience when students seem slow in discovering the obvious. The discovery technique allows students to play an active role in the learning process. All students may not "discover" but those who do not are often still able to follow the reasoning displayed by their classmates and hence appreciate the "why" something is true. A modern mathematics program emphasizes "why" along with "how" through this approach. It is not enough that the student be given "rules" to find answers. If rules are to be given, the student must see these as logical deductions from that which he already knows.

New ideas from learning theory suggest that mathematics instruction can be more effective than it has been. To determine whether or not these ideas are influencing instruction in your school, another set of questions needs consideration:

1. Are lessons organized so that many ideas are discovered by students?
2. Is the course content organized so that ideas are presented in a spiral approach?
3. How is the transfer of knowledge promoted from mathematics to other fields?
4. What basic principles are followed in building computational skills?
5. Are flexibility and originality fostered in solving problems?
6. How are positive attitudes developed?
7. How are students motivated?
8. What activities are planned to build skill in reading, writing, and speaking about mathematical ideas?
9. How is creativity nourished?

Individual Differences

The mathematics program should be a complete program for students of differing abilities, needs, and interests and provision should be made for these individual differences in setting student goals and in testing student accomplishments. The program should describe how students are selected for each specific course. Adequate time and flexibility are needed so that the program can be adapted to individual differences and correlated with other course content. An effective program will include both enrichment activities as well as remedial instruction. Although different courses at a particular grade level will assist in providing for individual difference, many differences must also be handled directly in the classroom. Individual help during the class period, or outside the classroom, grouping within the class, independent study, differentiated assignments, and other approaches should be given careful attention. A teacher's answer to the question, "What is done to motivate the maximum performance of each student?" will indicate what provisions are being made for individual differences.

Evaluating a Mathematics Program

The effective mathematics curriculum will need continuous evaluation. This evaluation can be done only partially by tests and examinations. The performances of the student outside the classroom, in other classes, in college, in his vocation, in his home, and in his community are all significant in evaluating a student's achievement. For classroom evaluation, the following principles are considered basic:

1. Achievement should be measured in terms of *all goals* of the curriculum.
2. Achievement should be measured in terms of *growth,* change and progress in the attainment of goals.
3. Achievement should be measured in terms of the ability to *use* the facts, skills and principles learned.
4. Achievement should be measured in terms of *retention* over a long period of time.
5. Achievement should be measured in terms of levels of *mastery* and understanding.

To abide by these evaluative principles, a variety of tests must be used including reading tests, problem solving tests, performance tests, open book tests as well as achievement tests. The evaluation should include observations, inventories, check lists, the evaluation of student products, teacher-made tests, and published tests. A schedule of standardized tests should be established so that information will be available for examining program outcomes in relation to norms, for research and for long range curriculum evaluation as well as for immediate counseling purposes.

An important point should be emphasized. Often a teacher attributes poor student performance to failure on the part of the student. Note that when specific objectives are considered for each student, evaluation shows how *the program has met these objectives.* Student performance is an indication of whether the instructional program has or has not met its objectives. If not, the implication is that either the objectives are not appropriate for the particular student, or that the techniques of instruction and materials of instruction are not the best for attaining the objectives selected. In either case, the need for a careful study of the instructional program is indicated.

The need for evaluating the new programs in mathematics has been a major factor in directing research in mathematics education. To attempt to answer the questions about the effectiveness of new programs, new materials, and new emphasis, many comparison studies have been made. Despite the availability of such studies it should be recognized that a major obstacle prevents valid comparisons, namely that adequate measuring instruments which are independent of content are not currently available. Hence, if the two groups study different content, how can one get a suitable common test for comparison?

Some valid comparisons have been made, however, in the areas of computational skill, success in problem solving, and success in college. The results of such studies unfortunately are largely inconclusive and suggest only that the new programs are equally successful in attaining such objectives.

Summary

The rapid development and acceptance of the new school mathematics programs demonstrate the remarkable production that can result when competent people work together with adequate resources of time, talent, and finances. Most of the experimental projects in school mathematics have involved the cooperative efforts of mathematicians, educators, psychologists, and teachers supported by federal or foundation grants. Early participation in these new programs was a stimulating experience for teachers and students. This enthusiasm was contagious and made other teachers and schools want to participate. Favorable publicity for the programs was widespread by the press and professional literature. As a result, many classroom teachers and administrators adopted new programs with few questions asked. It was tacitly assumed that any program produced by mathematicians would be an improvement over traditional mathematics programs. Some schools adopted new programs without having a staff prepared to teach the new content. Some programs were accepted without asking where they lead or for what students they are designed.

As we look at mathematics education today, it is clear that the trend is from narrow, less precise content to broad, new, sophisticated content and from narrow, limited goals to broad, boundless goals. The stepped-up pace and the new techniques require a level of teaching competence and a level of learning competence that make desired progress difficult. How these competing factors will forge the new school mathematics of tomorrow is yet unknown. The participation of the entire educated community will be required to build a new school mathematics curriculum.

REFERENCES

Books and Pamphlets

1. American Association of School Administrators, *Administrative Responsibility for Improving Mathematics Programs.* Washington, D.C., 1965, 24 pages.
2. Deans, Edwina. *Elementary School Mathematics: New Directions.* U. S. Department of Health, Education, and Welfare, Office of Education. Washington, D.C.: Government Printing Office, 1963, 116 pp.
3. Educational Services Incorporated. *Goals for School Mathematics: The Report of the Cambridge Conference on School Mathematics.* Boston: Houghton Mifflin Co. 1963. ix + 102 pp.
4. Johnson, Donovan A. and Rahtz, Robert, *The New Mathematics in Our Schools.* Macmillan Company, New York, 1966.
5. Kinsella, John, *Secondary School Mathematics.* The Center for Applied Research in Education, New York, 1965.
6. Mager, Robert F., *Preparing Educational Objectives.* Fearon Publishers, California, 1962.
7. Mathematical Association of America, Committee on the Undergraduate Program in Mathematics. *Recommendations for the Training of Mathematics: A Summary,* Buffalo, N.Y. 1961. 15 pp.
8. National Council of Teachers of Mathematics, Committee on Criteria for the Analysis of Instructional Materials. *Aids for Evaluators of Mathematics Textbooks.* Washington, D.C. 1965.
9. National Council of Teachers of Mathematics, *An Analysis of New Mathematics Programs.* Washington, D.C.: The Council, 1963. 72 pp.
10. National Council of Teachers of Mathematics. *Evaluation in Mathematics.* Twenty-Sixth Yearbook. Washington, D.C.: NCTM, 1961. 216 pp.
11. National Council of Teachers of Mathematics. *The Growth of Mathematical Ideas. Grades K-12.* Twenty-Fourth Yearbook. Washington, D.C.: NCTM, 1959. 507 pp.
12. National Council of Teachers of Mathematics. *The Revolution in School Mathematics.* Washington, D.C.: NCTM, 1961. 90 pp.

13. Phillips, Harry L. and Kluttz, Marguerite. *Modern Mathematics and Your Child.* U. S. Department of Health, Education, and Welfare, Office of Education. Washington, D.C.: Government Printing Office, 1963. 28 pp.
14. Schult, Veryl, and Abell, Theodore L. *Inservice Mathematics Education: Promising Practices for Elementary and Secondary School Teachers.* U. S. Department of Health, Education, and Welfare, Office of Education, Washington, D.C.: Government Printing Office, 1964. 129 pp.

Periodicals

1. Association for Supervision and Curriculum Development. "Mathematics in the School" *Educational Leadership* 19: 353–89; March, 1962.
2. Brown, Kenneth E., Edwina Deans and Veryl Schult, "The Lively Third R" *American Education.* June, 1966.
3. Fawcett, Harold P., "Guidelines in Mathematics Education," *Mathematics Teacher.* October, 1960.
4. Fehr, Howard, "Sense and Nonsense in A Modern School Mathematics Program" *Arithmetic Teacher* February, 1965.
5. Inbody, Donald, "Helping Parents Understand New Mathematics Programs," *Arithmetic Teacher* December, 1964.
6. Mueller, Francis J., "Five Recommendations to School Systems for Improving Secondary School Mathematics Instruction" *Mathematics Teacher* December, 1962.
7. Stone, Marshall, "The Revolution in Mathematics," *American Mathematical Monthly,* October, 1961.

Films

1. *Donald in Math-Magic Land.* 30 minutes, 16mm, sound color Disney Films.
2. *Mathematics for Elementary School Teachers.* 11 films, 30 minutes, 16mm, sound color. United World Films.
3. *Mathematics for Tomorrow.* 29 minutes, 16mm, sound color National Council of Teachers of Mathematics.
4. *SMSG Teacher Training Films.* 30 films. 30 min. 16mm, sound, color. Modern Learning Aids.

For Further Reading

Adler, Irving, "Some Thoughts About Curriculum Revision," *The Mathematics Teacher,* November, 1963, 56: 505–510.

Bowie, Harold E., "Recent Developments in Mathematics Education," *School and Society,* April 17, 1965, 93: 252–254.

Brown, Kenneth E., and Theodore L. Abell, *Analysis of Research in the Teaching of Mathematics,* Bulletin 1965, No. 28, U. S. Department of Health, Education, and Welfare, Office of Education, Washington, D.C., 1965.

Cambridge Conference on School Mathematics, *Goals for School Mathematics,* the Report of the Conference, Educational Services Inc., Houghton Mifflin Company, Boston, 1963.

Dessart, Donald J., "Mathematics in the Secondary School," *Review of Educational Research,* June, 1964, 34: 298–312.

Folsom, Mary, "Why the New Mathematics?" *The Instructor,* December, 1963, 7, 90–91, Vol. 73.

Johnson, Donovan A., "Evaluating a School Mathematics Curriculum," *School and Society,* December 1, 1962, 90: 424–426.

Kline, Morris, "A Proposal for the High School Mathematics Curriculum," *The Mathematics Teacher,* April, 1966, 59: 322–330.

Kline, Morris, "The Ancients Versus the Moderns, a New Battle of the Books," *The Mathematics Teacher,* October, 1958, 51: 418–427.

Mayor, John R., and John A. Brown, "New Mathematics in the Junior High Schools," *Educational Leadership,* December, 1960, 18: 165–169.

Meder, Albert, Jr., "The Ancients Versus the Moderns — a Reply," *The Mathematics Teacher,* October, 1958, 51: 428–433.

National Council of Teachers of Mathematics, *The Growth of Mathematical Ideas; Grades K-12,* Twenty-fourth Yearbook, National Council of Teachers of Mathematics, The Council, Washington, D.C., 1959.

National Council of Teachers of Mathematics, *Topics in Mathematics for Elementary School Teachers,* Twenty-ninth Yearbook, National Council of Teachers of Mathematics, The Council, Washington, D.C., 1964.

Moise, Edwin, "The New Mathematics Programs," *The Education Digest,* September, 1962, 28: 28–32.

Nielson, Ross A., "Evaluating the Secondary Mathematics Program," *The North Central Association Quarterly,* Winter, 1964, 38: 249–254.

Schutt, Veryl, "A New Look at the Old Mathematics," *NEA Journal,* April, 1964, 12–15, Vol. 53.

Scott, Foresman and Company, *Teaching Trends in Mathematics,* A Collection of Seven Professional Articles on Mathematics Teaching, 16 pages, Scott, Foresman and Company, Fair Lawn, New Jersey, undated.

Williams, Emmett D., and Robert V. Shuff, "Comparative Study of SMSG and Traditional Mathematics Text Material," *The Mathematics Teacher,* November, 1963, 56: 495–504.

Zant, James H., "A Proposal for the High School Mathematics Curriculum — What Does It Mean?" *The Mathematics Teacher,* April, 1966, 59: 331–334.

PART SIX

Health, Physical Education, Recreation

32. The Role of Physical Education in Health and Fitness

Delbert Oberteuffer

So far in the 20th century there have been four distinct periods of intensified interest in the role of physical education in fitness. We are today in the fourth discernible period. Theodore Roosevelt started the first one when he publicly advocated the vigorous life as a way of making

From Delbert Oberteuffer, "The Role of Physical Education in Health and Fitness," *American Journal of Public Health,* July, 1962, 52: 1155–1160. A noted spokesman for health education and physical education for nearly four decades, Delbert Oberteuffer is Emeritus Professor of Health Education and Physical Education at the Ohio State University. He is the editor of the *Journal of School Health* and the author of five books. His latest text is a 1966 revision of *School Health Education.* This article is reprinted by permission of Professor Oberteuffer and of the *American Journal of Public Health,* Copyright 1962, by the American Public Health Association, Inc.

our nation strong. The second was caused by the revelations of the physical examinations in World War I, which shocked legislators to the point where some 27 states passed laws in the succeeding ten years requiring that physical education be taught in schools as a way of improving the vigor of our youth. World War II brought the third national effort to improve physical fitness of the general as well as the school public. Those of us who were tapped for this sort of civilian service will remember that we were directed to rope off streets and by using available firemen and policemen lead the public in a program of exercises aimed at improving the fiber of the embattled American. And now for the fourth time in this century a wave of interest is felt. It is marked by Presidential citations of need and by extraordinary efforts from the Capitol to persuade communities to improve the fitness of youth by developing strong programs of health education and physical education including a recommended daily 15-minute period of vigorous exercises.

Historically, such developments have occurred before. At various times when nations have faced perils, either real or imaginary, efforts have been made to improve the fitness of youth as an important part of the solution to the problem. Programs of physical training in 19th century Germany and Sweden, and in 20th century Italy, Germany, and Russia have been used for national purposes in support of political or social ideologies. Youth has been captured in every instance and drilled, exercised, and strengthened to support the beneficent system, and, more importantly, to protect that system against its enemies.

So it is with us. Undoubtedly, we need a strong populace for either a warm peace or the cold war. To guard the health of the nation is a worthy ambition no matter what our destiny may be. To control disease, to improve nutrition, to prevent mental and nervous diseases, to seek emotional, social, and intellectual stability, and to secure appropriate growth and development of children and youth become almost an abiding national passion. We are committed to such effort and enthusiastically so. Our form of political life not only requires a nation of healthy citizens, but guarantees them the right to be healthy.

But, whenever we go through one of these periods of greater interest in fitness we should at least be in possession of an accurate picture of need in order to develop a true program in response. We should be able to distinguish fact from fiction in both areas of need and program. How is it today?

Some people have developed a test of muscular strength and flexibility of the spine, given it to several thousand children here and abroad, find our youth comparing unfavorably with Europeans, or Japanese, or whoever, and have immediately concluded (a) that our children, in fact all of us, are weak, and flabby, (b) that our technological culture is destructive of our capacity for survival, and (c) if we do not do something about it we will lose the cold war. This position, widely advertised in the popular press, has created quite a national stir.

So once again programs of physical education are asked to step up the intensity of their purpose and the vigor of their content in order to save youth, and thus our country, from desuetude, if not actual destruction! We have reemphasized an atrociously unscientific but popular term "physical fitness" and we are being told that our children are woefully deficient in it. It is alarming, in more ways than one because it is not a situation marked by clear fact, clear need, and clear response. In fact there is a great confusion in all three categories — of fact, of need, and of response or program.

For example, does one equate the sound advice and factual information of scientists in the area of child growth and development, or of pediatricians, with the television personality who advocates the criss-cross leg exercise for infants three months old? Does one equate the scientific papers appearing in the collection from the Institute of Normal Human Anatomy meeting in Rome in 1960, and bearing the imprint of such international names as Larson, Hollmann, Simon, Wolffe, Jokl, Missiuro, and the others who contributed, with the prattle of those who run the exercise emporiums for money and who are advertised as our greatest physical educators? Does one equate the sound advice on exercise coming from exercise physiologists such as Karpovich, Steinhaus, or Mayer with opportunistic entrepreneurs who would not know the myocardium from oxygen debt?

But we wander. Our problem is: What is the role of physical education in health and fitness? Let me see if my version of the answer comes anywhere near your version.

In the first place the need for activity on the part of the human organism has been well established. Documentation of this is unnecessary. The evidence is clear. Man is an active creature and activity is important to his growth, development, and survival. The need for exercise is here to stay.

But apparently nature does not care a bit how one gets the activity needed. The "form" the activity takes is biologically unimportant as long as no harm is done. Run around the block, play football, dance a jig, or go climb a telephone pole. The heart does not care. Muscle does not care. The rectus abdominus, which is a pretty important muscle in maintaining visceral order against visceral chaos does not care whether it is used in basketball, bowling, or burglary as long as it is used. If muscular strength is what we are after to correct the evil ways into which we have fallen, nature does not care how we get it — or at what price. Strength building activities can be anything that build strength — and thus they need to have no other purpose, no other meaning, no discernible relationship to anything significant except strength itself.

I am afraid this is the sort of thing that some are calling "physical" fitness — a sort of muscular development which comes from exercise and which can be used for any purpose at the discretion of the possessor.

In these terms there would be relatively few problems involved in making the nation muscularly strong. Just set 40 million school children to exercising with sufficient vigor and keep them at it and we will accomplish our objective!

There are only two things wrong with this concept: Exercise is only partially responsible for fitness, and strength is only one of the concerns of physical education.

Our scientists, our philosophers, our educators, the better informed physical educators, and even our poets have proclaimed that there is more to fitness than muscle strength. A conference of such people in 1956 described fitness as "That state which characterizes the degree to which the person is able to function."[1] It implies the ability of each person to develop most effectively his potentialities. And the conference agreed that fitness is maintained at a high level only if motivation is continuously present! This requires an inner desire — an egogenic stimulation. The activities which produce fitness must have meaning! The conference listed seven components of fitness, all of which are related to each other and are mutually interdependent. These are:

1. Optimum organic health consistent with heredity and the application of present health knowledge.
2. Sufficient coordination, strength, and vitality to meet emergencies, as well as the requirements of daily living.
3. Emotional stability to meet the stresses and strains of modern life.
4. Social consciousness and adaptability with respect to the requirements of group living.
5. Sufficient knowledge and insight to make suitable decisions and arrive at feasible solutions to problems.
6. Attitudes, values, and skills which stimulate satisfactory participation in a full range of daily activities.
7. Spiritual and moral qualities which contribute the fullest measure of living in a democratic society.

Now what does physical education have to do with fitness as described in those terms? Well, the relationship to all seven is the only thing that makes physical education physical "education." Otherwise it would be physical training — and there is a vast and uncomfortable difference between the two!

In the somewhat peculiar and not clearly understood combination of words which is "physical education," the noun "education" becomes of great importance. It is not the same thing as training — physical training. Physical training trains, just as you train a dog or a pony. Kelley and Rasey say:[2]

> "Much of our education is designed to train people rather than to educate them. When one individual trains another, he delimits the variety of possible responses, making the desired responses automatic and eliminating the possibility of other responses. We can train lower animals, but we cannot educate them. Training, limiting possible responses, is enslaving, while educating is liberating. It is not that one is trained not to think, but that the act of training by its very nature delimits thinking. In the degree that the individual thus trained does think, he has been robbed of confidence in his own thinking."

But physical education implies that someone, somehow, is being educated, through the games, sports, and dance culturally important to our race (and it is important to know the difference).

To educate means to enrich the capacities of human intelligence. It means to help the individual gain increasing possession of himself and his powers; it means to recapitulate his culture, to deepen and widen its social content, to give him control over the methods of living within that culture. Some would say that the essence of education is the development of intelligence, of powers of thought, of the capacity for reflection, of human reason. The task of education is to develop the fullest capacity to take thought, to reflect, to weigh, to foresee, to consider consequences, to choose among alternatives. There may be other descriptions of education but in the main they all describe a relationship between the learner and his environment in which the former is assisted to gain some personal control over and understanding of the latter by the cultivation of powers inherent within him. This is to make him fit in the terms the conference described. He learns to do this. He cannot do it as a child and as life goes on he develops his powers to the point where he can. Hullfish adds this thought:[3]

"The term learning may then be applied to any process within which potential stimuli become meaningful, change meaning, are discriminated with respect to possible meaning, and the like."

If we view meanings as the basic building blocks of learning, then any event which results in a reconstruction or reorganization of a meaning pattern may be called a learning experience. Any experience, then, which in consequence of its meaningfulness "increases ability to direct the course of subsequent experience" may be called an educative experience.

Now if physical education means that someone is educated through or by the "physical" experience, or in a "physical" environment, then the experience should be productive of the qualities described in the definitions. Can this happen? Does this happen? By accident, or by design? Maybe it is that no education at all takes place through the physical education experience. At least in these terms. Perhaps this is not what the term physical education is meant to imply. Perhaps the only relation physical education has to education is that experience in physical education so conditions the organism that it can receive the stimuli which permits the student to become educated! This is the idea of the sound body in which to house the sound "mind." This is the ancient dichotomous view. This belies man's unity. To many persons in physical education and to many from other fields other values from the physical education experience all loom larger and more important than the educational ones. Physical values come first — educational values a poor second, and only if something good happens to come along.

It should be clear, however, that if that point of view is held then it is hypocritical to use the term physical education. The term should be physical training, or physical exercise, or some other to describe what is happening. If "education" is the noun used then a clear, reasonable and demonstrable relationship to its substance must be developed in the physical education curricula. Someone must be educated. Educational outcomes must be sought, planned for, taught for, and obtained. They must be of prime concern, not secondary or incidental within a physical education program.

What kinds of outcomes could be considered educational? What experiences in physical education programs will be likely to cultivate this intelligence, develop this ability to think, to weigh, to reckon consequences, to assume possession of one's self and one's powers, to become a rational man?

The answer is inherent in the questions. Only those experiences which demand thinking will produce thinking! Only that kind of participation which requires the student to weigh, to reflect, to study will produce those qualities. It will not be likely that they will be produced by the kind of activity in which the participating individual does not become involved in some problem requiring solving, evaluating, thinking. Can a team have the chance to solve some of its own problems or must the coach always direct the strategy, call the plays? Can a class become involved in seeking desirable outcomes from their work? Is social, religious, racial integration of consequence to students? What responses can be developed to cheating at games, sportsmanship, values in athletics, and to appreciation of good play?

Experience in a well conceived physical education program can aid in the solution of such problems. The understanding of integrative processes and the relationship of the physiological, psychological, and other functional elements to development can be enhanced through physical education. Comprehension of strength, ability, courage, daring, and skill can be developed. One makes progress in the solution of such developmental tasks as achieving skill in motor control and coordination, independence in self-care, learning to live in groups, and in relation to competitors.

An analysis of the effects of these experiences from physical education relate directly to the stated components of fitness, and this kind of physical education has an important relation to fitness and health.

But, let us go one step farther. There is perhaps no more compelling problem facing our educational system than that of deepening and widening our understanding of democracy. Presidents have said that our young people must be physically, mentally, and spiritually prepared for American citizenship. This seems to relate to component numbers 4 and 7 from the conference report — social adaptability and qualities which make it possible to live in a democratic society.

How do you go about developing these qualities? By marching, drilling, exercising in groups and mobs under the impersonal supervision of an authoritarian drillmaster who counts the numbers while the victims pray they may be spared further boredom and when released from it vow never to have anything to do with physical exercise the rest of their lives? This is hardly a satisfying experience in adaptability to group living; hardly productive of the spiritual and moral qualities needed to live successfully in a democracy! This sort of thing may temporarily produce some muscular strength but it is also very likely to produce emotional and perhaps even spiritual trauma.

To preserve the democratic way, to bring the oncoming generations into a clear understanding of its meaning, to develop a deep and unmistakable sensitivity to what democracy really is — this is a compelling challenge. The program of physical education cannot afford to be caught napping in this respect; nor can it be found guilty of teaching by precept or practice the ways of behaving and thinking which are characteristic of authoritarian regimes.

We have said that schools in general and physical education programs in particular have always been used as instruments of political and social power. One shudders at the memory of the marching Hitler youth — fit, strong, singing their way through exercises and sports so they could better reflect the marching ruthlessness of the most inhuman regime the 20th century has known.

What social and political purpose then does 20th century American physical education serve? It cannot be culturally neutral. Opportunities abound in the physical education program to provide experience with democratic processes. It should be clearly said and clearly understood that as long as physical education remains an element in the curriculum of a school or college which is dedicated to the perpetuation of the democratic way, no teaching or administrative practice may, with conscience, demonstrate other and contrary values. The autocratic empirical administrator is as bad as the authoritarian teacher or coach. Each is a menace, in his or her own way, to the planned intellectualized approach to the perpetuation of democracy through the schools.

In some programs the students all wear the same kind of uniform, go through the same exercises, count the same cadence as they march, respond with the same imposed replies, affect the same posturing as they go through their exercises. They conform. The standard is set. The motive comes from outside, from above. It takes no intellectual response to "count-off" and to wave one's arms about in a calisthenic drill aimed at "physical condition."

It does, however, require self-initiated intellectual response to figure out the strategy of a game and execute it. Or to compose a dance, or to plot the course for an overnight hike. It requires self-initiated activity to practice what one has been shown on how to swim, or how to kick a soccer ball. This type of activity must come from within, and be willingly chosen as a rewarding experience. This sort of activity is within the cultural tradition of a free people.

The opportunity is here. Modern physical education can serve as an educative experience or it can frankly and honorably renounce its claims to education and direct its energies to producing the sound body in which to house the sound mind. There is something pathetically unscientific about that effort but there is nothing dishonorable in it — except that it must not use the term physical education.

But to seek the integrative development of the whole man, to be as concerned with his ethics as with his physiology, to be helpful in his interpretations of motives, to aid him in his understanding of human nature, to help explore those deep wells of yearning within himself, to help him see that excellence is not measured wholly by scores — these are some of the other outcomes which are within the reach of a well planned physical education curriculum.

And so we, at any rate, believe the role of physical education in health and fitness is clear — and important. It is indispensable to both. Physical training, on the other hand, or merely muscle exercises for strength alone may, paradoxically, be destructive of the many things they are designed to help. By their sheer meaninglessness and potential for boredom, and because they are almost invariably terminal experiences, and because they offer no intrinsic appeal, they may be so regarded by the self-directing individual to drive him away from any desire to be fit or from any practice which may contribute to his fitness.

We must be careful, not merely enthusiastic. Not just any activity as long as it produces sweat and strength is educative in the rational interpretation of that word. From modern physical education programs we expect lasting values in continuous participation — an accumulation of "fitness scores" is not only insignificant compared to this but may actually be defeating this goal.

REFERENCES

1. The AAHPER Fitness Conference reported in J. Health & Phys. Educ. 27,6:8 (Sept.), 1956.
2. Kelley, Earl C., and Rasey, Marie I. Education and the Nature of Man. New York, N.Y.: Harper, 1956, p. 106.
3. Hullfish, H. Gordon, and Smith, Philip G. Reflective Thinking: The Method of Education. New York, N.Y.: Dodd, Mead, 1961.

33. Recess Is Not Enough

Bruce L. Bennett

"Gee, Mother, these kids are lucky. They have a gymnasium!" exclaimed a fourth grader after visiting the large sixty-year-old school her mother attended as a child.

This youngster attended a modern suburban school. Faced with mounting costs and increased enrollments, many school boards have sought to economize by building new schools without gymnasiums or converting old gymnasiums into classroom use. Often, too, there is no physical education teacher or physical education class. Children have only recess periods under the supervision of the classroom teacher or older boys.

Many parents and some school administrators evidently feel that the recess period is sufficient for the children. Others consider that the baseball competition conducted after school by the local Boosters Club is a sufficient substitute for school physical education.[1] Is there justification for the organized and planned physical education class taught by a qualified and specially trained teacher? Should money be spent for a gymnasium when classrooms are in short supply? Should a school board buy extra acres of land to provide a playground?

Motor Development

Before going further, it may prove helpful to emphasize that motor skills and physical activities cannot be considered as an isolated or dis-

From Bruce L. Bennett, "Recess Is Not Enough," *Childhood Education,* May, 1959, 35: 398–402. Bruce L. Bennett is Professor of Physical Education and Chairman of the Graduate Committee for the Department of Physical Education at The Ohio State University. He is co-author of *World History of Physical Education.* Reprinted by permission of the Association for Childhood Education International, 3615 Wisconsin Avenue, N.W., Washington, D.C.

[1] Kenneth D. Miller, "Let's Quit Exploiting Children's Sports," *Today's Health,* XXXV, May 1957, pp. 18–20.

crete part of a child's education. Gates, an educational psychologist, expresses this fact in these words:

> Motor development is a handmaiden of mental development. The child experiments, manipulates, explores, and gratifies much of his intellectual curiosity by way of motor activities. In like manner, motor behavior serves as a vehicle for a large portion of the child's social contacts and his learning of ways of cooperating with others. Similarly, motor development also has an important bearing on a child's emotional behavior, since a child's strength, speed, coordination, and skill very often determine whether a child will experience success or failure, and whether he will be thwarted and angry or threatened and afraid.[2]

Motor activities therefore are an integral part of the total education and development of the child.

The significance of motor activities on physiological processes has been the subject of much research and study. Physiologists Schneider and Karpovich state that "experiments on human beings and animals have proved that a certain amount of physical exercise is indispensable in the cardiovascular and respiratory system."[3] Two physicians, Smiley and Gould, declare that "a considerable amount of muscle activity is almost as essential to the growth of a child as is proper nutrition."[4] The well-known physiologists, Carlson and Johnson, make a concise evaluation of the effects of exercise in these words:

> . . . the increased effectiveness of the circulatory and respiratory adjustments to exercise and the better muscular coordination and decreased waste movements that result are probably of much greater significance than mere increase in muscle size and strength.[5]

Many authorities have pointed out the effect of physical activities on posture. Olson says that "much exercise in running, jumping, climbing and throwing are basic approaches to development of suitable posture for a given child."[6] It should be stated that good posture is desirable

[2] Arthur I. Gates, Arthur T. Jersild, T. R. McConnell and Robert C. Challman, *Educational Psychology* (New York: The Macmillan Co., 1948), p. 61.

[3] Edward C. Schneider and Peter V. Karpovich, *Physiology of Muscular Activity* (Philadelphia: W. B. Saunders Co., 1948), p. 255.

[4] Dean F. Smiley and Adrian G. Gould, *Your Health* (New York: The Macmillan Co., 1951), p. 456.

[5] Anton J. Carlson and Victor Johnson, *The Machinery of the Body* (Chicago: University of Chicago Press, copyright 1953), pp. 359–60.

[6] Willard C. Olson, *Child Development* (Boston: D. C. Heath & Co., 1949), p. 84.

largely for esthetic reasons and probably does not confer any particular physiological benefits.

The values stated so far can certainly be achieved in large part through free play or the recess period. However, there are other values important for social and personality development which are less likely to be achieved through recess activities.

Bolster Social Prestige

Educational psychologists Breckenridge and Vincent discuss this matter in some detail. They point out the fact that much social contact evolves around physical skills and activities. "The boy who cannot throw a ball or run fast becomes a group liability. The girl who does not roller skate or ride a bicycle with skill is likely to have a lonely time."[7] Children need to be taught various skills which will bolster their confidence and prestige when they are with other children. "A child, once finding some confidence with other children in one skill or ability, is encouraged to try others, and can be led on into more and more ascendant behavior."[8]

Jones also emphasizes investigations which show the value of specific motor training in the treatment of early personality difficulties, such as fears, submissiveness and attitudes resulting from inferiority feelings.[9] A psychiatrist, Margaret Mahler, declares, "Motor release is the most important and soundest device of the growing child to serve ego growth, obtain balance, and form an always available safety valve against anxiety."[10] The well-known psychiatrist, William Menninger, in a study at his clinic, found that a well-adjusted person learns how to play and includes play as an important feature of his life much more frequently than the average maladjusted person.[11]

The evidence cited above provides concise but impressive testimony of the social and psychological significance of motor activities for individual boys and girls. The experts cited consider physical activity as something far more important than just "letting off steam" or "turn-

[7] Marian E. Breckenridge and E. Lee Vincent. *Child Development* (Philadelphia: W. B. Saunders Co., 1955), p. 272.

[8] *Ibid.*, p. 349.

[9] Harold E. Jones, *Motor Performance and Growth* (Berkeley: University of California Press, 1949), p. 161.

[10] Margaret Mahler, "Ego Psychology Applied to Behavior Problems," in Lewis, Nolan D. C., and Bernard L. Pacella, eds., *Modern Trends in Child Psychiatry* (New York: International Universities Press, 1945), p. 50.

[11] William Menninger, "Recreation and Mental Health," *Recreation*, XXXXII, Nov. 1948, p. 343.

ing young colts out to romp." These latter statements are completely untenable in the light of modern scientific knowledge about child growth and development.

Children Need Play

What further evidence is there that the recess period alone is insufficient and inadequate to meet the needs of children? Menninger declares that the ability to play is a *learned ability* and that children should have ample opportunities for play alone, with each other, and with their parents, both at home and elsewhere.[12] Smiley and Gould believe that the needs of children make a demand for children's playgrounds in much greater numbers than have been provided heretofore.[13] Breckenridge and Vincent challenge the opinion of those who see no need for supervision or instruction. Drawing upon certain experimental data, they conclude: ". . . we shall have to change the present *laissez faire* policy of most schools and playgrounds which assumes that children learn social lessons in free group play without teaching supervision."[14] Children do not necessarily learn to be cooperative, unselfish and respectful of the rights and feelings of others through free play alone. Recess can be a frightening and shattering experience for the timid, unassertive or poorly coordinated child.

Learn Other Skills

What, then, should be the nature of a sound physical education program which will achieve maximal results in the total growth and development of children? Breckenridge, Vincent, Olson and Gates all arrive at similar conclusions. Breckenridge and Vincent express their conviction that physical education programs "to be useful as well as interesting" to children must help them to enlarge on the variety of their skills as well as use skills already mastered.[15] This statement is based on the fact that as children master one skill, they quickly seek to add variations. What an opportunity this provides for the teacher of physical education! The natural interest of youngsters in hanging and climbing can be challenged by the competent teacher who demonstrates a single knee hang from the horizontal bar, a double-knee hang, a skin-the-cat hang, and who asks individual class members to think up and do other variations (with judicious spotting,* of course!). These activities will develop needed strength and coordination for rope or pole climbing

[12] *Ibid.*, p. 346.
[13] Smiley and Gould, *op. cit.*, p. 456.
[14] Breckenridge and Vincent, *op. cit.*, p. 349.
[15] *Ibid.*, p. 258.
* A term denoting safety procedures used to avoid possible injury.

and enhance the chances for successful and satisfying achievement for each child. A well-planned program of games, relays and rhythms can be so satisfying and challenging to children because new, useful and inherently enjoyable activities are offered. The recess period provides an occasion for the use of skills already mastered but cannot provide a chance for children to learn other skills.

The principle of offering a broad program of activities is strongly endorsed by Olson, who says:

> As a part of a desirable environment for children, extensive opportunity should be available for every suitable type of physical activity and sport, and for the development of skills which can be pursued into later life.[16]

He further stresses the need for exercise and instruction to facilitate the learning of skills such as swimming, skating and the like. Children will miss out on the acquisition of many such skills if they are not offered the chance to participate.[17] They will lose the opportunity to develop an initial interest in physical activities which they might be able to enjoy in later life. A child who learns to ice skate has acquired a skill which he can always draw upon for pleasure and satisfaction.

Gates sees other dangers in a physical education program limited to a few games, usually of a highly organized nature, such as basketball or baseball. Such a program may fail to give all children opportunities for their abilities and may also distort social relationships and emotional adjustments by providing opportunities for successful achievement and social prestige to children most competent in those few activities.[18] All children do not like basketball. Some will enjoy soccer much more if it is properly taught. Heavy emphasis on one or two team sports performs an injustice for other boys and girls who may want to participate in these sports at their own level of ability or may want to learn other activities.

Many adults can trace a distaste for certain games to some unpleasant experiences as children. As Breckenridge and Vincent suggest, a competent physical education teacher can work with the shy and unskilled youngster and teach him some of the skills so that he can perform creditably enough in the competitive situation to merit the good will of his teammates.[19] The results of some of these unfortunate experiences

[16] Olson, *op. cit.*, p. 85.
[17] *Ibid.*, p. 77.
[18] Gates, *op. cit.*, p. 78
[19] Breckenridge and Vincent, *op. cit.*, p. 349.

may be a partial explanation for the findings reported by Jersild that students at the high school age change their role from participant to spectator. Studies reveal that there is a marked decline in the number of different play activities used by children between the ages of ten and twenty.[20] Some of this decline may be due to poor and inadequate elementary school physical education programs and leadership, although other factors are involved.

The purpose of this article has been to try to show why elementary school children need physical education, regularly taught by the teacher and providing a broad and varied program of activities. Actually, one probably can demonstrate that physical education is even more important in the elementary school than in the high school, although such a comparison is not intended here. Yet it is no doubt true that physical education in the elementary schools today is generally more inadequate than physical education in the secondary schools, with the possible exception of some of the larger cities. Let it be earnestly hoped that parents and administrators throughout the country will recognize the validity of the need for physical education. Let's see to it that our children will no longer miss out on the values which physical education can contribute to their over-all growth and development in these formative years. Recess is not enough!

[20] Arthur T. Jersild, *Child Development and the Curriculum,* 38th Yearbook of the National Society for the Study of Education, Part I, 1939, p. 72.

34. An Image of a Future Program

J. Lloyd Trump

The secondary school program for health, physical education, and recreation proposed in this article does not exist in any school. You cannot visit a school to see how it works. No data can be presented to prove its worth.

The program is presented with considerable specificity in order to stimulate thinking and discussion. Actually, the proposals should be considered as hypotheses to be tested. Much research needs to be conducted. Many new approaches to the secondary school program need to be tried.

The writer's criticisms of today's schools are not based on belief that everything should be changed. As a matter of fact, nowhere in the world have so many been educated so well as in the United States. However, constant searching for better ways of doing things constitutes the essence of this superiority. The proposals made here are to stimulate thinking and discussion. Schools must serve the divergent needs of *all* students. What is known about the needs of youth, the social setting and the learning process must be utilized to the utmost. Organized education should not limit its efforts primarily to the training of the mind or to the development of an aristocracy of the intelligent few. Toughness in education has no inherent merit.

Today's schools through their organization and procedures inhibit the accomplishment of many of the stated goals of instruction, not only in physical education but in other subject areas as well. Basic changes are needed in the organization of instruction, in staffing patterns, the

From J. Lloyd Trump, "An Image of a Future Secondary School Health, Physical Education, and Recreation Program," *Journal of Health, Physical Education, Recreation,* January, 1961, 15–17, Vol. 32. J. Lloyd Trump, Associate Secretary of the National Association of Secondary School Principals, has published many works on curriculum and curriculum change, school reorganization, staff utilization, and school administration. Among the best-known are *Images of the Future: A New Approach to the Secondary School* and *Guide to Better Schools: Focus on Change,* coauthor. Reprinted by permission of JOHPER, the American Association for Health, Physical Education, and Recreation, and the author.

use of technology, and in curriculum content. This article shows how these needed changes can affect the health, physical education, and recreation program.

The new approaches have been suggested by experimental projects sponsored by the National Association of Secondary-School Principals (NEA). The ideas have come out of schools. Almost 100 junior and senior high schools were involved in one way or another during the past four years. Although only a few of the studies directly concerned health and physical education instruction, what was learned in other subject areas can be readily translated. That is what this article purports to do as it describes the future school.

Class Size

Class size in health, physical education, and recreation, as in other areas of the curriculum, will vary with the purposes and content of instruction. Actually, there will be three types of classes:

Classes of 100–150 students for large-group instruction
Classes of 15 or less for small-group discussion
Classes of 60, deployable in size at will, for work in laboratories

Large-group instruction. The most competent available person, on the school staff or from outside, will present ideas through talks and demonstrations to relatively large groups of students in order to save time and energy of staff as well as make these "best persons" logistically available to *all* of the students. Most of the time this instruction will be in face-to-face groups with the aid of an overhead projector. At other times, it will take place via television, video tape, or films, to groups even larger than 150.

Recreation interests will thus be stimulated by putting students in contact with someone "fired up" with an area of interest. A respected physician will describe health practices. Physical fitness will be explained and demonstrated. The most competent teacher will show how to develop basic skills in a sport.

Most of the time these large groups will be coeducational. Usually the make-up of the group will depend on past training and knowledge. The purposes will determine the constituency of the groups.

Small-group discussion. Classes of 15 or fewer students will meet regularly with a professional teacher to discuss problems and programs. The group is small so all will participate in the discussions. The teacher will be mainly a consultant and observer.

The make-up of these small classes can be changed at will as the needs of students change. The small group combines therapeutic and instructional services to students.

Work in the laboratories. The health, physical education, and recreation laboratory is a place where students individually, or in small groups, or in groups of 60 will learn by doing. They will learn and practice physical fitness exercises which they can also do at home. They will learn the fundamental skills of games that can be played at other times in gymnasiums and on playing fields at school and in the community. They will practice hobbies that can be recreational interests at home and in the community.

The laboratories will provide space for physical activities as described. They will also house automated learning devices (teaching machines for self-instruction by individuals and small groups). Students will be able to tell immediately whether or not they have learned, and what they need to do next. Other appropriate supplies will be provided so the varied needs of students can be served.

Student Schedules

The average student in the future program of health, physical education, and recreation will spend a minimum of 200 minutes per week in school in the following manner:

40 minutes — once a week as member of a large group
40 minutes — once a week as member of a class of 15
120 minutes — twice a week in the laboratory

The purpose of the program is to develop individual responsibility for the student's own learning. All students will be expected to follow systematic programs of fitness, games, recreation, and good physical and mental health habits outside these minimum times. Teachers will know about these practices of students as they listen to the discussions in the small groups, observe physical and mental adjustment and developments, and analyze records of home and community activities.

Some students will "study in depth" in these fields just as some other students concentrate on mathematics, science, or history. These students will spend many more minutes per week in large and small groups, in the laboratories, in gymnasiums, and on the playing fields. Some of them will play on intramural teams and others will represent the school on interscholastic teams. Who participates and to what extent will be based on professional decisions rather than on clerical decisions as in today's school. (Arbitrarily limiting participation on an interscholastic team to those "passing three subjects" is an example of a clerical decision.)

Student participation in programs of health, physical education, and recreation will be facilitated by the total schedule of the school. In the future other subjects will not meet on a five day a week basis, but like the health, physical education, and recreation classes will be related to the purposes and content of instruction. The average student will be scheduled in groups no more than 15–18 hours per week. Much greater flexibility in time use will result.

The building facilities for health, physical education, and recreation, like those for other subject areas, will be available to students more hours per day, more days per week, and for more weeks in the year. Students will be under the supervision of competent adults during these extra times, but not necessarily under professional teachers.

Staffing Patterns

The teacher of the future will be better utilized as a professional person. Today's teachers are expected to perform almost all educational services for the given group of students assigned to them. The term "self-contained classroom" has been coined to describe this condition. This concept denies in effect individual differences among teachers. It locks them into performing clerical, quasi-professional, and police-type tasks. The standard-size classes that result bring inflexible schedules and make difficult the utilization of modern technology in the classroom.

Six kinds of staff members will instruct and serve students in the health, physical education, and recreation program of the future:

Professional teachers — responsible for planning, supervising, and evaluating the total program, and for teaching in a team situation along with other teachers those phases of instruction for which each is most competent

Instruction assistants — persons with adequate training and competence to do specific parts of the teaching program, for example, assist in supervision and evaluation in the laboratories, supervise playing fields and gymnasiums at times, assist to develop specific skills etc.

General aides — perform such non-technical services as controlling corridors, managing crowds at games, selling tickets, etc.

Clerks — keep records, order and distribute supplies, and perform other clerical services

Community consultants — instruct large groups on some phase of the program when better qualified for that one thing than any professional teacher on the staff

Professional consultants — specialists in using technology in instruction, pupil personnel services, etc., brought in to help on specific problems

The purpose of this staffing pattern is to permit the teachers to perform professional services for which each is best qualified. The number of hours spent per week with groups of students will be reduced so there will be more time for preparing, planning, and evaluating in consultation with other teachers. Moreover, much of the time of the staff will be spent in working with students in groups of 15, something unheard of in today's school with its large classes, especially in physical education.

Logistics of the Program

Each school will need to make its own calculations regarding staff needs and costs of the health, physical education, and recreation program of the future. The data provided here are for purposes of directing thinking rather than providing definitive answers.

Let us assume a four-year school with 1200 students, 300 in each year. Further, let us assume that health and physical education is required for all students during each of the four years.

A defensible program in today's school would be to schedule the 1200 students in classes of 30, each with one teacher, five days per week. The normal work load of five classes per day would require eight teachers. If these teachers were paid an average salary of $6,000, that would cost $48,000.

The school of the future will require five professional teachers for the program presented here. However, these teachers will average less than 20 hours per week in scheduled activities with students in large and small groups and in the laboratories. Moreover, *more than one-half of that time will be with students in classes of 15 or fewer.* Most of the rest of the time will be spent in the laboratories where the use of two instruction assistants will make possible much small-group and individual work. When the teacher is working with the large group, an average of a little more than *one hour* per week, he will also have two instruction assistants to help.

The five professional teachers will have the services of a full-time clerk and 92 hours per week help by competent instruction assistants. These persons will be as carefully selected as are the teachers for the tasks assigned.

Assuming the average teacher salary of $6,000, as used in the example of today's school, and assuming paying instruction assistants and clerks at the going wages of today, the total costs of personnel in the future program would be $39,000.

Let us give the professional teachers an immediate salary increase of 25 percent, which is at least a step in the right direction. That will cost $6,500 and leave a considerable amount of money for purchasing technological aids to instruction.

This will only be a start in providing quality education in the program of health, physical education, and recreation. Of course, more money should be spent than in today's schools. Salaries of professional teachers should be much higher than 25 percent above today's figures. And more technological aids to instruction and more services of instruction assistants could be utilized.

Some Plus Factors

1. All students every year they are in school will receive motivation and assistance from the most able persons on the staff or in the community.
2. The professional competences, as well as individual differences in strength, of the professional teachers will be utilized.
3. Individual differences among students will be recognized more quickly in classes of 15, and in work in the laboratories.
4. Teachers will have more time to plan and evaluate instruction. Clerks and instruction assistants will help them accumulate data and keep better records of individual student needs and accomplishments.
5. The purpose of instruction will be to develop individual responsibility on the part of students for personal programs.
6. What happens in health, physical education, and recreation outside of school will be integrated more closely with what happens inside the classrooms.
7. The playing of games in either intramural or interscholastic competition will be an outgrowth of instruction in the classroom rather than the major determinant of how time is spent in the classroom and the nature of the spaces where instruction occurs.
8. Some significant steps will be taken to raise the professional standards of teachers. Teachers will do the teaching, clerks the clerking, instruction assistants and general aides the subprofessional tasks, and machines will automate some parts of teaching.

The Program of the Future

Today's school inevitably will become the school of tomorrow. We have no control over that. The only thing we can control is whether that school will be different and better than today's. That is the challenge to health, physical education, and recreation teachers and to those in charge of schools.

Some suggestions have been given here. Others have been made in recent publications by the writer. There is no standard blueprint for the future. Much experimentation and new approaches are needed. Will you do your part?

For Further Reading

American Association for Health, Physical Education, and Recreation, *Current Administrative Problems — Athletics, Health Education, Physical Education, Recreation,* The Association, Washington, D.C., 1960.

Clarke, H. Harrison, and Franklin B. Haar, *Health and Physical Education for the Elementary School Classroom Teacher,* Prentice-Hall, Inc., Englewood Cliffs, New Jersey, 1964.

Hein, Fred V., and Allan J. Ryan, "The Contributions of Physical Activity to Physical Health," *The Research Quarterly,* May, 1960, 31: 263–285.

Kilander, H. Frederick, *School Health Education,* The Macmillan Company, New York, 1962.

Miller, Arthur G., and M. Dorothy Massey, *A Dynamic Concept of Physical Education for Secondary Schools,* Prentice-Hall, Inc., Englewood Cliffs, New Jersey, 1963.

Oberteuffer, Delbert, and Celeste Ulrich, *Physical Education,* Third edition, Harper & Row, Inc., New York, 1962.

Patterson, Ann, and Edmond Hallberg, *Background Readings for Physical Education,* Holt, Rinehart and Winston, New York, 1965.

Sanborn, Marion, and Betty Hartman, *Issues in Physical Education,* Lea and Febiger, Philadelphia, 1964.

Smolensky, Jack, and Franklin B. Haar, *Principles of Community Health,* W. B. Saunders Company, Philadelphia, 1961.

Vendien, Lynn, "Are You Teaching Leisure Time Skills?" *JOHPER,* November, 1960, 31: 40–41.

PART SEVEN

Foreign Languages

35. The Foreign Language Curriculum

Robert L. Politzer

Throughout the 19th century, the firm foundation of the foreign language curriculum had been provided by a belief in the existence of logical grammatical universals and the psychological doctrine of Formal Discipline. Among the goals of foreign language instruction were "making the pupils aware of the grammar of his native language, teaching him to think logically, training his memory." The process of instruction itself and the abstract categories of logical grammar — rather than the

From Robert L. Politzer, "The Foreign Language Curriculum and Its Shifting Foundations," *School and Society,* April 17, 1965, 93:249–252. Robert L. Politzer is Professor of Education and Romance Languages, Stanford University. He has published numerous articles and books in such fields as French and Italian linguistics, and French literature, problems of language teaching and learning, and Latin. He is currently Editor of the Prentice-Hall French Series. Reprinted by permission of *School and Society,* official journal of the Society for the Advancement of Education.

achievement of the language skills — seemed the primary goal of instruction.

It is well known that the foreign language curriculum lost both of its foundations at about the onset of this century. The idea of Formal Discipline had received its first rebuttal through the investigations of William James.[1] The Transfer of Training controversy which ensued culminated in the conclusion that Formal Discipline was an illusion and that even Transfer of Training cannot be taken for granted.[2] As far as the existence of universal logical grammar is concerned, the early 19th-century scholar, Wilhelm von Humboldt, already had concluded that grammar and logic were to be associated with a particular linguistic system.[3] But the out-and-out assault on universal grammar came at the beginning of the 20th century, primarily as the result of the investigations of anthropologically oriented linguists. The latter found that the universal logical categories were a hindrance rather than a help in determining the real structure of the language they had to investigate. Not universal, logical, semantically defined categories, but formal categories defined with reference to a specific language seemed the only ones which made sense to the linguist.[4]

Thus, during the 1920's and '30's, foreign language education in the U. S. seemed in a state of flux and confusion. The grammar-translation method had lost its educational foundations and the very aims and purposes of foreign language education seemed uncertain. The high development of the language skills themselves, the immediacy of contact with a foreign language, literature, and culture — all were aims which, in spite of their appeal to the language teacher, did not seem to impress society as a whole. This situation changed drastically with the advent of World War II, the subsequent involvement in Korea, and the permanent, irrevocable involvement of the U. S. in world affairs.

[1] William James, "Principles of Psychology," 2 vols. (New York: Holt, 1890).

[2] For the developments in educational psychology from William James to and through the Transfer of Training controversy, see L. W. Webb, "Transfer of Training," in Charles E. Skinner, editor, "Educational Psychology," revised edition (New York: Prentice-Hall, 1945), pp. 250–273.

[3] Wilhelm von Humboldt's (1767–1835) essential statements on this point are found in his work, "Ueber die Verschiedenheit des menschlichen Sprachbaues," in "Wilhelm von Humboldt's Werke," Vol. VI (Berlin: Behr, 1907), pp. 110–303.

[4] An excellent representative statement of the linguists' attitude toward "logical grammar" is the one by E. Sapir, "Language" (New York: Harcourt, Brace, 1939), p. 125: "A part of speech outside of the limitations of syntactic form is but a will of the wisp. For this reason no logical scheme of the parts of speech — their number, nature and necessary confines — is of the slightest interest to the linguist. Each language has its own scheme. Everything depends on the formal demarcations which it recognizes."

It was within this setting of the sudden reversal in social attitudes toward language education that the new knowledge in the subject matter (namely, scientific linguistics) and the new educational psychology (namely, the various schools of behaviorism in learning theory) made their impact upon foreign language instruction. The impact came first in an area in which foreign language teaching had no considerable backlog of traditional experience which might have slowed down the innovators: the teaching of those foreign languages which previously had not been part of the curriculum, and the teaching of American English as a foreign language. The teaching of languages like Japanese, Hindi, Arabic, etc., became a necessity with the war effort. The teaching of American English as a foreign language received impetus as the result of the U. S. becoming a center to which military personnel and then students from foreign lands came (and still are coming in ever-increasing numbers) for the acquisition of skills and knowledge. Linguists were called upon to write the grammars and to conduct the courses in these new teaching situations. To the task they brought the skills, methods, and perhaps also the prejudices which were part of their learning and equipment.

In evaluating the contribution of a subject-matter specialist to the teaching of a discipline, it is imperative to keep apart the *what* and *how* of the teaching process. In the matter of *what* the contribution of the linguist has been in two areas, (1) scientific linguistic description has made explicit certain facts about language (*e.g.*, analysis of intonations) which we were unable to describe before; (2) the comparative linguistic analysis of the language to be learned and the native language of the pupil can show the exact points of conflict and their difficulty. Thus, the linguist can tell the language teacher where to put the emphasis in the foreign language course.

In assessing the linguists' impact in methodology, we must remember that linguistics not only is concerned with describing languages, but it also is concerned with developing "discovery procedures." Linguistics also implies a specific way of learning languages in the very specific situation of anthropological field work and investigation. The process by which the linguistic field worker "learns" the language of his informant is, by the very nature of the situation, audiolingual. To reduce the informant's language to writing is one of the goals of the learning procedure, but the written word cannot be the starting point; it just doesn't exist. The grammar of the language must be determined by the linguist through procedures which consist of the analytic comparison of utterances; *e.g.*, the hypothesis that two words belong to the same word class may be based on the observation that they can be substituted for each other in the same utterance, or that the same ending can be attached to them. Then this hypothesis can be confirmed if the native informant accepts the substitution of the one for the other within the same utterance or frame.

Whatever the purely pedagogical merits of the audio-lingual approach, there seems little doubt that its present vogue in language teaching is, in large measure, due to the impact of the "linguistic" type of language teaching which, through various channels (English as a foreign language, Army Specialized Training Program, and, more recently, Foreign Language Institutes sponsored by the National Defense Education Act), has made a tremendous impact in the American classroom. Even the methods of "pattern practice" (substitution, transformation exercises, etc.) are primarily the discovery procedures of the linguistic scientist converted into classroom teaching techniques.

The goal of the linguist who is investigating an unknown language is to establish communication for the ultimate purpose of exploring the culture of the speech community. Many of the facts concerning the culture under investigation often are learned in the process of analyzing the language. This intimate, inextricable connection between language and culture and this cultural aim of language learning also have become dominant aspects in foreign language education. Most statements of the aims of foreign language education place a heavy emphasis on cultural or international understanding and on the "understanding of language itself as a manifestation of culture."[5]

The "psychological foundation" of the foreign language curriculum also has made its primary impact via the influence of the linguistic scientist. American linguistic science, which in many ways began as a reaction to psychological speculation in the study of language,[6] has been in fact almost exclusively behavioristic in its approach. The very insistence that the object of the study of language must be the overt and observable speech acts testifies to this orientation.[7] Thus, linguistic scientists found it quite easy to adopt, in their teaching approaches,

[5] Bureau of Secondary Curriculum Development, "French for Secondary Schools" (Albany: New York State Education Department, 1960), p. 10.

[6] Leonard Bloomfield states in his preface to "Language" (New York: Holt, 1933), p. vii, that, in his "Introduction to the Study of Language" (New York: Holt, 1914), he accepted the psychology of Wilhelm Wundt, but that in his 1933 work he wanted to show that "we can pursue the study of language without reference to any one psychological doctrine."

[7] Bloomfield stated in the preface to "Language," "I believe that mechanism is the necessary form of scientific discourse." And in chapter 2 of "Language" (p. 24), he states, "Language enables one person to make a reaction (R) when another person has the stimulus (S)."

views of learning which analyze the learning process primarily as habit formation, as reinforcement of correct responses to appropriate stimuli, etc. The insistence on repetition, immediacy of reward of correct responses, and the widespread use of language laboratories are just some of the more important consequences of this view of the nature of language learning.

The change in the methods and aims of the foreign language curriculum was shaped primarily by forces which are outside of the field of language teaching and education as such. To some extent, this is neither surprising nor improper. A curriculum reflects the changing values of our society, and changes in the subject-matter field influence the content as well as the teaching method. At the same time, however, the very direct impact which linguistics, social pressure, and some theories of learning have had on the foreign language curriculum raises the question of the exact role of the foreign language teacher and educator. The linguistic scientist — the subject-matter specialist — can tell the educator *what* to teach; but to what extent are his teaching methods really the best? What is the evidence that language instruction contributes to cultural understanding? And if it does contribute, just what kind of language instruction can make this contribution? If international communication is the goal of language instruction, should we not remember that it is, of course, almost impossible to predict *which* language our pupils will need to know? Thus, instead of — or at least in addition to — teaching the skill of one particular language, is it possible to teach in such a way that the pupil learns a method or concepts which will facilitate the acquisition of another language in a situation of future need?[8] These are just some of the questions to which the language teacher and educator should address themselves. The answers will *not* be provided by society, linguists, or psychologists concerned with theory of learning. But they can be found through research by the teachers and educators who know how to use linguistics and psychology to build their curriculum. Much of what some educators like to call the "foundations" of the educational process perhaps should be named properly the *tools* of the educator. The real and solid foundation of the foreign language curriculum lies in the values which we want to create and in the pragmatic research that tells us how to achieve them.

[8] For instance, the "new mathematics" — unlike the "new key" in language instruction — is less concerned with the creation of particular skills than with the teaching of concepts, for the simple reason that the concepts are presumed to facilitate the learning of skills and that the specific skills required by future mathematicians and engineers are largely unpredictable.

36. The Case for Latin

William Riley Parker

In the "good old days" in the United States, as in Europe, which supplied the model, anyone who went to a secondary school and college studied Latin as a matter of course. Even in the first years of this century, when a half million students were enrolled in all our public high schools, fully half of them were still studying Latin. Those days are gone, and will never return. To regret their passing is to regret both mass education and mankind's phenomenal increase in scientific knowledge. Moreover, our world has shrunk while America's role in it has grown, and lately our society has recognized the increasing relevance of studying *modern* foreign languages. What, then, is the future place of Latin in American education? As one who long ago was taught both Latin and Greek, I want to try to answer this question as candidly and as objectively as I can.

For whatever reasons, Latin is still a significant factor in our educational system. Any report of its "death" is greatly exaggerated. In our public and private secondary schools, grades 7–12, about 1,167,000 boys and girls are now studying it, and in our colleges and universities nearly 1,000 students are annually choosing it as the major subject for their bachelor's degree. These numbers have been increasing, and they are not small numbers unless we are thinking in percentages: today, for example, only about five per cent of the students in our *public* secondary schools are enrolled in Latin classes, whereas thirty years ago the figure

From William Riley Parker, "The Case for Latin," *PMLA*, September, 1964, Part 2, 3–10, Vol. 79. William Riley Parker is Professor and Chairman of the Department of English at Indiana University. He is author of *The National Interest and Foreign Languages,* former executive secretary and past president of the Modern Language Association of America, and first chief of the Language Development Program in the U. S. Office of Education. Professor Parker has also written two books and more than fifty articles on John Milton. His two-volume *Milton: A Biography* will be published in 1967. This article, published by the Modern Language Association as a preprint in September, 1964, is recognized as the definitive statement presenting the case for Latin in the modern world.

was sixteen per cent. Should the current percentage be higher, or even lower? Many informed people believe that Latin is on its way out of the public high school curriculum. What is the objective (not accusative) case for Latin in American education in the second half of the twentieth century?

In any choice among languages to learn, the main argument that can be brought *against* Latin is that it is no longer spoken as a mother tongue by anyone. The case must be put this way, fairly, for Latin is today read by countless people, in many countries. It has really never been a "dead language" except in the sense that its natural growth has ended and that it is no longer learned as a first language by babies. Arguments that can reasonably be brought against Chinese and many other foreign languages in the course of choosing a second language to study — for example, the comparative difficulty of their writing- or sound-systems or of their grammars — cannot be brought against Latin. For more than five centuries English-speaking peoples have found Latin reasonably easy to learn, largely because there are so many Latin elements in English. Its literary content constitutes no argument against it, as the lack or thinness of literary content might for studying some languages. On the contrary, unless one insists on contemporaneity (of which, perhaps, there is enough in American education), the distinct social or political orientation of most of Latin literature gives it permanent relevance. The typical Latin curriculum introduces the student quickly to classical authors whose excellence is beyond question, whose substance is constantly referred to in Western literature and art, and whose literary genres and styles were models for writers up until very recent times.

One cannot even argue, reflecting an important contemporary concern, that Latin has no bearing on "international understanding" — unless this term is narrowed to mean only direct communication between people of two nationalities; and exceptions must even then be allowed, because Latin continues occasionally to fulfil this function, particularly among the Roman Catholic clergy — despite recent decisions to celebrate parts of the mass in vernaculars. If international understanding is ever facilitated by recognition of a common cultural heritage — as surely it is — then Latin has an extraordinary relevance. It is more than a permanent visa to a community of scholars, which it long has been. American tourists or businessmen or diplomats, meeting educated Europeans, can often earn their approval by talking their languages — if allowed to do so — but can earn more respect for American culture and education by making it clear that the classics have not been neglected in the New World — as they have, by official edict, in the Soviet Union. Let us face it: lack of knowledge of the classics makes us appear uneducated to Europeans, for whom such knowledge is the hallmark of an educated man.

Most, but not all, of the primary reasons for studying Latin are reasons universally recognized by informed people for studying *any* foreign language.[1] I am not talking about the reasons perhaps implied above, or about the various hoped-for by-products so often, and so confusingly, mentioned by partisans of language study. For example, the old claim that Latin is the best developer of logical thinking has been logically discredited, and it is clear that mathematics does as well, or better, at cultivating accuracy of detail. I do not know whether or not foreign language study normally brings more facility and precision in the use of the mother tongue. I have found it so in my own experience; many people have so testified in print (and many others to me in person); but I have listened to, and read, a number of American-born foreign language teachers whose awkward use of English belies the argument, and I strongly doubt that this pedagogical objective is often achieved unless it is *deliberately and intelligently sought for.*[2] In any case, let us distinguish between dependable results and occasional, or even frequent, by-products.

The strongest, most defensible reason for studying any foreign language, including Latin, is that such study, which is both a progressive experience and a progressive acquisition of a skill, enlarges the pupil's mental horizon by introducing him to a completely new medium of verbal expression and communication and consequently to a new cultural pattern. It also, of course, progressively adds to his sense of pleasurable achievement in the process; he can actually measure his own progress with some precision. To be honest, one must state the matter thus cautiously and moderately. At no point can such an experience be considered complete, or such a skill perfect; the expectancy of values to be derived from language study must be relative to the amount of time and effort devoted to it, to say nothing of aptitude and the enjoyment of skillful teaching under proper conditions. Talk about early "mastery" is usually misleading. While it has some value, language

[1] I resist all temptation to embellish my text with eloquent quotations favoring Latin study. It is easy to gather hundreds of these from well-known people, living or dead. The latest such collection that I have seen is *Latin: The Basic Language* (1964), edited by the students of Latin at Princeton (N. J.) High School.

[2] I suspect, but cannot prove, that Latin teachers more often set and really achieve this objective than do teachers of other languages, yet I am sure that not all of them do so. How polished English is learned is a complicated matter. Aspiring stylists frequently absorb the manners of good literary company.

study which does not go beyond the second high school year will predictably prove more frustrating than satisfying to the student. It can, however, be affirmed of language study that, granted competent teaching, at any stage the progress made will have positive educational values, in addition to providing a foundation upon which further progress can be built. Although Rome cannot be built in a day, or ever, what exists of it at any stage can both delight and inform.

In what lie the positive educational values of language study? Educators of a certain temperament or training insist on "proof" of the "value" of any given subject before they are willing to sanction its presence or its expansion in the curriculum. By proof they usually mean statistical proof; by value they too often mean "practical" value. But there are completely convincing proofs offered by the cumulative experience of the human race which do not lend themselves to statistics, and there are theoretically impractical values which education has immemorially sought. The best reason for studying physics is not to become a physicist or mechanical engineer, or even to be able to repair something — though these are possible, and welcome, outcomes. The best reason for studying Spanish is not to be able to talk with a businessman from Latin America — though in today's world this is an increasing, and important, possibility. One should study any "academic" or liberal arts subject primarily to stock and stretch and develop the mind, in the hope of becoming more civilized. This is arguably a very "practical" matter, involving objectives that can be clearly defined and tested, but let us not quibble over definitions. How does language study profit the mind?

The Educational Policies Commission of the National Education Association has recently (1961) decided that "the central purpose of American education" is the development of the ability to think. One may accept this dictum gratefully, but then ask: "Think only in the restrictive pattern of one's own language?" Until we have acquired a second language, we tend to assume the identity of words and things. Moreover, different language structures compel people to think differently; the limitations and historical development of a given vocabulary condition thought. For example, Norwegian Landsmal has five genders, Russian three, French two, and Hungarian none. The Spanish have no word for "honest" — only "honorable." What does a Communist mean by "democratic" in any language? What does a German or Frenchman mean by the untranslatable but socially important "du" or "tu"? Every language has its own, different way of organizing the data of "reality." Assuring first-hand awareness of these facts about language is becoming a purpose of American education, as it long has been in the education of all other countries in the Western world. It is one thing to be told these facts by someone, as here; it is another to experience and understand their reality, and to ponder their implications. It takes considerable time to learn to *think* in a second language; but when in Rome, it is less enlightening to "do as the Romans do" than it is to try to think as the Romans think, or, if this is impossible, to realize that the Romans will of course think differently (without definite and indefinite articles perhaps). Breaking the barriers of a single language and a single culture has been rightly called "a Copernican step," a positive educational value of primary and permanent importance.

This value can be recognized even in the early stages of language study, before genuine proficiency or the ability to think in a second language has been achieved. The recognition is, however, a progressive experience. In two high school years or one college year of instruction, a student cannot be expected to acquire an "active" vocabulary of more than 1,000 words (experts estimate only about 700 Latin words, with their compounds), and yet a very large majority of American students stop at this point, frequently because no further instruction is available. In the educational system of *no other nation on earth* has so little vocabulary been assumed to confer meaningful proficiency. When the student of a foreign language begins to acquire an adult-sized vocabulary — normally impossible in under four high school years — the intellectual rewards of course increase proportionately.

We are discussing the values of studying any foreign language, ancient or modern. Advocates of living languages add the very practical potential of direct communication with a contemporary culture. There can be no quarrel with this supplementary value, which in our modern world has an urgent, increasing pertinence — recognized by the Congress of the United States in 1958 when it included modern foreign language study in the provisions of a National Defense Education Act. We do need more and more Americans capable of "talking the other fellow's language"; and this no longer means merely French, German, Italian, and Spanish — since about 1920 the "usual" modern languages taught in our schools — but also Arabic, Chinese, Hindi, Portuguese, and Russian, to say nothing of the many important tongues of the new nations of Africa and Asia.

As for Latin and its literature, we have the back door of English translations. Such, we are often warned, are but sorry substitutes — produced by many of the finest classicists, of course. That one should study Latin for a few years because all translations are inadequate is a *non sequitur*. Translations from foreign languages into English inevitably vary in quality and accuracy, but the worst is better than the translating which any student must painfully do until his vocabulary and his knowledge of linguistic, literary, and cultural nuances approach that of the professional. It takes years to acquire enough proficiency to realize that translations of a given language are indeed inadequate — and one must even then continue to use translations from *other* languages, including, perhaps, the Hebrew of the Old Testament and the Greek of the New.[3]

With so much now needed, and so little room in the crowded curriculum for our attempts to supply it, what excuse can there be today for studying any ancient language? Few of us are at heart antiquarians. Should we not jettison Latin in the age of the jet? There are no ancient Romans to be met, and talked to, in the forums of current affairs.

Or are there? Rephrase it in sensible educational terms, and we are at the nub of the present matter.

Education that neglects the past is unthinkable, suicidal. Preoccupied as we may be with the present, we need roots in order to survive and to grow. One of the purposes of education has always been, and always must be, to *make us fully cognizant of our roots* — the continuum of our culture, our immense debt to the past, and the blessed timelessness of so much of our literary, artistic, and political heritage. Consciousness of these roots is not only instructive and reassuring; more importantly, it provides a perspective needed for intelligent, purposeful living in the present and the future. If we delude ourselves by assuming that today's pressing problems were all born yesterday (or since 1776), we stand little chance of understanding them and solving them wisely. Neglect of experience, personal or recorded, condemns us to repeating its follies.

[3] I do not want to be impaled on this touchy point. Translations are indispensable, but *literary* masterpieces often defy adequate rendering into another language. Let doubters who know a foreign language read any favorite English work in that language. Poetry, by its very nature, is a special use of language that defies translation, Similar or roughly equivalent effects can, with luck or ingenuity, be achieved, but the peculiar "meaning" of poetry depends, not only on the denotations of words. but also on their connotations, sounds, relationships, and arrangement. There is therefore no way of expressing in English (or any other language) what Catullus, Horace, Lucretius, and Vergil really "say" poetically. This is true also of unusually eloquent (i.e., poetic) prose.

Translations can convey *form,* but they convey thoughts without conveying the way of thinking, express feeling without giving us the true "feel" of the original. It is like being kissed through a veil — exciting contact of a sort, no doubt, if one has never been kissed directly. Emerson used another metaphor to defend the use of translations: why, he asked dryly, should one swim across the Charles River when one wishes to go to Boston? His figure is more revealing than he intended. Swimming is an exercise pleasurable and profitable *per se.* Getting to the other shore is only part of the experience.

We sorely need knowledge of the past, especially when the present presses upon us most insistently.

This knowledge can be even more serviceable if to it can be added *a sense of the past.* Knowledge of the past, most efficiently gained through the study of cultural and political history, can be both interesting and informing; a sense of that past, and of the varieties of our relationship to it, can be transforming. To live intellectually only *in one's own time* is as provincial and misleading as to live intellectually only *in one's own culture.*[4] Study of a modern foreign language fortunately enables one to break the bonds of his own peculiar culture, but Latin not only does this effectively but also, when studied beyond the elementary stage, enables one to live intellectually in the distant *past* out of which all Western cultures developed. One may gain some sense of this past by advanced study of any modern European language, including English if one reads *Beowulf,* Chaucer, and Shakespeare in addition to recent literature. The point is that the subject matter of Latin is the very roots of Western civilization. Latin is not, therefore, just another foreign language. It is the oldest variety of "area study." When one studies Latin, he directly encounters and experiences the significant past, whose most significant records still rank, for the most part, as belles lettres. The ancient Romans *do* have something to say to us: for example, a reminder that they handed on to us, through Englishmen of the sixteenth and seventeenth centuries, and hence Americans of the eighteenth century, our dearest concepts of political freedom. In a third-year Latin classroom, Cicero may ask us for a reckoning.[5] He is better read than "dead."

There are linguistic roots as well as cultural roots. Latin is the mother of five important languages of Europe and the Western Hemisphere, and is also the greatest benefactor of modern English, including a vast scientific and technical vocabulary to which it is still actively contributing. More than fifty per cent of our total vocabulary is derived, at first or second hand, from the parent of the Romance languages; or, to put it differently, approximately one out of every four Latin words has found its way into English.[6] This is the factual basis of the often heard

[4] This problem, Meriwether Stuart reminds me, was old in Cicero's day: "Nescire autem quid ante quam natus sis acciderit, id est semper esse puerum. Quid enim est aetas hominis, nisi ea memoria rerum veterum cum superiorum aetate contexitur?" (*Orator* 120).

[5] So also many Augustine and other Latin church fathers. I do not mean here to minimize our Christian heritage. The subject matter of Latin includes this too.

[6] James B. Greenough and George Lyman Kittredge long ago asserted: ". . . our vocabulary has appropriated a full quarter of the Latin vocabulary, besides what it has

claim that a knowledge of Latin helps one to understand and to write — even to spell — English with greater precision. The half of English vocabulary that is of Latin origin is the more difficult and important half for educated men, because it includes many scientific terms and a high proportion of words necessary to express abstract ideas and sophisticated concepts or distinctions.

The very different grammar of Latin provides an illuminating and much-needed perspective on how English grammar works. It may not invariably do so; that it often does many have testified and common sense would suggest. Unlike English, which has far fewer "signals" to indicate "gender," tense, number, and case, Latin is a highly inflected language, and the *contrast* can make us sensitive to the analytical syntax of our own language. The grammars of all foreign languages provide a contrast with English; the point is that Latin grammar provides an unusually sharp one. It also, of course, gives us much of our grammatical terminology, a heritage we have not always used wisely. Only of late have English teachers been learning the folly of trying to apply Latin grammar to English, instead of using it, as a good Latin teacher does, to clarify differences.

When a student's ultimate objective is to be able to read (not speak) a number of important foreign languages, knowledge of Latin can have extraordinary practicality. It would be ridiculous to argue that one should study Latin in order to learn French, but genuine competence in Latin can speed the informal acquisition of reading proficiency in not only French, but also Italian, Portuguese, Rumanian, and Spanish — more languages than most students, or most practising scientists, can find the time to study formally. In this respect, the study of Latin offers a certain advantage over the study of ancient Greek, rewarding as the

---

gained by transferring Latin meanings to native words" (*Words and Their Ways in English Speech,* New York, 1901, p. 106). See also the excellent essay by Gerald F. Else, "Classical Languages, Especially Latin," in *The Case for Basic Education,* ed. James D. Koerner (Boston, 1959), pp. 123–137.

In the above paragraphs I discuss what must be labelled a by-product of Latin study. It can be and has been said that "an English teacher should be able to teach the roots and the grammar as well in a small fraction of the time spent on Latin, and at least as effectively. Why should we go around Robin Hood's barn?" The question was asked by a classicist; as an English teacher let me reply, simply, that in *twelve or more years* of trying, we don't do the job. One reason is that familiarity with English breeds contempt for formal teaching of English. Another reason is the general confusion among English teachers about both ends and means. Only within the past 100 years or so have we thought that English can be taught exclusively by English teachers — a theory I often question.

latter can be.[7] In another respect, the fact that Latin differs so greatly from English in structure, the study of Latin offers an advantage over the study of the Romance languages if one's next foreign language is to be a highly inflected one — Russian, say. American education has been slow to realize that high school students rarely know — and no one can tell them — which of many foreign languages they will eventually need to use. There is thus a highly practical reason for choosing a *first* foreign language which is a demonstrable stepping-stone to others.

While we are being practical — but first reminding ourselves that we are now discussing, not general education, but the needs of comparatively few students in our schools — we might recall in passing the peculiar usefulness of Latin to students of law, medicine, pharmacology, and theology, as well as to advanced students of such subjects as educational history, philosophy, literature, Romance philology, linguistics, European history, and medieval studies of any kind. As a professor of English with a special interest in Renaissance literature, I deeply wish that all my students had proficiency in Latin and ability to recognize classical allusions. I am not so unrealistic as to expect American education to accommodate itself to those students who actually want to read Shakespeare and Milton with some understanding, but it might at least *advise* prospective English majors that they had better learn Latin.

Though the teaching and interpretation and influence of it may change, and do change, Latin no longer changes.[8] Of all the standard

[7] The case for the study of Greek is in most respects identical with that for the study of Latin. If I may be permitted an irrelevancy, as a student I enjoyed Greek more than I did Latin, and still find Greek literature and civilization more appealing. Nevertheless, I do not attempt here to plead both cases, partly because there are some differences (e.g., in alphabet and in structure), but chiefly because Greek is taught today in but a handful of public or private high schools and studied by only a small number of persons in college. I should like to see a revival of Greek, but in the present state of things Latin offers the only feasible opportunity for an early introduction to our Graeco-Roman heritage — despite the powerful and persistent influence of Plato, Aristotle, and other Greeks on modern thought. Ironically, the mansion of American education has numerous rooms, but the storehouse of many of its basic concepts and categories is the Attic.

[8] This statement is practically (or pedagogically) true for all except advanced students and scholars, but therefore in several technical senses needs qualification. For example, epigraphical and papyrological evidence continues to add to the specialist's knowledge of Latin and of Roman matters, and each new generation of critics reinterprets Latin literature. Latin as a language went through a number of fairly distinct phases of development, known to philologists as Old Latin, classical Latin, Late or Low Latin, Medieval or Middle Latin, and Modern or Neo-Latin (since about 1500). There is a scholarly newsletter for students of Neo-Latin. Vulgar Latin was the everyday speech of the Roman people, from which the Romance languages developed. Today, priests and scholars are constructing new forms of

subjects in the curricula of our secondary schools and colleges (most of the others added during the past 100 years), Latin is *the only one* which remains forever constant, its life not ended, but its age and development arrested — and given eternal youth. Physics and mathematics change, but not Latin. Each new decade adds to the stock of history, or of English literature and language, but not to that of classical Latin. In the anxious, transitory present, it is the permanent past. One can study Roman civilization under laboratory conditions. Little wonder that many students in our uncertain, rapidly changing world find Latin of almost therapeutic value.[9] It is reassuringly stable. It is tried and true. Studying it, young victims of insecurity and spiritual isolation are likely to realize that their culture has roots that are deep and firm. One can be told this, of course; it is something more to experience and feel it. The impact can be memorable and long sustaining. This is the bitter-sweet compensation for the decline of the classics: when the ancients no longer command customary respect, the thrill of personal discovery is greater.

A "dead language" is not a dead subject unless in a given classroom it is taught in deadly fashion; and when this happens, it is not the fault of the subject. Inadequate preparation yields poor instruction, and Latin has not escaped this general curse of American education. Many Latin teachers confuse language learning with memorizing of rules — or with the cultivation of humility! Moreover, in either enthusiasm or desperation, teachers of Latin have sometimes offended even sympathetic listeners or readers by claiming too much; I have read speeches and committee reports that practically equated success in Latin with good conduct and good hygiene. This is frantic, foolish pleading. Equating success in Latin with developing intelligence is, on the other hand, to misinterpret the surely significant fact — known to every college admissions officer — that the most intelligent students are

---

Modern Latin by coining words or phrases for contemporary things and activities. There is sometimes a playful spirit about this construction, as when Adlai Stevenson warns: *Via ovicipitum dura est* 'the way of the egghead is hard.'

[9] This is not intended as a sentimental argument, although I realize that it can easily be parodied and ridiculed as such. I state what I believe to be both true and important. I am not, of course, arguing that Latin study is a substitute for psychiatry, or that this particular by-product is experienced by all students. I am arguing the almost unique status of Latin as the inexhaustible mother lode of Western civilization. *All* great literature of the past can give us faith, or renew our faith, in the ageless dignity of the human spirit — in an age when our own literature often challenges that faith. An irony in what I am here arguing is the fact that the stability of Latin can attract *teachers* who are intellectually timid or sluggish. It can also, alas, encourage a false notion about the nature of *living* languages, unless the teacher does his job properly.

often, for whatever reasons, attracted to Latin. *All* academic subjects well taught develop intelligence. Other defenses have been too defensive, and a recent one that I have seen was insufferably snobbish, arguing in effect that Latin is only for the intellectual elite.

The case, when made quite soberly, turns out to be strong enough: Latin, simply as a foreign language, offers a demonstrably valuable experience, and, studied to the point of reasonable competence, it offers also *an educationally unique experience: a sense of our relevant past, cultural and linguistic.*

To argue that every American youngster should study Latin would be to ignore the history of American education, but to argue that we can now do without Latin would be idiotic. Ancient languages continue to offer much to those students in school or college who have the curiosity, or have had the good counsel, to elect them. May their numbers increase, in our public schools no less than in our private ones, in our state universities no less than in our Ivy-League colleges. Latin is not for an elite group; it is not, as the Communists sneer, a "tool of class discrimination"; it is for anyone who wants to be well-educated in the Western tradition. If a modern foreign language is studied first, or later, so much the better.[10] Tomorrow's leaders in all walks of life must listen intelligently to our past and be prepared to talk and read intelligently in our multilingual future.

Should school boards or school principals drop Latin in favor of modern foreign languages? Important as modern language study seems to me (and I have given eleven full years of my life to promoting this other good cause), I can see no valid educational reason for introducing Russian, say, at the expense of Latin. If — as might sometimes happen — we cannot have both, then let us never scrap a solid, time-tested sub-

[10] We need, however, an objective and reliable answer to this problem: at what educational level should Latin be introduced in order that it may *best* provide the chief benefits inherent in study of it? Like the modern languages, it can be, and is, taught at all levels, from elementary to graduate school. But when does its study give optimum results? In the competition with modern languages, a convincing answer might well strengthen the status of Latin in the total curriculum. I do know this: some students (I wonder how many) react adversely to the tension of audio-lingual methods of language teaching, but enjoy the more familiar, bookish methods of most Latin teaching. The chairman of a Spanish department tells me that, as an administrator and teacher in two universities, he has observed "over and over again that a significant number of students who failed in modern languages had a successful academic experience in Latin or Greek." This phenomenon, which other teachers have reported to me, should not be confused with a different, less important problem — the occasional relaxing of standards in Latin or Greek as a desperate bid for enrollment. Improve the status of the classics, and the football team will have to relax elsewhere.

ject for the sake of climbing aboard the latest educational bandwagon.[11] (When American education did just this in the 1930's and 1940's, it was the modern foreign languages that were often scrapped.) Should Latin, on the other hand, ever be made a required subject? Yes, as an alternative in every curriculum in which study of a modern foreign language is required, from elementary school to graduate school. Latin's values are not less; they are different. I am not here arguing for language requirements. I am saying that any language requirement which excludes Latin (or Greek) as an option is educationally indefensible.

These are difficult days for school administrators and, as a former administrator of sorts, I sympathize with them and wish them well. They and curriculum planners do their best under various and vexing pressures from single-minded groups and individuals. They know — what the faddish public too often forgets — that you cannot fill a glass beyond the brim. They also know that nourishing liquid can be added when there is less foam; for proof, look at the recent expansion of modern foreign language study in many of our schools. But this expansion has brought new problems, and educational supervisors now seek honest, reasonable answers to the troublesome questions of which language, and when, and for how long. Let me, therefore, suggest such answers as my own experience, enriched by the wisdom of many well-informed friends and colleagues, has thus far taught me.

One high school year of instruction — or study — in any foreign language is educational nonsense, a waste of time and money. *Two* years of any foreign language is close to nonsense (as Mr. Conant has said, "They might as well play basketball!"), but it is better than no instruction at all in a foreign language. A curricular offering of two years in *two* foreign languages is, however, nonsense, bad in every way, leading often to double frustration for students taking both. It is the worst possible administrative solution to the problem of competing needs. An absolute minimum of *four* years of *one* foreign language,

[11] I would make the same objection to hasty attempts to introduce our students to the non-Western cultures which we have so long and so foolishly ignored. They need this knowledge of civilizations in which they have no "roots," but not before, and certainly not at the expense of, a significant knowledge of their own culture. It is my impression that too many students have feelings of insecurity or doubt resulting from the various assaults upon Western tradition emanating from the Communist bloc — and more recently from the non-Western nations. It can be argued that what these nations really seek is some ideological equivalence with what the West has created by relating its vital heritage and traditions to its contemporary discoveries in science and technology. An American student ignorant of Graeco-Roman culture is unlikely to understand such an aspiration, and very likely to misunderstand it.

ancient or modern, makes sense, for it can provide meaningful proficiency. If a small school can offer four years of instruction in *only one* language, the choice of language should depend primarily upon the quality of instruction available, secondarily upon the wishes of the students and their parents. All things being equal — which they almost never are — I myself would choose to offer a living language, but better four years of Latin well taught than four years of badly taught Spanish. If a larger school can offer four years of instruction in *two* foreign languages without displacing equally valuable courses in something else, one of these languages, if practicable, should be Latin, for reasons I have tried to make clear. American boys and girls are entitled to this choice.

In the expansion of *any* foreign language program, the expansion should always be from the senior year backward, never from grade 7 or 9 forward. This is the only expansion that guarantees continuity by recognizing the shortage of qualified teachers, and it is the only one that is fair to the more than fifty per cent of our high school graduates who are now going on to college — many of whom will be required, and others of whom will wish in any case, to continue their foreign language study immediately, without serious loss of momentum.

Should the Congress of the United States use public funds for the improvement of Latin teaching, as it has done for the modern foreign languages? In the limited context of the National *Defense* Education Act of 1958, no. In the wider and equally defensible context of Government acting to strengthen the best in American education, yes! Both Government and the major foundations have done much in recent years to support modern foreign language study, especially study of many languages which had never or but rarely been taught. It is time, now, for both Government and the foundations to pay more attention to those solid, basic elements in the curriculum that do not have the additional advantage of sudden, temporary relevance in our competition with Communism; and for an appropriate beginning, I strongly recommend the subject that, in my considered opinion, has suffered, and otherwise will suffer far more, as a direct result of Federal and foundation interest in the modern languages.

Latin is unchanging, but exciting new ways of teaching it have been discovered, and are now known to a few.[12] They should be made known

[12] This writer cannot pretend to any expert knowledge of the reforms in methodology and curricula currently advocated by classicists, but he applauds the critical, questioning spirit of many teachers in this tradition-taut field. Some are concerned to see what can be learned from the audio-lingual *approach* now widely employed by

in summer institutes to the many who had their training long ago, and to the new teachers now being trained. Let us have better, truly modern instruction in this ancient language, so that our past can contribute more vitally to our future. American boys and girls, hopeful heirs to the best in Western civilization (whether or not they yet realize it), deserve nothing less at our hands.[13]

---

modern foreign language teachers; others are experimenting with applied linguistics, along lines set forth in Waldo E. Sweet's *Latin: A Structural Approach* (Ann Arbor, 1957). Professor Sweet has just completed the first year of a "programmed" course in Latin, for use with or without a language laboratory. The synthetic "made-Latin" that has crept into many textbooks is under vigorous attack, as are the trinity of Caesar, Cicero, and Vergil in their monopoly (since about 1894) of the second, third, and fourth years of secondary school instruction. The *Gallic Wars* may go, to give place to new, untraditional material (e.g., Erasmus) chosen for its permanent relevance. Prose composition may also go, or be minimized. Ovid may enjoy a revival — a development that would doubtless be cheered by English teachers, who have the cheerless task of explaining mythological allusions to students who should be happily recognizing them instead of merely understanding them.

In reporting these trends, I am neither predicting nor expressing any personal preferences — beyond the irresistible one above. Caesar, I should think, can be effectively taught today as a master of political self-justification, rather than as a dull reporter of strategy and tactics. Cicero can be taught as a voice of moderate conservatism. In any case, most Latin teachers are proud of the fact that *their* students quickly encounter real classics, and this is as it should be, for they can't have it both ways — offering to reveal the roots of Western culture while actually giving us diluted Latin and equally diluted ancient history. They have their clubs and contests and Roman banquets, but I have met no movement to substitute *Winnie Ille-Pu* for Vergil.

[13] A second draft of this essay was read and most helpfully criticized by 55 colleagues in 28 different schools, programs, or departments at Indiana University. A third draft was then seen and criticized — often at great length — by 115 persons throughout the United States and Canada. I regret the impracticality of thanking here individually so large a number of collaborators, to very many of whom I am deeply indebted — as they will realize upon reading my final version. I was greatly encouraged by the unanimous expression of genuine interest in my subject.

Some wondered why this piece should appear in *PMLA*. The Editor of *PMLA* invited me to write it, and reprints are available from the Modern Language Association (4 Washington Place, New York, N. Y. 10003) for all who wish to join me in getting it into the hands of those who most need to be informed and, perhaps, persuaded — guidance counsellors, school and college administrators, school boards, curriculum experts, and others. It is my earnest hope that, in this effort, teachers of English, linguistics, the modern foreign languages — indeed, all the humanities — will find common cause. My personal motive is to renew my allegiance to the humanistic tradition. The case for Latin seems to me a *crux* — in all senses of that word. My basic concern as an English teacher is the relation of language to wisdom. I like to believe that most members of the MLA share this concern. [Reprints of this article are available at the following rates from the address given above: single copy, 25 cents; 10 copies or more, 10 cents each — Ed.]

37. Foreign Languages and the Humanities

Georges J. Joyaux

More than a decade ago, Earl McGrath, then United States Commissioner of Education, opened a new era in the Foreign Language field with his now famous speech at the annual meeting of the Central States Modern Language Teachers Association in St. Louis. The much-needed re-assessment of our profession which followed, in turn set the stage for a general overhauling of foreign language teaching and led us into a period of unprecedented activity — though not necessarily of unprecedented success.

To be sure, McGrath alone cannot be given the full credit for what is going on in our field today; the field had been prepared by many events and factors which, furthermore, accelerated the revolution he set in motion. On the one hand, the ever-increasing flux of American tourists travelling abroad gave at first implicit, then louder support to the clamor for more "useful" foreign languages. As Robert F. Roeming, managing editor of *The Modern Language Journal,* points out, "it was from the members of the middle income group, finding themselves affluent enough to travel abroad, that came the greatest public support for the 'Speak the Language' approach."[1] On the other hand, America's growing economic, military, and strategic involvements around the world and the position of leadership she had inherited on the morrow of the war,

From Georges J. Joyaux, "Foreign Languages and the Humanities," *The Modern Language Journal,* February, 1965, 49: 102–105. Georges Jules Joyaux, Professor of French and Comparative Literature at Michigan State University, is the author of more than twenty-five contributions to scholarly journals in both France and the United States, centering on his major interests of twentieth century French Literature, comparative literature, and the teaching of foreign languages. He has translated or edited five books, the latest of which, *Lectures de France et D'Outre-Mer,* with A. Tukey, will be published by Prentice-Hall in 1967. Professor Joyaux has taught in French elementary schools and has served at Michigan State since 1947 with the exception of one year as a Guggenheim Fellow for research in France, and a second year as visiting professor at the University of Arizona. In 1962 he was awarded the Chevalier des Palmes Academiques by the French Government. This article is reprinted by permission of *The Modern Language Journal* and Professor Joyaux.

[1] Robert F. Roeming, "Traditional?"; *The Modern Language Journal,* Vol. XLVIII, No. 2 (February, 1964), p. 98.

made it imperative for her to remedy her tragic shortcomings in the field of foreign language competency. Finally, the *coup de grâce* to an antiquated state of affairs was given by Russia in 1957, when the launching of the Sputnik proved to be the greatest blow to their complacency the American people ever had.

As a result of this totally unexpected feat by Russia, the United States re-examined her whole educational system, many university officials and education specialists travelled to Europe to discover the "secret" of their successful instruction, much was written about Johnny and his schooling, and the foundations increased their financial support of education. Naturally, this soul-searching affected the study of foreign languages as well, and especially Russian, since, as was later revealed, we would have known about the Russian achievement six months earlier had we been able to read Russian scientific journals.

The climax of the uphill fight for more and better foreign language study was reached in 1958 when Congress enacted the National Defense Education Act which lumped foreign languages along with mathematics and sciences as academic subjects in dire need of help, financial and otherwise, and from whatever quarters, even the Federal Government!

Mention should be made also of another factor which undoubtedly contributed greatly to the present interest in, and concern for, foreign languages, that is the recent development of electronics and the resulting "interference" of this pressure group.

At any rate, and whatever the reasons might be, our profession is enjoying today an unprecedented boom and impressive statistics are readily available to attest to the successful adaptation of our discipline to the needs of the Nuclear Age. Thus, whereas language laboratories were practically non-existent a decade ago, today we can boast of more than 6,000 language laboratories across the nation. It is true that some of these laboratories are not used properly — whether it be because of lack of trained personnel, lack of materials, or simply indifference and lack of faith in them on the part of some teachers — and it is also true that in some cases they were built not to answer a need, but rather to take full advantage of the funds suddenly made available. After all, language laboratories have become a status symbol, and they provide schools with an undeniable center of attraction for visiting dignitaries and for PTA Meetings.

Likewise, we can — and do — boast the fact that more than a million and a quarter youngsters are at present *actually* studying foreign languages in our elementary schools. More precisely, it seems fairer to say, from my reading the many articles dealing with FLES and from my limited personal experience — my own children, direct participation in FLES programs and repeated visits to elementary schools — that more than a million and a quarter children are presently "dabbling" with foreign languages in elementary schools throughout the nation. In too many cases, FLES programs were introduced in a rather "hit and run" fashion, ranging from "extended play-time" to some kind of "foreign awareness" with, occasionally, an attempt to make it a genuine academic subject to be taken seriously and demanding accrued effort on the part of the learner.

Furthermore, the much discussed question of continuity and articulation is far from being solved and quite often the best FLES programs end in a *cul de sac* or, what is worse, in a disheartening constant re-beginning of the same language or a switching over to a new language — made possible by the availability of a newly-hired teacher whose departure, the following year, however, will mark the end of the program or a return to the very beginning of the language first started.

Time has come, it seems to me, and to others as well, if we judge by the large number of controversial articles appearing in our professional journals, to take hold of ourselves, to look with a critical eye at what is being done, at the results achieved — and not only at self-deluding figures. Time has come indeed to answer the question raised by a recent contributor to *The French Review*, "To what extent are we guilty of encouraging, at least tacitly, the expectation of miracles which will prove impossible?"[2] Time also has come to heed the warning of those who see "the non-utilitarian, unapplied and purely cultural aspects" of language study "in danger of being crowded out of the picture by electronic translating machines and communications laboratories."[3]

It is not my intention to argue for a return to the pre-atomic status quo with respect to foreign language teaching. Undoubtedly, much was wrong with the situation then, for reducing foreign language study to reading and translating is as unfair and as stultifying as reducing it to oral comprehension and speaking ability — especially when the latter is still further reduced to its least human aspect, the reflex mechanism.

It is not my intention, either, to advocate the rejection of language laboratories. Rather, I suggest that they be used for what they are, that is a new tool, a new device to alleviate the teacher's routine tasks while enlarging his scope. No more than the book — an older tool which we have been using for more than two centuries — did when it was first introduced into the classroom, the language laboratory should in no way dictate ends and means to the language teacher.

Since language is, on the one hand, a "branch of acoustics," it is

[2] Edward T. Heise, "Let's Talk Sense About Language Teaching"; *The French Review*, Vol. XXXVI, No. 4, (February, 1962), p. 176.

[3] Thomas Palfrey, "Literary Translation"; *The Bulletin of the Rocky Mountain MLA*, Vol. XVII (May, 1964), p. 8.

clear that laboratories and electronics can and should play an important role in developing this technical ability in our students; yet, on the other hand, language is also something else, and in this age of utilitarianism and technology, it might be well to remember that language is first and foremost a "vehicle of thought," (and there cannot be any real communication with a machine), and lastly, though of no lesser importance, that one must have something worthwhile to communicate.

It seems to me that too much emphasis is placed on "training" in our schools, as opposed to "educating" — and it appears that the blow struck against us by Russia, in 1957, increased still further this stress on "training." This attitude has reflected on foreign language teaching as well; today, the stress is on "training," just as it has always been with some teachers, even before Sputnik, though they had not yet heard of the "new key."

At the same time, and to answer in an erroneous democratic way the demands of ever-increasing numbers of students attending our colleges and universities, American education has tended to level down to the lowest common denominator, forgetting, as Louis B. Wright emphatically reminded us, that "somewhere, somehow, we must preserve the beauty and the wisdom that will never be found in mediocrity."

As we look over the past, and the present as well, one may well wonder whether the fault lies in the method, or even the objectives, or in the men themselves and their approach to their chosen profession. No matter the method in fashion, there have been, still are, and always will be teachers of foreign languages who succeed in maintaining the required equilibrium between the various facets of language learning, and what is more, who succeed in imparting to their students, besides a sound knowledge and command of the language, those very humane qualities which make them excellent students and teachers and thus responsible and needed members of the world community.

If the Sputnik fever which seized the United States after October, 1957, was salutary in that it brought about a needed re-examination of our educational system, that same fever can prove lethal if it leads us "to substitute mere technical training for the all-round education we must furnish our children."[4]

Education, let us insist, is not the mastering of a series of gestures and movements; neither is it the accumulation of a certain number of facts. It does not consist in filling a container to capacity with a large variety of products. On the contrary, in the education process, facts are first and foremost means, means toward the fullest possible development of the intellectual, emotional, and physical capacities of the student. As a matter of fact, what is important is not the amount of facts a student

[4] Arthur Beattie, "Language Study in the Space Age"; *The Arizona Foreign Language Teachers' Forum* (April, 1963), p. 8.

remembers at the end of his college career, but rather, to paraphrase a well-known statement, what is left in him once everything has been forgotten.

The present emphasis on science and technology has affected all areas of knowledge, including those disciplines which stand at the very heart of what we call the Humanities. As foreign language teachers, it is our duty to assert and to prove by our very attitude and practise that the "fundamental value of formal language study is humanistic and always has been."[5] To that effect, we must stand firm on our belief that the study of foreign languages must open up onto the study of literature. It is bad enough that we have to teach beginning language courses in our colleges and universities — especially in the so-called common languages — but let us not make this study an end in itself, rather let us bring it, as rapidly as possible, to its logical and rewarding conclusion, the reading of literature in the language.

Indeed there are signs — though often unnoticed, drowned out as they are by the rumble of the language laboratories — that serious consideration is being given this question, as witness the recent resolution unanimously approved by the Minnesota Chapter of the AATSP: "language departments of our colleges and universities should carry out their professional responsibility to the public by declaring the teaching of basic skills in a *first* foreign language to be *inappropriate for college* level courses."

Undoubtedly, foreign languages have to be taught as an end in themselves, just as other trades are and should be taught, but we do not feel that this limited goal should be the total objective of foreign language study in school, and particularly not in institutions of higher education. Let the commercial and technical schools perform this part of the task, in other words, let them assume the *training* while we concentrate on the *educating:*

> The teaching of foreign language in Universities must not be levelled down and reduced to the level of bilingual guides or Linguaphone records for hurried tourists. . . . We are not branches of the Berlitz school. . . . Our task is to form civilized and cultured young men and women, and not parrots who can only repeat sentences learned by heart or commonplaces prepared serially.[6]

We are all too aware of the tremendous progress made by science and technology in the last 25 years, and of the parallel decline of the humanities — at a time when they are more than ever needed. It is my contention that our profession, so long as it does not reduce language

[5] Roeming, *op. cit.,* p. 96.

[6] Roger Asselineau, "Language and Literature"; *The French Review,* Vol. XXXVII, No. 6 (May, 1964), p. 684.

learning to "something you do" that enables you to acquire "something you need,"[7] can and will play its part in the all-important fight ahead to prevent man from being completely outdistanced by science and technology and thus becoming their slave by default. Furthermore, if as Northrop Frye declared recently, the teaching of literature is best equipped "to train the imagination to fight for the sanity and dignity of mankind,"[8] the teaching of foreign literatures, adding the extra dimension of cosmopolitanism without which no true education can be achieved, should stand at the very heart of the fight for the rehabilitation of the humanities.

For ten years now, we have been witnessing a "drôle de révolution" in our field, a "révolution" which, as a critic pointed out recently, threatens to "totally *sapirize* and *skinnerize* our language field" and which, if unchecked "will lead to the eventual mechanization of subject matter and regimentation of human beings with whom we deal."[9]

Our task is immense, but not any more difficult than that of all those who, concerned with the fate of man — whether they be scientists or humanists, professors of foreign languages or professors of English — have chosen the teaching profession. As Professor Paul Hazard recalled, at the height of the Nazi onslaught, and with special reference to the professor of French,

> It is the task of the foreign language professors to get young minds accustomed to get out of themselves, to get out of their normal environment, to come into contact with other forms of expression and thought, and thus enrich them by making them more supple. It is their task to break down their narrow horizons and make them partake of the existence of the world. It is their task, also, to struggle against the invasion of technology and machines, by reminding them that man's ideal does not consist solely in enslaving matter for his needs but also to multiply his powers of life, through the acquisition of a better nourished thought, a more delicate sensibility, and a more fraternal soul. . . . It is their task to make others understand that humanity is not limited to a single moment — the present — nor to a single nation — however powerful it might be; rather, it is their task to link the present to the past, and the nation to all other nations, while preserving both the memory and the cult of the desperate shouts, songs of love, hymns of

[7] Herbert B. Myron, Jr., "Languages, Cultures, and Belles Lettres"; *The French Review,* Vol. XXXVII, No. 2, (December, 1963), p. 177.

[8] Northrop Frye, "Elementary Teaching and Elementary Scholarship"; *PMLA,* Vol. LXXIX, No. 2B, (May, 1964), p. 13.

[9] Myron, *op. cit.,* p. 179.

hope, epics, comedies, dramas, which the most divine of the sons of men, geniuses, have scattered in space and time.[10]

[10] Paul Hazard, "Le Professeur de français"; *The French Review,* Vol. XIV (February, 1941), pp. 277–283.

For Further Reading

Allen, E. V., "Role of Classics," *Journal of Secondary Education,* April, 1965, 40: 168–170.

Babbidge, Homer, D., Jr., "Thoughts for the Future," *The Modern Language Journal,* January, 1965, 49: 15–19.

Brooks, Nelson H., *Language and Language Learning,* Second edition, Harcourt, Brace & World, Inc., New York, 1960.

Eddy, Frederick D., "What Is Good About the Teaching and Learning of Modern Foreign Languages," *Teachers College Journal,* October, 1964, 36: 31–33.

Else, Gerald F., "The Role and Relevance of Classical Education Today," pp. 1–7 in the *Report* of the Planning Conference to Examine the Role of Classical Studies in American Education, John Francis Latimer, Project Director, The George Washington University, Washington, D.C., 1965.

Heller, John L., "Is Latin a Dead Language?" *The Classical Journal,* March, 1963, 58: 248–252.

Joseph, Sister Marie, "Status Report on Foreign Languages," *Catholic School Journal,* March, 1964, 64: 60–62.

Lindquist, Ed. "Latin and General Education," *Peabody Journal of Education,* March, 1965, 42: 285–289.

Lipp, Solomon, "Modern Foreign Languages," *Journal of Education,* April, 1966, 15–22, Vol. 148, No. 4.

Nostrand, Howard Lee, "New Perspectives of Foreign Language Learning," *School and Society,* October 21, 1961, 89: 335–337.

Politzer, Robert L., "Foreign Language Curriculum, Backgrounds and Problems," *The Journal of Secondary Education,* April, 1965, 40: 156–163.

Stack, Edward M., *The Language Laboratory and Modern Language Teaching,* Oxford University Press, 1960.

Starr, Wilmarth, "The Teaching of Foreign Languages: Current Issues and the Future," *School Life,* November, 1963, 7–10, Vol. 46.

Stewart, William McCausland, "The Western Literary Tradition and the Study of Languages," *The Journal of General Education,* January, 1965, 16: 317–326.

PART EIGHT

Business Education

38. The Case for Business Education in the Secondary School

John L. Rowe

Prior to the thirties, business education was known as commercial education; and its subject matter consisted largely of the three R's — shorthand, typewriting, and bookkeeping. The primary aim of commercial education was preparation for the office occupations.

During the twenties and early thirties, commercial education had

One of the nation's leading spokesmen for business education, John L. Rowe is Professor and Chairman of the Department of Business Education at the University of North Dakota, Grand Forks. He has published approximately 110 professional articles and research reports dealing with teacher education in shorthand, typewriting, basic business courses, student teaching, and vocational education. He was President, National Association for Business Teacher Education, 1957–58, and has edited numerous professional yearbooks, bulletins, quarterlies, and abstracts. The article which begins on this page was prepared as an original contribution to the present volume and is printed by permission of the author.

difficulty in being respected academically; but no one even remotely considered deemphasizing it in the schools. In fact, the trend was just the opposite. Commercial education continued to expand. Schools took pride in offering two or three years of training in shorthand, typewriting, and bookkeeping. By offering this amount of training, there was an assurance of developing the needed office skills for initial employment. In those early days of our work, there was no thought of curtailment or discontinuance. Commercial education was characterized by growth and expansion.

The growth of commercial education was not automatic, however. To combat the resentment of academicians toward practical courses required strong leadership on the part of commercial educators. The battle was won because the primary objective of our work at that time was vocational. Commercial subjects were offered so that people could obtain employment. There was no other objective. Commercial education became recognized and accepted, and it grew in respectability because it was successful in preparing young people for the work world. This was its reason for being, its basic defense; and no one could take exception to it. As a subject matter area, it became accepted because of this fact.

The great depression brought changes in our field. It was now difficult to obtain positions — regardless of how much training an individual possessed. We became alarmed and offered new justifications for our work — general education values, personal use values, and even cultural values. This lasted for about a decade and then came the great world conflict, World War II; and the demand for office workers was such that people with only marginal skills were readily accepted. Evidently not as much training was required because one could obtain an office position if he could type 30 words a minute. The businessman was afraid to ask if the applicant could take shorthand.

But the demand for office workers has continued ever since, and today it is the greatest in our nation's history. The most sought-after worker today is the efficient stenographer or secretary — one with an adequate competency in skills, and we are not training these people — despite the fact that high school graduates would be welcome. Why are we not preparing high school youth with adequate office occupations skills? Who is to blame for the deterioration of standards and the lack of intellectually qualified high school youth entering this type of work?

There are many factors responsible for our present plight. We are either doomed to oblivion as a business education department in the secondary school or we will continue to expand to new pinnacles of success.

Educational and Social Forces Affecting The Current Status of Vocational Business Education

National Unemployment and the Demand for Office Workers. There are more high school graduates today not attending college than there were in 1940. The percentage of high school students going on to college has increased, but we have more students graduating from high school.

The press has been filled with accounts of unemployment for the 18–25 age group. It has been stated that this group of idle workers lacks salable skills. They could be absorbed in the work force if they possessed sufficient skills. Not all of the presently unemployed young age group would be or could be effective office workers, but studies reveal that a considerable percentage could be salvaged for the office occupations.

The Manpower Training and Development Act has specifically provided for office occupations training programs; and it is reported that in many cities, large centers are filled to capacity with young people enrolled. They go to school six hours a day from 12 to 43 weeks — studying typewriting, shorthand, office machines, filing, and bookkeeping — to acquire the skills they did not get in our secondary school programs because we either did not provide this training or the guidance counselors were asleep on the job.

Significantly, it has been stated that the first graduates of these special training programs have been rapidly absorbed into business firms. This is truly an indictment against someone — the fact that these young people had to experience the degrading effect of unemployment and particularly so because it was unnecessary. Do we, as business teachers, want the Federal government assuming what is rightfully our responsibility?

The Space Age and Its Effect Upon the Curriculum. When the Russians first launched Sputnik, the public became concerned with what appeared to be a lack of adequate training in academic subjects, particularly in the sciences and mathematics. As a result, pressure groups (educational and public) were responsible for increasing the amount and number of academic subjects in the curriculum and, as we know, at the expense of vocational subjects. It was unfortunate that these groups failed to recognize that actually scientists and mathematicians and engineers cannot effectively produce without adequate support from business including the office occupations. Not everyone can become a scientist or a mathematician. Large numbers of very bright people may not have an aptitude for this type of work or even care to go into it.

But vocational subjects were curtailed. In general, most students were required to take science, math, foreign language, and the social studies, regardless of whether or not they entered college. It was assumed that by taking these academic subjects that one would have an appreciation of their importance, but appreciation is pretty hard to accept if one is unemployed.

There is just so much room in the high school curriculum, and something had to go. In many instances the subjects curtailed were advanced typewriting, advanced shorthand, and other specialized offerings in our field.

The hysteria has slackened somewhat, but a great deal of harm has been done to vocational business education; and it will be a challenge to regain our former stature.

Certain business education leaders have been our own worst enemies. Not all of the leaders in business education are vocationally oriented. Many of these leaders promote the general business subjects emphatically, declaring that our first aim in business education is that of general education. These leaders sometimes state that only one year of typewriting is necessary and that one can easily take dictation and produce a mailable transcript after only one year of shorthand. They implied that our instruction was unnecessarily time consuming and that we should be able to do the job in less time.

We can shorten some of the time required to develop skills in the office occupations, but it cannot be done by eliminating half of the program. Then, too, in our field, as well as in other fields, there is a vast area of new knowledge which must be taught. We, too, have had an explosion of knowledge.

The math teachers claim they need more time; the science teachers claim they need more time; and although we also need more time, we sometimes give in to the advocates of other phases of business education by shortening our skill training so that at best we offer a hodgepodge of many different subjects and produce a marginal worker or one who must be retrained. *Have we no pride?*

Current Trends in Business Education

Typewriting Enrollments Will Continue to Expand at a Dramatic Rate. This increase will be largely in the personal-use area. Seventy percent of all typewriting students today are taking it for personal use rather than for the office occupations. This is good because personal typewriting strengthens the vocational typewriting program.

Beginning typewriting is descending in the curriculum structure. The tenth grade has been our most popular year to offer this subject. However, at the present time nearly as many students are taking typewriting in the ninth grade as were taking it in the tenth. Last year there were 25,000 students taking typewriting in the elementary school — below grade 7.

Advanced typewriting as a subject is not as popular as it once was. Its content remains, however, and is being offered more and more in the subject of office practice. This is also true of advanced shorthand.

The Basic Business Subjects Will Be Re-evaluated, Redefined, and Reconstituted. The basic business subjects constitute such offerings as general business, consumer education, business law, economic geography, and economics. No one will deny the worthwhileness of these offerings provided they serve the needs of youth. There are many strong advocates for each of these subjects — those who state everyone should have general business, those who state everyone should have business law, and economic geography and economics. *But,* we cannot have all of these separate courses. Students would be taking only business subjects in the curriculum, and they would be narrowly trained.

Unfortunately basic business subjects are on the decline in some sections of the country; and when offered, these subjects frequently become a haven for the low-ability student.

There is a definite trend and need for integrated courses in the basic business subjects. This could be done by combining all elements of the various subjects — law, general business, economics. We would then have two integrated core courses — junior general business and senior general business.

The basic business subjects have been poorly taught — question–answer–workbook–lecture. Emphasis has been on facts and figures already obsolete in the textbook. The subject has been taught by poorly prepared teachers — both social studies and business education. The challenge is to teach understanding, attitudes, and ideals — not the repetition of facts some of which are already obsolete the day the book was published.

The Subject of Economics Will Expand, Due in Part to Pressure Groups. Communistic Russia, Fascist Germany, and Italy were effective in teaching economics — their brand of economics. The governments of these countries recognized the role of education in promoting their particular aims and isms. From the day the child entered school until he graduated, a way of living was taught to him.

In our country we believe in the free enterprise system, a democratic society, and a free interchange of ideas. Basic to our democratic way of life is an understanding of economics — the science of free enterprise in this country. Let's teach it. The challenge is how to relate theoretical college economics to the high school student.

Office Practice Offerings Will Greatly Expand in the Years to Come. This course offering will provide our greatest opportunity for vocational business education on the secondary school level. The most nebulous term in business education is office practice. But, it is a grand and glorious offering because our administrators think it is good although they don't know why. It is a subject where we are permitted to teach whatever we want to teach — whatever is left over to teach.

Many critics of business education — that is, administrators and academic personnel — frown upon advanced shorthand and typewriting. Even many prominent leaders in business education look down upon a second year of shorthand and a second year of typewriting. But, what's in a name anyway? Teach what you believe to be most appropriate or needed. Many office practice courses include such training as further skill in typewriting, further skill in shorthand, and the application of high shorthand and typewriting skills into integrated office projects. Advanced shorthand was really additional skill building plus the application of this skill in practical transcription. Advanced typewriting was really additional skill building plus the application of this skill to office situations. And is not the office situation phase of these skills office practice?

The Subject of Bookkeeping Is Being Questioned Concerning Its Value to All Students Enrolling in It. Bookkeeping enrollments are barely holding their own, and second-year bookkeeping is not as popular as it once was. This is unfortunate because the subject of bookkeeping is probably the best single offering we have in which to teach the organization of business, the importance of keeping adequate records, and the discipline of arithmetic and detail. It still remains the best general business course with some meat in it.

Bookkeeping is very much like shorthand. It takes an average or above-average IQ to master it. Recordkeeping should be considered as an offering for those students without an accounting aptitude. It is vocational in nature and is ideal for those possessing an aptitude for clerical work.

Automation Will Receive Some Additional Emphasis in the High School Business Department. Automation will affect the high school business education program, and there are many things we can do to provide for this technological change. For example, we must give more attention to numbers in typewriting. A good number touch typist will be invaluable in working with data processing machines.

Greater attention to the fundamental processes must be provided in our *adding and calculating machines* in the *Office Practice course.* We must provide bookkeeping as a background for data processing and teach voice-writing as an adjunct to shorthand. Key-punch training is definitely needed, and we should present the theory of records administration.

Newer Teaching Media Will Make It Possible to Provide More Effective Instruction in Business Education Subjects. There is a greater body of knowledge in business education today than ever before. We have more to teach, more to learn, and less time to do it in in all too many instances. We must work with more lower-ability students. Some very fine aids have been developed to accommodate instruction for larger classes and for individual differences in these classes.

Electronic dictation laboratories greatly assist in providing for individual differences in shorthand classes. There are currently programmed learning and teaching machines in the field of business arithmetic. Materials and new programs are being developed in other fields.

Distributive Education and Cooperative Part-Time Education Programs Will Expand in the Future. Distributive Education programs have been validated as being needed and worthwhile. They are truly vocational programs and prepare young people to assume responsible positions in selling and in the distributive occupations.

Cooperative office training programs have also been growing and expanding because of the realistic vocational training offered.

The Vocational Education Act of 1963 specifically includes aid to business education on the high school level as well as for distributive education. Federal aid will be offered to those providing cooperative part-time programs in office training.

It is easy to sell distributive education and cooperative office training to the public because it involves the cooperation of some of our most influential taxpayers.

Business Arithmetic and Economic Geography are Being Absorbed by the Mathematics and Social Studies Departments. Business arithmetic, for all practical purposes, has been lost to the math department. The math teachers claimed they were better qualified to teach it. They took it over, but they still teach mostly algebra and the pure math subjects. Supposedly, business arithmetic was to be offered in general math; but general math, in most instances, has become just another course in algebra.

The same has been true of economic geography. The social studies teachers took over this subject claiming it was a social science offering. But what have the social science teachers been doing? In general, they continue to offer more history, government, and political science with practically no attention to geography.

Will social studies take over economics? This is a very critical question. Business educators are best equipped by business education training to teach economics — particularly the free enterprise system.

Studies reveal we have more training in economics in the business teacher education curriculum.

Shorthand as a Secondary School Subject Is Receiving a New Look. Many communities are realizing the need for vocational shorthand regardless of the size of the community. Mobility is a characteristic of our population.

The importance of adequate training in shorthand is being recognized. The average businessman dictates 80 words per minute; but we should ask ourselves, "What constitutes this average?" At no time in the history of our country have we had a greater need for stenographers with the ability to take dictation at 80 words per minute on new matter.

Shorthand is being further simplified and should be easier to teach. There are newer teaching aids to facilitate learning. Notehand is growing rapidly.

What Can Be Done to Maintain An Effective Business Education Program On The Secondary School Level?

Provide Adequate Training in the Business Education Skills Used in the Office Occupations — Typewriting. Develop a skill of 50 words per minute on a five-minute timed writing with no more than one error for every two minutes. If you can obtain this skill in one year for 90 per cent of your students, then offer only one year of typewriting. Obtaining this skill in one year is usually possible because the development of a typewriting skill is a maturation process.

Develop typewriting production rates at approximately 90 to 95 percent of straight-copy rates. Students should be trained to arrange the following material at rapid and mailable rates of speed: letters, manuscripts, rough drafts, and tabulated reports. Develop the ability to type numbers by touch at the rate of 30 words per minute (150 digits).

Shorthand. Develop a dictation skill of 100 words per minute for three minutes on unpreviewed new material. Students should transcribe this dictation in mailable form and at acceptable rates of speed; obviously, to acquire these skills in shorthand and typewriting requires more than one year of training.

Every employment agency reports that dozens of unfilled positions exist for stenographers possessing the above skills. If we do not provide these skills, businessmen naturally question the validity of the high school business education department. Let us not be satisfied with training marginal workers. Of course, business will sometimes employ our graduates with marginal skills; but that doesn't mean they endorse what we are doing.

A knowledge of basic office machines and stenographic practices is needed. A high school business occupations graduate should have the following additional secretarial skills:

1. Skill with the 10-key adding machines.
2. Skill in typing ditto masters and stencils.
3. Skill with voice-writing machines.
4. An understanding of filing and finding.
5. A businesslike telephone technique.
6. A sense of how to meet people.
7. An appreciation of a full day's work for a full day's pay.

Promote the Teaching of Economics so as to Provide an Understanding of the American Free Enterprise System and How It Operates in a Democracy. Business teachers are best qualified to teach economics in the secondary school. Studies reveal that most business teachers not only have had college courses in economics; but they have had such courses as business law, business organization, management, marketing, and so forth. Business educators have a better background and understanding of how the free enterprise system works.

It is necessary to become more virile and articulate in assuming the role of teaching economics. A basic understanding of business democracy and how business works is essential to our way of life.

As business teachers, we must master the art of developing understandings and appreciations. One basic understanding is worth a thousand outdated facts. We could profit from some of the methodology used by social science teachers in developing understandings, but business teachers have a better subject-matter background to develop the important economic concepts needed to preserve our free enterprise system.

Objectively Determine the Need or Demand for Office Personnel. If your school administrator states that shorthand is going out, educate him that this is just not so. Present him with facts from the state employment agency, from the want ads of newspapers, from the private employment bureaus.

Don't take the office appliance salesman's word that voice-writing machines are replacing shorthand. Voice-writing is not a substitute for shorthand, but voice-writing should be offered because the secretary with shorthand also uses a transcription machine. She is just that more valuable because she can use both.

Promote the Profession of Business Teaching. Encourage your outstanding high school graduates to enter the business teaching profession. There is a real shortage of qualified business teachers with office occupations skills — not with marginal skills, but with high skills.

Obtain an advanced degree, but major in business education. Your administrator will respect you and the department a lot more if you do so.

Provide Visibility for the Business Education Department. Business education has never really had a very good press. We are sometimes taken for granted. When high school graduates obtain positions in business where they use their skills in earning a living, then we have a real human-interest story. We have done something worthwhile; let us tell about it. Tell the faculty; have it in your school newspaper.

Many of your graduates will go on to college where they will major in many different fields. A surprisingly large number of these young people earn part of their expenses in college by using the business education skills acquired in high school. Have you ever made a survey of those students who went on to college and used their business skills to earn part or all of their expenses? Wouldn't this make a wonderful news story?

Learn What the Critics Say About Our Work. School administrators and academicians, as well as our Rickovers and the Hutchinses, have frequently made questionable indictments concerning the merits of vocational education. In order to combat our adversaries, we must know what and how they think. There have been some excellent articles in business education publications recently concerning the criticisms of our work.

Become A Master Of The Skill And Of The Subjects You Teach

The best salesmen for vocational business education subjects on the secondary school level are those business teachers who have developed high skills in typewriting and shorthand, and those teachers who have had an adequate preparation in accounting. A business education teacher who can take dictation at 120 words a minute and transcribe it with speed and accuracy would never tolerate just one year of high school shorthand because he recognizes that more time is needed to attain adequate skills.

A business teacher who can type 60 words a minute also recognizes the value of sufficient time in training a typist. Then, too, we have gone through the process of acquiring these skills and can appreciate the difficulties encountered among our students when they attempt to acquire these skills.

A teacher of bookkeeping who has had at least two years of college accounting is not one to state that we should drop bookkeeping from the high school curriculum. And, finally, those teachers who have had a broad business administration and economics background plus a basic business methods course will be the ones fighting our battle to retain the important subject of economics in the curriculum.

39. Building the Business Curriculum

H. G. Enterline

The term "curriculum" is being used here in a somewhat restricted sense, referring specifically to an organized sequence of courses and other related learning activities designed to achieve a particular educational objective. In business education, the educational objective is usually vocational in nature. However, in some instances the end objective may be somewhat broad in nature so that it could refer to the attainment of unspecialized business knowledge and economic understanding with the thought that specialization will follow, either through later formal study or on-the-job training.

Broadly speaking, there are two approaches to building a business curriculum — or any other curriculum for that matter. One approach is that of planning a loosely structured curriculum; the other is that of building a tightly structured curriculum.

According to the loosely structured approach, relatively few courses are absolutely required. Essentially the curriculum is individually planned in terms of each student's particular objective. Such an approach is entirely workable *provided* that counseling service of the highest order is available to each student. Actually relatively few, if any, schools are equipped with this kind of counseling service. Consequently when the loosely structured approach to curriculum planning is attempted, what usually results is a kind of educational smorgasbord. Everything is on a more or less elective basis. (An analogy: giving young children the privilege of making unrestricted selections from a restaurant menu.) If students, young students particularly, are given an unrestricted opportunity to elect courses in an educational institution,

From H. G. Enterline, "Building the Business Curriculum," *American Vocational Journal,* May, 1961, 28–31, Vol. 36. At the time of his death in 1962, H. G. Enterline was a professor in the School of Business, Indiana University. Nationally recognized as an authority on the business curriculum, he was the author of many articles and textbooks in the field. This article, which explores the problems of structuring the business curriculum, is reprinted by permission of the *American Vocational Journal* and of Mrs. Ethel M. Enterline.

educational indigestion may result. Just as the planning of a meal involves balance, so must the curriculum, business curriculum or otherwise, represent a balanced educational effort.

On the other extreme is the tightly structured curriculum in which the student has no, or relatively few choices. The situation is comparable to that of taking meals at a boarding house where the meal is fixed. While a balanced diet may be maintained, the meals may not always be too palatable due to the lack of provision for individual tastes. A similar situation prevails in an educational institution which permits no electives.

Both points of view represent extremes, of course, but if a choice had to be made between a loosely structured curriculum and a tightly structured one, the latter obviously would be the better choice since the attainment of the educational objective is reasonably well assured. Ideally, some choice of electives is desirable, and some diversity of curriculum offerings is needed in order to provide for individual needs.

This presentation is concerned primarily with the basic framework for building a well-balanced business curriculum. Reference is being made primarily to the secondary-school business curriculum, although with slight modifications the basic framework presented could be adapted to building a business curriculum in a private business school or in a collegiate school of business.

All thinking business educators concur that a well-planned curriculum requires a balance of vocational business education and of basic business education. It is assumed that the curriculum is built upon a broad base of general education. There are, of course, differences over specifics.

All likewise concur that vocational business education involves two broad areas of preparation: (1) training for office occupations, and (2) training for distributive occupations. All likewise agree that vocational preparation involves more than the mere development of business skills; that accompanying such preparation there need to be adequate and proper kinds and amounts of related learnings, occupational intelligence, or whatever specific term is used to describe "vocational preparation plus." All likewise concur that every individual needs to have a fundamental knowledge of our economy, that all individuals develop competency in dealing with personal money management problems, and that the well-planned business curriculum will include work in this basic business education area.

The problem then is that of setting up a business curriculum which includes all of the foregoing important ingredients. Essentially the problem is not too difficult if one had X number of semesters in which to accomplish the task. But tradition, legislation, and logical principles and practices restrict both the amount of time available and the proportion of the total amount of the study program which may be applied to a particular area of learning.

With these considerations and limitations in mind, therefore, the framework for a well-balanced business curriculum resembles the pattern in the diagram below.

ADVANCED BASIC BUSINESS				
Stenographic Office Practice	Clerical Office Practice	Bookkeeping	Distributive Education	Unspecialized Basic Business Program
INTRODUCTORY BASIC BUSINESS (General Business)				

An introductory basic business course, commonly referred to as General Business, is required. This provides a background for the study of advanced business courses, acquaints the student with business terminology, and gives the student some comprehension of the nature of business occupational opportunities. At the same time it aids in the development of money management competency. It is generally agreed that such a course should be required of all business majors and that it should be effective for other students as well. The course is particularly valuable for drop-outs since this is the last opportunity for such students to gain some ability in money management competency through their formal education program.

The curriculum is concluded with an advanced basic business course. The course, or courses, serves two broad purposes: (1) it integrates and unifies all business-economic learnings to date, and (2) it provides orientation for dealing more effectively with the economic problems of adulthood. It must be remembered that approximately two-thirds of all students who enter high school terminate their formal education prior to high school graduation or with high school graduation. The advanced basic business course, therefore, needs to be required of all business students to provide the kind of balance described above. Likewise, it should be open to non-business students who terminate their education with high school graduation and to college-bound students — particularly those who plan to major in business or economics on the college level.

The advanced basic business course referred to above is commonly offered according to one of three different plans: (1) as two one-semester courses such as business principles, consumer economics, economics, economic geography, salesmanship (a general course), and business law; (2) as a "selected units" course in which students and teacher working together decide what units are of greatest concern, and then the two, three, or more books which give the best treatment of these materials are used as basic texts and reference materials; and (3) as a "problems" course, which is unstructured, wherein students working under the careful direction of the teacher in the first few weeks decide what problems are of greatest concern, and then use whatever text and reference material have a bearing on the problem.

The curriculum maker will be aware of other variations in practice in offering both the introductory basic business course and the advanced basic business course. In any event a maximum of two units of credit would be needed to offer the all-important basic business-economic material so essential in a well-balanced business curriculum.

Upon this base of business-economic understanding are built the various areas of vocational concentration. A basic principle to be kept in mind is that there needs to be enough concentration of work in one particular area so that the student will develop sufficient competency to obtain a satisfactory beginning position in business upon the completion of the curriculum. Assuming that a maximum of six units of credit in any area of study may be applied toward graduation, according to the plan suggested above a minimum of four units of work may be used to develop vocational competency in some one area.

On the diagram are shown four common vocational concentrations in business: stenographic office practice, clerical office practice, bookkeeping, and distributive education; with an additional non-specialized program in basic business education. The right side of the diagram has been left open intentionally to illustrate that in some situations other or additional areas of concentration may be offered. It is likewise possible that in a smaller school-community situation facilities and employment opportunities are such that not all five of the curriculum concentrations can be offered; so that the four, three, or two curricula which best meet the needs of the students in a particular school-community will be offered. However, in all cases, except in the very small high school where the facilities and number of students are such that no business curriculum, as such, can be offered at all, at least two curriculum paths need to be provided in order to allow at least this much diversity of business education opportunity.

Although the retention rate of students has gradually increased over the years, educators who have given careful study to the situation believe that while the number of persons attending college will continue to increase, the percentage of those doing so may level off, or actually decrease, due in part to a tightening up of college entrance requirements.

In either event the responsibility of educators in the secondary schools to provide the best kind of education for the masses of students who terminate their formal education in high school is great. As a consequence those responsible for business curriculum planning in the high school need to examine their curriculum provisions with great care to be sure that students who do study business are equipped with a high degree of vocational competency, with the basic knowledge needed to manage their personal business affairs, and with a healthy comprehension of our business-economic system. This objective can be realized only by requiring students to follow carefully planned business education "menus" rather than allowing them to take courses on a free elective, catch-as-catch-can basis, or by restricting offerings primarily to courses which teachers prefer to teach.

40. Basic Business and Vocational Education

Raymond B. Russell

Never before in the history of business education have the prospects for growth and development been brighter. The allocation of federal

From Raymond B. Russell, "Basic Business and Vocational Education," *Business Education Forum,* October 1964, 19, Vol. 19. Raymond B. Russell is Professor and Chairman of the Division of Business and Business Education, Kansas State Teachers College, Emporia. He has contributed many articles on basic business and the business curriculum to professional journals. In 1966–67 he served as President of the Kansas Business Education Association. Reprinted by permission of the *Business Education Forum,* a publication of the National Business Education Association, a Department of the National Education Association, Washington, D.C.

funds for vocational training, the emphasis for training of dropouts from school, and the retraining of the unemployed indicates an interest in vocational education never before experienced. Business education is a part of the total vocational education program, and we as business educators have a responsibility and an opportunity in this undertaking.

While the major emphasis at this time is on the vocational preparation of students and employees, certain implications are nevertheless evident that will, or should, have an effect on the basic business aspect of business education. Can we, as business educators, give competent training for the office and distributive occupations without including some work in the basic business area? A good employee possesses not only a marketable skill, but also must have an understanding of business and how it functions. This includes an understanding of our economic system.

It is, indeed, unfortunate that business educators have seen fit to divide themselves into two, or perhaps three, schools of thought concerning the primary purposes of business education. We have, on the one hand, the vocationally oriented group. This group is perhaps the largest and most vocal. On the other hand, there has been an increasing number of educators during the past several years who have indicated that high school and college offerings should be on a more academic level. They have been enthusiastic about the basic business, economic approach. This group will, if possible, eliminate the skill and technical training offered in our schools. Then, somewhere between these two extremes, there are those who believe that both the vocational and basic business education have their place and should be stressed. This latter group believes further that this can be done without sacrifice or hardship to either goal or objective. In fact, they believe that both objectives would be strengthened. The Policies Commission for Business and Economic Education in each of its pronouncements reminds administrators, counselors, and business teachers themselves that business education is concerned with two major aspects of the education of youth. These are:

A. The knowledge, attitudes, and nonvocational skills needed by all persons to be effective in their personal economics and in their understanding of our economic system.

B. The vocational knowledge and skills needed for initial employment and for advancement in a business career.

Certainly, today the need for vocational education in our public secondary schools was never greater. Lagging student interests, increased numbers of dropouts, and confused thinking are characteristic of many of our high school students today. Let those who recommend only the academic approach for our high schools continue in control for a few more years, and we will really have an unemployment and youth problem in this country. The urgent need for vocational training in our schools, however, does not imply that we should forego the offering of the basic business aspect of our program. On the other hand, it becomes more imperative than ever that this type of training be added to our offerings. As our business society becomes more technical and complex and jobs become more highly skilled and specialized, it is also necessary that each person have a better understanding of our economic system and how business operates.

At the present time there are a large number of so-called basic business courses offered in our schools. Among them are business arithmetic, general business, consumer economics, business law, business English, and business principles. While all of these courses have value and offer some information that every student should have, it is practically impossible for any school to include this array of subjects in the business curriculum. Certainly, no student could be expected to take all of these courses. The fact that there are so many basic business subjects is probably one of the reasons why more schools do not include one or more basic business courses in their offerings. They are confused as to which one would be the best for their students.

It is becoming evident that some consolidation and integration of the basic business courses must take place if we are to give a student the background and preparation he should receive. If, with the vocational or skill training, we could include a junior level (ninth or tenth grade) general business course and a senior level (eleventh or twelfth grade) course, we would accomplish much more than we do at present with our many different offerings. The junior level course should integrate general business, business arithmetic, and some basic economic concepts. The senior level course should emphasize and integrate economic understanding, business principles, and some aspects of business law. Our present general business textbooks do a fair job for the junior level, but they need to emphasize basic economic principles more than is done at present. The old idea that basic economic ideas cannot be taught to ninth graders, or even to grade school boys and girls, is completely false.

Business educators have before them one of the most challenging periods of growth and development. In order to meet effectively the demands of the times, we must adjust our offerings to meet the critical needs of the business community in which we live.

For Further Reading

American Business Education, May, 1961, 17: 195–272. (A special issue of the journal on the high school business program.)

Bahr, Gladys, "The Contribution of Secondary School Basic Business Education to General Education," *The National Business Education Quarterly,* December, 1961, 62–68, Vol. 30.

Forkner, Hamden L., "Educating for the Daily *Business* of Living," *NEA Journal,* December, 1953, 42: 565–566.

Lomax, Paul S., et al., "Curriculum Planning, Personnel Services (Guidance), and Teaching Methodology," *The National Business Education Quarterly,* December, 1963, 5–26, Vol. 32.

Mason, Louis D., "Business Education Offers Something of Value to All Pupils," *The Clearing House,* September, 1964, 39: 51–52.

Porter, Leonard J., "General Business at the Crossroads," *Business Education Forum,* December, 1963, 17–18, Vol. 18.

Roman, John C., *The Business Curriculum,* Monograph 100, South-Western Publishing Company, Cincinnati, Ohio, 1960.

Rowe, John L., "Economic and Social Forces Changing the Business Curriculum," *Catholic Business Education Review,* November, 1958, 29–39, Vol. 10.

Rowe, John L., "Developing Syllabi and Course Content in Business Education," *The National Business Education Quarterly,* Summer, 1965, 36–40, Vol. 33.

Samson, Harland E., and David A. Thompson, "High School Preparatory Education for Careers in Distribution," *Business Education Forum,* April, 1964, 10–12, Vol. 18.

Thompson, Pearle J., "The High School Stenographic Course and Then Some," *Business Education Forum,* May, 1964, 39, 48, Vol. 18.

Tonne, Herbert A., *Principles of Business Education,* McGraw-Hill Book Company, New York, Third Edition, 1961.

Tonne, Herbert A., "Building an Offense and a Defense for an Adequate Secondary School Business Education — Vocational and Basic Business," *The National Business Education Quarterly,* December, 1961, 78–82, Vol. 30.

Warmke, Roman F., *Supervision to Improve Instruction in Distributive Education,* Vocational Division Bulletin No. 278, U. S. Department of Health, Education, and Welfare, Office of Education, Washington, D.C., 1959.

Warren, Helen L., "New Addition to the Business Curriculum," *Journal of Business Education,* January, 1958, 33: 151–153.

PART NINE

Industrial Arts and Vocational Education

41. Curriculum Benefits from Industrial Arts

Rupert N. Evans

Industrial arts, as with every other subject in the curriculum, makes two distinct types of contributions to the accomplishments of the school. They are *direct* and *indirect* contributions.

The direct contribution of a subject comes through the increased knowledge, more highly developed skills, and changed attitudes which relate directly to that particular subject. For example, we expect that

From Rupert N. Evans, "Curriculum Benefits from Industrial Arts," *The Education Digest,* February, 1961, 29–31, Vol. 26. Reported from the *Illinois School Board Journal,* November–December, 1960, 18–22, Vol. 27. Rupert N. Evans is Dean of the College of Education and Professor of Vocational and Technical Education at the University of Illinois. Reprinted by permission of *The Education Digest.*

successful completion of a course in electricity will result in an increased knowledge of the functions of electrical circuits, a more highly developed skill in constructing and repairing electrical equipment, and a changed attitude toward symbols (together with other knowledge, skills, and attitudes).

The indirect contribution of a subject comes as it makes the learning of other subjects easier and more interesting. English makes other subjects easier to learn because of the indirect contribution of reading and writing skills. Physics makes music more interesting because it helps to explain relationships between different musical sounds.

If there is no "subject matter" in the subject it can make no direct contribution. If the student feels that the subject stops as soon as the period ends, there will be no indirect contribution. Sometimes we act as if we believe that the "nonacademic" subjects make only an indirect contribution to the development of students. This is not correct. Industrial arts has a subject matter, as do other nonacademic subjects. While it is essentially practical, there is sound theory behind each of the things it teaches.

Let's examine some of the direct contributions industrial arts can make:

Industrial arts develops an understanding of industry in our culture. If students do not know the principles of interchangeability of parts, of the relationship between amount of production and unit cost, of specialization of labor, of automation, and of industrial organization, they are not ready to live in our industrial society.

It may be claimed that these principles can be taught in the social studies. Certainly some students could learn them there, but more students understand these principles better if they see practical examples of the effects of the principles which are so easy to incorporate in industrial arts.

Another direct contribution is the discovering and developing of student talents in technology and applied science. Psychologists claim that intelligence tests, and most aptitude tests as well, do their best job in predicting success in verbal and numerical fields (the "academic" subjects). They are convinced that many students have other abilities which intelligence tests do not measure well.

Talents in music, art, spatial relations, and mechanical ability certainly exist but they are difficult to measure except through experience in courses which utilize them. To neglect the development of student talents simply because they are not in numerical or verbal fields seems unforgivable.

Students need an opportunity to discover whether or not they have the aptitudes and interests for occupations in the technical and applied science fields. Industrial-arts subjects provide that opportunity.

Engineering is a field of applied science that serves well to demonstrate the functioning of that opportunity and at the same time demonstrate how industrial arts serves the student with high intelligence. Many high schools have had success with engineering drawing, engineering mechanics, and similar industrial-arts courses which may have a year of physics and two years of mathematics as prerequisites. The attrition rate in engineering colleges would certainly be improved if more high-school students had an opportunity to learn what engineering is *before* they enrol in college.

Another direct contribution industrial arts makes is in developing problem-solving skills relating to materials and processes. We need people who can determine when a process is not operating efficiently and determine how to correct it. The housewife who calls the TV repairman when the set is not plugged in, and the chemical technician who allows a batch of boiling plastic to explode have some things in common.

Similarly, the home owner who buys shutters made of pine instead of hemlock because the "more expensive ones must be best," and the designer who specifies that a truck body be made of steel because it costs less per pound than aluminum also have some things in common. These people, along with all of us, need practice in solving problems related to materials and processes.

A direct contribution that is very close to all of us is the skill in the use of common tools and machines that can be developed in industrial-arts courses. In the last few years we have seen the beginning of the end for the domestic servant and the handyman as occupational groups. If a man (or his wife) can't use a hammer, saw, screwdriver, pliers, and drill effectively, he had better plan to increase his income in some way — he is going to need it. Moreover, each year brings us more leisure time and the use of tools is necessary for more than a few hobbies.

These, then, are some of the direct contributions of industrial arts. What of the indirect contributions?

Indirect Contributions

Every school should be concerned about its "under-achievers." Every year thousands of these students leave school when they have plenty of ability to succeed in school work. There are, apparently, many reasons why this happens. One reason is that these students don't see any immediate practical application of many of the things the school is trying to teach them.

This problem almost certainly will become more severe as our science and mathematics programs deliberately (and possibly necessarily) become more theoretical in nature. Industrial arts can show the immediate applicability, increase interest in these other subjects, and thereby aid in keeping the under-achiever in school.

Industrial arts can contribute significantly to the skill needed by professionals in other areas. Recently a group of physicists, all with Ph.D.'s, and all doing research work, said that they believed they should have taken industrial arts instead of physics in high school.

They explained that the content of the high-school physics course was repeated in college, but no one had taught them to build experimental apparatus. Because they did not know how to make orthographic drawings, a skill taught in all high-school drafting courses, they had difficulty in explaining what they wanted when they were provided with skilled workers to construct the needed equipment. Similar comments can be heard from dentists, engineers, and many other professional groups.

A third indirect contribution can be made to the students in special education classes. If classes are kept small enough, the individual instruction which is typical of industrial arts allows these students to work alongside their fellow students who are not in special education. All must work together outside of school and the school has an obligation to prepare them for this experience.

Here, then, are a few of the contributions industrial arts makes to the goals of the school. Your own industrial-arts teacher should be able to tell you about more.

42. Industrial Arts and the World of Work

Kenneth E. Dawson

Technology — automated machines! Technology — better living! Technology — complicated industrial processes! Technology — reduction of manpower! Technology — taxing pressures! Technology — research!

We live in an era often referred to as the technological age. The term technology seems to possess a thousand meanings and its implications are creative, mobile, dynamic, threatening, perplexing, and revolutionary. Technology and industry continuously influence our way of life. We can no longer think of technology as something that is purely mechanical. From the time of man the hunter, the trader, the builder, the manufacturer, the mass producer, up to the time of man the programer, we can see the various stages of technological development. Today this term is unique because society has become more aware of the complex integration of men and machines, of ideas, of industrial procedures, of management, and of the necessity to conquer the unknown.

In case not all readers are familiar with modern industrial arts, let us briefly explain this program of general education. Some have been exposed to "shop" or perhaps even the older concepts of "manual training" or "manual arts." The image of building an article or "project" for the project's sake is giving way to the building of men and women for the world of work.

From Kenneth E. Dawson, "Industrial Arts and the World of Work," *Educational Leadership*, January, 1965, 22: 236–238. Kenneth E. Dawson was Executive Secretary and Treasurer of the American Industrial Arts Association at the time this article appeared. He is now Dean of the School of Education, Morehead State University, Morehead, Kentucky. He has contributed many articles on industrial and vocational education to professional journals and has written reports for both the *Book of Knowledge* and for the *Universal Encyclopedia*. This article is reprinted by permission of the Association for Supervision and Curriculum Development and of the author.

Defining Industrial Arts

Industrial arts is that phase of education which offers individuals an insight into our industrial society through laboratory-classroom experiences. Through industrial arts, the role of industry and technology is unfolded as students study the history and development of industrial organizations, materials, products, processes, and related problems. Industrial arts provides experiences that develop basic skills and knowledge common to many occupations and professions. The study of industry helps students understand that the materials and products, which contribute to the comforts of everyday living, are the result of man's inquiring mind and his ability to solve industrial and technological problems. Actually, industrial arts provides a means by which students can apply in practical and meaningful situations the theoretical principles of science, mathematics, and other related subjects.

Industrial arts education is unique in its services to youth. It is the only curricular area devoted to the interpretation of industry and technology which comprise the dominant characteristic of 20th century American culture. The overarching objectives of industrial arts, as described in the U.S. Office of Education Conference report, *Improving Industrial Arts Teaching,* include the following:

1. To develop in each student an insight and understanding of industry and its place in our culture
2. To discover and develop talents of students in the technical fields and applied sciences
3. To develop technical problem-solving skills related to materials and processes
4. To develop in each student a measure of skill in the use of the common tools and machines.

Subject Areas Included

We have indicated that industrial arts provides for a basic understanding of the relationship between man and his industrial environment. It encompasses a study of many areas to include the broad aspects of construction, transportation, communication, manufacturing, and research development. More significantly, these may include subjects such as automotives, ceramics, design, drawing (previously called mechanical drawing), power mechanics, electricity/electronics, graphic arts, leather, lapidary, metalworking, plastics, textiles, and woodworking. Each of the preceding areas may involve a study of several subareas; for example, metalworking may include opportunities in foundry, welding, machining, sheet-metal, wrought iron, and art metal. Industrial arts laboratories provide students with the opportunity to become actively involved in studying, planning, organizing, creating, constructing, experimenting, testing, servicing, and evaluating materials, processes, and products associated with our industrial society.

Appeal of Industrial Arts

A trend in industrial arts education today is the increase in students throughout the country. In the school year 1948–49, the enrollment of students studying industrial arts courses totaled 1,762,262. In 1961–62 school year, the U. S. Office of Education estimated that over 3½ million students were studying industrial arts.

Industrial arts in the elementary grades is used to enrich and support the overall education program. Some school systems utilize industrial arts specialists to assist elementary school teachers in carrying out an activity-type learning program. Studying a community and its activities comes to life as children work with materials and associate themselves with the various occupational opportunities of their immediate surroundings.

Industrial arts is generally a required subject for all boys in junior high school. Students are introduced to various areas of industry, which include a study of natural and synthetic materials, production methods, and the resulting products. Junior high school boys and girls are encouraged to explore, plan, create, understand, and solve industrial and technological problems.

The world of work is experienced by each pupil as a teacher directs the class into a mass-production problem. Students may form a corporation, sell stock in order to obtain materials, determine and design a product to be manufactured, prepare jigs and fixtures, develop a flow chart representing the assembly line, carry out time and motion studies, continuously try to improve the product through research, etc.

During this time management may even be faced with a threatened strike. This, of course, may mean a wage increase which would affect the cost of the item being produced. If it is not practical to raise the price of the product, it will be necessary to improve production methods to increase output in order that cost may be held constant. As can be seen, there is no limit to the practical learning experiences in the industrial arts classes. And, of course, other methods such as the unit approach and group project are also used effectively in studying about various industries.

Preparing for Change

Senior high schools generally offer industrial arts as an elective. The individual interest of a student, whether it be professional, business, management, or technical, to a great extent determines the content and direction of senior high school industrial arts. The area of research and development offers the college bound student an opportunity to carry out individual research. Industrial arts provides further knowledge and depth of industrial techniques for those who desire to enter a technical school. For students entering the world of work immediately after high school, industrial arts may be the only opportunity they will have to develop a broad understanding of industry and become thoroughly familiar with the basic occupational skills. The basic knowledge derived from industrial arts will facilitate specialized training and perhaps even retraining at some later date. This factor is extremely important as it is predicted now that a person may change his occupational area seven times during his life.

Industrial arts education is devoted to the interpretation of industry, which is the most dominant characteristic of our society. Industrial arts education helps all kinds of students to prepare for living in an industrial democracy and provides a foundation for specific occupational and educational opportunities. Industrial arts gives basic education for the technician, engineer, scientist, and for the several occupational education programs.

Rather than being confined to the learning of a specific trade or skill which may be obsolete within a few years, today's concept of industrial arts emphasizes transferable skills and knowledge so that boys and girls may become more flexible and versatile in this rapidly changing world. By receiving basic information on the total scope of industry, students understand the necessity to equip themselves for future adjustment to employment changes due to scientific and technological innovations.

Industrial arts educators realize that more and more youth are entering the labor force. They are also aware of the fact that women are playing a significant role in industry since 27 percent of the labor force today is female. It is estimated that this proportion will be 45 percent by 1980. Industrial arts education is concentrating on meeting the needs of all young people. This area must provide motivation for the underachiever and the academically talented, the potential scientist and the pre-engineer, the future consumer and all other students. They must realize that their whole life will be influenced by the wonderful, but complex, world of work.

43. Vocational and Technical Education

William P. McLure

For some time the occupational structure in the United States has been undergoing rapid change. Job mobility is now the highest in the nation's history. Ten per cent of the persons employed change jobs each year, including five per cent who alter their occupations. The rate of vertical mobility or change in occupational status is high.

Not since the great westward migration of frontier days have so many youths and adults been uprooted from their home communities as in the last two decades to find employment in new surroundings. Occupational changes resulting from developments in science and technology have forced thousands of workers from the farm and the mine, from the shop and the corner grocery. All too often workers face new jobs which demand skills and knowledge that they do not possess. They and their families likewise are frequently unprepared to adjust to new social environments.

The United States Department of Labor[1] predicts an increase of about 13.5 million persons in the labor force from 1960 to 1970. Of this number six million will be women. The rates of increase in occupational groups to meet the predicted demands will vary greatly. The number of professional and technical workers needed in 1970 is estimated to be about 40 per cent greater than the number employed in 1960. Other major occupational groups for which formal education is necessary are: pro-

From William P. McLure, "The Challenge of Vocational and Technical Education," *Phi Delta Kappan,* February, 1962, 43: 212–217. William P. McLure is Professor of Educational Administration and Supervision and Director of the Bureau of Educational Research at the University of Illinois. His particular interests have been in school finance and cost analysis and the structure and function of educational government. In 1960 he directed a study of vocational education in Illinois, *Vocational and Technical Education in Illinois: Tomorrow's Challenge,* and in 1966 he served as Chairman for a comprehensive study of education in Illinois, *Education for the Future of Illinois.* This article reprinted by permission of the *Phi Delta Kappan.*

[1] U. S. Department of Labor, James P. Mitchell, Secretary. *Manpower Challenge of the 1960s.* Washington, D.C., 1960. pp. 11, 13.

prietors and managers, 23 per cent; clerks and salesmen, 26 per cent; skilled workers, 23 per cent; semi-skilled workers, 18 per cent; service workers, 25 per cent; unskilled workers, no change; and farmers, 16 per cent decrease.

Within these groups wide variations in rates of growth are expected among specific occupations. In the professional group the numbers of scientists, engineers, and teachers are estimated to have the highest rates of increase. The demand for technicians, clerical workers, craftsmen, and foremen will also increase rapidly.

These are the antecedent social and economic conditions which shape the role of formal education in our society. The nature of education is determined to a great extent by the character of individual occupational activity. A fast rate of change in the occupational sphere calls for prompt response in the educational pattern. For purposes of this discussion I should only emphasize the need for matching the demands of occupations with an adequate supply of individuals possessing requisite talents.

The maintenance of a reasonable balance between supply and demand of manpower in a dynamic society is among the chief educational problems of our nation. We now have some imbalance which must be corrected for our national economic health and welfare. We cannot move individuals around like characters on a chess board, nor do we wish to do so. Our solution is through public information, estimation, guidance, persuasion, education, and placement services.

Education in our society is conceived as the fullest development of each individual's capacities, including proficiency in a chosen occupation. In this discussion the terms *formal schooling* and *education* are used synonymously, even though all of the person's education includes contact with other agencies in society.

The Basic Components of Education

Education may be viewed as having two basic components. One is of general character, including knowledge and skills common to all men in all walks of life. This is often referred to as academic or liberal arts studies. The other is occupational specialization, which is concerned primarily with application of basic knowledge to a particular field of work. These components are related to each other in ways which are often difficult to explain, but nonetheless very real. The surgeon needs a broad and rich background in the humanities and the sciences. The manager or supervisor generally needs a background of academic knowledge superior to that of the skilled mechanic.

Specialization continues to grow, accompanied by higher and higher levels of general knowledge and skill. The two are inseparable. As increasing proportions of workers are needed with specialized training, the context of general education takes on greater significance for its contribution to the total educational experience of individuals.

The complexity of our society increasingly demands more education for more and more people. This is true for all occupational groups. Colleges and universities have done a much better job of meeting the needs in the so-called professional areas than in the sub-professional or technical fields. The most complicating factor is the large number of occupational areas requiring some specialized training within a context of adequate general education. The magnitude of the task is startling in terms of the numbers of people to be educated.

About six (or six plus) out of ten youths graduate from high school in the United States today. Three of these graduates continue education in some type of post-high-school institution. The other three, plus the four who failed to graduate, go directly into the labor force or into homemaking. Many of the girls in these groups who become housewives later enter employment. Thus about seven out of ten youths obtain only the vocational preparation which is available to them in high school before entering work.

These are the most disadvantaged groups in the total labor force. Having the least amount of education, they comprise the largest proportion of unemployed persons and of unskilled and semiskilled labor. The hope of most persons in these groups is in programs of adult education designed for upgrading on the job and training for new jobs.

Accurate statistics are not available to indicate the probable distribution of the population by educational level to meet the occupational needs of the future. If some recent estimates[2] for Illinois are extrapolated to the nation as a whole, a reasonable goal for 1970 appears to be about as follows: The high schools of the nation should be graduating eight (instead of six) out of ten youths. Four of the graduates should be entering college for four or more years of education in the professions. Two should be entering technical curricula of two or three years beyond high school. Only two should be entering work directly from high school, but better prepared vocationally than at present. It might be added that one of these probably should have a fifth year in high school to complete a more advanced level of training. The other one might be expected to pursue some further preparation in a program of adult education after a period of working. Eventually we should reach a goal of few high school drop-outs and a small proportion of graduates without some education beyond high school.

[2] William P. McLure and others. *Vocational and Technical Education in Illinois.* Urbana, Illinois: Bureau of Educational Research, College of Education, University of Illinois, 1960. 163 pp.

These estimates give a rough approximation of the educational task ahead. Some crucial changes will be needed at both the high-school and the post-high-school levels to accomplish this task.

Re-Definition of Vocational Education

At the high-school level a re-definition of "vocational" education is needed so that three major groups of students are put in proper perspective: (1) those who plan to enter college for the professions, (2) those who will choose technical fields requiring two or three years beyond high school, and (3) those who will enter occupational work either before or after graduation from high school. In this discussion I shall follow the conventional practice of applying the term "vocational" education to some of the second group and all of the third, when in the broad sense this term applies to all three.

Two major ideas seem to have merit for improving the program of "vocational" training at the high-school level. The first one calls for limiting the vocational or specialized occupational study primarily to the eleventh and twelfth grades. Few subjects below the eleventh grade can hardly be justified as anything except basic or general education. I would make an exception, of course, for students who are potential drop-outs. Some of them, particularly the over-aged ones, are ready for a vocational commitment at lower grades. About half of the student's program should consist of vocational subjects and the other half of general subjects common to most other students.

This program would be available for about half of the students who enter high school, including the potential drop-outs. Of the graduates, this would include all who plan to enter work immediately. Most of the students who plan to enter technical curricula beyond high school likewise should be in appropriate vocational subjects in high school. For example, a student who plans to enter a two-year post-high-school curriculum in dairy technology should have some study of agriculture in high school. On the other hand, a student who plans to pursue a curriculum in chemical technology might find that no occupational specialization in high school is suitable for him. He might be better prepared to enter this field of study by taking the usual college preparatory courses with emphasis on science and mathematics.

The second major idea calls for a fundamental reconstruction of vocational or occupational specialization in the high school. The existing program is a splintered patchwork of courses which, with the exception of too few schools, fails to give a rich and comprehensive experience for more than a small fraction of the number who should be served.

Limitations at the High-School Level

Obviously there are limitations on the degree of skill or competence that can be acquired at the high-school level. The specialization is limited mainly to the craft level, semi-skilled work such as carpentry, plumbing, auto mechanics, and radio and TV repair. Many students should be introduced to broad areas and to some extent to groups of occupations. The high school does not provide all students with either the general educational maturity or the time to develop specialized skills and knowledge to the extent required in the higher technical levels of work. Thus many individuals must plan to continue their education after high school if they wish to move into higher levels of specialization which are called for in sub-professional jobs.

One of the conditions essential to improvement of vocational education at the high-school level is adequate organization. The American people seem to be committed to a comprehensive type of high school in communities with only one school. In large school systems with several high schools it is more efficient to concentrate this work in a few schools rather than offer it in every one.

Requirements for a Comprehensive School

To be reasonably comprehensive today, a high school for four grades must have a minimum of around 2,000 students. Such a size cannot be attained in many communities through consolidation of small schools. The alternative is to have some administrative organization, not necessarily one school or even one school district, which has access to this minimum size high-school population. For rural areas and small cities a regional structure of some kind is needed to centralize vocational programs for part-time attendance of pupils in the eleventh and twelfth grades, for potential drop-outs, and for some drop-outs who might re-orient themselves in a new situation. For several years this idea has been advanced under the term "intermediate" district as an administrative arrangement to offer special programs such as this on a cooperative basis for two or more local districts. American citizens are not likely to consolidate the little high schools into ones of sufficient size to offer a truly comprehensive program. Thus a large regional structure constituted only for operation of special programs seems to be the most promising method of organizing adequate vocational programs for a third or more of the high-school population in the small communities.

The concentration of population and the means of transportation now make it possible to devise large regions in most states where it is feasible to consolidate vocational programs of varied character. Students could remain in their home high schools for academic subjects and attend the vocational center for part-time study. Actually, various types of area vocational schools and programs are beginning to emerge throughout the country. With few exceptions, however, they are not being developed within a well-conceived design of organization.

For nearly forty years most vocational education in the high school has been financed in part from special earmarked federal and state funds and in part from local district funds. This procedure developed in response to the fact that special federal funds were granted to states as a means to stimulate the development of this phase of education.

As time passed, some basic weaknesses of this approach became apparent. The original purpose of stimulation became lost in the practice of maintaining the programs within a fixed pattern. Only those courses which became approved for special federal and state funds tended to be defined as vocational, regardless of their basic character. The vocational program in its organization and operation tended to be separated from the context of the total educational program.

In recent years the trend of thought is to treat "vocational" education as something which is as basic as college preparatory work. To carry out this idea, two principles must be brought together in harmony. One is the foundation program; the other is the principle of effort, or the interest and willingness of citizens to meet an educational challenge.

The first principle calls for procedures which give full recognition to the variations in cost of adequate programs that are comparable among communities. The second one calls for methods to provide funds when communities are ready and willing to move ahead in the development and improvement of programs. Procedures long have been developed for distributing funds from local, state and federal levels of government to meet these principles.

Technical education is a term which is applied primarily to a wide range of occupational curricula requiring from one to three years beyond high school for completion. The curricula may be classified into semi-technical and technical groups for description. Most of them require two years of full-time study beyond high school. More than fifty of these curricula are found among institutions throughout the country. The number of curricula is increasing as occupational demands call for performance of individuals which necessitates further education beyond high school prior to entry into the field of work or for re-training on the job.

The areas of specialization at the technical levels are not always clearly distinguished in character from so-called vocational levels. The nomenclature in the field is not entirely consistent. But orderly classification is emerging rapidly. The crafts level vocational work is characterized generally by a high degree of manipulative skill and low emphasis on cognitive knowledge. Technical or sub-professional work places stronger demands on cognitive knowledge and less on manipulative skills. There is emphasis on planning, designing, and the application of knowledge from the basic disciplines.

The rates of student drop-out at all educational levels and in all types of curricula — vocational, technical, and professional — are of grave magnitude. High school drop-outs have been mentioned. Of junior college students, only about one-third who are in liberal arts or pre-professional curricula actually transfer to senior institutions. Of those in two-year technical curricula, only one-third graduate. The drop-out rates in professional curricula in colleges and universities are too high, especially in the freshman and sophomore years. Three causes appear to explain a large percentage of these drop-outs. The first is lack of adequate, individually adapted preparation from the elementary school up. The second is lack of sufficient knowledge about the occupational world in which choices are made. Too often choice is biased unwisely toward the "white-collar" job of high prestige. Education of the white-collar variety has been conceived generally as the path of upward mobility socially and economically. The third cause of high drop-out rates is the narrow scope of opportunity available to the students. This third reason has been acute, especially in the vocational and technical fields. Any one of the causes is alone sufficient to produce maladjustment. Frequently two if not all three are operating concurrently.

A variety of administrative arrangements exists throughout the country for the operation of technical curricula. There are junior colleges, technical institutes of both junior and senior college level, four-year colleges and universities.

Among the two-year institutions offering these curricula in 1958, 244 were public and 151 were private. The numbers offering engineering-related curricula were 152 public and 32 private. In contrast, the numbers offering non-engineering-related curricula were 233 public and 134 private. The four-year institutions offering these curricula numbered 143 public and 229 private.

In all, organized occupational curricula enrollments in the United States were reported as follows for 1958:[3]

[3] U. S. Department of Health, Education, and Welfare. Office of Education. *Organized Occupational Curriculums in Higher Education.* Enrollments and Graduates, 1958. Circular No. 632. Washington D.C.: U. S. Government Printing Office, 1961. pp. 10, 12.

	Full-time	*Part-time*
Four-year institutions	39,907	30,260
Two-year institutions	89,361	46,846

The distribution of full-time and part-time enrollments by type of institutional control was reported as follows:

	Full-time	*Part-time*
Publicly controlled institutions	80,274	47,438
Privately controlled institutions	48,994	29,668

Existing institutions are enrolling only a small fraction of the number of students needed in technical fields in the next few years. In Illinois it is estimated that by 1965 an annual enrollment of 62,000 full-time and an equal number of part-time students will be needed in two-year technical curricula to meet the demands in the 40 major occupations in that state. This rate would be sixty-two enrollees each of full-time and part-time students per 10,000 gross population. Projecting this rate to the entire nation would mean a need for over one million students or ten times the present enrollments.

As I shall point out, the junior college, properly organized, is the most promising type of institution to meet most of the increased need for technical education. In 1958 this institution had only a minor proportion of its students in technical curricula. If it takes on the responsibility of offering technical as well as pre-professional (college transfer) curricula, a fundamental reorganization of the structure must be undertaken. The aggregation of independent institutions operated mainly by local school districts for small communities must be replaced by large-scale units which function as parts of a state-wide system. The community is too small and too provincial to serve as the area for organizing the total educational opportunities of its citizens. The early notion of matching the educational program solely to the local occupational opportunities must give way to the state and even to the nation for many persons.

A Fundamental Policy Decision

This means that every state must make a fundamental policy decision. Are the technical and pre-professional (college transfer) curricula to be offered through one unified, comprehensive type of junior college? Or are these programs to be offered through separate types of institutions?

Four states — California, Connecticut, New York, and Florida — have adopted a positive answer to the first question.

In either case, many of the existing junior colleges will have to be reorganized. Those that are located in the largest population centers would be enlarged. Some in the smaller centers could be retained as extension centers within large regional systems. Others could be retained as separate entities to operate limited programs.

A small institution, public or private, may serve a very unique role in a community. Some students have preference for a small college. Others have difficulty adjusting to any institution except a small one. The institution is a prestige symbol and often a positive cultural force in the life of the community. On the other hand, when such an institution offers the sole educational opportunity to residents of the locality, many students have imposed upon them *de facto* a choice between what is available and nothing at all. I have asked a number of deans of small liberal arts junior colleges what proportion of the students would have been advised to enter technical curricula if such programs were available. The answers have ranged from 50 to 80 per cent.

The existence of some of the smallest institutions might be threatened if their students had a choice of attending them or of driving a reasonable distance to a central location where a preferred curriculum would be available. Thus the public interest in providing the best educational opportunity to youth and adults would seem to call for a design of organization which offers the unique role of the small institution and the widest possible choice to individuals.

Major conclusions about the future organization to meet the challenge in technical education are as follows:

1. Responsibility for accommodating most of the increased need must be met through public institutions.

2. The four-year colleges and universities which now have about one-third of the full-time enrollees in technical fields are not expected to fill more than a minor part of the increased need. Part of the reason appears to be the tremendous challenge facing them for expanding enrollments in the professions, the higher proportions of students needing advanced study, and the increased responsibility for research. Many of these institutions are not strategically located to provide a broad program within commuting distance of the majority of prospective students.

3. The most promising method of organization is a state-wide system of junior colleges which include the technical and the college transfer (pre-professional) curricula.

4. The junior college lends itself to serving a commuting population of full-time and part-time students. The increasing size of the part-time adult student population is a new phenomenon in technical education which must be accommodated.

5. The concentration of population in most states makes it possible to design a few large regions around the major cities and thus to serve a student body of sufficient size to justify a broad program of curricula on the most economical basis.

6. It is estimated that a base population of 500,000 is essential to provide a program of twenty to twenty-five technical curricula for 2,000 to 3,000 full-time students and an equal number of part-time students. Secondary size cities within such a region could serve as extension centers for some instruction.

7. Technical curricula are made up about half of general education and half of specialized occupational study. The former would be common to the liberal arts or pre-professional curricula. Hence an administrative unification of both types of programs would be in the interest of broader opportunity of choice for students, accessibility to students, and economy in operation.

8. Existing junior colleges can either collaborate as participants or reorganize and become incorporated into such a state-wide system of education.

9. It still must be recognized that even a large-scale organization as proposed herein will not serve all potential students within commuting distance of their homes. Even if half the curricula needed in the technical fields were available to all, many individuals would have to transfer to other regions for programs of their choice. Moreover, these large-scale junior colleges would be expected to attract substantial numbers of students who prefer to reside on or near the campus rather than to commute daily.

With few exceptions the financing of existing public junior colleges represents an extension of the theory of state and local support which is applied to the elementary and secondary schools. In the early days the junior college was conceived as an extension of two years to the high school. Even today this view still prevails in a few states. Under this practice it is natural to finance the junior college as part of the local school system or in a similar manner.

Financial systems must be designed to serve the administrative structures, which in turn should be designed to accomplish the educational objectives. Hence, so long as junior colleges are a responsibility of local school districts it is logical to have emphasis on local financing.

Wider Base Than the Community

If, as I believe, an administrative organization separate from the public schools is necessary for the junior college to meet the complexity of the challenge which appears to exist, the methods of finance must be changed accordingly. Since the state, and in some fields the nation, is the community for which educational training is directed, the community (or region) can no longer be the primary basis of financial support. The total economy of the state must shoulder at least the major part of the financial cost. The question of federal support for this phase of education should rest on the same basis as other higher education. Any support derived regionally should be supplementary in character. Thus the financial ability of a particular region to support a given curriculum would no longer be a criterion or necessarily a determinant of the educational offering. It is therefore obvious that a decentralized system of local junior colleges, operated piggy-back on an already overburdened and often inadequately financed local school district, is as much a system for denying as it is for providing educational opportunity to many persons.

44. Vocational Education: A Continuing Problem

Richard T. Avritch

The Problem

Perhaps the most important aspect of any problem is getting people to recognize that it exists, and then to arouse interest in it. A few minutes in almost any library will make it quite clear that there is a serious dearth of reliable information about vocational education. This situation indicates a lack of any real interest in the subject.

Plato recognized the potential of vocational education when he wrote that the basic purpose of education was to discover what each person was good for and to train him to mastery of that area because such development would also secure the fulfillment of social needs in the most harmonious way. Though Dewey considered Plato's interpretation too narrow, he was in basic agreement with its philosophy when he pointed out that the one thing that balances an individual's distinctive capacity with his social service is his occupation. The key to happiness lies in finding out what he is capable of doing and getting an opportunity to do it (1).

Marvin Barlow (2) expressed the view that, in the broadest sense, vocational education pertains to everybody and all occupations. Then he goes on to remind us that, because of federal participation, it is customary to think of it in a very restricted sense.

For over forty years, the Smith-Hughes Act of 1917 set the basic policy for federal aid to vocational education. It defined vocational education as "education of less than college grade for pupils at least

From Richard T. Avritch, "Vocational Education: A Continuing Problem," *Journal of Education,* October, 1965, 35–42, Vol. 148. Richard T. Avritch is an Assistant Professor in the Department of Business Education, Central Connecticut State College, New Britain. Reprinted by permission of the *Journal of Education,* a publication of the Boston University School of Education.

fourteen years old for the purpose of fitting them for useful employment or to render them more efficient in it."

Over the ages politicians, social planners, and educators have come to recognize the relationship between economic competence and social needs. Similarly the relationship between education and economic competence is now widely accepted. Private institutions designed to train students in vocational subjects and skills have flourished in this country since Franklin's Academy in 1751. The present problem is to decide how public education fits into this picture. The Vocational Education Act of 1963 offers us an excellent opportunity to assess the current position of vocational education and work toward its improvement. We are at the crossroads. Where do we go from here?

The Current Situation

There are few truly comprehensive high schools in this country. Most vocational education is being conducted in separate facilities, with the exceptions of commercial education and home economics. Until 1963 the federal funds available were restricted to a limited number of areas and were administered by state officials under a federal law based on the economic patterns of the United States in 1917. The Vocational Education Act of 1963 allows for some reorganization, but local administrators must still serve two masters. The authority of a local school committee is seriously limited in order to qualify for state and federal funds.

At present vocational education has fallen prey to many of the ills Dewey warned against. We have not really learned from its history. The separate facilities cause a social class distinction that discriminates against vocational education students and often restricts the availability of offerings to terminal students. A great problem exists in getting qualified shop teachers, let alone people who are qualified to teach the shop courses in addition to related technical and general educational courses.

In many areas vocational education has become a tool of industry, stressing skills at the expense of a broad general education. This provides industry with inexpensive skilled workers, but it does not train the worker to really accept responsibilities, nor does it pave the way for a truly democratic society. In many cases students are actually being trained for jobs that will shortly be automated out of existence. Wallace Fletcher (3) warns that most of the workers currently entering the labor force will find it necessary to accept jobs requiring completely different work skills and knowledges at least three times during their lives. Despite all the warnings of men like Thorndike and Dewey relative to transfer of learning, almost nothing is being done to prepare students to accept such an adjustment. At the age of fourteen many students are expected to choose from a narrow list of offerings the type of work they wish to pursue for the rest of their working lives.

Dewey also warned that though most Americans pay lip service to democratic principles, little if anything, is being done to develop a true economic democracy. In fact, in many areas it is possible that automation has resulted in dehumanizing the worker far more than he was under the feudal system. We now hear about the sins of urbanization and specialization, but little is being done to correct the situation. The barrier between those who work with their hands and those who enjoy more creative work is as strong as ever, though there have been a few minor changes.

Each year thousands of jobs go unfilled while unemployment becomes more and more of a problem. Still provincial interests attempt to block any plan broad enough to provide a possible solution. Opposition to the Poverty Program shows that we have not yet recognized the importance of Dewey's (4) statement that one who can not support his family is a potential social danger and parasite. We have not really accepted the importance of our experience with the Indians and the Fillipinos, which indicated that in the long run it is cheaper to educate people for economic competence and thus make them happy than to dole out charity and deprive them of their self-respect.

Many people today who oppose federal aid to education simply because their tax money may be used to support programs in other sections of the country lack the insight shown by those merchants close to 100 years ago who recognized that they had an important business interest in providing a good education for the masses — even in other sections of the country (5).

Educational Superstitions. Many "superstitions" about non-vocational education are as strong today as ever. Some people fail to recognize that though we do not live in ancient Greece we are living by some of their psychological beliefs and cultural prejudices. The disdain shown vocational education by the ancient Greeks still colors our thinking. Areas such as medicine and engineering have been strong enough to break through this barrier and win respectability, but we still face situations which describe a course of study for something like accounting as vocational, while the course of study for teaching history would be described as non-vocational — or even cultural or liberal.

The ancient Greeks may have believed in a theory of transfer of learning, but since Thorndike's studies we recognize its limitations. Yet we organize our courses of study — especially in secondary education — as though there were certain subjects which best prepare students for college. These so-called liberal subjects still have a strong hold on college preparatory education even though, as Ralph Wenrich (6) reports, there is no evidence to support the idea that they result in more success in college. In fact, he notes the studies have consistently shown that in instances where the measured scholastic aptitude of both groups of students was constant, there was no significant difference in college success.

Vocational education gets a great deal of support in times of need or emergency, but the support is usually restricted to the particular areas of need. H. G. Good (7) notes that wars have been especially effective in developing support for vocational education, but as soon as the emergency subsides the support is usually withdrawn and interest returns to the "cultural" subjects.

Recent events seem to be repeating the same procedure. Unemployment and poverty, two serious needs, have resulted in a renewed interest in vocational education, and federal funds have been made available to implement improvements. What is different is that present thinking is not as narrow as it has been for over four decades. The Vocational Education Act of 1963 offers the possibility of a far broader interpretation of vocational education than has been possible since 1917.

Control. Though funds are now available to provide a vastly improved vocational education program embracing all occupations, there are still problems. Pressure groups have already started to exert their influence for fear of losing their advantages under the present system. Many teachers and state directors of vocational education are staunch advocates of the status quo. A recent survey of the state directors of vocational education revealed that the majority simply wanted more money to expand their present programs. However any basic change or reorganization must have the support of these groups.

Who will control the organization or hopefully the reorganization of the system. Conant recognized a need for vocational education but he would probably favor control by a lay committee of interested citizens representing the dominant interests of the community, especially capital. Would this eventually lead to increased control by pressure groups utilizing vocational education as a tool of industry?

It is possible that control will fall into the hands of men like Rickover or Maritain, who advocate the classical view that school is to train the mind and believe that this is best done through cultural, bookish subjects. What would happen to vocational education in this case?

Professional educators might be a logical choice but historically they have not favored vocational education. Many people feel that the reason federal legislation has been limited in such a narrow way is that committees of professional educators are usually composed of people with a liberal arts background who recommend against any increased emphasis on vocational subjects.

Historical Overview of Development in the United States

Vocational education in the United States both on the secondary and post-secondary levels has followed a pattern from apprenticeship through private institutions to public schools and colleges. From the Colonial period through the 19th century most vocational training was done through some form of apprenticeship under the direction and control of industry or craft unions. No real movement for vocational education in public schools developed until the early 1920's. Still the basic ideas about vocational education were instituted by Benjamin Franklin as early as 1751, when he founded his famous Franklin's Academy (8).

Pre-1900's. The Lyceum movement was fairly popular in certain sections previous to the Civil War. This usually consisted of informal meetings about once a week where friends discussed mutual problems and interests. Vocational problems were naturally of great interest. Agricultural periodicals were also introduced about this time, but I doubt that the majority of people could read well enough to make much use of them.

Until the 1870's the basic concept of education did not include vocational subjects. Most of the secondary schools offered only a strict college preparatory course. The early colleges were designed solely to prepare men for the ministry — though they were soon expanded to include law and other professions. For some reason education for the professions was not considered as vocational. The Morrill Act of 1862 represented an important change in philosophy. By providing funds or land for the so-called land grant colleges, it provided for the development of courses to train people to work and teach in the areas of agriculture and the mechanical occupations.

About this time, polytechnic institutions developed to teach youths how to make practical application of the physical sciences — especially in those areas which might influence the economy. Many of these institutes developed into our present engineering colleges.

By 1871 people like U. S. Commissioner of Education, John Eaton, who were probably aware of the vocational education movement in Europe, began to produce statistical evidence to prove that if vocational subjects were made available to the masses, the entire community would benefit, including business.

In 1878 Emerson White (9) suggested that public schools teach the general aspects of vocational education and that employers teach the skills necessary for a specific job. This philosophy still holds today. Unfortunately its interpretation in the late 1800's resulted in a type of very general manual training which actually delayed the development of real vocational education for about fifty years.

Schools were very slow in accepting vocational education for a number of reasons. Employers did not believe it would have any practical value. Employees and unions feared it would be used to keep wages down and provide strike breakers. Educators, conservative as usual, still favored the liberal arts and could see no learning value in vocational education. During the last quarter of the nineteenth century a private technical school movement started to fill the gap. These teachers, apparently, were not adverse to making a profit by fulfilling a need that public educators felt had no value.

Just to keep all this information about schooling during the 1800's in perspective, remember that as late as 1890 the amount of schooling, including higher and specialized education, received by the average person was about four and one half years. If education of the masses is really an important aspect of a democracy, there was obviously room for a lot of improvement.

The 1900's. During the early 1900's the needs of agriculture, industry, and urbanization created a real interest in vocational education and re-education. Urbanization and industrialization created a concern for the health and welfare of working children — the only slaves remaining in Christendom (10). The Keating-Owen Bill of 1916 made it a misdemeanor to employ children under the age of fourteen in factories or sixteen in mines and quarries producing goods for interstate commerce. Though such attempts by the Federal Government to regulate child labor were later declared unconstitutional, they set the tone for state regulations which soon followed. The natural result was for the children to stay in school longer. Thus vocational education got another boost.

Mounting pressures from World War I and statistical studies showing that a proper education could help the lower classes improve their socioeconomic status resulted in the Smith-Hughes Act of 1917 (11). The funds appropriated encouraged vocational education of less than college level for children over fourteen. By 1920 a fairly strong public school movement was under way.

Additional federal legislation continued the basic policies established under the Smith-Hughes Act for over four decades. Not until the Vocational Education Act of 1963 and the Poverty Program of 1964 has there been any major attempt to modernize or improve the system established in 1917 and based on the economic and political problems of that era.

Something to Think About

Educational Theory. Whether or not one believes any substantial benefits might result from vocational education will, of course, vary with one's personal philosophy. Maritain sees it simply as play, a chance to relax from the real work of learning. Others, like Booker T. Washington, G. Stanley Hall, Edward L. Thorndike, and John Dewey, saw a real need based on potential economic, educational, and social benefits.

Thorndike's (12) highly successful attack on transfer of learning theories have given impetus to the need for special training. The democratic ideal of equality of education to all children caused men such as Horley Smith, Dean Russell, and David Snedden to severely criticize the assumption that all children profit from bookish training. They felt that at best such emphasis on education equipped a mere handful for academic culture and the professions.

Even the primitive tribes valued economic competence, and many took great pains to see that their young men learned the skills necessary for the survival and success of the tribe. This emphasis on vocational education and its relationship to the needs of society continued through the ages as a Western philosophy of education evolved.

Two schools of thought developed regarding the curriculum of vocational education. Each has its related benefits and problems. One stresses practical skills and well being. The other tends to put more emphasis on the cultural and sociological aspects without eliminating practical skills. Dewey was especially concerned over the narrow interpretation of vocational education and its potential dangers of social predestination. He placed great importance on the social effect of education and believed that industrial education could encourage cooperation, sharing, and group planning rather than competition. He believed it could bring intellectual culture within reach of the masses and help break down the classic barrier between those who toil with their hands and those who enjoy more creative activities of mind and spirit.

At times people have failed to see that their education was in fact vocational, but even the three R's were introduced for practical purposes. Luella Cole (13) noted that over the centuries developing nations usually emphasized the practical value of education while during periods of decline the cultural aims blossomed, often into grotesque forms.

Enlightened Self-Interest. Vocational education has been viewed by the masses as the basic means of social and economic improvement. Booker T. Washington (14) in his fight to improve the position of the

Negro in the South stressed a practical education. He argued that by equipping the Negroes with skilled services the entire South would benefit. He was appealing to the self-interest of the dominant whites, but it is worth noting that he convinced many people that they could help themselves by helping others. This is something many of us have never recognized, though as far back as the 1870's John Eaton produced evidence to back Mann's claim that proper public schools encouraged inventiveness and rendered labor more productive, thus enriching industry.

Some of the great capitalists of the late 1800's like Astor and Stewart stated that for selfish reasons they would gladly pay taxes for the education of the poor. Some northern merchants even went so far as to express a willingness to be taxed for support of schools in the South because they felt such education would produce better markets. These positions are interesting in the light of current arguments against using local tax money to support educational activities in other sections of the country.

The westward movement in the United States provides us with many examples of the power of vocational education. About 1835 Easterners began to realize that the glamour of the West was draining the factories and farmlands of qualified help and turned to vocational education as bait to retain the restless and ambitious workers. This was one of the incentives behind a public education movement in the early 1800's which stretched from New England to the Carolinas. This experience provided an impressive example of how the proper kind of education could meet the needs of the individual as well as those of the community.

Domination. As might be expected, industry and other pressure groups tend to favor a narrow vocational system which would provide immediate benefits. Professional educators tend to favor a broader interpretation. Either system could be developed with democratic ideals in mind, but note that the first is the quickest to rally support probably because it can easily be adapted to the selfish needs of particular groups. In 1897 Jane Addams (15) accused the majority of businessmen who supported public education of doing so simply in order to get trained help cheap.

Roger Babson in 1914 noted that, "However successful organized labor has been in many ways, it has never succeeded in directing the education of its children. Capital still prepares the school books and practically controls the school systems of the world." This domination did not seem to bother G. Stanley Hall, who justified it by his doctrine of heredity, explaining that class distinction corresponded to individual differences in capacity. He also argued that industrial education corresponded to the unfolding needs of the child and thus evoked interest and enthusiasm while cultivating truthfulness, integrity, and social solidarity. He noted that it should help alleviate the strife between capital and labor.

Hall was effective in winning support for the public school by his convincing arguments of its ability to make workers more efficient, thus conserving our most precious capital and raw material — the individual. He befriended capital by advocating education designed to meet the needs of industry in a competitive economy and he won the support of labor by insisting that it was criminal to allow dropouts to leave school unprepared for work and thus condemned to a life of unskilled labor. His arguments still echo today.

John Dewey (16) was not so willing to accept the domination of industry. He argued that such domination would eventually subordinate educational values to industrial interests and he did not want to see the schools evolve into merely tools of industry. He feared that industrial domination of specialized trade schools would not only deny vocational education to a large number of students but would lead to exploitation of education and eventually to a subtle form of master-subject relationship or social predestination.

A Question of Purpose. Thus the basic question to be answered is, "What is the purpose of public vocational education in a democracy?" Was G. Stanley Hall (17) correct when he advocated that the purpose of vocational education in the public school was to help meet the needs of industry? If he was, the specialized technical education available would be entirely different from the broad program which would be necessary under John Dewey's philosophy.

Other educators seriously question any type of vocational education in the schools. Jacques Maritain (18) made his position clear when he indicated that there are some school subjects "of most worth" with a high degree of knowledge value and others of "least worth," mainly useful for training, and which it is absurd to deal with as learning activities on the same plane as genuine learning.

The growing problems of poverty and unemployment are emphasizing vocational education the same way as the Great Depression and Sputnik did not so long ago. It finally appears possible that we might profit by our experiences. The 1963 Act is fairly liberal and allows for broad reorganization. Even the educational foundations, long considered arch foes of vocational education, have begun to express an interest in this area.

Perhaps some day we will be able to answer Erik H. Erikson's (19) question about the problems of man versus the machine by saying that a solution has come through the humanization of industry rather than by the mechanization of man.

REFERENCES

1. Dewey, John. *Democracy and Education.* New York: Macmillan Company, 1916. p. 308.
2. Barlow, Melvin L. "The Challenge to Vocational Education." *Vocational Education.* NSSE Yearbook; 1965. p. 5.
3. Fletcher, Wallace J. "A Ford Foundation Grant for Technical-Vocational Education." *Patterns;* Dec., 1964. p. 3.
4. Dewey John. *Democracy and Education.* New York: Macmillan Company, 1916. p. 38.
5. Curti, Merle. *The Social Ideas of American Educators.* Totowa, N. J.: Littlefield, Adams & Co., 1959, p. 228.
6. Wenrich, Ralph. "Vocational Education." *Encyclopedia of Educational Research.* New York: Macmillan Company, 1960. p. 1562.
7. Good, H. G. *A History of American Education.* New York: Macmillan Company, 1956. p. 508.
8. *Ibid.,* p. 73.
9. *Ibid.,* p. 450.
10. *Ibid.,* p. 381.
11. Vredevoe, Lawrence E. *An Introduction and Outline of Secondary Education.* Ann Arbor: G. W. Edwards Co., 1957. p. 154.
12. Curti, Merle. *The Social Ideas of American Educators.* Totowa, N. J.: Littlefield, Adams & Co., 1959. p. 1466.
13. Cole, Luella. *A History of Education.* New York: Holt, Rinehart & Winston, 1950. p. 619.
14. Curti, Merle. *The Social Ideas of American Educators.* Totowa, N. J.: Littlefield, Adams & Co., 1959. p. 293.
15. *Ibid.,* p. 203.
16. Dewey, John. *Democracy and Education.* New York: Macmillan and Company, 1916. p. 318.
17. Curti, Merle. *The Social Ideas of American Educators.* Totowa, N. J.: Littlefield, Adams & Co., 1959. p. 418.
18. Maritain, Jacques. *Education at the Crossroads.* New Haven: Yale University Press, 1943. p. 55.
19. Erikson, Erik H. *Identity and Life Cycle.* New York: International Universities Press, 1959. Monograph #1.

For Further Reading

American Vocational Association, *A Guide to Improving Instruction in Industrial Arts.* (A revision of standards of attainment in industrial arts and improving instruction in industrial arts), The Association, Washington, D.C., 1953.

Arnold, Walter M., "Area Vocational Education Programs," *School Life,* January, 1960, 16–21, Vol. 42.

Barlow, Melvin L., (ed.), *Vocational Education,* The Sixty-fourth Yearbook of the National Society for the Study of Education, Part I, The University of Chicago Press, Chicago, 1965.

Faulkner, T. L., "Updating Vocational Agriculture to Meet Present and Future Needs," *The Agricultural Educational Magazine,* October, 1965, 38: 84–85.

Greenfield, Donald, "Industrial Arts and Technical Training," *Industrial Arts and Vocational Education,* September, 1965, 42, Vol. 54.

Perry, Donald E., "Industrial Arts: The What, How and Why of Our Future," *Industrial Arts and Vocational Education,* January, 1964, 12–13, Vol. 53.

Phi Delta Kappan, April, 1965, 46: 353–424. (Theme of the issue: "The Swing to Vocational-Technical Education." Eighteen articles centering on various aspects of this theme.)

Roberts, Roy, *Vocational and Practical Arts Education,* Harper & Row, Inc., New York, 1957.

Rucker, Darnell, "The Liberal and the Manual Arts in Education," *School and Society,* November 16, 1963, 91: 350–352.

Swanson, Chester J., "Here's What the New Demands for Vocational Education Mean for Schoolmen," *The Nation's Schools,* February, 1963, 61–62, Vol. 71.

Willis, Benjamin C., "The Changing Story of Vocational Education and What's Needed Now," *The Nation's Schools,* February, 1963, 57–60, Vol. 71.

PART TEN

Homemaking

45. Home Economics in American Society

Gordon W. Blackwell

The challenge of change is perhaps greater for no single body of knowledge than for home economics. This challenge is necessitated not only by the rapid technological, social, and economic developments in modern American living but also by the enormous growth of the

From Gordon W. Blackwell, "The Place of Home Economics in American Society," *Journal of Home Economics,* June, 1962, 54: 447–450. Gordon W. Blackwell is President of Furman University, Greenville, South Carolina. Formerly President of Florida State University and Chancellor of Woman's College of the University of North Carolina, President Blackwell is author or co-author of five books and numerous academic and professional articles. This article is based on an address before the Home Economics Section of the Association of Southern Agricultural Workers in Jacksonville, Florida, February 5, 1962. Reprinted by permission of the *Journal of Home Economics,* official organ of the American Home Economics Association, and of the author.

educational institutions which offer instruction in home economics and by the expansion of their research programs and extension services. These changes must on occasion leave the home economist feeling very confused.

In such exigencies, one tends to forget his past accomplishments, and I would urge you to review now and then the accomplishments of your profession. From such perspectives as the excellent summary in "Home Economics—New Directions," you can better outline the future.

If the place of home economics in American society is to remain as vital a part as it has been in these last 50 years, it must, it seems to me, remain alert to the changes in our society — in particular, the changing role of women in our society. For her role is changing, and home economics will have to change with it. This being true, my remarks are largely devoted to some of the changes that sociologists have noted in recent studies, especially as they affect the women in our society.

Of profound significance is the steadily lowering age of marriage since World War II. Twenty is now the average age of marriage for women. Marriage has invaded not only college student bodies but our high schools as well. As aptly stated by Audrey K. Wilder, the "Pomp and Circumstance" of the commencement processional vies with the strains of Mendelssohn's Wedding March. Too frequently Mendelssohn wins out. Education takes a loss.

Looking at the other end of the life span, we know that women live longer than men by six years on the average. This means that there are more women than men in the population. Furthermore, there are economic implications for women who marry since they can expect to be widowed unless the marriage is broken for other reasons, as is more and more often the case.

It is clear also that an increasing proportion of our citizens will be in the older age brackets in the future. From 3 per cent over 65 years of age in 1850, the proportion increased to 9 per cent in 1960, with the prediction of almost 13 per cent by 1975. The psychological, social, and leisure needs of aging persons, *most of whom will be women*, present a challenge to the home economist.

The population of the United States has always been characterized by high mobility. In our history we have already seen the long-continuing westward movement, the great streams of immigrants from Europe, and the continual farm to city movement. Since 1920 many millions more people have left farms and gone to urban places than have migrated to farms. The majority of these cityward migrants have been women.

It is as though a giant egg beater has been at work in the nation's population. Families and single individuals have been spewed in all directions, with the main streams being from country to city, from South to North, and from East to Far West.

In addition to this relatively long-range migration, people have been quite mobile within their community of residence. Truly a high proportion of the American people are not anchored to hearth and home. And this high mobility can be expected to continue for some time. Young people, especially girls, must be prepared for high mobility of residence.

The growth of cities is reflected in changes in the occupational structure. In 1820, some 62 per cent of the labor force were agricultural workers; in 1960 it was approximately 8 per cent. This decline may be expected to continue slowly during the next several decades as agriculture becomes further mechanized and as more and more people enter industry, business, the professions, technical jobs, and service occupations. The proportion of workers who are in the professions has steadily increased as the American economy has become mature, and this trend will continue for some time yet.

Along with industrialization have come increasingly frequent opportunities for women in the world of work. In 1890 less than a fifth of American women were in the labor force at any given time; today the proportion is more than a third, with women earning $42 billion yearly in salaries and wages. Three out of every ten married women are working, and two out of every five mothers whose youngest child is of school age are in the labor force. Today the average age of a mother when the youngest child reaches six years is 32.

The more education a woman has, the more apt she is to be working. About half who are college graduates are working or seeking work at any given time. College girls today will work not three or five years but, some say, an average of more nearly 25 years — a prospect which most of our college students are currently not willing to accept.

There are many reasons which lead women to work in increasing numbers. Homemaking no longer need involve endless hours of manual labor as in former times. Furthermore, many women become dissatisfied with the chitchat of afternoon bridge parties or with listening to the perennial minutes being read in a so-called study club. They desire to feel productive. Many want to keep intellectually alive and consequently move into one of the professions. Many families find it difficult to make ends meet in the face of the high cost of living, and, therefore, the wife works as soon as the youngest child reaches school age.

There is every indication that these trends relative to women and work will continue in the future and, in fact, may accelerate.

Effects on Women

And now for a look at personality development. The individual in any society faces the necessity of charting his own course of development somewhere between putty-like conformity to prescribed cultural norms and legal prescriptions on the one hand and autonomous personal action on the other.

In American society, the pressure for conformity by women is great, varying from region to region, from community to community, and among different social strata and groups. Although these pressures are certainly real, we have a culture and social structure in considerable ferment and change. The many new social patterns provide a maze of multiple statuses and roles for each woman and often involve frustrating conflict. Her probable mobility adds to the complexities facing her. Changing values in the society make it difficult for her to keep her social moorings. The culture and social structure often do not provide her with sufficiently clear guidelines and high predictability in interpersonal relations. The social situation sometimes is not clearly defined for her. Social adjustment too frequently proves difficult. According to a noted sociologist, Robin Williams, "If such disillusion of the social pattern involves values central to the person's self-identity, the shattering of stable social expectations seems catastrophic for personality integration." It is not surprising, then, that psychiatrists bear witness to the high incidence of mental breakdowns among women.

Women are faced with a complexity of roles to play and frequently find themselves on shifting sand. There are indications that these problems of maintaining a stable personality at various points in the life cycle are more difficult to cope with for women than for men. For one thing, the stereotypic dependent feminine role comes into apparent conflict with intellectual role models and with concepts of independence and quality. These problems are of considerable concern to those engaged in working with girls and young women.

Global Outlook

Finally, global trends of the first half of the twentieth century dictate that we cannot confine ourselves to preparing the individual for life in a local community or for narrow nationalism. We must seek to develop a sense of responsibility that is no less than global, one which stretches even to the outer reaches of the universe. International shifts in power, technological developments in transportation, communication, and war making, as well as the spread of education among the masses of the world, have resulted in bringing international problems to our very doorstep as the oceans have become as mere lakes and as man probes into outer space. Women in tomorrow's world must be motivated to develop sympathetic understanding of complex foreign affairs.

In the past 50 to 100 years, women in America have achieved a large measure of equality of opportunity with men — equality in the ballot, in many occupations, in family life, and in most other important matters. Women now cast approximately as many ballots as men in the national elections, outnumber men as stockholders in America's great corporations, control at least 60 — some say as high as 85 — per cent of all personal expenditures.

Progress has been made also toward equality in education. For example, in 1890 fewer than 3,000 women graduated annually from American colleges and universities. Seventy years later the number is over 135,000, and it appears certain that women will obtain a college education with increasing frequency in the future.

And yet we know that many competent girls who graduate from high school with a high academic record do not enter college. Too often the girl or her parents do not see the values in a college education for her. If there is a brother, he will usually get first chance at the financial resources of the family. Whereas more than half of the graduates from our secondary schools are women, only a third of the college enrollment are women.

Based on ability tests, a study by the National Science Foundation of those in the top quarter of high school graduates who do not go on to college estimated the number at between 100,000 and 200,000 annually. Girls account for an alarming proportion of this loss of talented human resources. This "feminine fallout," to borrow a felicitous phrase from the *Wall Street Journal,* may be as serious as the threat of atomic fallout.

Kind of Preparation

This brings us then to the question of what kind of preparation is needed for women of tomorrow's world. And what will be the place of home economics in their education? What should be the pattern of extension services and of research? Whatever the specific answers, the home economist will have the continuous task of adapting to the realities of a rapidly changing society. Home economics will have to take into account a society in which there will be many more aged persons, especially women. It will have to take into account the trend toward early marriages, rapid mobility, continuing urbanization, and higher proportions of women in business, technical jobs, and the professions. Above all, it must prepare women for a society in which frustrations and role conflicts, resulting from these changes, will be the rule rather than the exception. Indeed, I venture to say that the place of home economics in American society will be directly determined by the extent to which its services, its curriculums, and its research programs are tailored to fit these realities.

I share with you a concern that home economics should take steps to adjust effectively to these changes. Although I realize that the number of earned degrees in home economics has not kept pace with the total enrollment of women in our colleges during the past decade, I am not among those who believe that home economics is sick. I know that your emphases in home economics education in the secondary schools, in college-level curriculums, in graduate programs, in research, and in extension services have been changing, particularly within the past 15 years. I believe the decreasing emphasis upon skills and the increasing attention to application of the social and natural sciences to problems relating to homemaking are illustrative of desirable changes.

"Yes, but what more can we do?" you ask. To this question, I'm afraid I see no easy answers. I am not trained in your discipline, and it would be presumptuous of me to make specific proposals even if I did imagine that I could be of help. As an outsider, however, particularly as a university president, I would propose certain general lines of endeavor.

First, as I've indicated earlier, you can make a rigorous effort to re-evaluate course offerings in the light of modern American society. How essential is the skill or the subject matter of this or that course to a woman as she actually lives her life today, not as she used to live it and not as she ought to live it — but as she does live it? In this connection, a continuation of the lessening of emphasis upon skills seems to be in order in educational programs, especially at the secondary school level. There is much evidence that the better students are not being sufficiently challenged by intellectual content of some of the courses. I need not remind you, I am sure, that no longer is it fashionable for a young woman to bank the fire of her brain.

Second, I suggest provisions in the college curriculum which would require home economics undergraduate and graduate students to go outside their department or school for a sound foundation in chemistry and biology, or in psychology and sociology, or in general economics. It is perhaps a truism to say that, as an applied discipline, home economics must have mastery of the fundamentals which are to be applied. After all, are not the really significant contributions in applied fields such as food and nutrition or clothing and textiles to be found in a thorough grounding in chemistry and biology? Do not the main avenues to new insights in child development, family living, and household management derive from psychology, sociology, and economics? Again I say that skills are less important in these kinds of activities than are basic scientific knowledge and decision-making ability regarding the management of family resources. And, as home economics comes to stress these matters universally — not just in the best universities — more men will be attracted into the field.

Third, I urge increased emphasis upon research and creative activity on the part of home economists. Most of this will take place either in the universities or in industry, sometimes on a co-operative basis between the two. If my previous suggestions are valid, then the requirement of greatly expanded research programs becomes clear, and the necessary dependence of home economics research upon the tools and concepts of the natural and social sciences need not be argued further.

Next, I would stress the obligation of schools of home economics and extension services to provide professional opportunities for women who, at age 30 to 40, find their youngest child in school and wish to engage in worthwhile work. Some of these have previous training in home economics and merely need retreading for a summer or two. Others will want to earn a master's degree in the process of job preparation. Still others will need to complete an undergraduate degree. Among hundreds of thousands of women such as these each year, there is a vast reservoir of potential professional womanpower which you must tap effectively with planned programs. In this endeavor, both the colleges and the extension services should be prepared to serve as educational and vocational counseling centers for these women who symbolize in their numbers and purpose a relatively new feature of American society.

Finally, I believe some serious thinking about the basic purposes of home economics is in order. From such thinking could emerge a modified concept of what home economics is and what it has to offer the modern homemaker. Conceivably, a fresh concept — perhaps even a new name — broadened to include more of the liberal arts and sciences, together with more concern for the attitudes, values, and decision-making ability of the homemaker than with skills, would open new and broader avenues of service. This emphasis on general culture, intellectual development, and the multiple possibilities of a strong undergirding in the natural and social sciences, together with the traditional concern for the ways and means to the best in family living which has always characterized home economics, could lead to an even more significant place for home economics in American society.

46. Home Economics in Secondary Education

Ruth Stovall

As home economists across the board, we are concerned with the problems of women, families, and homes. Home economics came into existence more than 50 years ago in response to those needs of society.

Because home economics is concerned with those things that are basic in society — people, families, and homes, home economics cannot be a transitory fad nor a frill course that has lost its usefulness in a school curriculum.

Because home economics is concerned with life in its broadest sense and the application of learning in its most personal sense, we may be living in the present "tense" since it takes a lot of "sense" to meet specific needs within so broad a scope in a changing world.

The program of home economics in the high school is affected by the influences upon general education as discussed by Dr. Tyler, because our program is an integral part of the total educational program.

The program of home economics in colleges has a direct relationship to the secondary program of home economics because the majority of the girls who major in home economics in college became interested in home economics as a professional field through their high school programs of home economics. The home economics education majors from

From Ruth Stovall, "Education in a World of Change: Secondary Education," *Journal of Home Economics,* September, 1962, 54: 537–540. Ruth Stovall is State Supervisor of Home Economics Education in Alabama. She has contributed extensively to many professional journals and is a past president of the National Association of State Supervisors, Home Economics Education, and former treasurer of the American Home Economics Association. This article is based on a paper presented at the opening session of the 1962 annual meeting of the American Home Economics Association, Miami Beach, Florida. Reprinted by permission of the *Journal of Home Economics,* official organ of the American Home Economics Association, and of the author.

the colleges in turn become the high school home economics teachers.

General education, home economics in higher education, and home economics education at the secondary level thus join hands in helping to shape the educational programs needed in a changing world.

That the world is changing is so obvious that the use of the term is almost trite. We have heard much about population explosion, mobility of families, industrial and scientific developments, automation, lengthening of the life span, early marriages, increase in number of women in the labor force, conquest of outer space, and the growing demand for quality education.

In the lifetime of even the youngest person among us today, the unthinkable has become thinkable.

The thinking home economics educators today must view these changes in terms of the life relatedness of home economics instruction to pupils, not only in their lives today but also in their roles as homemakers of tomorrow in which they will live in relation to even more rapid changes than we are now experiencing. The pupils in our classrooms today will not only be influenced by change but these same pupils will be the adults who will bring about the changes of tomorrow.

The parents of today who are demanding quality education in our schools were our classmates of yesterday. Today, they are influencing change.

In preparing pupils for a world of change, it appears that the instruction must be that which will help pupils "to learn how to learn" and thus become independent learners. This is real education in any era.

Margaret Mead said,

> The important things now in modern economics and industrial life are those that are not yet known. Much of education must become a process of sharing knowledge as we get hold of it rather than transmitting it.

We could add to her statement that education must include not only learning a body of knowledge and using it but learning education must also include how to get hold of knowledge not yet known. This kind of education will result in independent learners.

This concept does not confine itself to research on the doctoral level but to education at every level, because education in our world of change must be continuous from the outset of life to the end.

Home economics in secondary schools of the United States is not sitting on the sidelines. It is not honoring tradition by embalming it. It is not "out of season." It is not burying its head in the sands of the past. Instead, it is aware of the shifting sands and is not only adjusting to changes but it is helping to bring about changes that are desirable for people, families, and homes.

That home economics is a frill course — on its way out of the school curriculum because it has had its day — may be in some people's minds and may have been written in ink by a few, but this is not true.

According to the report of the U.S. Office of Education, home economics is offered in 95.5 per cent of all public secondary schools. Although home economics is an elective course in most schools, more than 2 million pupils are enrolled in home economics classes, which is nearly 50 per cent of all the girls in these schools. In addition, adult education in home economics is offered in 40 per cent of all secondary schools.[1]

The demand is great for additional programs of home economics at the secondary level, and the lag in meeting these requests is caused by lack of funds. In Alabama alone, we have on file from superintendents of education in 1961 requests for 163½ additional teachers of home economics when funds are available.

The program of home economics in secondary schools faces the future with confidence because there is an ever-growing need for what it has to offer and a demand for it. As Harold Benjamin of Peabody College said, "The most important subjects in the curricula are those which serve society." He added that "any curriculum which does not lead students to do the jobs that people need done is an inadequate one — for it is not a curriculum of action but merely a game of academic marbles."

Home economics at the secondary level is an action program which has been kept close to the needs of the pupils and families. Curriculum studies have been the responsibilities of states and local communities. The instruction has been based on real problems, and life relatedness of the learnings has been an important concern as problem-solving methods have been used, decision making based on sound values has been emphasized, and supervised home experiences have been an important part of the instructional program.

In today's world, the accelerated accumulation of new knowledge and the changing patterns of living have pointed up the need for broader concepts and greater depth in teaching home economics at the secondary level as well as for the teaching of other subjects in the school curriculum.

Perhaps the greatest challenge in home economics education today

[1] Home Economics in Public Secondary Schools, OE-83010. By Beulah I. Coon. U. S. Department of Health, Education, and Welfare, 1962. Available from the Superintendent of Documents, U. S. Government Printing Office, Washington 25, D.C., $1.25.

is to make sure that "Home Economics Is Education" in a world of change.

At the AHEA annual meeting in Denver, we had our first view of the Pillsbury filmstrip on home economics titled "Education in Essentials." This is a good title, because home economics has a body of essential knowledge and a supply of necessary skills. Speedy steps are being taken to sift out what these are in an effort to deepen the learnings within the broad scope of home economics. Because the program is so broad, we may have been guilty of teaching about something rather than teaching it. Pupils may have learned about science principles having some application to home economics, but they may not have learned what these principles are and may not have developed an understanding of the principle and how to apply it. Ruth Lehman wrote recently in the JOURNAL that home economics students don't need to know about the field; they need to know the field.

Edna Amidon has challenged us to re-examine our practices to see whether we are helping pupils see what the basic principles are and how to use them in new situations. This is important in making sure that home economics is education in a world of change.

This means that curriculum emphasis is on what is learned and how it can be applied to new as well as current situations. It also means developing a consciousness of how one is learning to learn so that independent learning can take place. This is as important in influencing change as adjusting to it.

This points up the urgent need to identify the elements which comprise our field of study. These elements are called concepts by some educators. Whatever is the label for home economics, Miss Amidon says, "It means that which pupils need to understand in order to function effectively as family members, as homemakers, and as parents in today's world."

The influence of home economics on the future might depend on the extent to which the concepts, along with the skills and values of our field, can be defined.

There are stirrings of a promising nature in identifying the concepts of home economics at the secondary level.

The committee of the home economics division of the American Association of Land-Grant Colleges and State Universities on "Articulation of Home Economics between the High School and the College" held a seminar last July at French Lick, Indiana. The seminar was largely devoted to the identification of concepts of home economics.[2]

[2] See Home Economics Seminar, A Progress Report. Available from College of Home Economics, Michigan State University.

Another heartening development in identifying concepts is the comprehensive curriculum study which is being sponsored by the Home Economics Education Branch of the U.S. Office of Education. Some of the basic questions that are being explored in this study are:

1. What is the place of home economics in the high school today and in the future?
2. What shall be the content, the subject-matter structure of home economics courses in junior and senior high schools?
3. How can home economics be more sensitive and adaptive to the problems and needs of young people in preparation for living in a changing society?
4. How can home economics in secondary schools contribute to the attainment of the broad over-all goals of education?

This curriculum study is now in progress with colleges and universities and state departments of education participating under the leadership of Miss Amidon and her staff.

To answer affirmatively the question "Is Home Economics Education?" many other new developments are in process in home economics in secondary schools.

In preparation of this report to you, I obtained information from the Home Economics Education Branch of the U.S. Office of Education, and I sent questionnaires to each state supervisor of home economics education in the United States. I asked for information on new programs, trends, and focus in home economics programs in the secondary schools in their states. I learned many things from this survey. Many of the existing patterns are being smashed and new ones are forged. There is only time to report a few of the many developments.

Over and over, states reported focus on depth and quality of instruction, including emphasis on principles, generalizations, concepts, and behavioral outcomes. As a part of this focus, many states reported the increased use of research and the recognition of the value of, and need for more, research.

More emphasis was reported on the areas of management, human growth and development, consumer economics, art, and relationships. These areas have always been included in the curriculum in most home economics programs, but larger blocks of time are being devoted to them, and these areas are being taught more effectively.

Some states reported that shorter blocks of time were devoted to the development of needed skills not because they were any less important but because they can be taught in less time now than previously through new techniques and materials and better equipment.

Because the secondary school program includes all the children of all people, a variety of programs are being set up to meet the varying needs. The redheads, the brunettes, the bright, the dull, the college bound, and the wage earners are the homemakers of tomorrow. All of them can profit from home economics instruction but not necessarily the same instruction. Experimental programs are in operation in many states. These include home economics classes on the 11th- and 12th-grade levels without prerequisites for pupils who have not previously had home economics; classes for the college bound, the academically talented, and the gifted students; classes for career girls; classes for those already married or "soon to be married"; classes for the educable, the special students, or slow learners; classes for boys; family living classes for both boys and girls; and semester courses for advanced students in a specialized area or areas of home economics, such as home management, advanced clothing, nutrition, and child development.

Some schools are experimenting with the scheduling of pupils in large groups, discussion groups, and personal work periods.

Experimental work was reported with team teaching with other home economics teachers and with art, science, physical education, and social studies teachers. Teaching machines and other new methods and material are being tried in order to achieve depth in teaching.

Many states reported an increased interest in home economics at the junior high school level with home economics curriculums planned to meet the developmental needs of these pupils. The junior high school program and the senior high school program are being planned in a "hook and eye" relationship without undue duplication.

One of the trends in nearly every state is the movement to provide education for both homemaking and wage earning. This has implications for both the high school and adult homemaking classes. Women are in the world of work, and this will doubtless prevail for some time to come.

Beth Peterson said that "woman has taken on two jobs — one for love and one for pay!" Home economics instruction helps prepare women for the dual role. There is a developing awareness of the relationship of home economics instruction not only to careers but also to jobs in restaurants, bakeries, florist shops, community and family service jobs, and many home-related occupations created because of the growing number of employed homemakers and other changed socioeconomic conditions.

Home economics in secondary schools is undergoing other changes.

State departments of education and local schools are making strides in discarding the obsolete and the unimportant and are eliminating duplication in the curriculum. Skills continue to be important — not the skills of yesterday but the skills needed today and tomorrow. I have in my files a printed bulletin interpreting the home economics program in Alabama in 1924. Two pictures were included — one was a group around a wood stove dyeing a garment; the other was a group around a black pot making soap. These skills were eliminated when no longer needed. Skills that are not outmoded are needed. The dentist, the surgeon, the nurse, and the technician must have skill to guard one's health. The homemaker needs skills to guard her home. Skills that are purposeful, skills that are creative, skills that are based on sound values in relation to a changing world form the support for home economics. Concepts, skills, and values are being increasingly recognized as the structure of the curriculum for home economics in high schools. In achieving depth, it is not necessary to eliminate the "how" in order to answer the "why." Through curriculum studies, we are thus cementing together what one should know and be able to do, and home economics itself is being cemented with the basic knowledges from the social sciences, physical sciences, biological sciences, and the arts. Today a stronger relationship is being built between home economics and the other disciplines. Home economics teachers and guidance personnel are working together more closely.

The areas of foods, clothing, and shelter are being viewed in their larger dimensions as forces for peace and harmony in the world. Instruction in these areas is being planned for greater depth and broader scope with more practical meanings.

Increased attention is being given to the woman in a world of work; the education and employment program has meaning and implications for home economics instruction.

The concern for the aging has given rise to the need for teaching in home economics the concept that aging is a natural part of the total life process and is not something to be feared or rejected. The secondary and elementary committee of the AHEA Workshop on Aging recognized that preparation for old age begins in the earliest years and home economics instruction can help develop attitudes, interests, and experiences in youth that will lead to rich and satisfying later years. Adult education programs as a part of the secondary program are being extended. It is foreseen that concern for the aged in the secondary home economics curriculum in the next few years will be comparable to the concern for children in the past decade.

In a changing world, more attention is being given to the identification of values in the home economics program. Values are guide lines. The theme for this year of the Future Homemakers of America was

"Youth Measure Your Values." Emphasis on values was insisted on by the youth themselves because they need direction in these times of change.

Our new kind of world has produced a new kind of pupil. Suddenly, it's smart to be smart. Suddenly, the brains and the eggheads are in and the slobs and dumbbells are out. Children are growing up faster and teachers are staying young longer. It's a new world in a new decade. We have new hopes — new dreams and new problems that call for the right answers.

In this world of change, our vision must be broad, our steps bold, our eyes bright, our voices low and clear, and our faith strong, because ours is a field of service that is designed to improve homes and families — basic units in a changing society. The merchandise of agriculture is food and fiber; the merchandise of industry is goods and services; but the merchandise of the home is people. By realizing our full potential, refraining from being defensive, and working together as home economists, we shall move forward as a field of strength, hope, and pride. To change with the changing world is necessary to education; but at the same time to take leadership in shaping the changes is our opportunity; and when you get home, post us a card telling us how you are interpreting the fact that "home economics is education in a world of change" in your home town.

For Further Reading

Barrow, Joseph M., and Elizabeth J. Simpson, "Where to Aim Home Economics Programs," *The Nation's Schools,* April, 1966, 68–69, 78, Vol. 77.

Bezant, Rozelle K., "Marriage and Family Living in the Homemaking Curriculum," *Journal of Home Economics,* January, 1965, 57: 11–16.

Bunting, Mary I., "Leadership in Education," *Journal of Home Economics,* November, 1964, 56: 647–650.

Bymers, Gwen J., "Economic Theory and the Home Economist," *Journal of Home Economics,* April, 1962, 54: 281–284.

Conafay, Katherine R., "Learning to Live: The Good in Home Economics," *Teachers College Journal,* October, 1964, 36: 34–36.

Fleming, R. S., "Home Economics Education: Next Steps in Curriculum Development," *American Vocational Journal,* February, 1964, 39: 23–25.

Leo Margaret, Sister, "Future Is Now: Home Economics Curriculum Today," *Bulletin* of the National Catholic Educational Association, August, 1963, 60: 343–345.

Luckey, Eleanore Brown, "Education for Family Living in the Twentieth Century," *Journal of Home Economics,* November, 1965, 57: 685–690.

Mallory, B., "Home Economics Curriculum Study," *American Vocational Journal,* September, 1963, 38: 34–36.

Ridder, C., "Central Part of Home Economics: The Core," *Journal of Home Economics,* October, 1963, 55: 617–619.

Simpson, Elizabeth J., "Home Economics Education at the Secondary Level," pp. 96–106 in Chapter V of *Vocational Education,* The Sixty-fourth Yearbook of the National Society for the Study of Education, Part I, The University of Chicago Press, Chicago, 1965.

Williamson, Maude, and Mary Stewart Lyle, *Homemaking Education in the High School,* Fourth edition, Appleton-Century-Crofts, Inc., New York, 1961.

PART ELEVEN

Art and Music

47. Art and Music in the Curriculum

Theodore R. Sizer

Let me justify my presence by arguing the paradox that because I have no important credentials in the fields of art and music, I have possibly the perspective often denied to the expert. This may be a lame rationale, but I see my task this afternoon to be just that and to be deliberately provocative in the hope that some general issues may be raised.

From Theodore R. Sizer, "Art and Music in the Curriculum," *New England Association Review,* Spring, 1964, 20–23. This article, which is based on an address presented at the annual meeting of the New England Association of Colleges and Secondary Schools, Wellesley, Massachusetts, October, 1963, was reprinted in the *Music Educators Journal,* June–July, 1965, 44–46, Vol. 51. Theodore R. Sizer is Dean, Graduate School of Education, Harvard University. He has contributed extensively to academic and professional journals and is the author of two books, *Secondary Schools at the Turn of the Century* and *The Age of the Academies.* Reprinted by permission of the New England Association and of Dean Sizer.

Let me start by lumping music and fine arts together under a single rubric, "art." In many schools' eyes this lumping takes place, so let us live with it for the next few minutes.

It is a cliché that "art" is neglected in our schools. It has to compete for periods in the week with science and mathematics and English and history and physical education and in this competition it all too often loses. It is also a cliché to deplore this state of affairs. It is this cliché that I object to because I think by and large we must expect, at least in the secondary schools and in the colleges, that subjects other than the aesthetic will draw the lion's share of the student's time. I would like to argue that "art" courses emphatically should not compete or indeed even attempt to compete in time with the main academic disciplines. This suggestion is not born entirely out of realism — that is, that art will always lose — but it is born out of a conviction that "art" is quite a different animal from these other subjects and that it must be handled in the schools and colleges in a way fundamentally different. I am suggesting that "art" is not a "subject" at all and that, like so many things that schools teach, it must be handled largely outside of a sequence of 53-minute periods with bells at each end.

I see "art" as two separate entities. On the one hand, I see the act of seeing and the act of hearing as *disciplined* — skills that call for training. I would argue that every human being should be functionally literate not only of the spoken and written word, but also in visual perception and the act of hearing. On the other hand, I see "art" as visual and musical expression, as distinctively creative and aesthetic experiences.

If one divides "art" in this fashion, I think one might argue that functional literacy in art is a skill to be taught in the schools. It might even qualify as a "subject," though, as my preceding remarks suggest, I am not sure of this. "Art" in the sense of an aesthetic experience cannot be taught in any systematic or predictable way. The parallel here with the subject we call English should be apparent. English teachers have a dual task: that of teaching functional literacy in the sense of the written and often of the spoken word, and at the same time of trying to get youngsters to appreciate and, indeed, even to create works so charged with emotional tension that they qualify as aesthetic. I think most English teachers would agree with me that in that latter task they are at sea to know how to handle it effectively. Therefore, in my discussion of "art" I might legitimately ask that the study of language be included, as I think its problems are similar to those of the visual arts and music.

Few schools now recognize in their curricula the two entities that I have suggested. In most art and music instruction that I am familiar with, the schools seem to favor the aesthetic entity — ironically the entity which, in my view, they have least chance of handling successfully. By attempting to compel youngsters to "appreciate" "art" in one period held in the cafeteria, they probably do more damage than anything else. In view of the general failure of art and music instruction in the schools — and I might guess in the colleges as well — the neglect of these fields is not really surprising.

I would argue that those in the schools and colleges who are concerned with the curriculum must redefine the field called "art" in some way similar to that which I have. If formal education does nothing else in this field, it must at least guarantee the society that its products are functually literate in every sense. Art and music as skills to be used by the non-performer, by the consumer, must be taught. I would argue that such literacy in the visual arts and music is achieved only by sequential and systematic study from kindergarten on. I would argue that such study has a place in the curriculum in one form or another in no less demanding a fashion than that expected for reading, writing, and arithmetic. I would argue that those who teach this aspect of "art" must ruthlessly prune their program so that it is tied centrally to the *disciplines* of seeing and hearing and *not* to what we call "appreciation" or the assessment of aesthetic values. Just as the first-grader starts with a saccharine little book called *Tip* rather than *Hamlet,* so too must the first-grader start with the rudiments of literacy in art and music — these hopefully not saccharine — rather than with Gustav Mahler or Jackson Pollock. I would argue that just as language study is tied to the child's reality, so too should the study of seeing and hearing be tied to those visual and audible facts that touch him most closely: the multiple picture, the animated picture, the canned music, the music of social revolt of our time. I am not an expert and therefore can speak with the assurance born of ignorance when I assert that a systematic and carefully limited course in literacy in "art" could be satisfactorily complete by the sixth or seventh grade. I would further assert that the elementary school is probably the best place to carry out a program of general education in this aspect of visual art and music as I think the children in elementary schools are not only more receptive to it but also may be yet the most malleable. If this instruction were well and truly carried out, few of the introductory courses that have been so carefully designed for the Carpenter Center of the Visual Arts at Harvard would be needed at all. By inference I am suggesting that the colleges are now trying to make good that which I think the elementary schools could quite handily accomplish, given perceptive teachers and a systematic program.

Let me not suggest that the problems of literacy in art and music be forgotten thereafter any more than the problem of clear exposition is forgotten. Ideally systematic or formal work in "literacy" should no longer be necessary. Literate perception, however, should continually be encouraged by example: the schools and universities should insist on nothing less than the most effective and persuasive — and, I should add, aesthetic — visual and audible presentations. By this I mean the insistence of the school and college faculties for books and catalogs and handwriting of unimpeachable clarity. I mean the insistence for a school's orchestra or band which is neither cheap nor inconsequential. At this point you might argue that I am talking about taste rather than literacy, and I would grant you this point. However I would argue that literacy is the beginning of good taste and in this way does aesthetic value inevitably intrude. Teaching the problems of aesthetics directly is still quite a different thing, particularly as the student will be a creator rather than a consumer. It is the consumer who must have a modicum of "general education."

If we can assume literacy produced in the elementary schools and encouraged informally thereafter, this leaves for the secondary schools and the colleges great opportunities in their art and music programs, because these programs need not suffer from the confusion between general education and specialized education. The aesthetic entity presents far more problems, I think, than the literacy entity. It rests on fuzzy words such as expression and creativity — words with which psychologists can help us little. Everyone has his prejudices about the ways and means a person achieves an aesthetic experience, and let me air mine.

First of all, I don't think the deeply emotional act which comes with creating or perceiving a visual or musical manifestation is taught by one person to another. The pedagogy of such emotion is quite beyond us and we should frankly admit it. In this admission we might re-examine the dictum which says that aesthetic matters are subjects taught sequentially as was literacy. It is my prejudice that when schools make this confusion and attempt to teach "creativity" on Monday, Wednesday, and Friday at 9 a.m., the result is very disappointing.

My second prejudice is that "art" in this sense is not a discipline and that the technical know-how which is necessary to have sophisticated expression *follows* rather than precedes a person's need to create. I suppose the counter argument would be that no one can fully savor the depths of a violin without having travelled the long road in learning the technique of its mastery, and I must grant this point. By and large, however, and particularly in the visual side of "art," the need for expression most probably precedes the desire for technical knowledge, and technical training should follow in the way most appropriate to the demands of the student.

My third prejudice comes from a conviction that the key problem of creative expression is to have something to express. This point, of course, bears on my preceding one. On this I would agree with the artist Millet: "An artist must himself first be moved if he is to move others."

But how does one who teaches in a school provide opportunities for the harnessing of deeply felt feelings in a creative way? Probably it means that the "art" teacher is as much a philosopher and a social critic as he is a technical expert.

To clarify this point let me give two examples which appear to me, at least, to be successful exercises in the aesthetic realm. Outstanding but admittedly extreme is the case of young Charles Knowles at the Putney School. This young man was doomed by an incurable illness almost at birth. He never knew when the malady would rise up and kill him, and he was promised but a few years of life at best. He had to grow up with this savage burden. By the time he went to Putney, he must have been an extraordinary and haunted young man. I did not know him nor do I know what happened at Putney. I only know the last product of his labors produced before his death at the age of eighteen. This is an extraordinary collection of large panels called a *Book of Psalms*. It is simply done on colored paper, with wood block and hand set type. His selections from the Bible, when one knows of the boy's affliction, are deeply moving and the largely abstract visual representations are crude but powerful. The *Book of Psalms* has a power rare indeed, and, in fact, transcends the boy. One need not know the emotional change that this creator had within him in order to "feel" his work.

In another, if less memorable way, is an exercise which I saw displayed at Phillips Exeter Academy this summer. Again I knew none of the boys involved nor have I met the teacher responsible for setting the exercise. I have only seen the results and thus can only guess at the problem set the boys. What appears to have happened was that the young men were asked to paint two self-portraits, the first to be an accurate representation of the reality of their faces, and the second to be a representation of how they thought themselves were — self-portraits not of superficial reality but of a deeper reality. The results were fascinating and would probably be even more fascinating if one knew the boys. In some cases nothing seemed to have happened, but in others a sense of self-understanding came through the abstract representations in a very rare way.

Similar examples could be stated for the field of music. One need only have a student observe protesting Negro groups join arms and sing this incredibly simple hymn, "We Shall Overcome," to see how the musical word can go deep indeed. But the point I am trying to make is that the kind of experience youngsters need to want to create is something intensely personal, something which is not hinged to a time schedule, something which probably starts and stops in an unpredictable fashion.

Let me present one final prejudice and that is that we should not confuse aesthetic work with public performance. It seems to me that the pressure to produce for Mummy and Daddy and the school committee is the kiss of death for most school and college "art" work. Youngsters never learn that creation is primarily for them and not for any one else, and thus they lose the creative meaning of "art."

Given my prejudices, you may now feel that I am arguing that formal education can do very little to nourish "art" in this aesthetic sense. On the contrary, I think it can do a great deal, but in ways quite different from those used to teach mathematics, French, and physics. First of all, the secondary schools and colleges should have the technical aid at hand to provide a range of courses of instruction in the tools necessary for a youngster to go ahead on his own. Describing courses in painting and drawing and harmony in this way may sound deprecating, but it need not. The instructors in these courses, while not expected to "teach" the creative act, can, if they are artists themselves, provide noble examples. They should be quietly at hand as apparently teachers were at hand at Putney and Exeter and they should provide the tools a youngster needs. Secondly, a school should be flexible enough to accommodate the youngster who seizes upon an idea and needs to be left alone with it. Now this is a tall order. It means that when something seems to be going right you let the student stay at it, at the expense of his other work. The principal of a high school with 3,000 students will surely laugh at the impossibility of this proposal, yet it seems to me that if we want those few of our students who may achieve the emotional satisfaction of aesthetic creation to achieve it, we must be prepared to get out of their way at those rare times when they seem to be taking off. There are difficulties here not only in scheduling, but also in identifying the truly creative person. All I am saying to the principal of a school is that when the art teacher bangs on his desk and says you must let Johnny Jones break the rules for a few days, Johnny Jones will be allowed to break the rules. It is no surprise that much of the most satisfactory work in art has been taught in boarding schools where flexible scheduling is possible and the sympathetic art and music teacher is nearby. Surely those of us who send our children to day schools, public or private, want an approximation of the same situation.

Finally, I suppose the most crucial point is that schools have an attitude of acceptance of the importance of the aesthetic and creative life. This is an undefinable thing, best called the "tone" of the school or college. It is the tone that will not tolerate the cheap and the tawdry and that is prepared to reward not only the intellectual but the creative as well. In a word, it all boils down to the teacher.

48. Music Education Faces the Scientific Age

Howard Hanson

My attention during the past year has been focused increasingly on the general subject of the arts and education in the scientific and technological age. This has resulted from having served as a member of the first Advisory Committee for the Ford Foundation in its program in humanities and the creative arts, having participated in a national television forum with consultants and members of the Educational Policies Commission, having met with the U.S. National Commission for UNESCO, and from having discussed the question of the use of manpower in the United States in the meeting called by the American Academy of Political Science and Senator Clark of Pennsylvania.

Throughout these activities I found a certain unanimity. In the meetings, each of which had no connection with the other, and each of which brought together a different group of consultants in the various fields, certain basic ideas and conclusions seemed to run as a continuing thread through the fabric of all the discussions.

There seemed to be a general recognition of the fact that we are being challenged strongly by Russia not only in matters directly related to the cold war but equally in the fields of education, technology, the creative arts and the humanities. There was, furthermore, the strong implication that, at least in the minds of many of the consultants at the various meetings, all is not well with American education and American culture.

The majority of consultants, for example, who had had the opportunity of first-hand observance of the Russian educational system,

From Howard Hanson, "Music Education Faces the Scientific Age," *Music Educators Journal*, June–July, 1959, 17–19, Vol. 45. One of the nation's most distinguished composers and conductors, Howard Hanson is Dean of the Eastman School of Music, University of Rochester. Reprinted by permission of the author and of the Music Educators National Conference.

expressed the conviction that, although they were strongly in favor of the American philosophy of intellectual freedom with its stress on the development of the individual in his own capacities, they nevertheless believed that the discipline and rigor of the Russian point of view were able to accomplish more in a shorter space of time.

Such criticism of education is, however, nothing new. All of us who have been in education for a long period of time remember that in every crisis in American life there seems to be a tendency to blame all of the ills of the world on the educational system. As a people we have always had an almost naive belief in what I have referred to before as "curricular tinkering," emanating from the belief that the maladies of civilization can be easily corrected by the addition of some courses of study and the deletion of others — a theory which has generally proven to be false.

The current criticisms, however, appear to be of a different order — more serious and at the same time more constructive. There was the belief frequently expressed that we needed more depth in education, even more than we need breadth; that we would accomplish more by a deeper concentration on fewer subjects rather than spreading the curriculum to the point where it produced, in the words of Oscar Levant, "a smattering of ignorance."

It was natural that, correlated with this point of view, should be a criticism of the theories of teacher training existing today in many of our colleges and universities, with the tremendous emphasis on the upgrading of courses in methodology, pedagogical materials and techniques, and "scientific" procedures, the validity of which was sometimes highly questionable, accompanied by downgrading of the importance of the subject matter to be taught.

This, of course, is again nothing new but expresses a general philosophy pertaining to all education with which we are thoroughly, and at times unhappily, acquainted.

Another area in the field of education which, especially at one meeting, was subjected to the sharpest criticism was the whole field of educational counseling which some members of the group considered to be carried on in a manner which was incompetent, irrelevant, but very material. Now I have the greatest respect for the work of the counselor and do not wish to subscribe to the statement that we create counselors for the same reason that we create deans — to get them out of the classroom!

At the same time we must admit that in these difficult times the task of the educational counselor becomes increasingly complicated. Most frequently expressed was a criticism against the attempt to fill what we may call the manpower needs of the nation by advising young students to go into those fields where the need was greatest, with sometimes no regard for the primary interest of the student himself.

The criticism of educational counseling was accompanied by the strong belief, expressed repeatedly, that what our country needs is not more scientists, but better scientists, not more musicians, but better musicians.

I was very happy to hear, particularly in the discussion of the manpower committee, the frequent use of the words "emotional involvement." I was especially happy to hear this phrase in a discussion of the best utilization of talent, since it emphasizes what has always seemed to me to be a basic philosophy essential to a free society: that every child should be given the opportunity of doing those things for which his talent best equips him, for developing his capacities as an individual rather than in conformity with a pattern which has been set by authoritarian control. "Emotional involvement," if I understand the term correctly, means simply enthusiasm, the opportunity for the individual to concentrate in the field in which he has personal enthusiasm, a field in which he is emotionally involved. The Russian plan may, perhaps, increase the number of scientists by converting a good poet into a bad physicist, but there is the strong possibility that such a political philosophy harms both poetry and physics!

There was another expression of opinion which was brought up again and again in every group and which greatly heartened me, although it did not surprise me. This was the repeated expression of the great importance of the humanities and the creative arts in a technological age. It was particularly heartening, although, again, not surprising, that this expression of opinion came not only from the educators themselves, but particularly from the scientists.

To those of us who have been concerned with the position of the creative arts in the world of today, for anyone who has been fearful that the creative arts might disappear in a world of science, the strong support of the creative arts coming from the scientists themselves should prove reassuring.

In the days ahead the arts in general and our own art of music may suffer some vicissitudes. These will come, if they come, not from the best minds of the nation but from less informed groups, perhaps from local boards of education who, spurred on by laudable but misguided patriotism, may seek to remove all of the so-called "frills" from the curricula of the public schools in order, once again, to convert talented poets, artists and musicians into bad scientists. This, I am sure, will pass; and I believe, pass quickly.

In the face of these problems what should be our attitude as musicians and teachers? Should we sit quietly by waiting for the day when the educational and cultural imbalance will right itself, or is there positive action which we may with profit pursue?

I believe that such a positive philosophy is not only possible but highly desirable. Such a philosophy would, I believe, have four important facets.

First, I believe that the creative arts should present their case in the court of public opinion more vigorously, more enthusiastically and with greater conviction. We, as musicians, for example, should not be apologetic because music is not a "useful" pursuit in a materialistic sense. We should, I believe, embrace the art — and for that matter all of the arts — as a great whole. Music as creation, music as performance, music as scholarship, music as history, music as therapy, music as a social force. We should, as teachers, first understand the power which lies hidden in the creative arts so that, being convinced ourselves, we may be able honestly to convince others. With such conviction, we would be able to admit freely that music is of little material value, that it is of little importance if importance is measured solely in terms of a materialistic philosophy. But if materialistic philosophy is, in fact, the basis of our American life — as some of our enemies insist — we would have to admit that none of the creative arts are important, that there is no importance in great literature, in philosophy or for that matter in religion itself. This is the materialism which I am convinced will never be accepted by our nation, certainly least of all by our educators.

Second, I believe that we should increase our search for depth in technical education. We should find out for ourselves the tremendous depth, breadth, and height of this art which we all serve so that again, being convinced ourselves, we may honestly convince others. But if we are willing to embrace this "philosophy of depth," are we equally willing to accept the increased demands that such a challenge would place upon our teacher training program? For it is obvious that, if we are to attain depth in the field of music education, the demands on the teacher would be greatly increased.

Perhaps I am speaking out of turn as a music educator who has never taught in the public schools. For this point of view I can present only two excuses. One is that I belong to the class of college deans and administrators who feel that the lack of knowledge of a subject should be no handicap in public speaking!

My other excuse is more valid, and that is that in my long experience in music education I am coming to believe increasingly that there is little or no difference between music education spelled with a capital M and a capital E and music education spelled in lower-case type. We are all doing essentially the same thing whether in grammar school, high school, college, professional school or graduate school. We are teaching at different levels, it is true, and using different materials, but the basic purpose at all levels is essentially the same.

At this point I think it might be appropriate to face squarely the question, "Is music one of the 'frills' in education?" The answer seems to me to be comparatively simple. If the highest ambition of the music department of the high school is to develop a marching band with slick formations, magnificently garbed in brilliant uniforms, and assisted by a champion group of baton twirlers, perhaps it is a frill — albeit a very attractive one.

This is a charge that can be leveled certainly at many of our great universities as well as our high schools. This brings up the whole vexing question of college football, bowl-games, Barnum and Bailey productions between halves, and last but not least the proud determination of all of the alumni of old Siwash "Siwash must win — buck that line — block that tackle." We must ask ourselves the question, "Is this also education?" This is a question which I would prefer to ask rather than to answer!

What I am trying to say, of course, is that important as the marching band may be in the matter of public relations, community spirit, and the like, we hardly can consider it as an end goal, particularly in a time when we are questioning frankly the matter of depth in American education.

On the other hand, if the purpose of the music department of any high school or college is to acquaint its students with the great literature of music through participation, through both active and passive experience, through history, theory and aesthetics, it is certainly not a frill. Or to put it another way, playing Beethoven may be considered a frill only if reading Shakespeare is also considered in the same category.

Here may I put in a still, small plea for a greater depth in music education at the high school level? At an age when students are more or less successfully studying the intricacies of algebra, trigonometry, physics and chemistry, is it too much to demand that music students of the same age and aptitude learn the structure of the major and minor scales, of the modes in which they are performing? Is the construction of the major and minor triad too involved? Is the ability to learn to read the tenor and alto clefs so much more difficult than the mastery of French irregular verbs? Can we not make some intellectual demands of our students comparable to those made in other areas of education? Must music always be "playing," must music always be "fun"? Perhaps this philosophy will prevail but, if it does, we must accept the warning that this is the highway to the kingdom of "frilldom."

Third, we should search for the best plan for the integrating of music with general education, and the integrating of general education with music. For the musician of the future — and, indeed the musician of the present — finds it increasingly difficult to live in his ivory tower. He has become more than ever a part of the main stream of life and he must be able to swim with confidence and strength in that current. This is a formidable task but one which, I believe, can, with imagination and enthusiasm, be successfully undertaken.

Fourth, we, as musicians, as artists, must convince ourselves that music in a democracy must exist on its own proven merits. The social philosophy of the support of the arts by the courts of the old world or the patronage of the immediate past — royal or otherwise — is probably over and gone. We must meet the challenge of the arts today in the framework of today's social structure.

Finally, I think that we must face again the problem of general music education for the student whether in the elementary school, secondary school, or college. As musicians, we are all, I am sure, convinced that the greatest contribution which the arts can make comes through personal involvement, through personal participation. We all know this so well that it is unnecessary to labor the point. Every one of us can recall, I am sure, times when we were lifted to spiritual heights by the performance of great and noble music under an inspired conductor. No amount of listening, no courses in music appreciation, theory or history, can ever take the place of this kind of experience.

But what of the students who are not able, for some reason or other, to enjoy such participation? What can music do for him or her? How can the magnificent but difficult language of music be made available to them? Probably through listening, but what kind of listening? Certainly by concentrated listening, but what do we mean by concentrated listening and how do we motivate such concentration? This is a question again which I can ask much more easily than answer, but it is a question which I believe we must solve eventually if music is to take an important place in the great area of what we term general education.

This, then, is the challenge which we face today. It is not a new challenge; it is as old as music itself; it is as old as education itself. It comes to us with particular force in the environment of the new age in which we must now live. It can be met successfully, I believe, only by drawing on the greatest resources of the art — and these resources are very great indeed. We must remember that the greatest contribution of the musician is music. Music for fun, music for recreation, is important. Music for dancing is important. Music for football games is important. But all of these vary greatly in importance. Let us never forget that the greatest importance of the art is as a communication of the most magnificent, the most inspiring of spiritual messages — messages which so transcend the power of the written or spoken word that their translation into speech would be utterly futile. Music at this level, like philosophy and like religion in their noblest moments, offers spiritual sustenance which the world greatly needs in this era of automation. For, although living in an age of automation, man is not an automaton. He is a living, breathing, spiritual being, and the nourishment of that spirit can be neglected only at our very great peril.

We have said often enough that the great purpose of education is the search for truth. With deep humility I would like to make an amendment. The greatest purpose of education is the search for truth and for beauty — and who may say which is more important? For the search for beauty is the search for God.

49. Art Education

Edward L. Mattil

If American public education is to function fully, it must provide for the preservation and strengthening of our democratic system. To accomplish this it must serve the individual member of our society by providing him with various opportunities for the fullest development of his capabilities.

From Edward L. Mattil, "What Is Good About Art Education?" *The Teachers College Journal,* October, 1964, 36: 27–28. Edward L. Mattil is Professor and Head of the Department of Art Education, College of Education, The Pennsylvania State University. President of the National Art Education Association in 1963–1965, his articles and research reports have appeared in many professional journals. He is editor of *Everyday Art,* author of *Meaning in Crafts,* and contributor to *Providing for Individual Differences in the Elementary School.* Reprinted by permission of Professor Mattil and *The Teachers College Journal.*

Art education has long regarded the individual as the most valuable part of the democratic society. It has worked toward the development of individual skills and sensitivities which are essential for sincere appreciation and has sought to teach the child to identify with others, for that is the basis for cooperative living and learning.

Beginning with the youngest children, art in our schools provides the kinds of experiences which help the child to become increasingly aware of his environment and thereby more sensitive to it and able to interpret it. Through art he becomes acquainted with his culture and becomes more conscious of his cultural heritage. Art provides the kinds of activities, materials, and processes which call upon each individual to use his resources as a creator and as a problem solver, presenting those conditions which elicit personal solutions of high aesthetic sensitivity. It places each child in the position of being both an individual producer depending upon his own resources, and a member of the group who learns to recognize, weigh, and value the solutions of others, no matter how different these contributions may be from his own.

Art education has moved a great distance from its introduction into the common schools of Massachusetts in the 1820's where it was regarded primarily as "drawing." Many of its steps forward have been both halting and shaky, perhaps even misdirected. But like the small child who stumbles, even falls before finding his sure means of walking forward, art education stumbled, fell and regained its balance and now is moving forward in an orderly direction. In the early years, art had limited goals and therefore limited acceptance as a useful part of education. The limited acceptance is still a major problem for art educators as attested in the recent study *The Status of Music and Art in the Public Schools,* a research study by the N. E. A. Though showing continuous growth, art is failing to meet widespread acceptance by the administrators of schools who are undoubtedly facing the pressures of increased demands of all subject matter areas.

Yet art is a subject, perhaps the only subject, which has continuously dedicated itself to the creative development of the individual through education. Because of increased attention and value now placed upon creativity, it is fashionable for virtually all subjects to lay some claim to the creative development of the child. Surely art education does not hold the exclusive answer to creative development, for people are creative in diverse ways and in many different disciplines; but art education, by its very nature, does open the doors to creative development at the earliest age and under sustained, supported programs is able to keep the doors open through childhood, adolescence and adulthood. Although modern education has had the shadow of "is it useful?"

cast over it for years, many have failed to see that following the development of one's senses, one's senses aid in all learning. For example, we live in a world of visual symbols, therefore, it is important to help children to become increasingly sensitive in visual perception. Our progress as a nation and as a culture depends upon inventive, imaginative, and more knowingly responsive individuals — people who can use their intuitive powers as well as their powers of logic. Perhaps it is the "uselessness" of art that makes it ever so valuable as a part of the balanced development of children and youth.

Art education in contemporary education values the creative urge of individuals, provides the conditions under which children develop and grow, and focuses upon the development of increased sensitivity of individuals in the areas of aesthetic, social, creative, mental, and emotional response. The teachers who are charged with this responsibility must be well grounded in the subject of art, have a sound knowledge of the creative needs of children and be aware of their patterns of development.

Art programs of great imagination and substance can be found in practically every region of this country. Increased interest in professional activities, serious research and scholarship, program re-evaluation, higher standards, and the artistic achievement of teachers have all added up to improve art education. Yet, much remains to be done, for remnants of poor practices exist in pockets here and there. There is still a great need to more carefully understand teaching and learning in art, art's place in the curriculum, the effects of social conditions on the learner, the content of art education, and the "why" of art education. But current activities are hopeful and the leaders in and out of education are aware that with the great progress of science and technology, it is necessary to continue to strengthen the other bases upon which civilization and human culture rest. Without attention to those values which exist in the arts, we are not likely to arrive at the solution to the many pressing practical problems of society.

50. The Role of Art in the Elementary School

Pauline Johnson

The subject of child art is of much interest to educators and psychologists today, for the visual imagery of young children is one of the most extraordinary phenomena found in the patterns of human growth and development. Amazing figurative depictions coming from the very young are indicative of the unlimited creative potential that all children possess. There seems to be no one explanation of how these mental images are formed or what their significance is; yet, obviously, they are closely identified with personal experience.

According to Langer[1] the child acquires the visual language of art in much the same way that he acquires a verbal language when he imitates and plays with sounds in learning to talk. As he "catches on to the language" he devises the forms that become the roots from which art and creativity spring. Langer states that the child works with symbols in art which he devises from his own intuitive mind and that the formation and use of these symbols are one of the primary functions of man — as natural as eating or walking. She refers to symbol-making as a fundamental process of mind that goes on all the time. In fact most thinking during the life span is in terms of or involves the use of pictorial elements.

Child art was first given recognition by Cizek,[2] while a young man

From Pauline Johnson, "The Role of Art in the Elementary School," pp. 51–56 in Chapter IV, "Art for the Young Child," *Art Education,* The Sixty-Fourth Yearbook of the National Society for the Study of Education, Part II, NSSE, Chicago, 1965. Pauline Johnson is Professor and Chairman of the Division of Art Education, University of Washington, Seattle. She is the author of *Creating With Paper and Creative Bookbinding* and co-author of *Crafts Design.* She is a member of the Editorial Board of *Art Education* and is on the Advisory Board of *School Arts.* Reprinted by permission of the National Society for the Study of Education.

[1] Suzanne K. Langer, *Philosophy in a New Key,* p. 32. New York: Penguin Books Inc., 1948.

[2] Wilhelm Viola, *Child Art.* Peoria, Illinois: Chas. A. Bennett Co., Inc., 1944 (second edition).

studying art in Vienna. He made the observation that children, when left to themselves, drew in entirely different ways than when they were taught in school. This observation led him to establish the classes in art for children for which he later became famous, and his explicit faith in the child's ability to produce art started a movement that later spread over the continent and to the United States.

Since Cizek's time, much research and study have been devoted to the art of the young child; the creative potential in all children has been recognized. Before the child starts to school and before he learns to read and write he makes extensive use of pictorial images as substitutes for verbal and written expressions. The act of picture-making serves as a natural outlet and a means of communication closely identified with play. It is sometimes difficult to separate it from those play activities which involve invention of stories and other imaginative ideas. For instance, a child may draw some forms on a piece of paper and then decide to cut out two wedge-like shapes between which he inserts the sketch, with the announcement that he has "made a sandwich for daddy's lunch."

To better understand the nature of the young child, one needs to observe him at play to learn how his play impulses are carried over into spontaneous rhythmic movements, original dramatizations, games, songs, poems, stories, and drawings. Such out-pourings come with only slight encouragement and opportunity. They involve the exercising of the imagination, an important factor of development that needs to be channeled and developed.

One of the greatest assets the child possesses is his creative mind, which provides for him another way to knowledge — the way that artists, poets, writers, and composers work. It is a way by which all persons can achieve greater depth and meaning in living. Education has not yet begun to recognize the significance of the creativeness of the child's mind, the implications of creative development, or what it can contribute to the child's mental growth. There seems to be little cognizance of the fact that creative people are the ones who mold the culture and give it a place in history, for it is the builders, artists, designers, writers, musicians, and statesmen who shape the character of civilizations. Although creativity is essential for the culture, it is a powerful force in the life of every individual regardless of his place or position. No matter what the child chooses to do for his life work, he can do it more effectively with the preparation he receives from the development of all his potential.

There is no better way to develop creative capacities in children than by means of the arts. They teach the child to be constructive and to bring forth something new and unique that has passed through his mind. As the great humanizers of life, the arts make him appreciative of life and sensitive to growing things and helpless creatures. As related to a great creation, he sees himself as part of the total plan of life.

The child is by nature a creator, inventor, and explorer, and his natural abilities need the nourishment of creative art activities. As with the unsophisticated primitive man, art is so much a part of the life of the child that it does not exist as something set apart as adults tend to make it. It is a natural activity partaken of by all without conscious thought. It has been said that all male Eskimos "can carve if they so wish" and, likewise, all people can exercise their creative abilities, in a form of their choice, for all possess the capacities to do so.

Children need the arts, and are hungry for them and for the release they provide for the emotions. When the arts are neglected, the child tends to become less flexible as he grows older, and his ability to create becomes stifled. One has only to compare the extent and freedom of output of the child in the first grade with that of the average child in the fifth or sixth grade whose creative development has been restricted, to see the loss of ability. If we are to have visual literacy in our culture, education must provide for it so that the language of art can be learned and used.

The school needs to recognize that art, music, poetry, drama, and rhythmic movement are not embellishments of life, but are fundamental to it, and to insist that they be given their rightful place in the curriculum to balance the areas of rationalization. Piaget[3] said that we need to "reintroduce into the framework of teaching that aesthetic life which the very logic of an education based upon intellectual authority tends to eliminate, or, at least, to weaken."

To the uninformed person, the arts may appear to be worthless, impractical, a waste of time, and luxuries, whereas that which is scientific, logical, and factual is practical and reasonable. This idea stems partly from the fact that we live in the most artless culture of any period of time in history. Although there are a few isolated artistic achievements in our present culture, and a resurgence of interest in the arts, one could say for the most part that our cities remain ugly, our homes are visually depressing, and our minds are often empty because they have never experienced the inward development that could be provided through the arts. These conditions will remain as long as we perpetuate the present illiteracy in the field of art and accept the present situation as normal.

[3] Jean Piaget, *Education and Art*, p. 23. Edited by Edwin Ziegfeld. Paris: UNESCO, 1953.

There are some engaged in teaching who would ignore the attributes of childhood and deny the child the kind of education that he deserves. They feel that play is a waste of time, that childish imaginations prevent him from acquiring "accurate concepts of reality." To them, logic and reasoning are the only elements of the human mind worth cultivating. So they go quietly about their task of devising workbooks and texts on reading containing dull and unimaginative exercises and stories guaranteed to provide a "good education," gradually leveling the child down to mediocrity in important aspects of his development. The child seeks approval and conforms, and soon learns that the education that is prized is concerned primarily with accumulating information, learning facts, and developing skills. These types of learning are necessary but should not be acquired at the expense of other vital types. In a few years, the child's senses will be dulled by such a curriculum, while fears and lack of confidence will supplant his self reliance and faith in his abilities. Imagination will be tempered by realism and gradually suppressed until it becomes almost dormant.

When education is focused on one aspect of the human personality we have a biased, distorted picture of what produces a developed, functioning individual. Scientific reasoning becomes the criterion of growth. It is felt the child must be learning something precise and specific, and that there must be "meat" in the program. No time is allowed for preparation and readiness, or to enjoy childhood, for the aim is to rush the child into adulthood as soon as possible. The earlier one learns to read the better, whether he has the background to understand the abstract concepts of the words or not. There is a time for certain types of learning, and the time for beginning to learn varies from type to type. Readiness for any experience is essential; if a child is forced into an activity before reaching a proper level of development, he may experience failure and emotional disturbance. When there is no previous opportunity to extend or sharpen awareness through the exercise of the sensibilities, the capacity to learn is severely restricted. When one is aware of the real nature of a child, one will see the fallacy of trying to accelerate development beyond his capacity to accept and comprehend meanings and to focus on one aspect of learning, the logical, to the exclusion of all others. Nearly thirty years ago Tomlinson said, "Let us take care that we do not develop in our children 'streamlined' minds lest they be not able to tarry along the way."[4]

It is the responsibility of the school to provide for the creative and artistic development of all children regardless of ability. When such

[4] R. R. Tomlinson. *Crafts for Children,* p. 118. New York: Studio Publications Inc., 1935.

development is neglected, the artistic dies or withers — to be revived, if at all, with considerable struggle. There is no certain way to predict which children will later excel in the arts, for many factors contribute to creative intensity. Interest, of course, is essential, and the child who appears to be imaginatively gifted should be encouraged to develop his full potential. We must accept as a fundamental principle that all children have talent to a greater or lesser degree in that all are creative. Since all are creative, a distinction must not be made between the so-called "talented" and "untalented." To do so produces an artificial situation — one that has no real validity.

Perhaps art is the least understood, the most difficult, and in many cases the poorest-taught subject of any in the elementary curriculum. This is most often due to the inadequate preparation of the teacher, whose only exposure may have been in a methods course in college or possibly in a teachers' workshop. Such superficial preparation does not provide a growing awareness of the part that art plays in the total realm of human culture and of the vital role of aesthetics in everyday living. The limited amount of time given to art and the poverty of the program testify to its lowly status in numerous school systems. Many may recall that the art lesson was scheduled for the last hour on Friday afternoon. Since it was not very important (its chief function being to provide relaxation from the intensity of the "more serious and significant subjects"), it made no really great difference whether it was offered or not. Because of the limited offerings, pupil enthusiasm was usually not too high. There are a number of factors contributing to the lowly position of art in the curriculum — a situation that should be of concern to those responsible for educational programs.

The success of the elementary art program is dependent upon the attitude of the principals and teachers toward it. Therefore, it is essential that both of these groups be required to present credits in basic art as a condition of their certification. The principal is responsible for the quality of the curriculum program in his school, and if he is not well informed on current professional practices he cannot very well expect to exert much influence on what happens in the classroom.

Alfred North Whitehead has written that "It would require no very great effort to use our schools to produce a population with some love of music, some enjoyment of drama, and some joy in beauty of form and color."[5]

[5] Alfred North Whitehead, *The Aims of Education,* p. 52. New York: Macmillan Co., 1952.

51. Art and the Pre-Adolescent

John A. Michael

School had just started, and David was on the playground with the other seventh-grade boys and girls when he unconsciously grabbed up a stick from the ground and held it in his hand, moving it in a swooping manner while making noises similar to those of a rocket. Suddenly he turned and looked around to see if anyone were watching. Upon seeing that a few of his classmates were observing, David dropped his head and looked sheepishly away. The stick which his imagination had transformed into a rocket or missile was thrown to the ground and once again became nothing but a stick.

Why did David stop playing with his imaginary rocket when he was noticed by his classmates? Why did he suddenly feel ashamed of his imaginary and uninhibited behavior? Here we see a basic change occurring which differentiates the child from the adult — a change in imaginative activity. The stick could easily become a rocket for a child but never for an adult. While a child may play without conscious planning and for the sake of play, an adult plays with rules and goals which he formulates for the game. David, being at the beginning of this in-between-childhood-and-adulthood period known as adolescence, may sometimes act as a child and sometimes as an adult. And he may feel somewhat insecure in either role.

In his creative art expression — whether it be drawing, painting, or working with clay and other materials — similar behavior naturally takes place, for it is in this that he projects himself into his own work, being motivated by his own experience. With paper and crayons or

From John A. Michael, "Creative Art Experiences Immediately Prior to Adolescence Are Important," pp. 86–89 in Chapter V, "Art Experience During Early Adolescence," *Art Education*, The Sixty-Fourth Yearbook of the National Society for the Study of Education, Part II, NSSE, Chicago, 1965. John A. Michael is Professor of Art Education, Miami University, Oxford, Ohio. He has contributed numerous articles and research reports to professional journals and yearbooks and is the author of a forthcoming report *Artists' Ideas About Art and Their Use in Education*. Reprinted by permission of the National Society for the Study of Education.

paints, he may play house with dolls or drive the family car; he may play hide-and-seek or work as an engineer; in fact, in his picture he may be anything he pleases, and all with equal success and with recognition from his peers, as well as from adults. Such constructive activity, and acceptance thereof, permits the child approaching adolescence to create in the art class in a manner which he feels is needed at the time. As a result, such art experiences help him adjust and prepare for his new and forthcoming role as a mature person.

As in the case of David, we see that unawareness is characteristic of children, whereas awareness is characteristic of adult behavior. For the child, imaginative activity is unconscious, while for the adult it is conscious and controlled. This change in imaginative activity from unconsciousness to critical awareness, brought about, in part, by changes in the body, is one of the most important characteristics of adolescence.[1]

With puberty come physical and psychological changes which affect every aspect of a person's life, and they frequently cause great difficulty. Many writers have called the period of this stage of growth and development one of crisis.

At a time just prior to the advent of adolescence, the art teacher has an excellent opportunity to help the individual hold onto his creativeness through art experiences. Frequently, this creativeness is lost forever during the period of adolescence.

In a report of research, Lowenfeld and Beittel write as follows:

> Through promoting creativeness in the arts we may be able to promote creativeness in general, regardless as to whether it will be applied to the arts or to the sciences. Thus the available data so far suggest confirmation of the common assumption that art education can promote creativeness beyond the arts.[2]

Conversely, if we thwart creativity in one area, in all probability we will thwart it in another. The adolescent period is a crucial period. If we fail to help the individual hold onto creativeness at this time, his creative ability may become atrophied for the rest of his life. Because of the strong tendency of the adolescent to be critical of his imaginative activity, he tends to lose confidence in his own creative ability, and he expresses himself less and less in a visual manner. The resulting rigidity in his visual expression is frequently mirrored in his personality. He often reacts to his art work negatively since he suddenly feels it to be

[1] Viktor Lowenfeld, *Creative and Mental Growth,* p. 216. New York: Macmillan Co., 1957 (3rd edition).

[2] Viktor Lowenfeld and Kenneth R. Beittel, "Interdisciplinary Criteria in the Arts and Sciences: A Progress Report," in *Research in Art Education,* p. 43. Washington: National Art Education Association, 1959.

childish when evaluated in terms of his new-found but often not fully understood system of values. Now, the final product becomes more important to him, if not all-important. If the adolescent cannot create a product which will satisfy himself, he will feel the effort was not worth while, regardless of how much he enjoyed the attempt, i.e., the process.

Knowing the importance which the adolescent will attribute to his art product, the art teacher can help alleviate any negative feelings concerning his creative art ability by helping the individual, before the advent of adolescence, to develop and to become aware of the many creative and aesthetic abilities, sensitivities, and skills shown in his work. If we are able to make the individual knowledgeable concerning his own accomplishments, in all probability he will feel confident in his own work. This may be accomplished by asking questions, such as "How did you make those trees seem so far back into your picture whereas these trees seem so close to us?" "How did you achieve that stormy effect in the sky?" "How did you make the man look as though he is running?" Questions such as these make the individual aware of his own accomplishments, and, coupled with words of praise, they tend to build confidence, as well as awareness. As a result of a newly developed conscious sensitivity concerning his art expression, the child may tend to lose some spontaneity in his work; however, at this time in his life it is far more important that he maintain confidence in his ability to do creative art work. Because, as a child, he is made aware and confident of his creative art ability, in all probability, as an adolescent, he will experiment, be free and spontaneous, and become more and more involved in his art work if given appropriate stimulation from the art teacher, his peers, or his parents.

Another factor contributing to a turning away from art expression by some boys during adolescence is the acceptance of the attitude that the arts are "sissy" and not manly. As a result, the arts are rejected by some boys, and with this rejection practically all aesthetic and creative development ceases. Prior to the adolescent period, the art teacher should make both boys and girls aware of the field of art and design, the importance of these in our society, and the place of both men and women in the art field.

Just as the healthy individual is best prepared to undergo surgery, so is the properly conditioned individual prepared for adolescence. If we can get the child immediately prior to adolescence to express himself spontaneously, freely, and sincerely with an awareness, sensitivity, and confidence in his ability to do so through line, shape, value, texture, and color organized in a consistent manner, he will undoubtedly undergo the period of adolescence without difficulty, or perhaps even without hesitation, in his creative art expression.

For Further Reading

Choate, Robert A., "The Shaping Forces of Music in the Changing Curriculum," *Music Educators Journal,* April–May, 1961, 29–32, Vol. 47.

D'Andrea, Frank, "A New Basis for Music in the Secondary Schools," *Music Educators Journal,* February, 1963, 33–36, Vol. 49.

Gould, Morton, "Sound of a Band," *Music Educators Journal,* April–May, 1962, 36–37, 46, Vol. 48.

Hastie, W. Reid, (ed.), *Art Education,* The Sixty-fourth Yearbook of the National Society for the Study of Education, Part II, The University of Chicago Press, Chicago, 1965.

Henry, Nelson B., (ed.), *Basic Concepts in Music Education,* The Fifty-seventh Yearbook of the National Society for the Study of Education, Part I, The University of Chicago Press, Chicago, 1958.

Housman, J. J., "Contemporary Art and Art Education," (bibliography of studies), *Art Education,* Fall, 1963, 5: 82–91.

Keel, John L., "Sir Herbert Read on the Teaching of Art," *School Arts,* December, 1963, 19–20, Vol. 63.

Miller, Thomas W., "Musical Taste Influences Curriculum," *Music Journal,* March, 1966, 64, 66, 107, Vol. 24, No. 3.

National Association of Secondary School Principals, *The Arts in the Comprehensive Secondary School,* NASSP *Bulletin,* September, 1962, Vol. 46. (The 1961–62 Major Project of the NASSP Committee on Curriculum Planning and Development, Delmas F. Miller, Chairman.)

Reimer, Bennett, "The Curriculum Reform Explosion and the Problem of Secondary General Music," *Music Educators Journal,* January, 1966, 38–41, 117–121, Vol. 52.

Schoenbach, Sol, "Chamber Music in Secondary Schools," *Music Educators Journal,* February, 1963, 73–74, Vol. 49.

Wilson, Harriet, "Art as Education," *School Arts,* December, 1963, 63: 31–32.

Wright, G. Scott, "The Subject Matter of Art," *School Arts,* December, 1964, 64: 37–38.

Zeiger, A. L., "The Case for Jazz in the Classroom," *Music Educators Journal,* February, 1963, 137–139, Vol. 49.

PART TWELVE

Specialized Subjects and Activities

52. Sex Education

Helen Manley

Surely the home should be the source of the child's first sex education. Here he receives his conception of love, security, and family interrelations. Here he should learn that all parts of his body are good and should receive as much approval on his discovery of his penis as his

From Helen Manley, "Sex Education, Where, When, and How Should It Be Taught?" *Journal of Health, Physical Education, Recreation,* March, 1964, 21–24, Vol. 35. Helen Manley is Executive Director of the Social Health Association of Greater St. Louis. She served as President of the American Association of Health, Physical Education, and Recreation in 1946–47. Reprinted by permission of JOHPER and the American Association for Health, Physical Education, and Recreation.

toes. Here he should see that love means warmth and understanding along with some disagreements. His questions should be answered factually, with warmth and understanding, and the correct names of all parts of his body should be known to him. Hopefully we expect him to gain standards of acceptable behavior, self-control, and a realization of the role of his sex in adult life.

Unfortunately, many children enter kindergarten or the first grade with such a diversion of terms for even the bowel movement that school nurses have difficulty in getting health data. Sex organs have been labeled "naughty" and bodily functions dirty. At school at very early ages, children discuss their bodies and answer their questions in the toilets, and with a guilty feeling. As the child reaches preadolescence and the teen age, his natural withdrawal from adults increases his reliance on his peers for sex information.

A Purdue Poll of 1,000 teenagers revealed that sex information was gained as follows:

32% of the girls and 15% of the boys were informed by parents
6% learned from courses in school
7% learned from older people not their parents
53% of the boys and 42% of the girls found out from friends and people of their own age
15% pieced together the information they had from other sources
56% of these young people acquired their sex knowledge between 6th and 9th grades and 18% learned about it between grades 1 and 5
88% of these young people said they would like more information.

School-age children and youth today have acquired much sex information. Their peers and mass media have filled them with images and challenging suggestions for behavior which has produced alarming statistics. Radio and television programs depict prekindergarten children being asked "Who is your boy friend?"; advertising insists that its products give sex allure, which alone makes one attractive; marriage is shown as forever playing house with all the latest gadgets. Aroused with curiosity, the children may try to get answers and further information from parents, but too often they find them busy, embarrassed, or uninformed — or they just can't find their parents — they are out. So the answers come from elsewhere.

Teenage marriages have increased notably. The December 1962 issue of the *Catholic Family Leader* gives this data.

Increase in teenage marriages
1940–58 — all marriages rose 231%; teenage marriages 500%

1961—2/5 of girls marrying were teenagers; average age of girls at marriage was 18 years

One study — 50% of high school girls were pregnant at time of marriage; 80% of wives of high school boys were pregnant at time of marriage.

Stability of teenage marriages

One study — within five years most of the couples studied were engaged in adulterous relations with someone else

United States Census Bureau — rate of divorce of teenage marriages is three times as high as for those married between 21–25 (12.6 per 1000 vs 4.8)

One study — three out of four teenage marriages break up

These marriages not only tend to shorten the schooling and job preparation of the youth but also affect the next generation. Teenage parents produce a higher percentage of premature babies, there is a rise of 26% in death rate of babies, and more babies born ill due to lack of prenatal care. Infectious syphilis among teenagers aged 12–19 has increased 200% in the last six years.

A recent research study of 346 young people in the New York metropolitan area revealed the following:

32% did not know venereal disease can be cured if treated in time
44% did not know syphilis and gonorrhea are two different diseases
60% did not know these diseases were transmitted through sexual intercourse

In 1960 Dr. Celia Deschin made a study of 600 teenagers who came to venereal disease clinics in New York. Through this it was learned that:

64% received all sex information from peers
21% received all sex information from parents
15% received all sex information from other adults

Only 10% of these young people had an adequate knowledge of the disease for which they were being treated. In spite of the known easy cure for venereal disease, the rise in the instances of infectious syphilis from 1959 to 1963 was 448%, and the under twenty-four year olds accounted for 54.7%.

Pressures and changes in society have deprived children of the security, example, and values they need for mature adulthood. Problems of teenage delinquency, tensions, and general inadequacies are making the headlines. Young people are thrown into a society for which they are not prepared and are given freedoms for which they are unable to accept the responsibilities. Without information, restrictions, or guidelines they drive miles away from parents, relatives, or friends to park and pet; they go steady at 12; some find easy access to liquor. They feel that they only have understanding and appreciation from other frustrated teenagers.

All agencies which touch the lives of children and youth have an obligation to prepare them for their functions as members of a family now, and as potential husbands, wives, and parents later. The school, however, is the only institution which receives all children over a prolonged period. It has the challenging opportunity and obligation to supplement and contribute to this education and in some instances to offset the unfavorable teachings the child has picked up from various sources. The school has definite responsibility for the total education of the child, and this includes the important phase of his living — his sex and family interests.

For many years there has been an awareness of the need for this kind of education in our schools.

In 1941 the American Association of School Administrators recommended that sex education be included in the curriculum.

In 1948 the National Conference on Education of Teachers recommended sex education as part of the curriculum for all teachers.

In 1960 the White House Conference on Children and Youth recommended that "family life courses, including preparation for marriage and parenthood, be instituted as an integral and major part of public education from elementary school through high school."

Still the schools are lagging. School administrators seem to have three fears. The first is public response: It is too controversial; there will be too much criticism. The second problem is how to get it into the curriculum. What should be the actual procedure of handling this type of education? A third qualm is the question of finding qualified teachers.

The administrator of a public school system is rightly concerned about the opinion of the public. He is charged with giving to the children the state-required education in a manner approved by the citizens. The will of the people will decide the depth and breadth of this education. The home, school, and entire community must have a common and thorough understanding of purposes and objectives. Parents today are very concerned about the sex behavior of their children and are pleading for help. They realize that the problem cannot be solved by one or a few families but involve the whole community, and even the world. A few vocal citizens who do not understand the program or whose personal experiences may be a bit warped should not prevent the introduction of this area of education.

Pioneers in Sex Education Programs in Schools

Thought, time, and expert leadership are needed in planning and initiating a program. Various methods have been tried. The Toms River system described in *Teaching Family Life Education,* by Elizabeth Force, is perhaps best known. Mrs. Force stated the procedure as follows: (1) A dedicated high school principal recognized the needs of the students, (2) he brought this to the attention of the school board, (3) the board approved the introduction of a new course, (4) a faculty committee prepared the guide, (5) a teacher was chosen, (6) the course was started and (7) it was constantly evaluated. It took three years of careful preparation with constant advice from a "citizen faculty" composed of adults in the community to get it under way.

Washington, D.C. began a curriculum project in personal and family living in 1958 in eleven pilot schools. It was constantly changed and evaluated, and by 1961 the program reached all schools.

In some school systems, such as the one with which I am most familiar, University City, Missouri, the program grew somewhat like Topsy. Health was taught by the physical education teacher in the senior high school, and as early as 1930, the teacher recognized the need for a sex education unit, and added to the curriculum without excitement or commotion. Students were informed on the sequence of the teaching units, and parents were invited to come to class or discussions with the teacher. An evaluation of this work showed the main criticism to be that much of the material should have been taught at a younger age. As a result, a unit was added in the ninth grade, and later in the sixth, until now University City has a plan of definite instruction at three times during the child's school life with less formal teaching supplementing this throughout the twelve years.

Two policies cannot be overemphasized: (1) The community must be ready for whatever program is initiated, and (2) the parents must be constantly informed. Parents should be invited to view the films, books, and other teaching materials which the students will use and should know exactly what is going on. This will give them the opportunity to make suggestions, allay any doubts or fears, and help them correlate the home and school information. Parents who have difficulty in presenting sex information to their youngsters find that the school experience creates a teachable moment to open up communication.

In the Early Elementary Grades

When the child enters school, the schools have the opportunity of helping him assume his responsibilities for living in a world made up of individuals or groups and of those intimate groups called families. The teacher of the young child takes him with his good, bad, or lack of sex information, satisfies his curiosity, and relieves any of his anxieties on this subject. There are certain routines in school which are strongly connected with preschool family living. The child needs to take care of himself in the toilets and to develop habits of neatness, sanitation, and courtesy to others in the bathroom. He becomes aware of the difference in the girls and boys toilets, and his curiosity is satisfied by teaching him the location and use of the toilet, including the stools and urinals and the flushing of these.

In the homes of these young children, baby sisters and brothers often arrive. This furnishes a natural opportunity to supplement home teaching with acceptable terminology instead of babyish terms. Raising animals in the classroom, visiting the farm, observing pictures of the life of people in other countries, and children's questions will bring occasions for further information. Teachers answer children when a question is asked, whether it is about South America or sex, but only in terms of the child's maturity and understanding.

Briefly, the objectives for a program in sex education in the primary grades may be expressed as follows:

1. To help each child develop a wholesome attitude toward sex
2. To establish the use of the proper terminology in reference to the body
3. To help children understand that there are sex differences of boys and girls
4. To discuss with frankness and lack of embarrassment their problems of growing up and living in a sex-oriented world
5. To discourage the unnecessary handling of parts of the body
6. To give correct and understandable answers to his questions on reproduction
7. To help each child be a good family member — with loyalty, love, and appreciation of his family.

A suggested list of materials and activities would include:

1. Many books and other visual aids
2. Plants and animals in the classroom
3. Visits to the zoo, to the farm, and, if possible to a family that has a new litter of kittens or puppies

4. Hand-washing checks after going to the toilet and before eating
5. Stories of younger brothers and sisters.

In the Intermediate Grades

In the intermediate grades children are ready for scientific and direct teaching in health and are interested in the physiology of their bodies. They can understand and appreciate the human body and how its parts work. Through discussion, charts, films, and books they observe growth, see first hand its variance, and note the differences in individuals and in sex. The reproduction of plants and animals can form an excellent background for a unit of sex education which might be placed in an area of the curriculum for the sixth grade. This might tie into health, social studies, or science.

In many school systems sex education receives stronger emphasis in the sixth or seventh grades. In situations which use the 6–3–3 plan, it seems logical to place this in the sixth grade. The boy and girl feel they have reached a transitional point in their lives; they are about to leave elementary school and consider themselves grown up. It is also the chronological age for the use of bad words, a beginning of boy-girl interests, mixed parties, and kissing games. Puberty is advancing, sexual identity is being established, and sex per se is holding interest.

The objectives of the program at this level may be stated as follows:

1. To continually stress a wholesome attitude toward sex
2. To give students an understanding of the scientific vocabulary for discussion of natural processes
3. To help preadolescents understand the changes that are and will be taking place in their bodies
4. To develop a mature attitude toward sex (to talk freely without embarrassment and to know the facts scientifically)
5. To help boys and girls understand growth and how it is tied into physiology and inheritance
6. To develop respect for social customs
7. To deepen family loyalties
8. To respect the miracle of life

The science program in the intermediate grades includes plant and animal growth and reproduction, which is a logical forerunner of the processes of human growth. How do I grow — why am I taller or shorter than others — are natural questions of this age youngster. The knowledge that human animals have definite growth patterns which vary in length and size for individuals and for sexes is essential.

In some schools boys and girls are separated in this area of instruction. Sex education should be taught naturally and not as something unusual. If boys and girls are separated for any part of the curriculum, this unit might fit into that part. In most situations, boys and girls of this age level are mature enough to work in this unit together. A well-prepared teacher can make this as free from tittering and embarrassment as an arithmetic lesson.

Boys and girls need to understand the function of menstruation in its relation to reproduction. Girls, however, should be given more time on this area and some opportunity to ask questions of a woman and in the presence of girls alone. Their fears and mislearnings must be dispelled so that they can enter or continue this experience with a wholesome attitude toward the process.

The study of reproduction follows in logical order. Children need to know that all living things produce their own kind. They should develop an appreciation of the wonder and meaning of reproduction, understand that male and female are necessary for reproduction, and know that there are definite growth patterns before birth. They should be helped to regard reproduction as a privilege and a function only in marriage.

A suggested list of materials and activities would include:

1. Read books, pamphlets, and visual aids, including such films as the *Story of Menstruation, Miracle of Reproduction,* and *Human Growth*
2. Observe stages of reproduction of animals (hamsters, puppies)
3. Study physiology of human growth
4. Chart age and size of students in class
5. Visit Hall of Health, Science Institute, museums
6. Conduct question and answer sessions with teacher, nurse, or doctor
7. Discuss ancestry, inheritance, and their effect on growth

In the Junior High School

Incidental teaching in many situations and in various subject matter areas will continue throughout the twelve years, but sex education should be specifically emphasized in the junior high school.

This is an age of transition. Boys and girls are eager to assume sex roles and also have a keen interest in scientific knowledge. Inner sex tension is acute; there is great interest in body development and sex changes. Social competence, especially with the opposite sex, is much desired yet these youngsters are insecure. They are vulnerable and will accept the wrong as well as the right. Emotions are volatile; intellectual maturity is being established. It is the job of the schools to help these boys and girls understand themselves and develop values and skills for living in and later establishing a family of their own.

It cannot be left to chance or accident, but needs a definite place. Some schools include this unit in the seventh grade, others in the eighth or ninth. The young adolescent is apt to be embarrassed and lacks poise in the discussion of intimate aspects of sex. Many educators, therefore, feel that the sexes should be segregated in this area. Boys and girls can well be brought together for the discussion of dating and boy-girl behavior. Physical education classes which are separated by sex and yet offer coeducational opportunities in phases of the program have been found to be a good, natural medium for this instruction.

The objectives of this unit in the junior high school might be stated as follows:

1. To continue to develop a wholesome and mature attitude toward sex
2. To give students a scientific background and vocabulary for dignified discussion of sex
3. To establish respect for social standards
4. To help students understand the reasons for proper behavior
5. To develop fine family relations
6. To encourage students to talk frankly and to help them find answers to their questions.

The subject matter areas to be covered by this age level include:

1. Growth (the causes and the many changes in growth)
2. The physiology of reproduction for both male and female
3. Growth and birth of a baby
4. Inheritance
5. Boy-girl relations; dating and its responsibilities
6. Venereal diseases
7. Family relations
8. Responsibilities of being grown up.

Many teaching aids are available and helpful for this unit. Films especially appropriate are: *It's Wonderful Being a Girl* (7th or 8th grade); *Boy to Man* (8th or 9th); *Human Growth* (7th or 8th); *Your Body During Adolescence* (8th or 9th) and *Physical Aspects of Puberty* (9th).

In the Senior High School

Sex education in senior high schools is placed in various areas of the curriculum, such as sciences, health, home economics, psychology, social studies, social problems, or sometimes as a special family living course.

It may appear in the tenth, eleventh, or twelfth grade. If sex education is given strong emphasis in the ninth grade, it seems advisable to hold this course for the eleventh and twelfth grades and use it to pull together in a systematic and mature way all things learned before. At this age level, the sexes may profit from a class on a coeducational basis. Separating boys and girls conspicuously may engender unwholesome attitudes. The objectives of this unit are:

1. To give youth the knowledge and appreciation of the place the family holds in our culture, his place in his own family, and his responsibilities to the family he may wish to establish later
2. To give boys and girls the scientific and physiological information for understanding sex and its relation to life and the family, including the knowledge of the power of the sex drive, the tensions that arise, and the need of controlling the sex urge by will power and self-discipline; also the need for separating sex desire from love
3. To help youth acquire a background of ideals, standards, and attitudes which will be of value to him in choosing a mate and building his own family.

The subject matter would include:

1. The family — history, types
2. Adolescence — its meaning and its responsibilities; sex growth and development; boy-girl relations; dating
3. Selecting a mate; qualifications
4. Preparing for marriage
5. Understanding the process of reproduction (pregnancy, child birth)
6. Promiscuity (dangers, ethics); illegitimacy; prostitution; venereal disease
7. Population explosion and answers to it
8. Ideal of life

The senior high school students have high intellectual potential. They need and want to know the scientific why and are able to understand it. The task of adjusting to adult life in today's world needs understanding. Sane education for family living, including an understanding of the basic urge of sex at this age level, is essential. The teacher must be honest, know the subject matter, and avoid moralizing. No specific birth control methods should be discussed, and the view of continence during adolescence should be upheld.

Teaching aids would include books, pamphlets, charts, and films, including: *Human Reproduction*, *Early Marriage*, *Human Heredity:*

From Generation to Generation, Innocent Party, Social Sex Attitudes in Adolescence; and *Dance Little Children.* Much time should be given to discussion and answering questions.

The Teacher Is All-Important

Perhaps the biggest problem in introducing sex education in the schools is the teacher. Some schools develop teachers through an inservice program of conferences and workshops, and through the help of a local university. In most primary schools, the teacher will tie sex education into the curriculum; in the intermediate grades sometimes the nurse or physical education teacher will assist the classroom teacher in teaching this unit.

In the departmentalized schools, at the junior or senior high school level, this area of education is often taught in such departments as science, home economics, physical education, or health. The choice of the teacher is more important than the department in which it is taught. Research and experience seem to indicate that in the secondary school men, women, married or single, with or without children have equal success with boys or girls or mixed groups.

Having a program of sex education in the schools will not be a panacea for all social ills, nor will facts necessarily be a motivation for improved behavior. They are, however, essential when motivation is stimulated. Boys and girls need the truth, the right answers, and factual knowledge to counteract the fantasies and half-truths they are getting from their peers and mass media. The school is the place where the children are; it has a responsibility for helping boys and girls to make accurate choices among competing moral codes, to understand and assume their sex roles, and to crystallize their ideals, standards, and attitudes toward loyality to the family in which they are born and the one which they will establish.

53. Health and Safety Education

Fred V. Hein

In preparation for this discussion I polled a group of respected colleagues in the fields of health and safety education with respect to crucial issues facing these fields today. Replies were singularly similar allowing for differences of expression.

I might say, also, that I could have presented these same problems based on my own feelings about critical problems without making the poll. It was a reinforcing experience, nevertheless, to receive supporting statements from each of the individuals who replied.

One thing came out of the poll that I had not anticipated. Almost without exception those who replied were militant in their comments. "Its time to stop pulling punches!" "We haven't gotten anywhere buttering up people!" "Let's put the cards on the table!" and other comparable expressions were indicative of the mood of those who responded.

Basic Issues

It is somewhat disheartening to report that the critical issues in health and safety education are not what shall be taught, or how this teaching shall be done or even how students should be motivated to apply what they learn. They are more basic than that and are concerned with deep-down problems like (1) how to get any time whatsoever for teaching health and safety, (2) how to find teachers with even basic competency

From Fred V. Hein, "Critical Issues in Health and Safety Education," *The Journal of School Health*, February, 1965, 35: 70–72. Fred V. Hein is Director, Department of Health Education, Division of Socio-Economic Activities, of the American Medical Association. He has served as President of the American School Health Association, Chairman of the School Health Section of the American Public Health Association, Vice President for Health Education of the American Association for Health, Physical Education, and Recreation, and President of the American Academy of Physical Education. He has written and edited several textbooks in the field of health and has contributed extensively in health education to professional periodicals and to the popular press. This article was presented before the American Association for Health, Physical Education, and Recreation, Washington, D.C., 1964. Reprinted by permission of the American School Health Association.

in the fields of health and safety, (3) how to deal with uninformed critics of health and safety education (both in and out of the profession), (4) how to gain administrative support for health and safety education, (5) how to impress pupils and parents with the importance of instruction in health and safety, and (6) how to combat the irregular, unreliable health education to which the public is exposed over public media.

Teaching Approaches

Obviously unless you are given time to teach health and safety there is little need to worry about what specifics you are going to teach or how you are going to teach them. Often, because of the attitudes of teaching colleagues, lack of support of the administration, and failure of parents to appreciate the need, health and safety education is sort of a stepchild in the curriculum. Where this is true, you have little chance to motivate pupils to accept the subject seriously.

"Health and safety education permeates our total school program," is a favorite expression of those who won't concede that health and safety instruction are deserving of equal rights in the curriculum. "We teach health in science, through the social studies, in physical education, and 'incidentally' every day in every way," these people say. This is fine, and in some schools a good job of correlation and integration is being done. Even so, it isn't enough. Several studies have indicated that direct health teaching cannot be replaced by correlated and integrated instruction. Science teachers and others try hard to do a good job in health education, but they are not specifically prepared for this assignment.

We should remind the well-meaning people who think that correlation and integration are enough that English is also being taught in many other areas of the curriculum. Supposedly it is also being correlated and integrated throughout the school program. But who has heard of doing away with English courses because English is being taught elsewhere on a concomitant basis? As is true in English, there has to be a special place, a special time, where health and safety is given first place, where learning from other areas is tied together, where gaps are filled, where relationships are defined. More important, there needs to be a special time and place where a properly prepared person, whose first concern is health and safety, can communicate his knowledge, attitudes, and example to students.

Consider the health problems of youth today — venereal disease, illegitimacy, the use of habit forming substances. Where are these problems being adequately dealt with in the curriculum?

On the American scene today nearly half of all advertising on public media is health-oriented or health-related. Yet in many of our schools we have no time to teach discriminatory techniques with respect to this advertising. The American people spend an estimated billion dollars a year on unneeded and sometimes harmful health products. Yet today's curriculums generally include little if any instruction on the wise use of health products and health services.

Accidents kill more young people each year than the several most serious diseases combined. But where is the time in the curriculum for "preventive medicine" with respect to these accidents. It has been statistically demonstrated that water safety, first aid, and driver training courses can markedly cut the terrible toll that accidents take in disability and death each year. Wherever organized instruction in health and safety has been incorporated in the curriculum, this has been the case.

Other Problems

All of the foregoing relates to only the first subject on my list of basic issues and it is evident that I have been carried away with the intensity of my feeling that Time for Teaching is the first and foremost need today. Here I think we know which comes first — the chicken or the egg. It is the egg of *time for teaching* from which all the rest can grow.

Today in institutions where a health education major is offered only half of the graduates are placed in school jobs. The others, because of lack of opportunity or better pay elsewhere, take positions in health agencies or go into other work apart from that for which they are prepared.

Once there is a definite time and place for health and safety instruction in the curriculum and once school administrators begin to ask for competent health and safety teachers, the rest will come. Colleges and universities will begin to prepare qualified teachers to fill the need. Accreditation of professional programs and certification for teaching will follow.

In the schools students would demand a scope and sequence of instruction that challenges them at each school level. Qualified instructors would begin to adapt and apply the vast reservoir of motivational research in the classroom situation. Relationships between health and safety instruction in the classroom and physical education in its play area and movement areas would be clarified. Health and safety education would no longer be a step-child in the curriculum.

Facing Reality

Too often, health and safety education has been given only borrowed time grudgingly allotted from physical education. There is no reason why the two areas should be related in this particular way. Each is entitled to its own integrity, its own proper position in relation to the other within the total school curriculum. We cannot live on borrowed time.

Most of us who call ourselves health educators feel that we have done a great deal to bolster the place of physical education in the school curriculum. The health objective of physical education has probably been used more often than any other to substantiate the program. Also the use of the term *health* and physical education has strengthened the standing of physical education in the educational community. If this term is to be used, however, it should mean what it says. It should refer to two distinct but allied curricular fields each of which has its own allotment of time, its own teaching stations, its own equipment and facilities, and qualified professional staff.

There is an unwritten but nominal agreement among health educators that we need and must have the things I have outlined above if we are to achieve our professional objectives. We feel that it is time to take the offensive in attaining these goals for health and safety education.

54. Controversial Areas

Gilbert M. Shimmel

Ordinarily before discussing the content and methods of teaching in the areas of tobacco, narcotics, and alcohol some attention would be

From Gilbert M. Shimmel, "Content and Method in Controversial Areas," *The Journal of School Health,* September, 1961, 31: 230–235. Gilbert M. Shimmel is Associate Professor of Health Education, Teachers College, Columbia University. He has contributed articles dealing with specific health problems to several professional journals. This article was presented at the thirty-fourth annual meeting of the American School Health Association, San Francisco, 1960, and in 1962 was issued as a pamphlet by the Ohio State Department of Health, Alcoholism Unit. Reprinted by permission of the American School Health Association.

given to the prior question as to whether we should teach about them at all, but this one has been answered for us. True to tradition, anytime society recognizes a problem it has failed to deal with, it is handed to the school. Every state *requires* teaching about alcohol in elementary grades and some two thirds of them require such teaching at the secondary level. Most states tie in alcohol and narcotics in the same legislation and some specify that the *harmful effects* shall be taught. Many spell out in detail the place in the curriculum it shall be taught as well as specifying the length of time devoted to it and even the number of pages a textbook must contain on the subject. It behooves each teacher to find out what the requirements are in her situation.

> Section 10191 of the California Education Code says:
> Instruction shall be given in all grades of school and in all classes during the entire school course, in manners and morals. Instruction upon the nature of alcohol and narcotics and their effects upon the human system as determined by science shall be included in the curriculum of all elementary and secondary schools. The governing board of the district shall adopt regulations specifying the grade or grades and the course or courses in which such instruction with respect to alcohol and narcotics shall be included.

Variations in meeting this requirement are extreme. Many districts set up special units in courses such as Biology, Hygiene, or the increasingly used "Required Course in State Requirements." Some meet this by having an assembly in which an outside speaker is utilized. While the quality of the speaker is of major concern this, it seems to me, disregards the difference in atmosphere between classroom and assemblies which are often associated with entertainment rather than instruction. It further fails to capitalize on already existing relationships between teachers and pupils which may work towards reinforcing behavior already effective or to accomplish desired changes in attitude and behavior.

In attempting to influence such change it is essential to understand factors which influence decision making which have been discovered by researchers in the field of social psychology. It is easy to point out that there are differences of opinion and we don't have all the final answers about motivation and behavior but it is just as pertinent to indicate that we aren't utilizing what we do know. While we debate the finality of our knowledge, Madison Avenue pounces on the concepts of identification, reference groups, participation, and ego-involvement and uses them to sell everything from breakfast cereals to tractors. They may be used to sell a specific brand of cigarettes or liquor or just to create a favorable climate of opinion to smoking and drinking in general.

Disavowing any claims of originality, I would like to amalgamate findings by such social psychologists as Allport, Festinger, Lewin, Sherif and others and offer these three principles as pertinent to this discussion. (1, 2)

1. To effect a change in norms of behavior, the change must give promise of beneficial results (the more immediate and obvious, the more effective) or be offered by a person or group who has prestige in the eyes of the one asked to change.
2. When there is conflict between the norms of one reference group and that of another, the group with more salience at the moment will prevail. Hartley says "The more pressing the importance of a group for the individual, the earlier and more persistently he is exposed to its norms, the greater the multiplicity of agencies supporting each other in enforcing conformity, the more the norms come to resemble a categorical imperative and the less they are subject to change." (2)
3. If an individual actively participates in the decision making process, he is more apt to accept the decision and maintain it for a longer time.

Looking at these principles, let's examine our efforts in regard to alcohol and tobacco education.

Ninety percent of alcohol education is directed at total abstinence but over sixty five percent of all adults drink. Surveys in America and Canada have shown remarkably close correlation in this regard, all showing between sixty and seventy percent of all adults, about three-fourths of all men, and from fifty to sixty-four percent of all women who drink. (3) These percentages are highest in age groups from 21 to 50 where strongest likelihood of identification by high school students occurs. It has also been shown that higher amounts of education, economic level, and urbanization are correlated with higher percentages of drinkers. In effect the school is attempting to educate against other socialization forces which got the student earlier and have more consistency of contact with him, including such primary groups as family and peer groups. This applies too to groups to which he aspires to belong. This so-called "anticipatory socialization" is really at the heart of all criticism of teenagers who smoke or drink to be "smart" or pretend they're grown up. This is not a deviance of behavior but one rather of timing. When the teenager perceives himself as being grown up, he assumes prerogatives of the adult as he observes them. Advertising which unceasingly portrays smoking and drinking in an atmosphere of glamour, virility, adventure, and sophistication takes the nod over arguments that "it's bad for you."

Most of the teaching in the past and too much in the present is based on arguments that smoking and drinking are inherently sinful and that engaging in either is tantamount to automatic forfeiture of salvation. Without entering the debate on whether or not there is sin involved, I would suggest that this argument is effective mainly on people who already believe it and stirs strong resentments in those who believe otherwise. A teacher quoting the Bible in favor of abstinence may be confounded by students gleefully quoting verses to the contrary. Most of the major churches now do not take a stand against drinking itself but only against its abuse and the resulting misbehavior. Studies which purport to find differences in drinking behavior among members of different faiths are difficult to evaluate because of the differences in tolerance among the different denominations. Degree of devoutness is difficult to pin down and a church listed by a respondent who doesn't attend its services should neither be blamed if he drinks nor credited if he doesn't. Some faiths have interdictions against drinking almost of taboo strength. Studies of members of such groups show smallest percentages of drinkers but reveal the highest rates of problem drinkers among those who do drink.

There are a great number of misstatements or misuses of fact in exhortations against smoking and drinking. Nicotine is a deadly poison, true, and there may be enough nicotine in one cigar to kill two men but when the student hears the teacher say this and remembers seeing a man smoke a cigar without dropping dead, it reduces the efficacy of her teaching not only in that area but in other areas as well. A student hearing a teacher say that two cigarettes contain enough nicotine to kill an elephant may be so bemused by speculating as to possible ways to effect this that he doesn't hear the rest of the discussion. Statements that alcohol contains no food value, that it rots the stomach, or destroys the brain are in the same general category and appear in statements explaining why teachers are against drinking.

Albert Schweitzer is quoted as saying "EXAMPLE is not the *best* way to teach, it is the *only* way." "Practice what you preach" is an old adage and research points to the futility of doing otherwise with much degree of effectiveness. The Portland study of smoking among high school students (4) showed the highest predictive factor as to whether a student smoked was whether his parents smoked. The greatest percent of abstainers was found where both parents abstained, the highest percent or smokers where both parents smoked. Where only one parent smoked, children tended to imitate the behavior of the same sex parent. Many surveys have shown that drinking behavior among high school and college students is similarly correlated to parental practice.

This raises the knotty question: What of the smoking and drinking behavior of the teacher, or of anyone else, attempting to influence behavior in this regard? If one advocates the cessation of either but continues to practice it, is he not open to charges of hypocrisy or stupidity or both? The common defense is that there are differences between children and adults which make the argument inappropriate so let's focus on adults. How effective is the health counseling of a physician who tells a patient to quit smoking because of any one of a dozen reasons when the doctor is himself smoking? The most vexing question a teacher will be asked by her students is "If smoking is so bad for the health, why don't all doctors quit smoking?" This is a question which each teacher (and doctor) must answer for himself. Speaking as an experimentalist, the obligation upon us is to make certain that each student has recognition of the consequences: the choice then is his alone.

When someone is speaking out against alcohol a common charge is to cite the billions of dollars spent annually and compare it to that spent for education or recreation or whatever else he favors. The conclusions from some of these charges demand closer inspection. Though the amount spent for alcohol in all forms has risen from $3.1 billion in 1936 to $9.2 billion in 1958, the percentage of disposable income spent for that purpose has dropped from 5.1% to 3.1% in the same time. In those same years, the amount spent for food rose from $15.25 to $67.4 billion, tobacco rose from $1.5 to $6.4 billion, and recreation from $3.0 to $17.0 billion. (3) There is also evidence that while the number of drinkers and percentage of population who drink is on the rise, there has been significant change in drinking pattern (more beer and wine, less distilled spirits) so the absolute alcohol consumption per person has dropped. It is felt that this change in taste has been due more to stepped up advertising by wine and beer producers than to attempts of schools.

A common charge against speakers is that it's easier to raise questions than to give answers. To provide ammunition and targets, here are some specific suggestions for those teaching in this area.

Be informed. If this seems to be flogging the obvious, there are school administrators who exert every effort to hire the best prepared teachers in other fields who will assign these areas to anyone regardless of interest or preparation because "everyone knows about them." Similarly, there are teachers who would resist assignment to math or history class without a good background but who sally forth to tackle demon rum and the noxious weed armed with little more than a mantle of righteousness. Such a person is blissfully undisturbed by fact of physiological effects, psychological or social implications and rambles on scattering unsubstantiated specifics and unwarranted generalizations. There is available more and more a wealth of modern, factual, well-written material to be used by student and teacher alike. Districts often have money available for such purposes as subscription to *Quarterly Journal of Alcohol Studies* or to purchase some of the excellent films that have been produced recently. An excellent summary of smoking and advertising appeared in a recent *Journal of School Health* (5) and other professional journals and popular magazines have excellent articles in the area. Alcoholics Anonymous can provide much useful literature and other community agencies, such as the American Cancer Society (4) are good sources.

In teaching about alcohol, let abstinence be a live option as an acceptable way of life and reenforce it in any way you can by identification with individuals and reference groups but don't teach that anything short of total abstinence is indecent and reprehensible. Don't stress the harmful effects as being inevitable or even common and don't be afraid to let your students know that some people use alcohol in moderation and without any complications. This will have the double effect of letting the students know that you're not completely out of touch with reality and will also enhance cooperation from parents who can espouse a policy of moderation but would be threatened by advocation of abstinence alone as being critical of their practices.

Start out by finding out what students know and what they want to know and provide opportunity for full and uninhibited discussion. This can serve as a real learning experience in evaluation of testimony by "experts." To learn to look at what is said, who says it, and possible interests which might cloud objectivity is an experience useful in many choices for individual and community issues. Side benefits of discussions will be the fact that if a group decision is to not smoke, indications are that it will be more apt to be accepted and followed by the individuals than if they make the same statement of intent after a lecture. Even those rejecting the decision will be influenced to some degree by the discussion.

It would appear more feasible in these discussions to focus on short range and intermediate goals. Rather than dwelling on such distant and relatively rare possibilities as lung cancer from smoking, or of alcoholism as an eventual outcome of drinking, one can more effectively and with complete sincerity talk about the harm in our complex society that might result from even a single instance of over-imbibing. These are people to whom the newly won right to drive is precious and a discussion centered around drinking and driving has almost certain attention. Specific topics could be such things as whether a high school student should ride with a person who has been drinking, whether conviction of drunk driving should result in revocation of license, whether a person should be required by law to submit to a blood or breath test for alcohol concentration if he is suspected of being "under the influence." To answer the questions originating from this kind of focus, attention will be directed outward to many other aspects of drinking.

Another area of concern to this age group is the relation between drinking and dating behavior and the possibilities for discussion in this general area are boundless. The effects on inhibitions by even fairly moderate amounts of alcohol is so well known that the following story needs no explanation: A girl writing to a columnist specializing in advice to teenagers wrote that she had had a date the previous evening at which she had had two cocktails before dinner, wine with dinner, and a liqueur after dinner. Had she done wrong? The columnist's reply was "probably!"

REFERENCES

1. Macoby, E., Newcomb, T., and Hartley, E., (editors). *Readings in Social Psychology,* 3rd edition, Henry Holt and Co., N. Y., 1958.
2. Hartley, Eugene, and Hartley, Ruth, *Fundamentals of Social Psychology,* Alfred A. Knopf, N. Y., 1955.
3. Keller, Mark and Efron, Vera, *Selected Statistical Tables,* illustrating two lectures delivered by Mark Keller at Yale Summer School of Alcohol Studies, Summer 1960.
4. American Cancer Society, *Smoking and Lung Cancer Materials,* 1959.
5. Mitchell, Roger S., "Cigarette Smoking, Cigarette Advertising, and Health," *Journal of School Health,* vol. xxx, no. 7, Sept. 1960, pp. 251–258.

55. The School Library as an Instructional Materials Center

Richard L. Darling

The school library, which once was outside the mainstream of education, today is at its very center, thoroughly a part of the school's basic program.

This change springs from many sources. School libraries have felt the impact of the past decade of innovation and change. To team teaching, ungraded schools, advanced placement programs, new emphasis on independent study — to these and other trends — the school library has responded by developing new and relevant services.

The philosophy of the school library as an instructional materials center was made the policy of the American Association of School Librarians at its 1956 conference, when members adopted an official statement affirming the belief that school libraries should be administered as comprehensive instructional materials centers.

The 1960 AASL publication, *Standards for School Library Programs,* soon to be revised to accommodate later developments, outlined a dynamic program of school library services in which listening and viewing assumed a vital place beside reading and research. These standards, prepared in cooperation with nineteen other educational organizations, have had enormous influence on the continuing revolution in school libraries.

Library programs developed to help meet general school objectives present a markedly different range of services than traditional programs.

From Richard L. Darling, "The School Library as an Instructional Materials Center," *Education Age,* May–June, 1966, 45–46, Vol. 2. Richard L. Darling is Director, Department of Instructional Materials, Montgomery County Public Schools, Rockville, Maryland, and a former School Library Specialist with the U. S. Office of Education. He is President of the American Association of School Librarians, 1966–1967. Reprinted by permission of *Education Age,* Copyright 1966 by Visual Products Division, Minnesota Mining and Manufacturing Company.

The instructional materials center offers a wider range of services, includes more varied types of materials in its collections, provides different physical facilities and requires more imaginative use of the library staff.

Books and printed matter may still form a major part of the library's collection. In fact, these collections usually become larger and more varied as the library acts to meet the needs of vitalized curricula in science, mathematics, social studies, the humanities and languages. These enlarged collections include reference works at an advanced level formerly found only in college libraries and an increasing number of paperbound books, valuable in that they may quickly support new courses at relatively low cost.

Challenging courses in the social studies have created a demand for original documents and large periodical collections. Instructional center libraries are meeting this demand with microfilmed copies of documents — and microfilm readers and reader-printers — and long runs of back volumes of periodicals. A few libraries with microfilm cameras microfilm teacher prepared materials.

The principal difference in the instructional center library, however, is in its wide use of auditory and visual materials — 8 and 16mm motion picture films, filmstrips, slides, transparencies, disc and tape recordings.

Teachers obtain these materials and the necessary accompanying equipment from the library for classroom use; students use the materials in the library. To encourage student use many libraries now are open evenings, Saturdays and holidays. A few let students borrow equipment and material for study at home. Most offer flexible loan periods; equipment and materials may be kept for extended periods in classrooms, laboratories and other study centers.

The governing principle is that materials and equipment should be available where needed for as long as needed.

Instructional center libraries also provide materials and equipment which enable teachers and students to create and prepare their own instructional materials. The old library work-room has become a combination work-materials preparation room where teachers make transparencies for classroom use with overhead projectors and students make transparencies or mount pictures for reports. Here, too, the library staff may prepare materials for busy teachers.

Librarians have modified their card catalogs in the instructional centers. Non-print materials are cataloged with books in one continuous alphabetical arrangement; thus all materials on a single subject are listed together. Many libraries use color-coded cards for different types of non-print materials.

Libraries providing service with many media must have facilities for these media. The reading rooms in new libraries frequently are subdivided into smaller areas to create an atmosphere more congenial to serious study. Much of the space formerly devoted to rows of tables is used instead for individual study carrels, some wired for use with projectors, filmstrip viewers and recordings.

Some libraries now consist of several rooms planned for reading, listening and viewing. Small group projection rooms often have a wall-mounted television receiver in addition to a screen.

A few schools, developing still more sophisticated programs, have begun to install automatic equipment. The Montgomery County (Md.) public school system, for example, is planning an elementary library in which pupils working at individual stations will be able to dial and play automatically tape recordings in a central tape deck. Each classroom also will have access by dial to recordings in the library deck.

Instructional center libraries must offer augmented guidance programs if students are to study and profit effectively from this wealth of new material. Library staffs train students to use projectors, viewers, tape-recorders and transparency producing equipment, and teach them to use indexes and advanced subject reference tools. Most important, the librarians train students to discriminate in the use of these materials and to appraise the value, strengths and limitations of each.

Librarians in instructional centers find their professional role enhanced. By using technicians and aides for mechanical and clerical duties, they are freed to work in the instructional program. They serve on curriculum committees and meet with teachers planning instructional units. They also work more with individual students; their understanding of course objectives enables them to advise students in the selection of study material.

In effect, the librarians serve as helping teachers who are responsible for important aspects of the individual study program.

It follows, of course, that instructional centers have created a demand for a new kind of school librarian. Library education institutions have responded with revised curricula and several NDEA Title XI institutes for library personnel have been designed especially for this purpose. The U.S. Office of Education sponsored a 1962 conference on The School Library as a Materials Center: Educational Needs of Librarians and Teachers in Its Administration and Use. The proceedings of this conference — available from the Superintendent of Documents (OE-15042, Circular No. 708), provides valuable guidelines for in-service and pre-service education in the use of instructional materials.

The evolution of the school library from a book-centered agency to an agency supplying the broadest range of instructional materials has radically altered the library's role in the school. From the wings the library has moved front and center and developed into a dynamic new force in elementary and secondary education. By adopting new materials and new methods, the school library has become a vital part of instruction.

56. Athletics

Justice Byron R. White

Ladies and gentlemen, it is said in the books that Darius, the Persian king in the sixth and fifth centuries B. C., determined to conquer the Greeks, considering them to be an inferior race. He accordingly sent a spy among them to see how they trained for battle and to determine their capabilities. This spy disguised himself as a merchant and infiltrated the Greek army. What he saw was Greek soldiers, their bodies naked and oiled, practicing a variety of athletics. They did much dancing, too, clad only in a bronze shield. And they walked together, arm in arm, hand in hand. These soldiers seemed strong enough, but they sat and paid close attention when Greek poems were read aloud to them. The spy reported to Darius that the Greeks spent their time cavorting around in the nude or sitting, partially clothed, while listening to idiots propound ridiculous ideas about freedom and equality for the individual citizen.

Darius and his luxurious court were greatly amused and thought

From Byron R. White, "Athletics: '. . . Unquenchably The Same'?" *School Activities,* November, 1965, 11–14. Vol. 37. Byron R. White is an Associate Justice of the Supreme Court of the United States. This article is an adaptation of an address given by Justice White at the annual meeting of the National Federation of State High School Athletic Associations held in Williamsburg, Virginia, June 27, 1965. Reprinted by permission of *School Activities* and of Justice Bryon R. White.

conquest of Greece would be a terribly easy job. What a rude shock it was when at Marathon the Persian army was driven out to sea. All of this was beyond the comprehension of the powerful emperor.

The same can be said of his son, Xerxes, who succeeded his father and also tried to conquer Greece. The night before his naval forces were to battle the Greeks at Salamis, word came to Xerxes that Themistocles, aboard his flagship, was in a deep discussion about certain passages in a Pindor ode. Xerxes, like his father had been, was amused. But the next day he wept when he saw his naval forces routed by the art loving Greeks whose only weapons were their virile bodies and steel minds.

I don't know how much fact or myth these stories contain but they do express a basic idea about the Greeks: For them intellectual power and physical vigor were not incompatible but were natural allies; together, they counted for much more than either one alone and even more than the sum of the individual parts.

Scholars and Athletes

The ancient Greeks made what were probably history's greatest contributions to philosophy, government and the arts. But at the same time, athletics were an essential part of education and training, and no other nation has ever produced so high an average of physical development as the Greeks did in this classical period. The result was a standard of athletic excellence perhaps never again equaled.

The historian Isocrates expressed the idea well when he said this:

> . . . certain of our ancestors, long before our time, invented and bequeathed to us two disciplines: physical training for the body of which gymnastics is a part and for the mind, philosophy. These twin arts are parallel and complementary by which their masters prepare the mind to become more intelligent and the body to become more serviceable, nor separating sharply the two kinds of education, but using similar methods of instruction, exercise and discipline.

For the Greeks, a strong body was not only of great utility for simple survival. Athletics were a joy in themselves. Strong and graceful performance was inherently satisfying. A vigorous body did much for personality and much for the mind. Moreover, physical training and competitive sports were thought productive of that sound character and noble vision so essential to wise government which was a central concern of the serious minded Greek.

The representative nature of the Panhellenic athlete and the connection of the games with the national religion perhaps explain the great honor which came to winning athletes. Whole cities turned out to welcome the returning heroes. Songs were composed and their exploits recorded on pillars of stone. Athletic poetry and art were common. Statues were raised in some public places. It became common to give substantial prizes to winning athletes, and they also enjoyed important public privileges. They were even exempt from taxation at a later date.

It is probably true that the victorious athlete in Greece enjoyed a distinction such as he has never had, before or since.

Specialization Was Corrupting

But the sad story is that Greek athletics destroyed themselves. Even in those ancient days, sports without serious competition became meaningless. Competition begat specialization, trainers, coaches and winners who had time for little else. Professionalism followed, with the excessive prizes and the accompanying corruption.

Even in Socrates' day, many youths were turning away from sport. He once lectured a young man for his poor physical condition. The youth haughtily said he was not competing because he was an amateur. Socrates replied that there was no such thing as an amateur as far as physical condition was concerned and that it was the young man's duty to be strong and healthy.

Plato and Aristotle decried the trend. Euripides, himself fond of athletics, said,

> Of all the countless evils throughout Tellas, there is none worse than the race of athletes . . . In youth they strut about in splendor, the pride of their city, but when bitter old age comes upon them, they are cast aside like threadbare garments.

Xenophanes added these words about the athlete: "Yet he is not so worthy as I, and my wisdom is better than the strength of men and horse. Nay, this is a foolish custom, nor is it right to honor strength more than wisdom."

The historian Isocrates, whom I have quoted before, lucidly posed the problem, and he might well have written speeches which are given today.

> Many times, have I wondered at those who first convoked the national assemblies and established the athletic games, amazed that they should have thought the powers of men's bodies to be deserving of so great bounties, while to those who had toiled in private for the public good and trained their own minds so as to be able to help also their fellowmen, they apportioned no reward whatsoever, when in all reason they ought rather to have made provision for the latter, for if all the athletes would acquire twice the strength they

now possess, the rest of the world would not be better off, but let a single man attain to wisdom and all men will reap the benefit who are willing to share his insight.

Bribery Is Not New

The first case of bribery in Greek athletics was reported in 388 B.C. when one boxer bribed another to give the match away. Other instances followed. It took some time, but in a span of 100 years athletics had fallen into a corrupt and deplorable state, and the country had developed into an unathletic nation of spectators. The glory and value of athletics were dead.

All of this has a familiar ring. Neither the fascination with other athletics nor the problems which beset them are unique to the Greeks. Many other periods have become heavily involved with sports, which in some instances have entered into the very social fabric of the community. The British, for example, have an old and solid commitment to athletics. Indeed, among their most valuable exports in the eighteenth and nineteenth centuries were their athletic games and all that the idea of sports implied. This tradition is very much alive today. On July 17, 1956, at the Guildhall in London in the presence of Her Majesty the Queen, the Lord Mayor interrupted the city's reception for King Faisal of Iraq to announce the score in the cricket match with Australia. And in January 1957, there was widespread surprise, disappointment and anger that the famous football player, Stanley Matthews, had not been knighted. The *New Statesman* went so far as to say that Sir Anthony Eden would lose more votes over this than over the Suez Canal or petrol rationing. English athletics, of course, have their problems but their rather firm tradition of the amateurism has not yet been seriously eroded by the overlay of their immensely popular professional sports.

As for ourselves, massive involvement in athletics is an aspect of our culture. Our investments in facilities and manpower are astronomical at both the amateur and professional levels. Millions are engaged in some form of athletic recreation each week and millions more are spectators. Interschool and intercollege competitions are of consuming interest to large groups of people. The current group of heroes always includes a number of athletes. The professional games have grown enormously and promise great financial return. Professional football has even revolutionized family life on Sundays.

I would hesitate to assess the total picture in America. Others have tried and I refer you to them. A much narrower focus is the situation in the high schools and colleges, indeed in the handling of athletics and sports in any of our schools as part of the educational process. Here the debate has been intense and continues to be so.

Why Have Athletics?

The basic question, I suppose, is why we put up with physical training or athletics in any form in any of our schools or colleges. But I think this is primarily a rhetorical inquiry, for I doubt that any significant number of thinking people would advocate excising from the schools any and all forms of physical education and training. This is so for a number of reasons.

In the first place, athletic games are immense fun. Young people, given a little room, an opportunity and a minimum of intelligent supervision can easily have an exhilarating time. And this, I must confess, I consider to be a worthy end in itself, at least for children who live in a predominantly gray atmosphere of our great cities. Secondly, there is the matter of health and physical fitness, which are also seminal values and which need no further justification. Our gigantic health programs aimed at curing disease are perhaps limited only by the preventive measures which the young should learn at an early age, including as a primary matter the whole process of physical training and conditioning. The immediate and practical benefits of a strong and healthy body — and I am not talking here of those who make a fetish of their physiques — are very great indeed. There is a considerable difference between health on the one hand and strength and vigor on the other. I am sure you can count among your friends many who are perfectly healthy but not very energetic; who are seldom sick but tire easily; who don't seem to need a doctor but who do seem to need a rest, a nap or a coffee break; or who appear perfectly normal but wear out in the middle of that sustained, emergency effort which everyone of us has from time to time, whatever his line of work.

Appearance, demeanor and personality are equally basic considerations in pleasant and effective living and subject to measurable improvement by significant involvement by some form of vigorous athletic or recreational activity.

The Elusive Qualities

It is also said, and I am one of those who believe it, that our athletics afford one of the few opportunities for our youth to nourish and develop those important qualities of character which are absolutely essential to the great performances required of this Nation in the next few decades. Native ability plus formal education may be an inadequate formula to produce the excellence we so urgently require. We need those mysterious and elusive qualities of courage, determination, presence of mind, self-control and concentration upon a given task — these are the traits which we hope will be inevitably developed when the athlete is repeatedly confronted with situations demanding them and which he will carry with him to his other endeavors.

The late President Kennedy said all this in these well chosen words:

> . . . the physical vigor of our citizens is one of America's most precious resources . . . It is not only one of the most important keys to a healthy body; it is the basis of dynamic and creative intellectual activity. The relationship between the soundness of the body and the activities of the mind is subtle and complex. Much is not yet understood. But we do know what the Greeks knew; that intelligence and skill can only function at the peak of their capacity when the body is healthy and strong; that hardy spirits and tough minds usually inhabit sound bodies.
>
> In this sense, physical fitness is the basis of all the activities of our society. And if our bodies grow soft and inactive, if we fail to encourage physical development and prowess; we will undermine our capacity for thought, for work and for the use of those skills vital to an expanding and complex America.
>
> Thus, the physical fitness of our citizens is a vital prerequisite to America's realization of its full potential as a nation, and to the opportunity of each individual citizen to make full and fruitful use of his capacities.

But with all this undergirding for our athletic programs, there are troublesome areas left to consider. Of course, the schools should concern themselves with the body as well as the mind, for it is the schools who have the only really consistent access to our youth; and if room for recreation is not available in the schools, it will not be available at all. But all this may be admitted without accepting the validity of our existing athletic system. Perceptive critics argue that a physical fitness program can produce a strong and healthy youth without the elaborate overlay of competitive athletics on an interscholastic basis. The system of school against school, it is said, inevitably has unfortunate consequences for a truly comprehensive program: energy and effort are concentrated upon producing the school team; it is an exclusive system which leaves all but the chosen few sitting in the grandstands to cheer; the participants themselves are so pressured into peak performance and pushed to such limits that they neglect their minds and overtax their bodies, the very antithesis of a sound program. Moreover, if these unfortunate conditions exist in the high schools, it is said that the colleges are even worse, much worse.

To what extent these criticisms are true, you know better than I.

Certainly, in some schools and in some areas they have considerable validity. And wherever valid, they prove what history has taught before — that athletics carry the seeds of their own destruction and without sound direction the suicide will most surely occur.

Many Should Participate

No one can justify a school program which benefits only the few and neglects the many. No one can defend a system which discourages the many who cannot compete with the best and see no reason, therefore, to compete at all. No one can fairly close his eyes to those many young people who do not put athletic skill high on their priority list, but who urgently need and would enjoy athletic participation, given more inviting conditions. Is it really necessary for the schools to choose between the school team on the one hand, and no athletics and no physical fitness programs on the other?

The answer is clearly in the negative. There is no incompatibility between a broadly focused physical education program and the team sports. There is no necessity to discard either. On the contrary, there is ample justification for both. Such a program presents few problems that able management and direction cannot cure, particularly when it is tied to the schools, which have the responsibility of producing whole men and women who are stunted in neither mind nor body, who are neither mental nor physical cripples and who must be willing and able to face the rigors of the future.

This is familiar territory to all of you and to your organization. The basic criteria under which you operate reveal your awareness of these problems and of the goals for which you strive. Your handbook says that athletics are to be an integral part of the secondary school program; that athletics are for the benefit of all youths; that the aim is maximum participation in a well balanced intramural and interscholastic program with emphasis on safe and healthful standards of competition; and that your task is concerned primarily with extending benefits of athletics to all participants and to spreading these benefits to constantly increasing numbers.

There is, as I have said, no mystery about what your problems are; and your goals are reasonably clear. The difficulties lie more in day-to-day performance and in closing the gap between principle and practice, between theory and reality in everyday life. I have no illusions, and I am sure you don't either, about the difficulties which you consistently encounter in implementing admittedly sound ideas. Solving public problems in a democracy is not an easy task, nor should it be. It is a job for the patient and the hardy and a job that deserves doing, not for some impersonal notions about athletics, but for the generation of the young.

Many Talents Are Needed

There is not a shadow of a doubt these days as to our need for men and women of intellect, energy and character. Since its very beginning, this country, along with others, has been in constant change and flux. The rate of change has been steadily increasing and there is every indication that the trend will continue. Change in our country has ridden on an unfolding technology which has left nothing untouched, on a rapidly growing population and on a socio-economic system which has emphasized shared values. With rapid change has come a vast complexity and the imposition of almost an absolute demand for not only an adequate, but an extended education. Whatever the unemployment figures seem to indicate, there is today, and there will be, an almost inexhaustible demand for talent to manage the private business world, to man essential government positions and to devote itself to solving the critical problems swirling around our position in what we sometimes call the family of nations.

But this kind of talent must prove itself and this process of proof which goes on in our schools all across the land can be an unnerving thing to the average young person who has begun to think and ask questions about his future. There seems to be that rather awesome necessity to shape up and measure up, and the entrance requirements to any kind of meaningful life are constantly on the rise. Energy, brains, character and motivation seem basic ingredients for a successful formula.

Unquestionably, difficult demands are imposed on the young. But the rate of obsolescence of their elders is very high indeed and for the young who want it, there is almost unlimited opportunity in the challenges which lie ahead.

Herein, I suppose, lies the importance of organizations like yours, which are tied to the overall academic institution but are dedicated to producing those nonacademic consequences which bear so heavily on achievement and the way a young man makes his peace with the world.

Substantially, you are dealing with human nature in a specialized context. This, as was said by Dr. George Norlin, long-time president of the University of Colorado, is a very old problem. Using his words,

> Lo, all these centuries human nature remains unchanged . . . Perhaps we had better accept this unflattering fact and make the best of it. Perhaps the time will come when college students will hold pep meetings to stir the philosophy department to do or die or will root with enthusiasm when the department of chemistry discovers a

new element, but that time has not come nor will the Carnegie report on athletics (or others like it) bring it about in our day or our generation.

Human nature and athletics as Shelly said about another subject are "through time and change, unquenchably the same."

We have our particular problems in the judiciary, ladies and gentlemen, but your distinctive tasks involve the management of the young and their athletics. Fortunately, I can leave these tasks with you during the forthcoming week, and I wish you the very best of things.

57. Religious Issues

Sheldon Stoff

The Supreme Court ruling against Bible-reading and recitation of the Lord's Prayer in public schools as part of required classroom exercises should cause educators and laymen to evaluate the relationship between religion and the public schools. This Supreme Court ruling is not antireligious. It is consistent with the basic ideal of a separation of church and state so that both may flourish. It is consistent with past Supreme Court statements in the Zorach case:

> We are a religious people whose institutions presuppose a Supreme Being. We guarantee the freedom to worship as one chooses. We make room for as wide a variety of beliefs and creeds as the spiritual needs of man deem necessary. . . . Government may not finance religious groups nor undertake religious instruction nor

From Sheldon Stoff, "How Can the Public Schools Manage Religious Issues?" *The Clearing House,* January, 1964, 38: 271–274. Sheldon Stoff is Assistant Professor of Education, Queens College of The City University of New York. He has completed two works which are forthcoming, *Martin Buber on Education* and *The Two-way Street: Guideposts to Peaceful School Desegregation.* This article is reprinted by permission of *The Clearing House.*

blend secular and sectarian educators, nor use secular institutions to force one or some religion on any person.[1]

What then should be the role of the public school in the area of religion? It would be wishful thinking to believe that the issue is now clearly resolved. The religious influence in the schools is far deeper than simply Bible-reading and the recitation of the Lord's Prayer. Basic moral and educational implications must be dealt with.

In many parts of our nation the Christmas season is heralded by emotional controversies regarding certain practices in the public schools. Religious issues become the subjects of heated debate during a period of time in which thoughts of good will are supposed to dominate. For many decades this season of the year has brought forth decorations, trees, crosses, plays, hymns, and nativity scenes for the Christmas celebration in our public schools. This outward display of religious observance quickly brings forth cries for the separation of church and state, and for the public disestablishment of religious favoritism. The results are tears, suspicion, discord, and no concrete solution.

With or without conflict or controversy, the situation is not being properly managed. The Constitutional view is further classified by the Supreme Court in *Zorach vs Clauson:*

> The government must be neutral when it comes to competition between sects. It may not thrust any sect on any person. It may not make a religious observance compulsory. It may not coerce anyone to attend church, to observe a religious holiday, or to take religious instruction.[2]

The public schools, functioning with compulsory attendance laws in a pluralistic society, cannot justify any religious participation and ritual on public property. Religious services and celebrations should be conducted in the home, church, synagogue, or church-supported school. Religious observance should not enter into a pluralistic public forum supported by public funds.

On the other hand, such observances of Christmas celebration cannot often be completely removed from the schools without initiating strong public clamor. The public observance of Christmas has become firmly entrenched in much of our national culture, and many of the population expect its preservation.

A dilemma? Partially, but a third alternative does exist that should

[1] *Zorach vs Clauson,* 343 U. S. 306, 1952. Mr. Justice Douglas delivered the opinion of the Court.

[2] *Ibid.*

satisfy the majority, conform to the Constitution, safe-guard minorities, and strengthen the ability of the schools to perform a basic role of enriching and disseminating the culture and enabling the student to grow, mature, and broaden his horizons. Justice Douglas' statement that "We are a religious people" is completely supported by the U.S. Census (95 per cent of those polled classified themselves into one of our three major religious groupings),[3] by the *Catholic Digest* (95 per cent of those interviewed stated that religion was either very important or of medium importance to them),[4] and by statements by every President of the United States (as detailed by James Keller in *All God's Children*).[5] This religious facet of our lives cannot be ignored without distorting the world culture as it is presented in our schools. It is equally important to remember that it is not the function of the schools to indoctrinate religious dogma. We are historically a nation of many backgrounds and beliefs and we have thrived on this principle. The rights of the religious and the nonreligious should be respected.

> The school cannot and should not try to decide whether the religious need has an answer and, if it does, which one it must be. The school is only obliged, if it would inform its students, to remind them that men have made and lived out a variety of answers. . . .
>
> No man can be regarded as informed, awakened, and free unless he has learned as much as he can about himself and about the examples of others like him in history. No man can call himself educated unless he knows what his religious potentialities are, no matter how unreal, foolish or otherwise objectionable he judges them.[6]

This statement by Professor Harper can be practically applied to our public school situation by assigning the education for a particular religious orientation to the home or church and encouraging the schools to perform the function which neither is performing. I am referring to teaching comparative religion in a specialized course of study. Through this democratic approach, in keeping with our nation's pluralistic and cultural heritages, the school would open students to a broader under-

[3] U. S. Bureau of the Census, *Current Population Reports,* Series No. 79 (Washington: Government Printing Office, 1958), p. 20.

[4] B. Gaffin and Associates, "Who Belongs to What Church," in *The Catholic Digest* (January, 1953), p. 5.

[5] James Keller, *All God's Children* (Garden City, New York: Hanover House, 1953), p. 237.

[6] Ralph Harper, "Significance of Existence and Recognition for Education," in *Modern Philosophies and Education,* N. Henry, Ed. (Chicago, Illinois: The National Society for the Study of Education, 1955), p. 248.

standing of life rather than indoctrinate them with specific religious dogma or even force them into a general religious orientation.

The program presented here, to manage the controversy over religious practices in public education, is both practical and educational. It was developed after communication with religious leaders from each of the six religions concerned. A sincere effort was made to meet their recommendations and also meet the general goals many desire for public education.[7] In the development of the program it was desirable to set goals which were compatible with the basic aims of the schools and the nation's Constitution. The goals are these:

1. A greater understanding of other people by the student.
2. A more mature development of the student.
   a. An enriching process for the student because of the broad spectrum of ideas explored.
   b. A more significant insight by the student into his own life, which could lead to a deeper character development.

The basic program is divided into two areas. The first (part A) could be adopted by the schools immediately. It involves no great expense and would help resolve the pressing issues which have gained the most notoriety. The implementation of the second (part B) involves the teacher training institutions' cooperating with the schools in an attempt to meet their responsibilities in this vital area.

Part A — Immediate Action

The proposals in this phase center on the celebrations of religious holidays in the schools. Christmas is the most notable example. In our society, the schools cannot defend holding religious celebrations on public property. For the most part, Christmas observance cannot be eliminated from the schools without causing considerable public clamor. This total separation should not be attempted. Instead of promoting a religious view by one religious celebration, the schools should seriously consider the several major religious holy days of the world's great religions as resources for the dissemination of knowledge and understanding. The dogma, the ritual, the affirmation is to be avoided; the educational message is to be promoted.

The question which most quickly comes to mind is: "How do you accomplish this education without indoctrination?"

At this preliminary stage in the program I would suggest that a qualified social studies teacher make the presentation to a general assembly or lead a panel discussion in which the "why" of the holy day

[7] Approval on the part of these religious leaders for this program is not here suggested or rejected.

should be considered. As material becomes more available in the future, dramas could be added to this type of presentation.[8]

We need not have ritual at Christmas in the public schools, but the message inherent in Christmas can be explored. The holy days of Hinduism, Judaism, Buddhism, and Islam could be explained and "respected" in their turns. If the emphasis is placed on promoting broad knowledge and understanding instead of narrow ritual, even the atheist cannot be offended.

A brief understanding of the world's religions is made possible without favoritism, by overcoming existing provincialism. The views of other local religions which are not already represented by the aforementioned should also be considered.

The schools would then have the power to outgrow localism. They could continue to fulfill their basic responsibility — education — in the full knowledge that people must learn to live with, and respect, their neighbors.

Part B — The Long-Term Solution

The proposal in this part centers on the role of the school. It is the job of the school and all structures of society to disseminate and enforce that which is beneficial in the culture. The school has responsibilities in the area of knowledge about religion that no other agency can render as well. In outgrowing a concentration on local practices, beliefs, and attitudes, the schools have deep obligations to meet.

I. *Course Content.* This proposal advocates that a specific course dealing with the religions of mankind be taught in the social studies area of our senior high schools. It would be taught by a specifically trained teacher. The prime content of the course would be concerned with the study of six major religions: Islam, Buddhism, Catholicism, Judaism, Protestantism, and Hinduism. In areas where other religions are present, they would also be explored.

The study of these religions should concern itself with:

[8] Some sources of material are:

The National Conference of Christians and Jews, Inc., 43 West 57th Street, New York 19, New York.

Buddhism: Dr. Kurt F. Leiderker, 306 Caroline Street, Fredericksburg, Virginia; Washington Friends of Buddhism, Washington, D.C.

Islam: The Islamic Foundation of New York, One Riverside Drive, New York 23, New York; Diyanet Isleri Reisilgi, Ankara, Turkey.

Hinduism: Ramakrishna-Vivekananda Society, 17 East 94th Street, New York, New York; Vedanta Society, 34 West 71st Street, New York, New York.

For Buddhism, Catholicism, Protestantism, Hinduism, Islam, Judaism: *Great Religions of Modern Man* (6 volumes), published by George Braziller, New York.

A. History and leaders
B. Ethics
C. Rituals and customs
D. Present application

The material for each of the religions under discussion should be provided by or acceptable to the individual religions.

II. *Religious Practices.* No religious practices would enter into the curriculum. No religious dogmas would be inculcated. This course could develop a broad area of enlightenment and understanding. No one religion would be favored. No expression of faith would be asked of the student. There would be no worship or ritual. The separation of church and state would be maintained as constitutionally intended.

III. *Role of the Teacher.* The teacher would be sympathetic to each religion as it was studied. He would help his students gain a knowledge and appreciation of each. In the classroom he would not be a partisan supporter of any individual faith.

IV. *Teacher Training.* The teacher should be specifically trained for this task. His training would be in the area of social studies, with a major concentration in the area of comparative religion. Specific knowledge of each of the religions would be included in this training program. The program offered by the Department of Religious Education of New York University could well provide a guide in this area.

Conclusion

The above proposal is both practical and far reaching. Interested persons could well take immediate steps toward action. Part A needs no elaborate preparation. Part B would require strong support in order to be executed. This program would help fill a void in present public school curricula. It is designed to present six of the world's great religions as a part of the total world's culture. Some will view this proposal as a program charged with risks. Most certainly some risk is involved. Most steps forward require daring, but the greatest risks are those of inaction. Ignorance should not be preferred to an honest, careful attempt at understanding.

The Supreme Court decision of June 17, 1963, may yet awaken educators and the general public to this serious void existing in much of the American education system.

58. The Band

Lloyd Schmidt

Pendulums swing quickly in current educational thought, and once again, as Howard Hanson ably pointed out in a recent issue of this magazine, music educators appear to have re-discovered their common element — music itself.

In evaluating the role of the band in this revival of emphasis on the *musical* values, it is easy to understand the strong suspicions on the part of educators concerning the band's function in music education. Many aspects of the school music program have long been educationally embarrassing and the time has come when they must be challenged. What is needed, however, is not merely an airing of views, but a consideration of aims generally, and a review of the role that the various facets of the total program may play in the fulfillment of those aims. The band program needs no apology for hundreds of hard-working and dedicated music educators, yet its unique values may be least understood by those who champion it so actively.

The goals of music education have been stated often; the purpose here will be to develop one view of those goals and to establish the validity of the band program in the fulfillment of those goals. The fundamental concepts of music education as listed in the more recent publications of the MENC and other organizations (most recently in *The Music Curriculum in the Secondary School*, MENC 1959) substantiate earlier goals and principles formulated by educational groups. These emphasize the appreciation of music as an art force through direct experience involving quality music literature. This emphasis on music as an art of sound, again echoing Mr. Hanson, points up the simple truth that the function

From Lloyd Schmidt, "The Role of the Band in Music Education," *Music Educators Journal*, February–March, 1961, 81–83, Vol. 47. Lloyd Schmidt is the Music Consultant for the Connecticut State Department of Education, Hartford. He has published a number of articles centering on specific content and activities in instrumental music. This article is reprinted by permission of the author and of the Music Educators National Conference.

of music is musical; the function of music education must be in terms of musical experience; skills in performance, though important, are therefore primarily means and are only secondary as ends.

Once this point of view is accepted, music education is no longer basically concerned with producing musicians for professional groups, symphonic or otherwise (although ability to perform in after-school years is high on any list of objectives); there is, instead, an artistic objective in appreciation gained through an *aural* vocabulary. In these terms, quality becomes an important factor. There is a parallel in written literature which cannot be experienced with a vocabulary of one syllable words and one syllable experiences. Further, as emphasized by Howard Hanson: "As musicians we are all, I am sure, convinced that the greatest contribution which the arts can make comes through personal involvement, through personal particiption. We all know this so well that it is unnecessary to labor the point. No amount of listening, no courses in music appreciation, theory or history, can ever take the place of this kind of experience."[1]

This is basic to current American school music practice. It may be carried further; performance *is* musical experience in this sense of involvement. A good listening lesson will produce a roomful of youngsters who are thrilled by a phonograph presentation because somehow the wizardry of the teacher has broken sound barriers, and the aural and intellectual attention of the students is real. But how difficult this is to achieve!

Singing groups and instrumental groups also seek this musical experience. Through the process of making music, every student of a performing group *necessarily* gives physical evidence of the musical experience, which in most cases far exceeds the individual's ability to achieve by himself. The total program does provide listening and similar experiences for the nonperformer, but the same goal is reached directly (in a most practical manner for young people) through participation in performing ensembles. The vocabulary of aural experience encompasses rhythm, harmony, tone color, melody, and the thematic processes — in short, the very substance of music. At its best, a rehearsal becomes a laboratory for the study of the arts of sound.

What has this to do with band? Band has little place in the world of the finest concert halls. On the surface, this common challenge to the band seems to be a real indictment; however, the band can lead to loftier goals in unique fashion. Herein lies its real value.

Band shares with orchestra and chorus the elemental *musical* experi-

[1] Hanson, Howard. "Music Education Faces the Scientific Age." *Music Educators Journal,* June–July 1959. p. 19.

ence; all of these groups offer perfect classroom situations wherein all students recite constantly with the finest of motivation; each student experiences music at his own individual level in a group which appeals to social feelings and to adolescent urges for activity. All of these groups develop skills which enlarge the aural vocabulary, the very warp and woof of music itself. The process in no way hinders the development of skills for future personal use, but vitalizes them, giving full measure of personal satisfaction and achievement in the musical arts. All this takes place in a practical school situation open to all in large numbers.

It can be seen that the band represents an ideal group for these musical experiences. Holding a semipopular position musically, the band attracts large numbers of participants and is in good position to guide many, who would otherwise be missed, to better musical experiences. The amazingly quick results of band education have proved to be lasting, and a very high level of achievement in music itself can be expected from such a group. Strange as it may seem, in spite of the superiority of the professional orchestral and chamber literature, the band usually attains a more superior level in technical and musical performance than does the average high school orchestra we are producing in these days.

Few works of the standard literature reach the high school orchestra. This by no means intends to belittle the splendid work evident in many school orchestras, and by no means does it imply that the situation should remain as it is. To visualize potentials one need only remember the well-deserved standing ovation received by the New York All State Orchestra conducted by Frederick Fennell after an almost unbelievable performance of the Stravinsky *Firebird Suite* at the 1959 MENC Eastern Division meeting in Buffalo.

In actuality, the band is far from its origins in the park band-stand and street parade. Its musical accomplishments now gain increasing interest in musical and university circles, and a great bulk of good, original literature, as well as innumerable quality transcriptions, serve to give experience in all styles, developing a musical vocabulary which includes the most complex of modern textures. As a training device for music education, the band can hardly be equalled.

That uniforms, parades, and football have little to do with the above picture must be readily admitted. Efforts to call the football band a new art form can only appear ridiculous. However, many non-musical elements may produce values not immediately apparent. Uniforms, majorettes, and the "frills" generally catch the adolescent eye; such "nonsense" has caught many a youngster unawares and has led him to a meaningful musical situation. Pride, service, self-discipline, and real social values may not be musical values, but they have not as yet surrendered to the new scientific age. Many a critic of such "frills" could do well to see to his own public relations and weigh the good in musical as well as in social values that results from such "nonsense."

The real educator will see to it, of course, that the tail does not wag the dog. This is his job. Such wagging is not inevitable. The problem is squarely one for the conscience and ability of individual teachers and administrators rather than one due to any intrinsic weaknesses of the band program itself.

Parents need no justification for these things; they understand the values in terms of their children. The strongest band supporters, as parents or citizens, are the former band members who know band values from experience. These values are not calculated; they are simple, strong, fundamental, and clear. Others, as Mr. Hanson suggests may defend marching and majorettes, but may it be said here, the band itself does the job in attaining the goals of education.

59. Why Driver Education?

Howard R. DeNike

In all fairness, let's look at both sides of the coin.

Ever since the first orbit of the first Sputnik we have seen considerable pressures — occasionally taking the form of near-frantic crash programs — to revise the curriculums of our high schools and colleges. Driver education, along with a number of other so-called "non-academic" courses, has taken a beating.

From Howard R. DeNike, "Why Driver Education?" *Safety Education,* November, 1962, 23–25, Vol. 42. Howard R. DeNike is Associate Professor in the Department of Health and Physical Education and Director of Intramural Sports at the State College, East Stroudsburg, Pennsylvania. He has written extensively on various topics in health and safety education for professional journals and has been a contributing author to several textbooks in safety education and driver education. Reprinted by permission of the National Safety Council, Chicago.

Recent newspaper and magazine articles seem to be renewing the attack. Claiming that it is an expensive, virtually ineffective, academic "frill," they loudly clamor for the elimination of driver education from the curriculum.

Now let's flip the coin and look at the other side of their arguments. Let's look at the facts:

Is It a Fad?

During the past 30 years, driver education has shown a strong and steady growth in our nation's schools. In the last 10 years alone, the number of students enrolled in standard driver education courses has leaped from 335,000 in 1952 to more than one million this year. The number of high schools offering the recommended course rose 66 per cent, from 6,000 to 10,000, in the same period.

It is a firmly established school subject. In the last school year, more than half of the American students eligible to study driver education were taking a course in it.

Driver education has received the rousing endorsement of leading police officials, state authorities, insurance companies, parents' organizations, school administrators, and Presidents Hoover, Truman, Eisenhower, and Kennedy. It has been introduced into the curriculums of many European schools — including some in Russia, a country supposedly not given to adopting worthless educational fads.

Is It Worth The Money?

A research report on driver education in this country for the past two decades, prepared by Earl Allgaier of the American Automobile Association, has just been released. He states that more than six million high school students have completed classroom-practice driving courses at a cost (including teachers' salaries, texts and materials, auto operation costs, and incidentals) of between \$34–\$44 per student. That's less than is usually charged by garages for the repair of a damaged fender.

Allgaier also reports that, in terms of accidents prevented, the past 24 years of driver education have averted an economic loss of \$697 million, or \$113 per student trained. This means that for every one dollar invested by the schools, about three dollars have been saved in economic costs of the accidents prevented. More important, Allgaier estimates that 5,570 lives have been saved, and nearly 200,000 injuries prevented as the result of driver education programs in our schools.

Does It Make Better Drivers?

American drivers are probably even worse than you think. Several years ago, some 10,800 licensed drivers (about 75 per cent of them teenagers) were given actual road checks in a survey conducted by Pennsylvania State University and the Atlantic Refining Company. The survey, which was made by thoroughly trained and experienced personnel, involved more than 50,000 miles of travel — approximately five miles for each driver checked.

It revealed some interesting items. A total of 143,696 driving errors were noted — an average of 13 per motorist. That's equivalent to an error committed for each 0.4 miles of travel. If this is typical of all drivers, it means that a person who drives 10,000 miles per year will commit about 25,000 driving errors annually!

A more recent Pennsylvania study made some specific comparisons of driving records. It involved 7,200 subjects, half were formally trained in driver education, half were not. The groups were matched according to age, sex, and years of driving experience. The conclusions reached clearly indicate that driver education has served a worthwhile purpose in the secondary schools of Pennsylvania. For the academically trained drivers, the number of suspensions and arrests, and the number of accidents for which the motorist was responsible was *far below* that of the untrained group.

We have had many other carefully conducted research surveys which measure the efficacy of driver education programs. After reviewing 26 of these studies, the National Commission on Safety Education formed the following generalizations:

Driver education course graduates have fewer accidents and violations than drivers with no formal training.

Trained males seem to show a superiority in performance of from 30–50 per cent during the initial period of driving.

There is strong evidence to show that drivers who completed a course in classroom and practice driving were better than those who completed only the classroom phase of instruction.

It appears that the salutary effect of driver education is most evident in the early stages of driving.

Is It An "Academic" Pursuit?

In my opinion, the materials of instruction, teaching methods, testing and evaluation procedures of a good course in driver education compare very favorably with *any* of the so-called "academic" subjects.

Teacher preparation courses for driver education instructors have come a long way in a short time. At present, a fairly large number of colleges and universities are offering driver education courses at the undergraduate and graduate levels (see *SE*, May, 1962). Among the various states, the trend has been to continually raise the teacher certification requirements.

The standard driver education course consists of 30 hours of classroom work, and at least six hours of behind-the-wheel training. To teach it, we have at our disposal a number of excellent modern textbooks, work books, manuals, standardized tests, audio-visual aids of all kinds, and even some fine laboratory psycho-physical testing and teaching equipment. The driving simulators provide us with a most valuable — and relatively inexpensive — teaching machine. Certainly, we have all the accoutrements of an "academic" course.

As a matter of fact, driver education reaches out to a number of the solidly "academic" subjects — to physics, science, mathematics, chemistry, biology, economics, history, and others.

You have only to look at the units of instruction ordinarily taught in the driver education classroom to see the relationship to other courses in the curriculum. Here are some sample topics: Socio-economic impact of the automobile upon American life; Driving as a privilege; Laws of nature and of man; How the car runs, and how to maintain it properly and economically; Fitness of the driver and his car, and how to measure them; Safe use of the eyes; Reaction and reflex time; Effects of alcohol and drugs; Psychology of the driver; Engineering modern roads and highways.

If the above aren't academic studies, I wonder what else to call them.

Does It Produce The "Best" Drivers?

Who are the *best* drivers anyway? In a recent research project, Columbia University defined them as the motorists with the best actual driving records. Nine thousand of these "best" drivers were studied by trained traffic experts, doctors, and psychologists.

Some of their findings appear below. As you read down the list of traits of these "best" drivers, I think you will agree that many of their behaviors are the kind of thing we try to engender in driver education courses.

These drivers all exhibited a marked degree of courtesy, caution and care.

They always signaled their intentions.

They drove smoothly and steadily, showing a light touch on the accelerator and brakes.

They used good timing when passing other vehicles and when selecting lanes.

They used their eyes efficiently and effectively, moving them about to increase side vision and take in the picture of the whole road. They made certain that other drivers saw them, and were careful always to "leave an out" in case of an emergency.

They were concerned with the control of their cars and the ease and comfort of their passengers.

As a group, they were found to be definitely above average in their knowledge of the elements of safe driving, and of the vehicle and its maintenance.

Why Driver Education?

The facts are clear; the conclusions seem obvious. Driver education is neither fad nor frill, it is a well established course of study, as worthy of the label "academic" as any other.

When measured against the economic loss of potential accidents prevented, the cost of driver education becomes small. When measured in terms of human lives saved, it becomes infinitesimal.

The driver education course aims at producing the best drivers possible. In fact, it has been proven that driver education produces motorists who are better drivers than the average.

The course is a necessary and worthwhile part of the curriculum. Why driver education? Because we need it.

60. Psychology

Ann F. Lucas

Whether psychology should be taught at the precollege level has become little more than an academic question among psychologists.

From Ann F. Lucas, "A Guide to Upgrade the High School Psychology Course," *The Clearing House,* May, 1963, 37: 523–528. Ann F. Lucas is Associate Professor of Psychology, Fairleigh Dickinson University, Teaneck, New Jersey, and Director of the Montessori Teacher Training Program at that institution. She has had extensive experience as a consultant and clinical psychologist in hospitals and guidance centers in New York and New Jersey. This article is reprinted by permission of *The Clearing House.*

On the basis of a questionnaire survey done in 1960 (7), it was reported that psychology has been in the secondary curriculum by title since 1895 and at present is being taught in all but seven of the 50 states.

The questionnaires, completed by superintendents, principals, and high school teachers of psychology, revealed other interesting facts: Psychology seems to be a popular course. Once introduced into the curriculum, it not only stays, but class enrollment usually increases. In those high schools where psychology is not being taught, the reasons given were: (*a*) an already crowded curriculum, (*b*) a lack of trained teachers, and (*c*) the trend toward more intense development of science.

The first two reasons are true enough, but the last seems rather ironic since psychology is an important behavioral science, a science by virtue of its emphasis on gathering data through carefully planned experiments and observations, and the rigorous use of controls, in order to arrive at a systematized body of knowledge.

Psychologists, then, are no longer debating about whether psychology should be included in the secondary curriculum, since this seems to be an accomplished fact. There is, instead, an increasing interest in offering assistance to high school teachers of psychology who are often cut off from the mainstream of professional psychology. Since the psychology instructor at the precollege level seldom has the doctorate which would be required for membership in the American Psychological Association, he often functions with limited contacts in the field of psychology and with little access to the psychological journals.

This article concerns itself with: (*a*) suggestions by psychologists on the objectives of high school psychology courses, (*b*) the wide variety of materials which are being made available for use in the classroom, and (*c*) some of the attempts being made to keep secondary teachers in contact with current major developments in the field of psychology.

The Nature and Purpose of a High School Psychology Course

In organizing the material for any course, an instructor usually tries first to establish clear-cut objectives around which a well-integrated course may be built. What are the long-range goals of a high school psychology course? Three major objectives (6) have been suggested: (*a*) the development of a more nearly accurate image of psychology by presenting it as a science, (*b*) advising youth of career opportunities in the profession of psychology, and (*c*) the development of a better informed public.

Presenting Psychology as a Science. With respect to the first course objective, there is wide agreement among psychologists that regardless of whether psychology is taught as a scientific course with heavy emphasis on the biological, or as a social studies course with emphasis on good emotional adjustment, the scientific nature of the course should be stressed. (6, 10) This may be accomplished in discussion by contrasting (*a*) the organization of knowledge through experimentation, surveys, and measurement, with (*b*) drawing conclusions which are based on reasoning alone or simply on opinion. But students will undoubtedly have a better understanding of the empirical approach if they are permitted to participate in experiments.

High school teachers may be handicapped by lack of a budget for psychological apparatus. The trend, however, is changing. A survey conducted in 1954 on teaching methods used by psychology instructors in the secondary schools (14) revealed that about one-third of 217 teachers who responded had some experiments performed by all members of their class and about 40 percent used experiments as classroom demonstrations.

Several psychologists, encouraged by the American Psychological Association, have been collecting information on experiments which can be performed by high school students.

One of the most productive people in this field is Dr. Snellgrove (18). He has mimeographed material which is available at a nominal charge on: (*a*) the construction and use of inexpensive psychological apparatuses, (*b*) an annotated bibliography on companies having psychological apparatuses, and (*c*) a collection of short paper-and-pencil psychological experiments.

Another good source of information is a book written by Bugelski (1). It includes a discussion of laboratory equipment which can be secured or easily made for this level student.

Have you thought of using psychology demonstrations in your science fair? Not too many projects in psychology are set up for science fairs. Yet this is an effective way of helping large numbers of high school students to appreciate the scientific nature of psychology. Some excellent books (2, 3) and an article (8) have been written for high school students who are interested in scientific research and who might be contemplating the preparation of a project of a psychological nature for a science fair.

To recapitulate: Discussion of the scientific method used in psychology, demonstrations of it, student participation in experiments, and psychological projects at science fairs will help accomplish the objective of presenting psychology as a science.

But a word might be added on the role of examinations in fulfilling this course objective. Examinations can be tailored to emphasize the falsity of: "Psychology is nothing more than common sense" (12).

Carefully constructed multiple choice items or essay questions that tap factual information help students realize that psychology is not a subject which relies on opinions.

Career Opportunities in Psychology. The United States Department of Labor (20) has estimated that the number of individuals in the profession of psychology tripled between 1945 and 1955 and has since grown by 1,500 annually. "Employment of psychologists is expected to grow substantially during the 1960's," the Bureau of Labor Statistics (20) predicts. Talented youth can find tremendous diversification in this rapidly growing profession which is spreading into so many new fields. A greater number of psychologists will be employed both in student personnel work and in teaching at the college level. Federal, state, and local government agencies will hire more psychologists. Within the federal government, psychologists will be needed in the Veterans Administration, in the Public Health Service, and as commissioned officers in the Armed Forces. More will be needed in the elementary and secondary schools, in private industry, and in nonprofit foundations, hospitals, and clinics. Of the estimated 24,000 psychologists professionally employed in 1959, one-fourth were women. This profession, which often has appeal for women, is one where opportunities for them are many and varied.

Helping high school youth to be aware of the many possibilities for them within the field of psychology is accomplishing the second major objective of the course. Someone from a nearby university may be invited to the school to speak on career opportunities in the field. Or an instructor could use some of the very fine material on "Career Conferences in Psychology," which has been prepared by the Illinois State Psychological Association (17) to help make high school students aware of the wide range of possibilities open to them.

Development of a Better Informed Public. A large number of high school students never go on to college. For many who are taking a course in psychology in high school, this may be their only opportunity to develop an informed opinion about the field. With varying degrees of success, authors of elementary psychology textbooks attempt to inform readers about the field of psychology and to clear up common misconceptions. To cite a few examples: Students are helped to understand that seeking professional help when life's conflicts are overwhelming is a wise decision, not a sign of weakness; mental illness is nothing to be ashamed of and, in most cases, is curable; psychology is not "just common sense."

Instructors, however, have an opportunity to accomplish what cannot be done in a textbook. As erroneous ideas are expressed in a class discussion, they can be cleared up immediately by an alert teacher; otherwise, distortions about the field of psychology may persist as an individual goes through life. Thus, the third major objective of a high school psychology course will be fulfilled by the teacher who keeps in mind the long-range value of a student's having the proper understanding of psychology.

Hazards of Field Trips and Class Discussions

Although preparing students to be better informed adults is one of the major goals of a high school psychology course, there are some dangers which must be avoided. In particular, the use of field trips to acquaint students with the problem of mental illness might be mentioned.

About two-fifths (14) of high school psychology teachers have used visits to various institutions to help their students become better informed about community problems. The type of institution most frequently visited is the mental hospital. While such trips often present information in a more vivid fashion than does a classroom lecture, there are certain hazards involved.

Even when they are carefully prepared, sensitive students are often quite disturbed by their visits to mental institutions. Students frequently leave a mental hospital with the impression that patients with emotional difficulties are quite different from normal individuals. Students may have reinforced for them the idea that emotional illness is a stigma, something frightening and incomprehensible, something about which to be ashamed. Yet, these are the very misconceptions which should be dispelled by an understanding of psychology.

Conservative estimates are that one in ten people born today will experience mental illness some time during his life. Many students will some day have to face the problem of mental illness in their own families. Seeing crowded state mental hospitals may make students aware of the need to allocate more tax money so that the institution can function more effectively, but one also takes the risk that as adults, they will be less apt to take a member of their family for treatment because of what they have observed in mental institutions.

There is another related problem for the instructor of high school psychology classes. Students in any psychology course tend to relate what they learn about human behavior to themselves. When they learn about emotional maladjustment, they sometimes begin to fear for their own stability. It is difficult, yet necessary, that teachers discourage students from talking about their own personal problems in class discussions. Students will sometimes bring up experiences in a classroom which would be more appropriate for the psychologist or psychiatrist's office. Their classmates are usually not the best ones to tell them how to handle situations which they may only partially understand. So unless the instructor is also a trained psychotherapist, such problems might better be left undisclosed.

Textbooks, Reading Materials, and Supplementary Aids

The choice of textbook and other teaching aids is sometimes a problem for the high school teacher. He may be much more familiar with the material available in his major field. Several very good psychology books have been written especially for high school students. The titles of two of the better, more recent texts (13, 19) have been included in the bibliography. Only those textbooks having the word psychology in the title were considered.

The assignment of supplementary readings presents another quandary for the teacher of psychology at the secondary level. Most high schools are necessarily more interested in building libraries around the required major fields. Local libraries are also fairly limited in the number and quality of psychology books which they have. As a result, a large number of teachers assign "psychological" articles in popular magazines which are of questionable value.

High school students of psychology often write to state psychological associations or to universities asking for information because there are so few books available to them where they can obtain the answers to their questions.

In order to satisfy this need, Dr. Coffield (4), while chairman of the Committee on Psychology in the Secondary Schools for the American Psychological Association, compiled an excellent bibliography for high school teachers and students. Included is a variety of paperbacks so that an excellent psychology library can be secured at low cost. Also listed in his bibliography are two sources of tape recordings on psychology and guidance, a number of which may be re-recorded at a nominal fee for the use of secondary schools and colleges. The second part of Coffield's bibliography includes published studies in the area of high school psychology with the hope of stimulating investigations by such teachers as are now conducting classes in high school psychology. Dr. Elder (9), in an attempt to satisfy the requests he has been receiving at the State College of Washington, has made up a "kit" of nine books which are available for $10. Selection of books was based on: (*a*) numerous inquiries from students about some material for term reports, and (*b*) the judgment of approximately 50 psychologists as to the type of material which would be most beneficial.

Audio-visual aids are also frequently used with some effectiveness in high school psychology classes. In 1956, the films found to be used most often (14) were: Emotional Health, Feelings of Hostility, Feelings of Rejection, Angry Boy, and Shy Guy. Other good recent films may be available free of charge through your state department of education.

Qualifications of High School Teachers of Psychology

High school teachers of psychology have had on the average only eight or nine undergraduate hours of psychology, excluding educational psychology (11). Compare this with the background of the high school instructor who is teaching in an area in which he has had 30 hours of undergraduate work, and sometimes additional graduate credits. Plainly, by accepted measurements, high school psychology teachers are not well trained to teach psychology. On the positive side, however, is the fact that those who are teaching psychology tend to be the more experienced instructors. It was found (16) that almost three-quarters of the psychology teachers had had more than five years of teaching experience.

In 1959 a questionnaire (11) was sent to all of the psychologists in Division 2 (representing college and university teachers) of the American Psychological Association to ask their opinion on the training and qualifications of high school teachers of psychology. According to 100 psychologists who cooperated in the survey, the average number of hours to be considered a *minimum* of preparation for psychology teachers at the secondary level was 27. When the same group of 100 psychologists was asked about the number of hours thought to be *desirable* as preparation, the average was 43 hours of psychology. Obviously, the difference between what psychologists felt should be the minimum or the desirable preparation for teaching psychology on the secondary level, and the actual average preparation of high school teachers of psychology is quite different.

For those who are teaching psychology and wish better to qualify themselves, the next part of the survey will be of interest. Psychologists were asked to rank a number of courses in terms of their importance for the high school teacher of psychology. In terms of specific preparation, the psychology courses listed in their ranked order of importance were: general introductory, experimental, tests and measures, statistics, personal adjustment, adolescence, social, personality, educational, learning, abnormal, and history of psychology.

This year the National Science Foundation is sponsoring a summer institute in psychology being prepared by Dr. Graham Bell at Claremont College, Claremont, California. This is an intensive six-week course in statistics, testing, research design, and adolescent psychology for high school and junior high school teachers of psychology, biology, and social sciences. Tuition is waived for students who are accepted. In addition, stipends of up to $75 a week, an allowance for dependents, and travel allowances are provided. Although the February 15 deadline makes it too late to apply for admission to such a program this year, there is a good possibility that similar programs will be offered in the future better to prepare the high school psychology teacher.

Closer Relationship Between Psychology and Secondary Schools

The American Psychological Association has continually encouraged the state psychological associations and the state universities to do more to aid the high school teachers of psychology. For instance, the psychology teachers at the precollege level need a journal of their own, a link between secondary school personnel and the national and state organizations of psychology.

Much of the source material mentioned in this article was developed by psychologists who are especially interested in making information of all kinds available for high school psychology teachers.

A mailing list (5) has been compiled of persons in secondary schools, in colleges and universities, and in state psychological associations who are interested in the teaching of psychology in high school. They are listed by states. Additional names may be sent to Dr. Kenneth Coffield, Department of Psychology, University of Missouri, Columbia, Missouri, looking toward a more comprehensive future list. Copies of the present list may also be obtained from him.

In the 1962 business meeting of Division 2 (teaching) of the American Psychological Association, a motion was passed to provide for a class of divisional affiliates to include teachers of psychology in high schools (contingent on revision of the bylaws by the membership). This could be another important step on the part of psychologists to provide for a better *rapprochement* with high school teachers of psychology. Your suggestions on what psychological associations can do to help you would be welcomed!

REFERENCES

(1) Bugelski, B. R. *A First Course in Experimental Psychology.* New York: Henry Holt and Co., Inc., 1951.

(2) Candland, D. K., and Campbell, J. F. *Exploring Behavior.* New York: Basic Books, Inc., October, 1961.

(3) Candland, D. K., and Campbell, J. F. *Psychology: a Guide to Research.* New York: Basic Books, Inc., September, 1961.

(4) Coffield, K. E., Chairman. Committee on High School Psychology of Division 2 of the American Psychological Association. "Bibliography for High School

Psychology Teachers and Students." Unpublished material. (Available from: Dr. Kenneth E. Coffield, Chairman, Department of Psychology, University of Missouri, Columbia, Missouri.)

(5) Coffield, K. E.; Engle, T. L.; McNeely, P.; Milton, O.; and Campbell, J. "Mailing List for High School Psychology." Unpublished material. (Available from: Dr. Kenneth E. Coffield, Chairman, Department of Psychology, University of Missouri, Columbia, Missouri.)

(6) Coffield, K. E. "The Role and Responsibility of High School Psychology." Unpublished material. Presented at the American Psychological Association convention, 1961.

(7) Coffield, K. E., and Engle, T. L. "High School Psychology: a History and Some Observations." *American Psychologist,* 15: 350–352 (June, 1960).

(8) Darley, J. G. "Use Psychology in Your Science Fair." *Current Science,* 46: 59–61 (October 31, 1960). (Weekly science newspaper published by American Education Publications for Wesleyan University.)

(9) Elder, J. H. "Collateral Reading List for High School Courses in Psychology, Biology, or Social Science." Unpublished material. (Available from: Dr. J. H. Elder, Chairman, Department of Psychology, State College of Washington, Pullman, Washington.)

(10) Elder, J. H. "Potential Relationships of State Associations and High Schools, Symposium No. IV." Unpublished material. Presented at the American Psychological Association convention, 1962.

(11) Engle, T. L. "Preparation for Teaching Psychology in High School." *American Psychologist,* 15: 353–5. (June, 1960).

(12) Engle, T. L. "Psychology as a High School Science," *Science Teacher,* 22: 235–7 (October, 1955).

(13) Engle, T. L. *Psychology: Its Principles and Applications* (3d ed.). New York: Harcourt, Brace, and World, Inc., 1957.

(14) Engle, T. L. "Teaching Psychology in High Schools," *Social Education,* 19: 346–8 (December, 1955).

(15) Engle, T. L. "The Training and Experience of High School Teachers of Psychology." *Educational Administration and Supervision,* 38: 91–6 (February, 1952).

(16) Engle, T. L., and Bunch, M. E. "The Teaching of Psychology in High School." *American Psychologist,* 11: 188–193 (April, 1956).

(17) Jones, D. R., Chairman. Standards and Training Committee of the Illinois Psychological Association. "Career Conferences on Psychology for High School Students." Unpublished material. (Available from: Dr. Donald Jones, Leo Burnett Co., Inc., Prudential Plaza, Chicago, Illinois.)

(18) Snellgrove, L., Chairman. Committee on Apparatus Assistance to Small Colleges of Division 2 of the American Psychological Association. "(a) The Construction and Use of Inexpensive Psychological Apparatuses, (b) An Annotated Bibliography on Companies Having Psychological Apparatuses, and (c) A Collection of Short Paper and Pencil Psychological Experiments." Unpublished material. (Available for 50 cents for each of the three from: Dr. Louis Snellgrove, Box 944, Union University, Jackson, Tennessee.)

(19) Sorenson, H., and Malm, Marguerite. *Psychology for Living* (2d ed.). New York: McGraw-Hill Book Co., Inc., 1957.

(20) United States Department of Labor, Bureau of Labor Statistics, in cooperation with Veterans Administration *et al. Occupational Outlook Handbook,* Bulletin No. 1255. Washington, D.C.: Superintendent of Documents, United States Government Printing Office, 1959.

For Further Reading

Athletics in Education, A Platform Statement by the Division of Men's Athletics, American Association of Health, Physical Education, and Recreation, Washington, D.C., 1965.

Bathurst, Effie G., and Wilhelmina Hill, *Conservation Experiences for Children,* U.S. Department of Health, Education, and Welfare, Office of Education, Washington, D.C., 1957.

Berry, James R., "Where We Stand in Driver Education," *Safety Education,* February, 1965, 44: 10–13.

Florio, A. E., and G. T. Stafford, *Safety Education,* Second edition, McGraw-Hill Book Company, New York, 1962.

Gaver, Mary Virginia, *Every Child Needs a School Library,* American Library Association, Chicago, undated, approx. 1960.

Gregg, Walter, "Teaching About Alcohol," *NEA Journal,* December, 1961, 53, Vol. 50.

Journal of Education, February, 1960, 1–76, Vol. 142. (Theme of the issue: "Character Education: Methods and Materials.")

Keeler, Otis, "Let's Be Realistic About Alcohol — Narcotics Education," *Illinois Education,* March, 1966, 54: 314–315.

Kronhausen, Phyllis and Eberhard Kronhausen, "Sex Education — the Orphan Annie of American Schools," *Phi Delta Kappan,* December, 1961, 43: 128–132.

Marland, S. P., Jr., "Placing Sex Education in the Curriculum," *Phi Delta Kappan,* December, 1961, 43: 132–134.

National Association of Secondary School Principals, *The Effective Secondary School Library,* NASSP *Bulletin,* November, 1959, Vol. 43, No. 250. (The entire issue.)

NEA *Journal,* March, 1964, 57–71. Vol. 53. (Special feature on health education. Nine articles dealing with alcohol, smoking, venereal diseases, consumer purchasing, diet, and air and water pollution.)

Phi Delta Kappan, October, 1964, 46: 41–96. (Theme of the issue: "The Schools' Responsibility for Moral Education." Twelve articles centered on moral education, religion, sex education, controversial topics, and freedom.)

Pollack, Jack Harrison, "Teen-age Drinking and Drug Addiction," NEA *Journal,* May, 1966, 8–12, Vol. 55.

Russell, Robert D., "Alcohol," NEA *Journal,* March, 1964, 66–67, Vol. 53.

Russell, Robert D., "What Do You Mean — Alcohol Education?" *The Journal of School Health,* October, 1965, 35: 351–355.

Sperry, Gale L., "The Importance of a Band Course of Study," *The School Musician,* September, 1962, 34, 36, Vol. 34.

Staley, Edwin J., "Critical Issues in Recreation and Outdoor Education," *JOHPER,* June, 1964, 17, Vol. 35.

Thompson, Clem W., "Smoking," NEA *Journal,* March, 1964, 66–69, Vol. 53.

Wallace, Charles E., "Driver Education," *Journal of Secondary Education,* May, 1964, 39: 217–222.

Ward, Douglas S., "A Proposal To Put Interscholastic Athletics in Their Proper Place," *Phi Delta Kappan,* April, 1961, 42: 276–278.

Index